CW01300995

The Derbyshire Chronicles
*Cricket's Lost and Found Champions
of 1874 and 1936*

ALSO BY EDWARD GILES IN DESERT ISLAND BOOKS
Derby County: Champions of England 1972 & 1975

The Derbyshire Chronicles

*Cricket's Lost and Found Champions
of 1874 and 1936*

Edward Giles

DESERT ISLAND BOOKS

First published in 2007
by
DESERT ISLAND BOOKS LIMITED
7 Clarence Road, Southend on Sea, Essex SS1 1AN
United Kingdom
www.desertislandbooks.com

© 2007 Edward Giles

The right of Edward Giles to be identified as author of this work has
been asserted under The Copyright Designs and Patents Act 1988

British Library Cataloguing-in-Publication Data
A catalogue record for this book is available from the British Library

ISBN 978-1-905328-25-3

All rights reserved. No part of this book may be reproduced or utilised in any form or by any means, electronic or mechanical, including photocopying, recording or by any information storage and retrieval system, without prior permission in writing from the Publisher

Printed in Great Britain
by
Biddles Ltd

Contents

		Page
1	The Lost Title of 1874	7
2	An Amateur About-Face	18
3	The Turning Point	29
4	Keeping it in the Family	40
5	Expulsion from First-Class	52
6	The Demon Spofforth	64
7	Seasons in Exile	76
8	Death of a Record-Breaker	88
9	Bestwick's All-10 Comeback	99
10	Chesterfield Run Feast	112
11	From Glory to Gloom	123
12	Talent from the Nursery	135
13	Cricketing Footballers	148
14	Townsend and Worthington	162
15	The Rise of Denis Smith	181
16	Copson and Mitchell	193
17	The Pope Brothers	206
18	Third in 1934	218
19	Second in 1935	232
20	Champions in 1936	247
21	Final Steps to the Title	258
22	Undermined by Unrest	274
23	The Other Honours	286
	Appendix 1. Final Averages for 1874 and 1936	292
	Appendix 2. Scorecards from 1874	294
	Appendix 3. Scorecards from 1936	299
	Appendix 4. Miscellaneaous Scorecards	329
	Index	342

Author's Note

For many years I have kept my own records of Derbyshire cricket, but I could never have attempted an undertaking of this kind had I not also been able to refer to such invaluable publications as *Wisden Cricketers' Almanack*, *The Cricketer*, *Derbyshire County Cricket Year Books*, Roy Webber's *The County Cricket Championship*, *Cricket in England 1894-1939* by E L Roberts, and that miracle of the internet age, the *Cricket Archive*.

I have also been indebted to Walter J Piper Junior's *History of the Derbyshire County Cricket Club* that covers the years from its foundation in 1870 up to the end of the 1898 season, and *The Rise of Derbyshire Cricket 1919-1935*, a booklet compiled by Major L Eardley-Simpson. Other sources are acknowledged in the text.

On a personal level, I wish to express my heartfelt gratitude to David Baggett, who has been the official archivist and historian to Derbyshire CCC since 1991, and who edited the county *Year Book* from 2001-06, and to Peter Griffiths and Philip Bailey of the *Archive*. They have been unfailingly prompt and patient in answering questions with which I have pestered them in seeking clarification on a number of points. As I have not bothered them further with a check through the completed manuscript, any errors that may remain are mine alone.

I am also grateful to have been given permission to make use of scoreboards that appear on the *Archive*. Acknowledgement of the sources of photographs in the centre of the book is made where known.

Last, but certainly not least, a big thank-you to my wife Joan for the tolerance she has shown as I have tapped away on my computer keyboard for so many hours when in her view, no doubt, I could have been doing something more useful around the house or in the garden. I just hope that anyone who reads this book will think that at least some of those hours will not have been wasted.

EDWARD GILES

Dedication

This book is for my old friend Ernest Oakland, a Second World War survivor of Dunkirk and the Italian campaign, and for the memory of his late wife May.

1. The Lost Title of 1874

For just over a quarter of a century, from 1936 to 1963, Derbyshire were officially recognised as twice winners of cricket's County Championship. Then, at a stroke as sudden and sharp as a guillotine, they had their title tally halved. *Wisden,* the revered Cricketers' Bible, decreed in its one-hundredth edition that they be deprived of their 1874 crown, leaving them with just their triumph of the mid-Thirties to cherish. The reason? In that far-off year of the nineteenth century fewest defeats had been the controversial criterion by which top place had been decided, and although Derbyshire had alone been unbeaten they had fulfilled only four Championship fixtures.

That questionable dethroning in favour of Gloucestershire, who had played just two matches more and lost one of them, came only four years after *Wisden's* editor, then Norman Preston, had appended a disassociating note to an article in the yellow-backed annual in which Rowland Bowen, a cricket historian of provocative views, had detailed his differences with the list of county champions in the game's early seasons. One of those differences applied most emphatically to Derbyshire, but the editor then classed it with Bowen's other forceful opinions in observing: 'Without in any way disputing the conclusions reached by the author, I do not think we can alter the accepted list as regularly published in *Wisden* for over forty years, even where there are good grounds for disagreeing with it.'

It was at the editor's request, because attention had recently been drawn to doubts frequently expressed down the years, that Major Bowen conducted his extensive research. In addition to county club histories, he consulted a large number of contemporary annuals – four of them in particular: *Fred Lillywhite's Guide, John and James Lillywhite's Companion, James Lillywhite's Annual,* and *Wisden.* Foremost among the conclusions he arrived at was that 'there has been an uncritical acceptance and repetition of statements concerning earlier periods, or statistics about earlier cricket, which would horrify a professional historian.' He could find no evidence that the Championship started in 1873, even though it had hitherto been generally accepted that the competition had been instituted that year with the introduction of the rules of qualification that prevented a player from representing more than one county in the same season (as James Southerton, for one, had done with Sussex and Surrey). There is still a line in *Wisden,* referring to 1873, which states: 'First regulations restricting county qualification, often regarded as the official start of the County Championship.'

Bowen also maintained that the concept of first-class cricket, let alone the Championship, was 'quite alien' to the minds of cricket enthusiasts and writers of those days, yet *Wisden* itself has recorded that when those qualification rules were first agreed in April 1873 nine counties *were* considered first-class

(Derbyshire, Gloucestershire, Kent, Lancashire, Middlesex, Notts, Surrey, Sussex and Yorkshire). Indeed, a special commemorative stamp was issued by the Post Office in 1873. Since then, however, Hampshire have come to be recognised as having had first-class status at that time, as is recalled in more detail in Chapter Three.

The *James Lillywhite's Annual*, which ceased production with the turn of the century, shied away from definite decisions in giving the counties in alphabetical order, but contended that in the 1874 season 'the most partial supporter would hardly venture to compare Derbyshire with Gloucestershire'. Rowland Bowen used that quotation to strengthen his argument, and continued:

'Both *Annual* and *Companion* were in no doubt that Gloucestershire were champions, and *Wisden* listed them second to the conventionally placed Surrey (listing Derbyshire last!). *The History of Gloucestershire County Cricket Club* made the definite claim that Gloucestershire were champions in 1874; *Derbyshire County Cricket,* by [Walter] Piper, published 1897, made no claim for Derbyshire to have been champions in 1874, though it said they were the only unbeaten county, but it is fair to say that the unofficial *Derbyshire Cricket Guide* for 1896 did make the claim (prompted no doubt by [Alfred] Gibson). On the other hand, 'Feats and Facts of Derbyshire Cricket' in the *Derbyshire Cricket Annual* for 1887 did not mention Derbyshire as champions in 1874 – surely it would have done if anyone in or out of the county had made the claim? In the face of contemporary unanimity on the subject, there can be no doubt that the present list is wrong, both in supposing that the champions were designated with reference to fewest matches lost, and in designating Derbyshire as champions. At the time, Gloucestershire were accepted as champions, and claimed to be champions; Derbyshire were not, and did not, and the modern list should therefore be corrected.'

Bowen appears to have put most of the blame for what he saw as faults in the list on Alfred Gibson, whose *County Cricket Championship* was published in 1895, dismissing him in a manner that might just as well have been applied to himself – as 'the statistician who tried to read back into the minds of writers of twenty years earlier his own ideas'. Gibson's version, which gave the 1874 title to Derbyshire, was copied and brought up to date by the Rev R S Holmes in a publication brought out in 1896, three years after Holmes had compiled the first history of the County Championship. *Wisden* was the first annual to show Gibson's list, in 1901, but at that time it omitted 1873 (when Gloucestershire and Nottinghamshire, both unbeaten, had been shown to share the title) and 1874. Not until 1911 did it add those years in accordance with what Gibson had stipulated. And that was how things stood until 1963, when *Wisden's* editor so abruptly had thoughts second to those he had formed only four years before by deciding to accept Bowen's amendments.

The reference in Bowen's remarks on 1874 to the 'conventionally placed Surrey' is explained by the fact that until *Wisden* first published a table in 1889 the order in which it placed the counties was headed by Surrey up to 1877, then by Middlesex, and the next county shown was, in Bowen's words, 'usually found to have been considered champions.' All very quaint and confusing. No wonder there was so much debate and argument about the various title interpretations of the Press and cricket annuals in those days before the Championship was officially recognised. Tables appeared in other annuals long before *Wisden* got round to giving one (though there had first been mention of a champion, Yorkshire, in that august publication as far back as 1871), but right until the late 1880s another exalted cricket institution, the MCC, had considered 'all counties equal' in refusing to acknowledge any classification.

Even when Rowland Bowen stepped in to influence, eventually, *Wisden's* outlook, the list in the 1963 almanack differed in only two respects from the one published the year before, apart from beginning in 1864 instead of 1873 so that it could cover the *Wisden* century (taking account of the seasons lost to the two world wars). Besides Gloucestershire's replacement of Derbyshire for 1874, the title of 1878, hitherto awarded to Middlesex, was deemed 'undecided'. No specific explanation for these changes was made in another article by Bowen. Readers were merely referred back to what he had had to say in the 1959 edition. Middlesex joined Derbyshire as a dethroned county because, although also alone undefeated and having made no title claim, they were involved in a muddled situation arising from their own club history's concession that 'probably Nottinghamshire, and certainly Yorkshire, were stronger'. Middlesex won three of only six games, with the others drawn. Notts (seven wins, four draws and three defeats) and Yorkshire (seven wins, two draws and five defeats) both played fourteen matches.

Other anomalies went unheeded at that time. A case, for instance, could be made against Notts in all but one of the five successive seasons, starting jointly with Lancashire in 1882, in which they continued to be named champions. Even the zealous Bowen had no objection to Notts (seven wins, seven draws and no defeats) being rated above Surrey (twelve wins, one draw and three defeats) in 1886, despite his denigration of the 'least matches lost' deciding factor that so debatably counted in Derbyshire's favour until the purge of 1963. To accentuate the anomaly, Notts are still shown in *Wisden* as the unofficial champions of 1886. It was admittedly a suspect system, and a clear encouragement to play for a draw if a win were not viable, to make fewest defeats a guide, if not a rule, in allocating the title. Indeed, the unsatisfactory manner of Notts' fourth consecutive outright success was the catalyst for the introduction of a 'new' method of points scoring (one for a win, half of one for a draw) for the 1887 season. The word 'new' is in quotes because, as Rowland Bowen pointed out, the publication *Cricket* used that method to determine the placings in 1882.

For all Bowen's protests that it had been 'repeated blindly', the fact remains that from 1873 to 1886 the method of deciding the order of merit – though, it has to be said, not consistently applied – was generally regarded as being by the smallest number of matches lost. Bowen had another dig at Derbyshire in saying that Kent and Lancashire, the only counties they played, home and away, in 1874, were 'both very weak teams at that time'. Maybe so, but it certainly was not Derbyshire's fault that their fixture list was so restricted. The more powerful counties could have avoided all the 1874 objections if only at least one of them had condescended to play the smaller fry such as Derbyshire undeniably were in that era. Not until 1886, for example, did Gloucestershire deign to meet them, and that, at Derby, was just an isolated instance even though the result was close enough (victory for the visitors by 47 runs) to justify further encounters during that period. Indeed, the outstanding individual performance was given by a Derbyshire player, George Davidson surpassing the match bowling figures of W G Grace (7-76) and his colleague William Woof (9-69) with thirteen for 83 – nine of them for 42 in Gloucestershire's second innings.

Gloucestershire did not again provide the opposition until 1901, when Derbyshire had the better of two drawn games, and after that there was another gap until they started regular fixtures in 1921. Middlesex also met Derbyshire just the once in the nineteenth century, and, as recalled in a later chapter, they were even more tardy than Gloucestershire in arranging a second fixture.

As it was – as W T Taylor, Derbyshire's secretary into a record 52nd year up to the end of 1959, told us in his *History of Derbyshire Cricket* in the 1953 *Wisden* – only Lancashire were willing to arrange fixtures with the Peak county in the first three seasons following the Derbyshire club's formation in the winter of 1870. Taylor recalled that the inability to attract additional opponents in the county's early seasons 'caused a great deal of despondency among officials and supporters'. What could be interpreted as a boycott by certain counties which existed for most of the years before Derbyshire were cast out into the second-class cold from 1888 to 1893 was partly due to the bad state of the pitch at the County Ground in Derby – so bad that it was widely regarded as the worst in England on which first-class cricket was played.

This was attributable to the fact that it was then shared by the Derbyshire club's soccer offshoot, Derby County, and was scarred by not only the footballers' boots but also the feet of spectators who encroached towards the cricket square. Big crowds were not anticipated when the football club came into existence in 1884, and to begin with only stout ropes fixed to stakes separated the players from the onlookers. More formidable barriers were not erected until the larger crowds were attracted to the ground for an international match between England and Ireland, four FA Cup semi-finals, and the first replayed final. In 1886, the attendance of just over 16,000 at Derby for the replay in which Blackburn Rovers won the Cup for the third successive year by beating West Bromwich Albion was a thousand bigger than the gate at the Kennington Oval's drawn game in London, despite an early-April snowstorm which did not peter out until less than two hours before the kick-off.

Almost ten years later, only a few months before Derby County departed to the Baseball Ground, more than 25,000 saw the Albion defeat the Wednesday in their semi-final replay at Derbyshire's cricket headquarters.

The football pitch at the County Ground was described around that time as 'a magnificent piece of turf,' but the one used for cricket often played so 'queerly' (an adjective among the less objectionable attributed to it) that 'many a famous batsman carried away the marks of the punishment he received from rising deliveries at Derby', according to one contemporary account. The casualties most notably included John Shuter, captain of Surrey. It could be said that he twice came a Cropper when he first played at Derby in 1883, for in both innings he was dismissed cheaply by the bowler of that name, but a year later he was unfortunately undone in a much more painful manner. Top scorer with 61 in Surrey's first innings, he had to retire before getting off the mark when he batted again, bleeding profusely from an ugly head cut, after being felled by a fierce rising delivery from George Walker, a Yorkshire-born farmer on the Duke of Portland's estate at Whitwell whose switch from slow bowling to erratic left-arm pace and lift from short of a length regularly had batsmen hopping about. It brought him more than 300 wickets, at nearly 21 runs each, over eighteen seasons up to 1898.

It was against Surrey at Derby, in 1886, that Walker had his best match figures of 12 for 113. He took six of their last seven first-innings wickets for only eleven runs on a pitch that was so bad that the captains decided to change to another one after the first day. An inspection of the new pitch was even less encouraging, however, so Derbyshire slumped to another defeat on the original one, collapsing for 68 in their second innings. Surrey were then such a power in the land that they were champions in each of the next six seasons (once shared) and in eight out of nine, though the first three of those titles are among those now classed unofficial. After that purple patch, Surrey claimed the crown only twice more, in 1899 and 1914, until they topped the table in eight years out of nine in the 1950s, the last seven in succession.

William Cropper, to whom John Shuter twice lost his wicket on his first appearance at Derby, was a promising all-round cricketer, with a hat-trick in his best bowling return of seven for 25 against Hampshire at Southampton, and twice unfortunate not to complete a century with scores of 93 against Surrey at the Oval and 92 not out against Middlesex at Derby. He was also an accomplished footballer, but his double career was tragically cut short in 1889, just after his twenty-sixth birthday, by an injury suffered while playing soccer for Staveley, a Derbyshire club, against Grimsby Town. He was carried off after being accidentally struck in the stomach by the knee of defender Dan Doyle in going up to head the ball, and he died the next day of a ruptured bowel. Ironically, the pair would not have been in direct opposition if Cropper had not turned out on the right wing, instead of in his usual position of centre-forward, because he was due to play against Glasgow on the following Saturday and therefore wished to keep out of the thick of the action to avoid injury. Moreover, Doyle was also out of his regular place in appearing at left-half, and had not wished to play there.

The death, at thirty-six in May 1873, of the opening bowler who was known as Dove Gregory, although his real name was Gregory Dove, had already deprived Derbyshire of a player who had taken 25 wickets for ten runs apiece in the four meetings with Lancashire that comprised their county programme of their first two seasons, and a young professional named Thornhill had been killed in a railway accident. Another loss to the county, from typhoid fever at the age of only nineteen while under treatment for an eyesight problem towards the end of 1886, was that of Joe Chatterton, whose elder brother William was one of four Derbyshire cricketers and Derby County footballers to play Test cricket for England (the others were William Storer, Frank Sugg and Arnold Warren). Joe, who was the first to make his Derbyshire debut at the age of seventeen (and 165 days), against Sussex at Derby in 1884, had shown encouraging form as an all-rounder in the two seasons since the formation of Derbyshire's Club and Ground side, and a bright future had been predicted for him once his sight defect had been cured.

By the time Derby County's switch to the Baseball Ground was precipitated by the refusal of the owners of the County Ground to allow them to meet the Corinthians amateur side there because of an Easter fixture clash with a horseracing meeting, strong protests about the state of Derby's cricket area had forced a solution that transformed the pitch from one of the worst in the country into one of the best. A committee member, James Ragg, had the brainwave of having the pavilion moved (at his own expense) from its position about a hundred yards from the canal bridge entrance so that access could be gained to it from both sides – for cricketers on one, footballers on the other. At the same time, the cricket square was relaid, and, no longer under threat from soccer, it became, so the local paper reported, 'if not the best in England, then at least one on which the greatest batsmen of the time delighted to disport themselves.' One visitor went as far as to claim that Derby then had 'the finest racing, football and cricket ground in England', but that was far from the view of the many cricketers who came to regard it as the least appealing on the county circuit because of its exposure to bleak weather conditions. And so it remained until some years after the Second World War, since when the county's officials are to be complimented on the considerable improvements that were carried out in making it their only home venue for the seven seasons from 1999 to 2005, though at the regrettable expense of the attractive Queen's Park ground in Chesterfield.

Back in those far-off days of 1874, however, the circumstances under which Derbyshire played at home gave them much less to be pleased about, and their enjoyment of elevation to a title that was to be taken away from them nearly ninety years later was also diluted by the inability to attract sufficient Championship opponents that was to persist until after their six-season banishment into the second class.

Kent, the only county that condescended to join Lancashire in playing home and away games against them in 1874, were, like Derbyshire, confined to four fixtures in the competition that year. Like Derbyshire, too, they had been formed only four years earlier – or re-formed, to be exact, and for the second time at that. Having originally come into some form of existence in 1842, they had first been officially launched in 1859, and in 1870 were revived again chiefly under the impetus provided by a man, Lord Harris, who was to be the dominant power in that county's cricket for almost sixty years. His lordship, born George Robert Canning Harris, enjoyed himself on the field at Derbyshire's expense with a couple of centuries and twice got into the eighties against them.

This was the final table of 1874, as published in Roy Webber's *County Cricket Championship* in 1957, with the fewest defeats determining the order:

	P	W	D	L
Derbyshire	4	3	1	0
Gloucestershire	6	4	1	1
Kent	4	1	1	2
Lancashire	6	1	2	3
Nottinghamshire	8	5	0	3
Yorkshire	12	8	1	3
Middlesex	6	1	1	4
Sussex	8	1	2	5
Surrey	10	3	1	6

The striking feature of those positions is that if Derbyshire were not to be considered in some quarters as worthy champions, because they had played so few matches, Yorkshire were more deserving to displace them than Gloucestershire, considering that they gained twice as many victories as the men from the West Country. Not even *Cricket*, circulated under the name of W G Grace, the game's towering figure in ability as well as build, supported the cause of the good doctor's own county for that 1874 title. It gave the distinction to Yorkshire, though to do so it had to resort to the system of points scoring that was not introduced until the competition's official recognition from 1890 – when, up to 1894, losses were deducted from wins and drawn games ignored, the county with the highest number of points (one for each win that counted) being adjudged champions. And Yorkshire would still have come out ahead of Gloucestershire under the 1887 change to one point for a win and half a point for a draw.

That made *Wisden's* preference for Gloucestershire, when Derbyshire belatedly had the title taken away from them, all the more perplexing, quite apart from the fact that cricket's equivalent of soccer's moving of the goalposts, a realignment of the stumps as it were, on a no longer level playing field, was needed to do it. Ironically, it was not until Derbyshire undisputedly finished first in 1936 that the doubts about the validity of their title of sixty-two years earlier, having long since died down, were resurrected.

The big question then raised was: Is this their first Championship or their second? Many expressed themselves unhappy about the 1874 issue, but it was generally accepted at the time that it was their second. In its review of the 1936 season, *Wisden* contradicted what Rowland Bowen was later to maintain by stating that 'no claim has been made to the Championship of 1874 by any other county'. *The Cricketer Annual* of 1936-37 agreed there was room for a difference of opinion, but added:

'It is important to bear in mind that in those early days of county cricket there was no reason at all that the team which happened to come out first in the season's results should be the strongest in the competition. The champions might be, and often were, the best, but this was not necessarily so by any means. It must be remembered that there were very few fixtures, and that there was a very marked difference in strength between a few of the counties and the rest, a much greater difference than there is today. More than this, there was a tendency to arrange matches which promised a good fight, so that strong teams played against strong teams, and weak teams played against weak teams. Each game stood out by itself, and not as one of a series upon which points depended. No genuine test of general merit was possible until larger programmes allowed a more extensive campaign in which all, or nearly all, the competitors could meet each other. This position was not reached until many years later. Problems like this one, of ancient county championships, are interesting, but the interest is, after all, only academic. We settle them half a century after the event on modern lines, and by the application of modern tests. Such a settlement can never be anything but arbitrary, for each critic can lay down his own condition and make his figures prove anything.'

Even so, the writer drew what he called 'the inevitable conclusion' that Derbyshire headed the table in 1874, given the conditions that then applied, although he emphasised that there was no suggestion, least of all by Derbyshire themselves, that they were among the stronger counties, let alone the strongest. The article ended with the Championship table of 1874 as it would have been according to the 1936 method of reckoning. From 1933 to 1937, that method was:

'Fifteen points for a win;
Seven and a half points to each side in match ending with the scores level;
Five points for lead on first innings in a drawn match;
Three points for the county behind on first innings in a drawn match;

Four points to each side in a match without result on first innings, or if the scores on first innings were level, or if no play had taken place;

Ten points to side winning on first innings, three points to their opponents, in a match restricted to play on the third day.'

How much more complicated than merely relying on fewest defeats! And after all that still to find Derbyshire on top. This was the 1874 final table in 1936 style:

	P	W	D	L	Poss pts/Act pts		%
Derbyshire	4	3	1	0	60	48	80.00
Gloucestershire	6	4	1	1	90	65	72.22
Yorkshire	12	8	1	3	180	125	69.44
Nottinghamshire	8	5	0	3	120	75	62.50
Surrey	10	3	1	6	150	50	33.33
Kent	4	1	1	2	60	20	33.33
Lancashire	6	1	2	3	90	23	25.55
Middlesex	6	1	1	4	90	18	20.00
Sussex	8	1	2	5	120	21	17.50

Further backing for Derbyshire came two decades later from Roy Webber, the widely respected cricket statistician who preceded 'Bearded Wonder' Bill Frindall in the BBC's commentary box. He omitted to emphasise that Derbyshire made strenuous, though unavailing, efforts to arrange more matches in 1874, but went on to say: 'If the results in 1874 are related to the points-scoring method in use today [the late 1950s], Derbyshire are still at the top of the table, and this appears to prove that, however hard the position might be on some of the other counties [with bigger fixture lists], the assessment of Derbyshire as champions does carry some justification.'

When I took this up with Matthew Engel, then in the first of his two spells as editor of *Wisden,* he said that he admired my pursuit of this subject, but could not really offer me an authoritative view. He added:

'As editor of *Wisden,* I have made a clear division between the pre-1890 unofficial Championship and the official Championship after that. Since we are talking about an unofficial Championship, decided only by newspaper interpretations, uncertainty seems to me inevitable. I disapprove of official bodies trying to interfere with cricket retrospectively, and this is not an area in which I would wish to meddle.'

Yet only a few years later meddle he did. Since the 1997 edition champions have been tabulated only from the year of 1890 in which the competition was at last put on an approved official basis. In one paragraph an unofficial list dating back to 1864 has continued to be incorporated in accordance with Bowen's findings, but not equated with what the editor called 'the real champions', and still with all the contentious interpretations among which Gloucestershire's ousting of Derbyshire for 1874 stands out. Even the official list is not free from flaws either. In 1903, for example, Middlesex, top on percentages with draws ignored, fulfilled ten fewer fixtures than third-placed Yorkshire, who gained the biggest number of victories – thirteen to Middlesex's eight. The fact that all the teams did not have to play the same number of matches remained a most unsatisfactory aspect of the calculations for more than fifty years.

After all, as *The Cricket Annual* so rightly noted, figures can be manipulated to prove anything. There have been several other debatable title outcomes since the Championship was placed on a proper footing, and frequent changes in the ways of deciding them have given some counties cause to regret that they could not also benefit from retrospective reassessments on 1874 lines. In 1910, Kent, winners of all but six of their 25 games, retained the title when a new method of deciding it, percentage of wins to matches played, worked to their advantage (*Wisden* complained that 'its defects were obvious'), but another adjustment, introducing first-innings points with the order determined by the greatest proportionate number of points obtained to points possible – how complex it all sounds! – narrowly denied them a third successive title the following season. Instead, that alteration allowed Warwickshire to edge above Kent to become champions for the first time. Good luck to them, but they played neither Kent nor Middlesex, who were third, and most of their matches were against counties in the lower half of the table.

Matthew Engel, who had described Derbyshire's right to the 1874 title as a 'romantic notion', changed *Wisden's* position on the pre-1890 County Championship because he felt 'we were failing in our duty in regard to the annual's historic mission to separate cricketing fact from fiction'. It was ironic that Gloucestershire became one of the major victims of the cull, for it took away their four titles (one shared) in the years from 1873 to 1877 and left them with not one to their name – 'the county of the Graces joining the disgraces, I am afraid to say,' remarked Engel. Nottinghamshire were the other county to be hard hit, losing ten outright titles and five shared ones, though they still had four left. The 'avenging' Engel expected to be 'burned in effigy in Mansfield Woodhouse and Wootton-under-Edge,' but could see no honest alternative.

It is also interesting to recall the peculiar addition to the conditions of the Championship when it was expanded to fourteen counties (including the reinstated Derbyshire) for the 1895 season. It read: 'At the close of each season the committee of the MCC shall decide the County Championship.' This ambiguity was accentuated by the fact that it was then not specifically stated that the title would go to the county gaining the most points or achieving the highest percentage, alternative criteria that have applied down the years. More than sixty years after that the MCC were still emphasising that they had the power to award the title. One sports writer of a national newspaper tried to make a big story out if this by intimating that the team finishing at the top need not automatically be the champions, but, as *Wisden* had for many years made clear, by that time it was stipulated that 'the side which has the highest aggregate on points gained at the end of the season shall be the Champion County'.

Just imagine the hullabaloo if, in modern times, the MCC had ever given the title to a county ending below first place on points or percentage. Any other feelings of injustice over title amendments would have paled into insignificance by comparison.

2. *An Amateur About-Face*

Derbyshire County Cricket Club came into existence on 4 November 1870, at a well-attended meeting at the Guild Hall in Derby, chiefly on the initiative of Walter Boden, the club's honorary secretary for the first dozen years and president for four consecutive years from 1895. His brother Henry also played a prominent part in the venture.

The county's first president was the Earl of Chesterfield, but he died before the club was a year old and was succeeded by the Hon William Monk Jervis, a Londoner who made his home at Quarndon Hall only a few miles outside Derby. William Jervis, brother of the third Viscount St Vincent and uncle of Lord Harris, held the post until taking over as honorary secretary for just the one year of 1887 in which he made the removal of the club's debt of £1,000, then a considerable sum, his principal objective. With the help of George Henry Strutt (that year's president), Walter Boden and James Ragg, the liabilities were liquidated by the time Jervis handed the secretarial duties back to Boden's successor in the post, Arthur Wilson.

Though not without some success as a player in his youth, Jervis was past his best by the time the Derbyshire club started out. It was therefore no big surprise when, in his forty-seventh year, he failed in opening the innings with Robert Smith against Lancashire at Derby in 1873, twice bowled by William McIntyre – first for nought, then six. That was the only game in which he played for Derbyshire. Walter Boden also turned out just the once for the county in a first-class match, and with even less success. When Kent were beaten at Wirksworth in 1874 he began by scoring two runs without being dismissed, but in his second innings was also out for a duck.

For their entry onto the county cricketing scene in 1871 Derbyshire drew players mainly from the South Derbyshire club, which, so Walter Piper tells us, 'had for many years held a leading position in the country.' Others came from the 'team of Derbyshire gentlemen' whose opposition had included the MCC, Lincolnshire and Gentlemen of Kent. A few trial matches were also arranged, those between Colts of the North and South of the county among them. Derbyshire fulfilled five fixtures in their first season, but only the two against Lancashire were rated first-class. Only amateurs took part in home and away games against Lincolnshire, both drawn, and a Derbyshire XI lost to a team of seventeen Colts by 106 runs.

Rain prevented play on the opening day, Thursday, 25 May, of the first meeting with Lancashire in Manchester, but Derbyshire got off to an encouraging start with victory by an innings and eleven runs. The home side were hustled out for a mere 25 runs in their first innings, still their smallest total in first-class cricket. Ironically, they lost their first four wickets to a player who only the year before had excelled for them at the same ground by taking all ten wickets in Hampshire's second innings. This was William Hickton, an all-rounder born at Hardstoft, a hamlet near Clay Cross in Derbyshire where there used to be a colliery. He switched to his home county at the first opportunity. In his five seasons with Lancashire, Hickton totalled nearly 150 wickets; in eight with Derbyshire he took just over 130 more, including three of Kent's in four balls when he had match figures of 11 for 93 at Derby in 1876.

The six other wickets in Lancashire's collapse on Derbyshire's debut fell at a cost of just nine runs to the ill-fated Dove Gregory. Derbyshire managed only 147 in reply, but, although they had to work harder in Lancashire's second innings, that proved sufficient to ensure that they did not have to bat again.

The scoreboard (see p.329) differs from the one published in those far-off days in that the amateurs are not indicated by the prefix 'Mr'. And an even more respectful mode of address than that had to be adopted towards their captain by members of teams led by the lords Harris (Kent), Hawke (Yorkshire) and Tennyson (Hampshire). More often than not, only the 'Mr' amateurs were given their initials, professionals usually having theirs appended in brackets only if there happened to be more than one of them with the same surname. When initials were given for all the professionals they were put after the surname instead of before it, as was the case with the amateurs. Such were the sticklers for this practice that Alex Bannister, the *Daily Mail's* cricket correspondent for many years, recalled hearing this pre-match announcement at Lord's: 'In the match card, for F J Titmus please read Titmus F J.'

There was one chap, the great grandson of a Wicklow chieftain who had been among the leaders of the Irish insurrection of 1798 before being exiled to Australia, who was entitled to no fewer than seven initials before his surname. He was John Elicius Benedict Bernard Placid Quirk Carrington Dwyer, who was known in cricket simply as E B Dwyer when he spent a few seasons with Sussex early last century. In 1906 he achieved what are still that county's best individual bowling figures in a Derbyshire innings when he took nine wickets for 35 runs at Hove.

Four initials before the surname were uncommon enough, though Derbyshire provided an immediate instance with John Thomas Brown Dumelow Platts. Among the best-known players with that number was John William Henry Tyler Douglas, an Essex and England captain whose frequent extremely slow batting had those initials renamed by some exasperated spectators as Johnny Won't Hit Today. One barracker in Australia felt constrained to call for a policeman to arrest him for loitering, and Douglas told a story against himself about a member of the Melbourne club who bet him that more trains would pass the ground in an hour than he would make runs. The trains were said to have won by twenty-three. On one memorable occasion when Douglas dug in and resisted all attempts to get him out, he made his highest score of 210 not out against Derbyshire at Leyton in 1921.

As a captain, Douglas was described by *Wisden* as 'more brusque of manner than might be wished of a leader', yet Herbert Sutcliffe, the immaculate Yorkshire and England batsman who was one of the most determined batsmen he bowled against, considered him 'as charming a gentleman as ever donned flannels'. In also saying that he was 'a fighter second to none', Sutcliffe could have been taken literally, for in his earlier days Douglas became the British amateur middleweight boxing champion and won an Olympic title. It was tragic indeed that such a talented and respected figure should meet a premature and violent end. Having survived the 1914-18 war, in which he was a Lieutenant-Colonel in the Bedfordshire Regiment, and a car accident that killed the driver alongside him during the 1924-25 tour of Australia, he was drowned while returning to England from a business trip to Scandinavia in 1930. He and his father, who also perished, were passengers aboard the *Oberon* when it was in collision with another steamship, the *Arcturus,* in the Kattegat between Denmark and Sweden.

The distinct divide between cricket's amateurs, mainly products of public schools and universities, and the professionals from more modest backgrounds was a Victorian-type throwback nurtured in the annual match between the Gentlemen and the Players that reached its 150th anniversary in 1956, but died out six years later as amateur status was abolished and all first-class cricketers became players with a small 'p'. It was an historic and long-overdue change, yet one that caused a big surprise because only four years earlier, following a full inquiry conducted by the MCC, the Advisory County Cricket Committee had expressed a 'wish to preserve in first-class cricket the leadership and general approach to the game traditionally associated with the amateur player' and had 'rejected any solution to the problem on the lines of abolishing the distinction between amateur and professional'. Far from being obsolete, that distinctive status of the amateur cricketer was then considered to be 'of great value to the game', and well worth preserving.

For some seasons before the committee's sudden about-face in 1962, the number of amateurs had dwindled to approximately forty, with only about half as many as that before the holidays of the universities and schools, whereas two hundred or more took part at various times during a season around the turn into the twentieth century. One of the greatest of the professionals, Sir Jack Hobbs, said he was 'sad to see the passing of the amateurs because it signals the end of an era in cricket', and it cannot reasonably be denied that the best of the amateurs brought into the game what *Wisden* called 'the spirit of freedom and gaiety' that is much less frequently seen nowadays. Against that, however, the thorny subject of the expenses the amateurs were paid was not the only undesirable aspect of having players of unequal status. Not least was the snobbish 'Mr' element that prevailed for so long – and which was not discarded in *Wisden's* list of births and deaths until some twenty years after the hierarchy had at last seen fit to make all players of equal standing.

It can be argued that the ending of amateurism has not entirely cut class distinction out of English cricket, for snobbery still exists in most forms of life, but thank goodness we are far removed from the days when amateurs did not stay at the same hotel as the professionals and had a separate dressing room in the pavilion, with an imperious bell sounding to summon the rest of the team out of theirs to join the amateurs on the field. And thereby hangs a tale that Fred Trueman, the former Yorkshire and England fast bowler, was fond of telling, passed on to him by Herbert Sutcliffe. It is of one match at Lord's concerning Brian Sellers, Yorkshire's autocratic captain. This is how Trueman retold it:

'When Sellers was seen, through the dressing-room window, to walk through the amateurs' gate and onto the field, Herbert Sutcliffe, the senior pro – and very much a believer in doing things in a proper manner – halted the professionals as they prepared to follow the captain: "Wait just a minute or two." And they allowed Sellers to walk right to the middle and stand, for a moment, on his own. He must have felt the loneliest man in the world: Lord's on a Saturday in high summer ... the ground full ... a captain on parade, but no team. It was only then that Sutcliffe said, "Right, let's get out there".'

Sellers, so the story goes, did not complain about the incident. Nor did he again make the mistake of not going to see his men before that start of a game.

John Bentley, when president of the Football League, was not slow to point out, as a plain-speaking Lancastrian and strong opponent of bogus amateurism, the hypocrisy of such arrangements in hitting back at the criticism of professionalism in soccer late in the nineteenth century. He contrasted the honesty of the paid player to the cricketer 'who comes out of the amateurs' tent, who expects a salute from the common professional, and who is paid as much as, or more than, any recognised professional breathing'. On this theme, in his book about *Trevor Bailey: A Life in Cricket,* Jack Bailey, an MCC secretary after also, like his namesake, playing for Essex, pointed out that on the 1958 tour of Australia the England amateur all-rounder earned £1,000, whereas Surrey's Jim Laker received only £800 for playing in the same MCC side as a professional.

The story has also been told of the 'revenge' extracted by G H Cartland, one of the big names of Warwickshire cricket, when the Yorkshire amateurs Lord Hawke, Stanley Jackson and Frank Milligan stayed at his home while their professional colleagues were installed at a hotel for a match between those counties in Birmingham. After Yorkshire had batted for two days in running up the then record county score of nearly 900 he withdrew the champagne to which he had intended to treat his guests.

There were four amateurs in the first team Derbyshire put into the field for that 1871 match with Lancashire in Manchester – Robert Smith, John Smith, Unwin Sowter, who for many years after finishing playing was a vice-president of the club and a member of the committee, and Sam Richardson, the captain and wicketkeeper. Eighteen years later Richardson was the central figure in a scandal that rocked the county when he absconded and was alleged to have embezzled the funds of both the cricket club, with which he was assistant secretary, and Derby County, where he was secretary. He left the country and was at the ripe old age of ninety-three when he died in Madrid during the spring of 1938.

By an unhappy coincidence, three members of that first Derbyshire team, Jack Platts and the two Smiths, died within the space of nine months towards the end of the nineteenth century. Platts, of whom more later, and Robert Smith both missed only one of just over eighty matches Derbyshire played in their first dozen years, and Platts was an ever-present for one further season before his remarkable run came to an end with the last three of his games for the county in 1884. That was also the year in which Robert Smith finally bowed out, both narrowly failing to reach a century of appearances all told – outstanding examples of consistency in those days when so few matches were played.

Robert Smith, who was born at Sawley, near the county border with Nottinghamshire, and educated at Castle Donington, just over the border in Leicestershire, made his reputation as a dependable batsman but was also an accomplished footballer, oarsman and hurdler besides being one of the best shots in Derbyshire and, said *Wisden,* 'a bold rider to hounds.' In his obituary, the almanack also remarked that as a captain (he succeeded Sam Richardson in that role for the eight years from 1876) 'he was somewhat lacking in judgment, but there can be no two opinions as to the value of his services to Derbyshire cricket at a time when the county was none too rich in high-class batsmen'. It was added that 'the one thing that possibly stood in the way of his achieving the highest distinction was a somewhat indolent temperament'. Soon after his retirement from the captaincy, Smith inherited a large estate on condition that he changed his surname to Stevens (the name of his mother's side of the family), and he settled comfortably into the life of a country gentleman at Staunton Grange in the Newark area of Nottinghamshire. It was there that he died on May Day 1899.

For Derbyshire's return match with Lancashire at Derby in August 1871, John Smith, who hailed from the village of Clifton near Ashbourne, was replaced as Robert Smith's opening partner by the Rev A A Wilmot, one of three more amateurs (the others were Edward Foley and James Billyeald) who were brought into the side for what was to be their only first-class match. It was a particularly chastening experience for the clergyman and Foley. They were both out twice without scoring as Lancashire avenged their Manchester defeat in a low-scoring game after heavy showers, winning by 62 runs. Gregory, Hickton and Platts were again Derbyshire's most successful bowlers in the dismissal of the home side for 116 and 84, but all were outshone by

Arthur Appleby, whose thirteen wickets cost only 59 runs in Derbyshire's replies of 80 and 58. Appleby, one of five changes in the Lancashire team, was one of the best of amateur bowlers in his dozen seasons with the county, quite quick with an easy left-arm action, and he would have twice toured Australia but for having to decline invitations from W G Grace and Lord Harris through pressure of business.

One of the professionals replaced by amateurs in Derbyshire's team for their first home game against Lancashire was Joseph Davidson, a right-arm medium-pace or off-break bowler whose sons George and Frank followed him into the county side in the 1880s. Joe did nothing special in his four matches for Derbyshire, but in one season with the Carlisle club he collected nearly 150 wickets for fewer than two runs each. One of the other Derbyshire games in which he took part was the first the county played at Chesterfield – not at the picturesque Queen's Park venue that housed a record crowd of 14,000 for the opening day's play against Yorkshire in 1948, but at the Recreation Ground at Saltergate, home of the football club since 1884. In those days the Recreation Ground was little more than an enclosed field, with a clear view from one side of it to the famous crooked spire on the fourteenth-century church in the heart of the town.

During the seven years from 1999 while Queen's Park was deprived of County Championship cricket, after exactly one hundred years of staging it, the belated considerable improvements at the County Ground in Derby included a complex, known as the Gateway Centre, containing an indoor school and cricket academy in addition to a new pavilion which came with the unexpected drawback of incurring the payment of rent when the club wished to use the sponsors' accommodation on the top deck. Funded through grants and the sale of surrounding land, the building replaced the decaying grandstand that had been erected in 1911 for the horseracing meetings that were held up to 1939 on a track noted for its straight mile. The concentration on Derby had represented a compete reversal of the policy temporarily adopted when only one first-class match (the opening one of 1975) was played there for two seasons as cricket was taken around the county to seven other venues – Chesterfield, Ilkeston, Buxton, Darley Dale, Trent College (where there were record one-day takings), and the Allied Breweries and Bass Worthington grounds at Burton-upon-Trent.

The two matches with Lancashire in the 'title' year of 1874 were among the very few in which Derbyshire avoided defeat by the men of the Red Rose from the time of their victory in the first meeting up to their six-year loss of first-class status after the 1887 season. And even then the result at Chesterfield was influenced by bad weather that restricted both teams to one innings. Of the thirty-three matches played between these two counties during that period of seventeen years, Derbyshire won four, drew three, and lost the twenty-six others – a dozen in succession, eleven by an innings, and four by ten wickets.

Two of those innings defeats were suffered in the only matches Derbyshire played against a county in their second season of 1872. They were bundled out for 75 and 51 in Manchester, where William McIntyre took ten of their wickets and Alec Watson six (two of the others fell to Arthur Appleby and two were run-outs), and for 42 and 69 in Derby, where, in the absence of Appleby, McIntyre claimed a dozen more victims and Watson seven, with one run out. Ilkestonian Tom Attenborough's 27 at Manchester was Derbyshire's highest individual score in those two matches, and only Joe Flint reached double figures in both innings of either of them.

McIntyre, a prominent fast bowler for many years, had transferred his allegiance to Lancashire from his home county of Nottinghamshire, for which his brothers Martin and Michael also played. Watson, a Scot, was an extremely accurate slow bowler with a potent off-break whose professional engagement with a club in the Manchester area led to his joining Lancashire, for whom he took more than 1,500 wickets in a career that lasted for over twenty years. And it might have lasted even longer, for in 1898, five years after his final appearance, he was invited back again, but decided that, at the age of fifty-four, it would not be a wise move.

Between them, McIntyre and Watson amassed more than 450 Derbyshire wickets – McIntyre 122 in nine seasons, Watson 330 in seventeen. McIntyre's best match figures in those encounters were 14 for 72 in totals of 60 and 78 in one of the innings victories in Manchester in 1876. He twice had a dozen Derbyshire scalps in a game, and captured ten on two other occasions. Watson six times took ten or more in a match with Derbyshire, most notably when he claimed twelve at Derby in 1883 for only 67 runs. That was the last of the four occasions on which Watson shared the attack unchanged through both Derbyshire innings – the first three with McIntyre, this final one with Dick Barlow, who took the six other wickets that fell. Derbyshire, already deprived of the injured Robert Smith, were reduced to ten men for both those innings because George Hay, a fast bowler from Staveley, also became a casualty. Hay, whose younger brother John was crushed to death in a colliery accident after playing just one match for Derbyshire Colts, had his career with the county shortened by rheumatism, but went on to head the ground staff at Lord's.

Although Barlow, born in the Barrow Bridge district of Bolton, was a Lancashire player for some twenty seasons, an all-rounder of Test standard, it could be said that he also turned out for Derbyshire – just the once. The county club would not agree to the team for which he played being called Derbyshire, but that was the name it went under for a game against a United North of England XI at Saltergate at the end of August in 1875, the second and last first-class fixture to be fulfilled there. Barlow opened the 'Derbyshire' innings first with William Rigley, a Somercotes blacksmith, then with Robert Smith, but accumulated fewer than two dozen runs in his two innings, and took only one wicket, as the home side slumped to defeat inside two days despite all but two of the visitors' wickets (the other one was a run-out) falling cheaply to Mycroft and Hickton.

Barlow scored nearly 12,000 runs as an opening right-hand batsman and took nearly 1,000 wickets as a left-arm medium-pace bowler (the first one with his first delivery in first-class cricket, against Yorkshire at Sheffield in 1871). He made only four first-class hundreds, but one of them, for the North of England, came in a match with the Australian tourists of 1884 in which he also took ten wickets. For the Players in the same year he dismissed three distinguished Gentlemen, W G Grace, John Shuter and Walter Read, with successive deliveries. His other hat-trick, in 1881, was performed at Derby, in one of Lancashire's four now unofficial title-winning seasons, during a match that marked the debut for Derbyshire of George Porter, who swept chimneys when he was not playing cricket.

Porter, a tall fast bowler from the Spondon district of Derby who had been attracting attention in club cricket in Lancashire, earned that chance by taking seven wickets for 20 runs while playing for a team of twenty-two Colts against the Derbyshire first eleven in Easter week, but that was to be his only appearance for his home county for seven years. When he was brought back he developed into one of the best bowlers in the team for several seasons. He had his biggest match haul of ten wickets (4-60 and 6-61) in a ten-wicket defeat of champions Surrey at The Oval in 1891 as he shared the attack throughout with George Davidson (6-41 and 3-41) apart from a couple of overs by Walter Hall, an all-rounder from the Whitfield district of Glossop who bowled at medium pace. In his decade with Derbyshire, Hall had his best figures of 6-47 during the 1885 home match with Lancashire in which Nottinghamshire-born Johnny Briggs added to that county's tormentors of their Peak neighbours with 9-29 in a ten-wicket win for the visitors. Briggs, one of the giants of the game until stricken, during a Test match at Leeds in 1899, with the first of the attacks of epilepsy that were to shorten his life, also excelled in other big defeats of Derbyshire with twelve wickets at Long Eaton in 1887, then thirteen in Manchester the next year. And he emphasised that he was no mean batsman either by scoring a century in another of their beatings at Old Trafford.

George Porter had his most successful season in 1895, Derbyshire's first back in the Championship after their seven-year exile. During that year, he took 78 wickets and made his top score of 93 in the follow-on of a drawn game at Nottingham after being out without scoring in the first-innings collapse. Against Lancashire at Derby, he snatched an unlikely win as the visitors got to within 73 of victory but then lost their last five wickets to him for the addition of only nine runs. Porter became an umpire after ending his first-class playing career the following season, but only twelve years later he died, back at Spondon, from an illness caused by sunstroke.

Eleven of Derbyshire's wickets in that 1895 match in Manchester were taken by Arthur Mold, a Lancashire import from Northamptonshire who had claimed thirteen on a winning visit to Derby two years earlier. Mold was one of the deadliest fast bowlers of his day, but also one whose action was widely questioned throughout his career. Although he played for England in home Tests he was never chosen for a tour of Australia, no doubt for that reason, and it could fairly be said that he was fortunate to get away for so long without being no-balled. Not until 1900, by which time he was in his twelfth season with his adopted county, was he called for throwing by umpire James Phillips in the only over he bowled in Lancashire's match at Trent Bridge. Soon afterwards, county captains who met to look into the growing bugbear of unfair bowling condemned Mold's delivery by eleven votes to one, and he was forced out of the first-class game after being no-balled by Phillips sixteen times in ten overs during the match with Somerset at Manchester in 1901.

There was a great deal of throwing by bowlers in English cricket towards the end of the nineteenth century, and it was not only because of Mold that Lancashire were at the centre of the controversy. Middlesex, Notts and Kent all refused to make fixtures with them because of it at various times during the 1880s. Even the remarkably consistent and effective Alec Watson had an action that was queried. He did not come in for the fierce criticism levelled at Mold and two other members of the Lancashire attack who were Watson's contemporaries, John Crossland and George Nash, but many of the batsmen who faced him had very unfavourable views of his methods. They were especially suspicious of how well he could keep his length, for a slow bowler against the wind, and there was little doubt that all this scepticism was the reaon why he never played in Test cricket.

Selection for England also eluded Crossland and Nash. Crossland was the particular target of the critics, working up such a tremendous pace that, as *Wisden* recalled, he was 'rather dreaded' by even the best batsmen. He provoked one crowd demonstration that almost caused a game against Surrey at The Oval to be abandoned, and the influential Lord Harris was so vehement in his unfavourable views that he sent a letter of protest to the Lancashire committee.

With the editor of *Wisden* leading a campaign that stamped out throwing at that time, the aboriginal fast bowler Eddie Gilbert became the most prominent player to have his Test claims nullified by his suspect action before an alarming spread of bent elbows again made this a burning issue in the middle of the twentieth century. It was then that the doubtful deliveries of several Australian bowlers threatened to scupper a tour of England, the South African Geoff Griffin became the first to be no-balled for throwing in a Test in England (after doing the hat-trick), and Derbyshire's Harold Rhodes also had his international career brought to an abrupt end for the same reason.

George Nash, who assisted Buckinghamshire after dropping out of first-class cricket in the mid-1880s, twice took nine wickets in a game against Derbyshire with his slow left-arm deliveries. Crossland, ironically lost to

Lancashire not through his action but because he broke his qualification by going back to live in his home county of Nottinghamshire one winter, also had nine in a match against Derbyshire – the one at Derby in 1882 in which William Chatterton, who hailed from the Peak district village of Thornsett not far from the border with Cheshire, made his first appearance for the home county in one of Lancashire's innings victories. With Watson taking eight of the others as Derbyshire were caught in conditions made difficult by heavy rain, Chatterton had no opportunity to show his worth on that occasion, but he was to total nearly 11,000 first-class runs over the next twenty seasons and compile the top aggregate on the 1891-92 tour of South Africa, only 45 short of 1,000, in a team captained by Walter Read. Chatterton, the first to play in Test cricket while with Derbyshire, missed a half-century by only two runs as an opener in the only Test of that tour, which England won by an innings in Cape Town, but he had the misfortune never to be called up by his country again, such was the strength of the batting available to the selectors at that time.

Chatterton, a regular choice for the Players against the Gentlemen, had a liking for Essex bowling and Leyton, taking four centuries off it at that ground and denied the chance of a fifth (what would have been his second of the match) by a declaration when he was unbeaten on 85 in his second innings. The first of those centuries, however, came before Essex rose to first-class status and the second one was made while Derbyshire were themselves rated second-class. Chatterton scored two of his other hundreds before Derbyshire were restored to the elite, both against Yorkshire. At the top level, he compiled six centuries for his county and two for MCC, and although the biggest of those was his 169 against Gloucestershire at Bristol in 1901, he doubtless derived greater satisfaction from the one at Manchester in 1896 with which he dimmed memories of his disappointing debut. That was the match in which George Davidson, with whom Chatterton shared in the county's then record third-wicket partnership of 208, made what still stands as Derbyshire's highest individual score of 274 in a total of 577 that was also the county's biggest up to that point. In becoming the third century-maker in that innings, William Storer narrowly beat both Chatterton and Davidson to the distinction of being the first batsman to complete a thousand runs in a season for Derbyshire.

Only two years later Chatterton had even more cause for celebration as he was one of four century-makers, with 142 in three hours, when Derbyshire's record total was boosted to 645 against Hampshire at Derby. More about that, and Davidson's record score, later. Suffice to say for the moment that only Yorkshire, against Warwickshire in Birmingham, had previously had four individual hundreds in one innings.

It was not just as a batsman that Chatterton was one of the most prominent players of his time. He also took only one short of 200 wickets for Derbyshire and altogether held nearly 250 catches – a few of them as an emergency wicketkeeper, in which role he also made four stumpings. Twice he took six catches in a match – a double feat, apart from wicketkeepers, equalled for Derbyshire only by Derek Morgan, holder of the county's overall record of 563 catches. Small wonder *Wisden* said of Chatterton that 'it was largely due to him that his county was reinstated among the first-class sides in 1894'.

As a footballing forward, Chatterton played in Derby County's first FA Cup-tie and five matches in their first Football League season of 1888-89, but he was heavily on the losing side each time. The Rams conceded seven goals at home to Walsall Town without reply in the Cup game, and twenty-two in those League matches – sixteen in the three successive appearances Chatterton made, in one of which, at home to Everton, he scored his only goal.

Two other cricketers who played for Derbyshire, Percy Exham and Frank Sugg, were also among the sufferers of the Cup defeat. That was the only time they turned out for the Rams, and Exham, a Cork-born Cambridge Blue, also played just the once for Derbyshire, scoring a dozen runs in a rain-curtailed draw with Yorkshire in Derby in 1883. Exham was then newly an assistant master at Repton School, which he had attended as a pupil. He remained on the teaching staff there, becoming a housemaster, until his death in the autumn of 1922. For a number of years he suffered from narcolepsy, a disease that makes it difficult to stay awake.

Sugg, who, with his elder brother Walter, features prominently in later chapters, accumulated almost 1,500 runs in his three seasons with Derbyshire, making what was then their highest score on debut, 73 against Lancashire in Manchester in 1884, and their biggest before George Davidson's 274 with 187 against Hampshire at Southampton in 1885.

William Chatterton, who had not long turned fifty when he died in Cheshire in 1913, was the first professional to captain Derbyshire. He took over when Edmund Maynard relinquished the post in 1887, and held it for the next two seasons. Maynard, a Chesterfield man who was educated at Harrow and Cambridge University, gave up the captaincy because of his indifferent form, but before that he missed a maiden century by only sixteen runs against Surrey at The Oval and carried his bat through a completed innings, if for only 28 in a total of 55, in another of the big defeats by Lancashire, at Derby.

3. The Turning Point

At Wirksworth on the evening of Friday, 5 September 1873, Derbyshire completed a victory inside two days that was hailed as 'a turning point in their career' by Walter J Piper Junior, who was the county's official honorary scorer until his journalistic work with the *Derby Daily Telegraph* confined him mainly to the office. And, as the long-serving secretary W T Taylor said in his recollections of high points in the club's history, 'that thrilling victory created intense interest in Derbyshire's fortunes the following season' (the season of the disputed title success).

It was gained by an innings and eight runs against Nottinghamshire, then a cricketing power in the land, a class above the rest alongside Gloucestershire and Yorkshire. Because, however, Derbyshire were regarded as being so firmly among those 'inferior rest', they were permitted to field sixteen men against the regulation eleven (see p.330). Furthermore, a tale went the rounds about the Derby-shire supporter who owned a wine and spirits business that specialised in a potent brand of whisky. He was said to have lavishly entertained the Notts players at his premises on the morning before they first batted. Even so, whether or not he overdid the hospitality, Derbyshire, according to one report, 'demonstrated their right to be treated with greater respect by their hitherto more favoured rivals and took something like a position in the cricketing world.'

The events of those two days in North Derbyshire were nothing short of staggering. Derbyshire, having totalled an unconvincing 114 for the fall of their fifteen wickets, shot out their mighty neighbours for a beggarly 14, and then dismissed them again for 92. The havoc in Notts' first innings was wrought by two bowlers of sharply contrasting styles who were prominent figures in Derbyshire's early years as a first-class county. They were William Mycroft, from Brimington, near Chesterfield, and Wirksworth-born Joe Flint, who shared the attack unchanged. The powerfully built left-arm Mycroft, who cleverly mixed speed with spin and specialised in a lethal fast yorker, took four wickets for six runs, and twelve of his sixteen overs, which in those days each comprised only four deliveries (rising to five in 1889 and six in 1900), were maidens. Flint, a slow bowler with a disconcerting break-back, snapped up six for seven, no runs coming off ten of his sixteen overs.

James Shaw, the main destroyer of Derbyshire's batting, was then nearing the end of a career with Nottinghamshire that had begun in 1865. He was a right-hand batsman as an undistinguished tail-ender, but his left-arm fast bowling altogether claimed almost 650 wickets, five or more of them in an innings some sixty times.

The fact that Derbyshire needed sixteen men to put themselves on the cricketing map in 1873 by accounting for the eleven of Notts gave Rowland

Bowen more ammunition in the case he built up in denigrating their worth as champions of the following season. He claimed that 'the question arises whether, even in the vague terminology of those days, they were one of the counties', adding that 'no county generally accepted as "first-class" ever batted odds against another county'. But that game against Notts did not count in the Championship, and there cannot be the slightest doubt that Derbyshire did then hold first-class status as it was generally recognised in those days. How else could they have had it temporarily taken away from them after the 1887 season because their fortunes had gone into steep decline?

For William Mycroft, called upon by Derbyshire to fill the vacancy caused by the untimely death of Dove Gregory, the 1873 season was his first with the county at the advanced cricketing age of thirty-two, just a few months older than Joe Flint had been when introduced into the side a year earlier. In view of that, it was perhaps not surprising that Flint played for the county for only six seasons up to 1879 (he missed a couple along the way), but Mycroft was such a mainstay of the bowling that he would no doubt have gone on beyond 1885 but for being afflicted by rheumatism after being the team's top wicket-taker for eight successive seasons. And it would have been ten if Flint had not narrowly interrupted his sequence in the year of the contentious title.

Mycroft touched his summit in 1877, when he amassed 157 wickets in a mere twenty-two first-class games at an average of 12.27. As, however, fourteen of those matches were with other teams, including an England XI, MCC, the North, the Players, and, most incongruously considering he was a professional, the Gentlemen of the North against the Players of the North (the Players won despite Mycroft's 7-52 and 6-55), only 63 of his wickets were for Derbyshire. It was not until the following season that he became the first to take a hundred in one season for the county alone. His 101 then cost only 9.45 runs each – still the lowest bowling average for the county in one season, most closely approached by Les Jackson's 135 at 10.09 in 1958 (the year in which Jackson topped the national list with 143 in all at 10.99). Next come Harold Rhodes, 119 at 11.04, and Brian Jackson, 120 at 12.42, who were first and second nationally in 1965.

For his century of wickets in 1878 (he had 116 in all), Mycroft required only a dozen Derbyshire games, one of which was arranged at short notice at the beginning of July to coincide with what was then a popular holiday in Derby, known as Arboretum Day. That match, which Derbyshire lost by seven wickets inside two days after following on, was played against a team comprising nine men from Notts and two from Lancashire, grandly labelled 'All-England'. It was one of the few in which Mycroft's half-brother Tom was among his team-mates. Tom, an iron moulder away from cricket, played in only two dozen first-class matches, sixteen of them for Derbyshire spread over eleven seasons from 1877, but he was on the ground staff at Lord's for just over twenty years and was also an umpire good enough to stand in a couple of

Tests besides more than a hundred County Championship games. His opportunities with Derbyshire were limited because, as a wicketkeeper, he had the misfortune to find his career coinciding with those of the county's regulars in that position during his time, Alfort Smith and James Disney.

Smith, a cotton weaver who was born at Bury, entered county cricket in 1867 with Lancashire, but he qualified for Derbyshire by residence, having been taken by his parents to live in Glossop at an early age, and he came to the fore with the Glossop club in his mid-teens. He played just four times for Lancashire, but only one game short of fifty in first-class matches for Derbyshire, with whom he proved so reliable in standing up to the wicket for the hostile bowling of William Mycroft, George Hay and Bill Hickton – a very courageous thing to do considering the indifferent pitch surfaces of those days – that the county's regular use of a long-stop was dispensed with for the first time. Several other wicketkeepers of that period, notably Dick Pilling (Lancashire), George Pinder (Yorkshire) and the Australian John Blackham, also stood up to the wicket without the 'safety net' of a long-stop in coping efficiently with speedy deliveries that often flew about dangerously and disconcertingly in beating the bat.

In briefly turning to umpiring after finishing playing, Alfort Smith was unwittingly at the centre of some controversy when Yorkshire protested about him because of his place of birth after he had stood in one of their games against Lancashire – but that failed protest was not made until after they had been beaten by five runs. He had umpired previously at Old Trafford, the MCC having given their approval in believing that he came from Derbyshire. Curiously, there was a similar mix-up in the 1901 Census, which transposed the findings of the previous one of 1881 by giving Smith's place of birth as Glossop and his wife Mary Jane's as Bury.

Butterley-born Jim Disney, a plumber by trade, took over from Smith behind the stumps for Derbyshire in 1881, the year in which he first played at Lord's as one of the Twenty-three Colts of England against the MCC. He completed a half-century of first-class appearances for Derbyshire over the next thirteen seasons, towards the end of which he was professional with the Stockport club – an appointment that led to his winding up his county career with Cheshire.

Although William Mycroft, acknowledged as one of the country's best left-arm bowlers of the time, missed Test selection, his appearances in an England XI included a drawn game with the Australians, in which he took four wickets, at Derby in 1882. The national selectors may well have been influenced against awarding him a Test cap because of some questioning of his action in sending down one particular type of delivery. *Wisden* asserted that there was 'little doubt that his fast yorker with which he used to get so many wickets was open to serious question on the score of fairness'. In saying that, when recording his death, after months of impaired health, during the summer of 1894, the almanack conceded that 'on this point there is now no occasion to dwell'. No indeed. Walter Piper, though open to some accusation of bias, hailed Mycroft as 'a bowler whose superior the world has scarcely seen' in his history of the Derbyshire club published towards the end of the nineteenth century. The benefit awarded in the August of 1883 to this formidable forerunner in the county's envied line of exceptional opening bowlers was truly well earned, with the occasion marked by a match at Derby in which an England XI defeated a combined Lancashire and Yorkshire side by an innings and nineteen runs.

Season after season Mycroft produced the most remarkable bowling figures, right from the first of his seventy-eight games for Derbyshire in which he took 6-35 in Lancashire's first innings at Derby at the beginning of the 1873 season. He snapped up ten or more wickets in a match for Derbyshire eighteen times, and twenty-eight in all with the inclusion of the sixty first-class fixtures in which he played for other teams. Too often, however, his efforts went without the reward of a win, so unreliable were his colleagues in batting. Derbyshire were beaten despite his fine start in 1873, and two years later they contrived to lose at home again to Lancashire, and by an innings at that, despite his 9-80.

Most frustrating of all, in the following season he took all but two of the nineteen Hampshire wickets that fell at Southampton's Antelope Ground, only to see the home county edge to victory with their last pair together. Mycroft had a hand in every wicket in Hampshire's first innings, taking 9-25 and catching the other batsman off the bowling of George Hay, who three years later equally shared Yorkshire's twenty wickets with Mycroft as Derbyshire, winners by an innings at Derby after also succeeding at Sheffield three weeks earlier, completed a season's double over that county for what is still the only time. In the 27-run win at sodden Bramall Lane, Mycroft returned the best match figures of 13-65 by a Derbyshire bowler against Yorkshire. His return of 12-42 at Maidstone in 1875 also has yet to be bettered for the county against Kent. The sole wicket to elude Mycroft in his second-innings 8-78 at Southampton in 1876, apart from either of the unbeaten last pair's, was that of opener Hector Hyslop, who was caught off Jack Platts. Hyslop, who also played a few matches for the first Australian tourists in England a couple of years later, was to be one of those tragic cricketers who were plunged into the depression of taking their own lives.

Mycroft, whose match figures of 17-103 not surprisingly remain the best for any team against Hampshire to this day, was the first bowler to take so many wickets in one game and finish on the losing side, a bitter-sweet feat equalled by Walter Mead for Essex, also against Hampshire at Southampton, in 1895. That made Mead, a slow-medium bowler with exceptional powers of spin, the first twice to claim seventeen victims in one game, for two years earlier he had also done so against the Australians. 'Tich' Freeman, the Kent spinner whose tally of 3,776 first-class wickets is second only to the 4,187 of Yorkshire's Wilfred Rhodes, has alone matched that achievement (against Sussex at Hove, and Warwickshire at Folkestone).

My researches into Mycroft's Match at Southampton in 1876 at first led me to believe that it was a second-class fixture, causing me to look upon Cliff Gladwin's sixteen wickets for 84 runs against Worcestershire at Stourbridge in 1952 as the best match figures by a Derbyshire player at the first-class level – as, indeed, they were given in the *Playfair Cricket Annual* up to 1987. Desmond Eagar, who was with the Hampshire club, first as captain and joint secretary, then as secretary, from 1946 until his death while on holiday in Devon in 1977, said in *Wisden* that 'the story of Hampshire cricket from 1793 until the county became first-class over 100 years later is one of apathy and constant disappointment'.

An inquiry direct to the county's headquarters a few years ago brought the reply that 'Hampshire CCC achieved first-class status in 1895', with the bold added assertion: 'This fact is not in doubt.' Two well-known statisticians of their time, Maurice Golesworthy and Roy Webber, were of the opinion that Hampshire did not achieve first-class status until they were brought into the County Championship in 1895, although Webber did admit to some 'confusion'. In his book *County Cricket Championship,* he wrote:

'Hampshire played first-class counties in some seasons, but did not undertake such matches in other years, so that further confusion occurs in the 1880s. Somerset come into the same category and in 1882, at least, there is a strong claim for both Hampshire and Somerset to be regarded as partaking in the Championship. The 1920 *Wisden* is the first to include a consolidated match results table for all Championship matches from 1873, and as Hampshire and Somerset matches are excluded before the 1890s this seems to tell against their claims to first-class status at that time. The MCC promoted Somerset to first-class status in 1891 and Hampshire in 1895, a ruling that would not have been necessary if they had been regarded as first-class in previous years.'

As I have since discovered, however, that 'official' response from the Hampshire club has been emphatically contradicted by the fact that the match Derbyshire played at Southampton in 1876 is among those that have been rated first-class in the Hampshire Yearbook for quite some time. Moreover, since Eagar, Golesworthy and Webber went into print with their differing information, the Association of Cricket Statisticians has been formed and gone to considerable trouble to study all debatable matches on their merits, taking note of contemporary opinions and the strength of the sides involved. The outcome of that tremendous amount of research – 'a miraculous creation' is how it has so rightly been described to me – has included the decision, now widely accepted throughout the statistical world, that Hampshire *were* first-class from 1864-70, 1875-78 and 1880-85, but were again temporarily reduced to second-class from 1886 to 1894. Their form in 1894 justified their addition in the October of that year to the four counties (Derbyshire, Essex, Leicestershire and Warwickshire) which had been admitted to the Championship at the previous May's meeting of county captains, with effect from the following season.

Wisden's list of each county's final seasonal positions now dates back only to 1890, the first year of what have become the official champions, but the almanack's summary of first-class match results in relation to Hampshire is firmly in line with the ACS's findings. So there you have it. Mycroft, after well over one hundred years, is still regarded as Derbyshire's most prolific wicket-taker in one match of first-class standing.

First-class though counties that competed in the Championship were considered to be, even during its unofficial phase, it is interesting, and not a little surprising, to note that, as Bill Frindall stated in his *Wisden Book of Cricket Records,* the term 'first-class match' was not officially defined until as late as 19 May 1947 – and even then it did not have retrospective effect. On that date the six countries represented at the Imperial Cricket Conference at Lord's (Australia, England, India, New Zealand, South Africa and West Indies) agreed that 'a match of three of more days' duration between two sides of eleven players officially adjudged first-class, shall be regarded as a first-class fixture. Matches in which either team has more than eleven players or which are scheduled for less than three days shall not be regarded as first-class. The governing body in each country shall decide the status of the teams.'

This ruling, which, as not retrospective, had no bearing on the 1919 season in which the promptly discarded experiment was tried of limiting matches in the County Championship to two days, gave MCC the authority to decide the status of all matches in Britain for the first time. 'Although they had controlled the status of the counties since 1895,' said Frindall, 'the classification of matches outside the County Championship had rested largely with the Cricket Reporting Agency, who compiled the "first-class averages" for the leading publications of the day. Only occasionally did the agency consult the MCC.' In compiling his records, Frindall accepted that the Association of Cricket Statisticians' guide to the ranking of matches from 1864 until the 1947 ruling removed all problems of classification. It was from 1864, the year in which 'overhand bowling' was authorised and *Wisden* was first published, that, as Frindall put it, 'the division between first-class and other matches becomes more obvious.'

After 1876, Derbyshire paid only two more visits to Southampton before their fixtures with Hampshire were temporarily discontinued until both counties were restored to the Championship in 1895, and on both those occasions they did manage to exploit Mycroft's mastery with convincing victories. In 1877 he took six wickets in each home innings at a total cost of only 47 runs; a year later he not only had match figures of 10-82 but also made his highest score in county cricket, 44 not out.

However, in the match immediately after the first of those visits to the south coast, at Lord's in the late May of 1877, Mycroft was back in the familiar groove of having all his good work undone. Against the MCC, he took thirteen wickets, eleven of them clean bowled, for 104 runs (8-47 and 5-57). He hit the stumps three times in four balls, four times in six, without having a run scored off him. Yet MCC won by forty runs thanks to one of W G Grace's outstanding all-round performances. In addition to outdoing Mycroft with fourteen wickets for 109 runs, the illustrious Gloucestershire doctor was top scorer in each MCC innings – after being missed at point off the very first ball of the game. The unfortunate bowler was, of course, Mycroft, who himself took fourteen wickets in one match while playing for the North against the South at Loughborough in 1875.

Considering that he left it so late to start out with Derbyshire, Mycroft did astonishingly well to total almost 550 wickets in just 78 matches for the county, and 863 in 138 first-class games overall, at the cheap cost of around twelve runs apiece, even though batting techniques in wet conditions, and the preparation of pitches, then lacked the sophistication of later years. His appearances were limited by his rheumatism in 1883 and 1885, his final season with Derbyshire, and he did not play county cricket at all during the intervening year. By that time he was an innkeeper in Chesterfield, where he and his wife Sarah lived with their five sons and three daughters.

Mycroft was promptly engaged by the MCC after he had played at Lord's against them for the first time in 1876, taking 6-30 and 5-44 in Derbyshire's innings victory, and he was a member of their ground staff until as late as 1893. So well known did he become, also as an umpire, it has been suggested he was the inspiration for the name Mycroft being given by Sir Arthur Conan Doyle (no mean cricketer himself) to Sherlock Holmes's brother. Not only that, there was another Derbyshire player, Frank Shacklock, who was said to have influenced the choice of the great detective's own name. Shacklock, who was also on the MCC ground staff, was born in Derbyshire but came from a Nottinghamshire family at Kirkby-in-Ashfield, and he spent the greater part of his career with Notts on either side of two seasons of considerable success for his home county.

While on this subject, it is also interesting to recall that it was from cricket that P G Wodehouse derived the name Jeeves for Bertie Wooster's butler. The novelist who caricatured the English upper classes happened to see Percy Jeeves playing for Warwickshire against Gloucestershire at Cheltenham in 1913. 'I suppose,' he later wrote, 'that Jeeves's bowling must have impressed me, for I remembered him in 1916 when I was in New York and starting the Jeeves and Bertie saga.'

In one of the matches in which Mycroft umpired, he controversially gave Worcestershire wicketkeeper Tom Straw out for obstructing the field at Worcester in 1899. Straw lofted the ball towards the middle of the pitch and began to run while a Warwickshire fielder, Alfred Glover, ran in to try to catch it. Straw was ruled out by Mycroft when he and Glover collided, though many of the onlookers saw it as accidental. Straw became the only player to be given out twice for obstructing the field when, two years later – and again against Warwickshire, but this time at Edgbaston – he barged into 'Dick' Lilley as the wicketkeeper came from behind the stumps to take a simple popped-up catch. This was far more flagrant obstruction, and *Wisden* suggested that, in view of Mycroft's earlier decision, it was possible Straw was 'taking the mickey'.

Having offset his failure to score in either innings of his solitary appearance for Notts in 1883 by taking five MCC wickets for 48 runs, Frank Shacklock achieved his finest performance for Derbyshire with returns of 8-45 and 5-97 in the benefit match, drawn with Yorkshire, awarded in 1885 to Jack Platts, the left-hand batsman and right-arm bowler who scored the club's first century, 115, against Hampshire at Derby in 1877 (he took an unbeaten 90 off Yorkshire in the next match) and achieved their first hat-trick, against Yorkshire, also at Derby, in 1880.

Tragedy changed Platts from being a very fast bowler. It was a ball delivered by him in a match between MCC and Notts at Lord's in 1870 that caused the death of George Summers. Platts lessened his pace after that, and he was so badly affected by such a horrendous occurrence that he never again played with any pleasure at the headquarters of cricket. His remarkably consistent career with Derbyshire spanned fourteen seasons, after which he continued in the game as a first-class umpire until not long before his death at the early age of forty-nine in 1898.

Shacklock took eight wickets in an innings on four other occasions during his eight seasons back with Notts, whom he helped to share the now-unofficial 1889 title with Surrey and Lancashire by claiming eighty at low cost. His 8-46 against Somerset at Trent Bridge in 1893 included four in four balls. He subsequently gave some excellent displays for Lasswade in Scottish cricket – most notably all eleven wickets in a 12-a-side match with Edinburgh University and all ten against Loretto – before emigrating to coach in New Zealand, where he died in 1937, aged seventy-five.

Much, no doubt, to Rowland Bowen's disapproval, Derbyshire prefaced their big year of 1874 with another victory when they again fielded sixteen men against the Notts XI in the return match at Nottingham, this time by fourteen wickets (more about that in the next chapter). But when it came to meeting on level terms Derbyshire were very much second best, going without a win against those neighbours from 1875, when Alfred Shaw's match figures of 12 for 62, including a hat-trick, outsmarted Mycroft's 12 for 119 in their first Championship encounter, through to 1903, when, after twenty-five unsuccessful attempts, they finally won by 114 runs at Derby. And it was not until 1934 that they triumphed for the first time at Trent Bridge – by 28 runs, despite having to contend with the daunting Larwood-Voce opening attack.

Derbyshire's nearest approach to ending their bleak run of results against Notts before at long last managing it came at Derby in July 1898, when they finished only twenty runs short with two wickets left. Frank Davidson was the hat-trick man on that occasion, polishing off the visitors' first innings. His brother George – who that season also did the hat-trick, for the second time, against MCC at Lord's – struck two key blows when Notts batted again by dismissing century-maker Arthur Shrewsbury and his partner in a big second-wicket stand, William Gunn, senior member of a famous Notts cricketing family.

Shrewsbury, who only five years later plunged into such deep depression because of illness and the end of his career that he committed suicide, was widely regarded as the finest professional batsman of his day, though George Gunn, nephew of William, later earned in his obituary the *Wisden* accolade of being 'probably the greatest batsman who played for Nottinghamshire'. That home draw with Notts in 1898 was one of seven in eight successive matches between the clubs. Derbyshire were again losers in the exception, but rain had an important influence on most of the others. William Chatterton was the unfortunate beneficiary when the weather intervened after Derbyshire, caught on a treacherous pitch, had narrowly failed to get into three figures in reply to a total of 466, compiled in far more favourable conditions, to which William Gunn contributed an unbeaten double-century. Gunn was again the main obstacle when George Davidson, who had him caught at the wicket for 152, was also awarded a benefit. That match ran its full uninterrupted course, but with no time left for Notts to attempt a target of just under 150.

Revenge for that sensational collapse of 1873 against the home county's sixteen men at Wirksworth was sweet and very near precise for Notts at Trent Bridge only six years later when they dismissed Derbyshire for their record low total of 16 and then whipped them out again for 44 to win by an innings and 99 runs. Tommy Foster, son of a Glossop cotton weaver, was top scorer with a paltry seven runs in that deplorable first innings in which seven Derbyshire batsmen failed to get off the mark, and he alone reached double figures, with 19, in the follow-on. The renowned Alfred Shaw and Fred Morley shared all twenty wickets, twelve of them falling to the fast left-arm bowling of Morley, whose seven in the first innings cost only seven runs. In the return game at Nottingham, which Notts also won by an innings, Morley took seven wickets in both innings, his 14-53 still standing as his county's match-best against Derbyshire.

Morley, four times a Test player, remained a force with Notts until the early 1880s. He broke a rib when the ship on which he was travelling for the 1882-83 tour of Australia was in collision with another off Colombo, but recovered in time to play a prominent part in the creation of the famous Ashes. It was after England's victory at Sydney, where Morley and Dick Barlow bowled unchanged in Australia's dismissal for 83, that some Melbourne women gave substance to the mock obituary notice, written by the son of an editor of *Punch*, which the *Sporting Times* had published 'in affectionate remembrance of English cricket' following Australia's first Test victory in England, by seven runs at The Oval on 29 August 1882. After Australia had lost at home in the following series, those women presented the England captain, the Hon Ivo Bligh, later Lord Darnley, with an urn in which they had placed the ashes from the burning of a stump used in the deciding third game of that rubber. When Lord Darnley died in 1927, he bequeathed it to the MCC in his will, and, contrary to the *nota bene* in the *Sporting Times* that 'the body [deeply lamented by a large circle of sorrowing friends and acquaintances] will be cremated and the Ashes taken to Australia', it has since stayed at Lord's, no matter who the holders have been. It was in the Long Room there until 1953, when, with other cricket treasures, it was moved to the newly built Imperial Cricket Memorial near the pavilion. There it stands with the velvet bag in which the urn was originally given, and the scorecard of the 1882 match.

Sadly, Morley was only thirty-three when he died during the year after returning from his trip to Australia. Alfred Shaw, another of the truly great players of his day, had a career in cricket that lasted for more than forty years. It began in 1864 when he took thirteen wickets in his debut at Lord's for the Colts of England against the MCC, and ended with his omission from the umpires' list for 1906 only because of failing health. Having started out at medium-pace, he was the best slow bowler in England at the time of that first confrontation with Derbyshire. His five tours of Australia included the inaugural Test at Melbourne in 1887 in which he played the first of his seven matches for England. Notts discarded him for being too old at 44 after the 1886 season, but eight years later he took the last of more than two thousand wickets after being persuaded to come out of retirement with Sussex, whose bowling averages he topped, on taking up an engagement in that county with Lord Sheffield.

Derbyshire lost to Notts three more times by an innings, and twice by ten wickets, before that sequence of drawn games with them began on their return to the Championship in 1895. The biggest of those beatings was by an innings and 250 runs at Derby in 1885, when another England player, Billy Barnes, an all-rounder whose brother Tom and son Jim also played for Notts, took thirteen wickets cheaply as the home side collapsed after two other Test men, Arthur Shrewsbury and Wilfred Flowers, had taken centuries off an attack deprived of the injured Shacklock.

Flowers, whose 173 was the highest score of his career, was also an exceptional slow bowler, and two years earlier Derbyshire had felt the full force of his all-round ability in a match with the MCC at Lord's in which he had taken ten of their wickets and scored a century. In view of the splendid service he gave to his county, and to cricket generally, it was most unfortunate, however, that Flowers did not have the best of luck with his benefits. The one Notts gave him at Trent Bridge finished early on the second day thanks to the fifteen wickets Arthur Mold took for Lancashire. Then MCC arranged one at Lord's in recognition of his efforts for them over a good many years, only for the first day's play on the Whitsun Bank Holiday of 1899 to be washed out, and the game, between Middlesex and Somerset, to be all over in three hours and five minutes on a drying pitch the next day. It remains the shortest first-class match on record. Notts later made up for all that by awarding him part of the proceeds from another match at Trent Bridge, but misfortune still dogged him as failing eyesight forced him to give up the umpiring to which he had turned after giving up playing.

4. Keeping it in the Family

The repetition of Derbyshire's defeat of Nottinghamshire with sixteen men against eleven in the return match in Nottingham at the start of the 1874 season was again mainly due to the bowling of William Mycroft and Joe Flint – if on a less spectacular scale. Both took eight wickets as Notts were dismissed for 65 and 125 in reply to a total of 163. That set Derbyshire to get just 28 runs to win, and they obtained them for the loss of only the wicket of Robert Smith, top scorer in their first innings, eight runs from a half-century.

Derbyshire also ended the season by fielding a team of sixteen against the regulation eleven – in this case a United XI of some of the leading players in the south of England. The most distinguished of those visitors to Derby was the great man himself, Dr W G Grace, who fittingly was their top scorer with 51 in their first innings and also their most successful bowler with eight wickets in the match at a cost of 84 runs.

On another visit to Derby, with his London County team in 1900, W G had a very different, most unhappy, experience. With the pitch turned into a gluepot by rain that cut play to just under three hours on the first day and completely washed it out on the second, he fell lbw for two runs in his first innings, and for nought in his second. James Gilman, one of his colleagues, had this memory of it in an interview he gave to Jack Arlidge, published in *Wisden*, shortly before his death at the age of ninety-seven in 1976:

'The first decision did not seem a good one. Grace stalked off to the dressing room, and there was a rare old rumpus. Grace had one leg out of his flannels and kept saying: "I won't be cheated out. I've a good mind to go home." We tried to calm him down, and a whisky and seltzer came to the rescue. The real hero was that same umpire who gave him out again!'

That game was drawn because of the time lost to the weather. A week earlier, W G had scored 87 and 44 in London County's defeat of Derbyshire at the Crystal Palace. In 1874, however, his typically effective all-round effort was not enough to deny Derbyshire victory. Flint was once more to the fore with 6-51 and 5-36 in the United's dismissal for 167 and 86, and Derbyshire scored the 52 runs they needed for the loss of two wickets after Bill Hickton (52) and John Tye (43) had done most to help them to a first-innings total of 202. Apart from the Champion, the only batsman to trouble the home attack unduly was Frank Silcock, of Essex, who was caught off Flint when needing just a single for a half-century.

Mycroft had to be content with four wickets in that match, but it was again his combination with Flint that carried Derbyshire to success when they played the first of their four Championship games of 1874 in Manchester at the end of the week following their sixteen's defeat of Notts. In two days Lancashire were beaten by nine wickets, forced into an improved but still unavailing uphill battle after being routed for 38 in their first innings as Mycroft (6-23) and Flint (4-14) shared the attack unchanged with fifteen four-ball overs apiece. Following on 152 runs behind, Lancashire had their late-order batsmen chiefly to thank for totalling 181, William McIntyre making the biggest individual score of 48 before being caught by Flint off Mycroft.

Derbyshire's opening pair both had eight wickets in the match, but, with McIntyre for once going unrewarded as a bowler, they were upstaged by Alec Watson. The Scottish spinner took 9-117 in Derbyshire's first innings of 190, the only wicket to elude him being that of Sam Richardson, who was run out, and he also claimed the only one to fall, that of Smith, as the 30 runs required were knocked off. Smith's opening partner was top scorer when Derbyshire first batted, fellow amateur Abraham Shuker marking his first-class debut with a steady innings of 41. A Shropshire man, Shuker qualified for Derbyshire by living at Trent College, where he was a master, but he made only infrequent appearances over the next eight years and not until his final one, against Sussex at Brighton in 1882, did he make his biggest score of 86 – only his second half-century. He had previously played for Staffordshire while a member of the Wolverhampton club.

The return match with Lancashire at Chesterfield in 1874 resulted in a draw, bad weather limiting both sides to just one innings as the third day's play was washed out. In the absence of Mycroft, Flint shared the opening attack with Bill Hickton, who had the best figures of 6-61 in the visitors' dismissal for 161. Flint had the rare experience of being left wicketless, and it was scant compensation for him to be the most successful batsman, with a modest two dozen runs, in a Derbyshire reply that ended 57 runs in arrears. Watson (6-43) and McIntyre (3-41) again did the damage. The one man to escape them in being run out was Edward Estridge, an amateur from Middlesex whose four runs in what was to be his only innings in first-class cricket made him the first player from Repton College, where he was on the teaching staff, to get on the scoresheet for the county.

Kent, Derbyshire's other opponents in the Championship that year, were beaten at both Wirksworth and Tunbridge Wells. Their first-innings total of 25 on their first venture into Derbyshire was the smallest by any county during the season, Mycroft conceding only eight runs for his five wickets and Flint taking 4-17, but Derbyshire also found it hard going as Edgar Willsher, a fast left-arm bowler who claimed more than a thousand victims in his career, completed a match return of 13 for 58 with seven wickets in their second-innings dismissal for 36. That presented Kent with a reasonable victory target of 109, yet it proved 34 beyond them, Mycroft and Flint sharing seven more of their wickets.

Stiffer resistance was offered by a stronger Kent team in the return match, but Derbyshire edged ahead on first innings and then obtained the 195 runs required for the loss of seven wickets. This time their redoubtable opening bowlers had to take a back seat as Hickton followed up his 6-15 on the opening day with 5-68 as Kent battled to within two runs of 200 in their second innings. Willsher, too, was overshadowed, William Draper's nine wickets including his best figures of 5-51 in Derbyshire's victory chase.

Outside the Championship, Derbyshire met Yorkshire for the first time in 1874. They gave a good account of themselves in a drawn game at Derby, but had the worst of another draw at Leeds when both teams were below strength. Half-centuries by Charles Ullathorne and Walter Smith, and one run shy of one by John Hicks, helped Yorkshire, under their 'United' label, to a substantial lead on first innings in the first encounter despite another five-wicket haul for Mycroft, but Dr W G Curgenven led a fine fight-back when Derbyshire batted again, with sound support from Robert Smith. Top scorer with 34 in a home first innings of 105 that was marred by three run-outs, Curgenven made 74, Derbyshire's highest individual score up to that time, and Smith reached exactly 50. At the finish Derbyshire were almost 100 ahead with three wickets in hand.

There was time for Derbyshire to bat only once in the return game in Yorkshire, where they trailed by 54 runs on first innings after an attack deprived of Mycroft and Hickton had done reasonably well to restrict the home team to a total of 183. The end came with Yorkshire's last-wicket pair together in their second innings, and the lead increased to just beyond 200.

William Grafton Curgenven, to give him his full name, also missed that match. Plymouth-born, he played his early cricket in Devon before moving to a medical practice in Derby, and it was for the Gentlemen of Devon that he first appeared at Lord's, against the MCC, in 1864. He headed the batting averages (if with very ordinary figures in those days of much moderate scoring) in the first three of his six seasons with Derbyshire, making his biggest first-class score of 71 in an innings defeat of Kent at Derby in 1875, and he afterwards served on the county's committee for many years.

His sons Gilbert and Henry also played for Derbyshire. Gilbert, the younger brother, enjoyed the greater success over nearly one hundred matches during ten of the seasons from 1901 to 1922, but Henry, a medium-pace bowler who played in fewer than a dozen games for the county, came up with the more memorable achievement in taking a wicket with his first ball in first-class cricket. His victim, lbw for 21 at Leyton in 1896, was Frederick Luther Fane, an Essex and England batsman who much later was also the subject of something very unusual. In the 1956 *Wisden,* Fane had his death reported four years before it actually occurred, the error arising from a similarity of initials. He had been confused with his cousin Francis L Fane. And that was not all. 'By a coincidence,' reported *Wisden* in making the correction, 'Mr Fane informs us his father also once read his own obituary.'

Gilbert Curgenven, stylish but also a hearty striker of the ball, was one of the most gifted of the players from Repton School to turn out for Derbyshire

– a line that dates right back to two old boys, the Rev A A Wilmot and Edward Foley, who, as has already been noted, both made their only appearance in the county's very first home match and were both out twice without scoring. Although the call never came for them again, they were useful cricketers – Wilmot especially. He was only fourteen when he played for Repton against the Old Reptonians in 1859, and while at Oxford he was admitted to the Harlequins club that was limited to those judged to be the best sixteen players at the university. In the year of his Derbyshire debut, 1871, he was appointed rector of the Morley-cum-Smalley parish near Derby, but he died only five years later at the early age of 31. Foley's father was also a clergyman, but he himself became a solicitor.

After captaining the Repton team and heading their batting averages, Gilbert Curgenven earned the distinction of being the first Reptonian to exceed a thousand runs for the county. He altogether went close to 3,500 in a first-class career that was interrupted for six seasons (1906-08 and 1911-13) by a spell in Canada and his running of a milk business in Birmingham, then by the First World War.

He was most regularly available to Derbyshire in 1904, 1914 and 1921 (the only year in which he did not miss a match), but he scored two of his three centuries in 1910, when he played in only seven games. He reached three figures in just over 100 minutes in a defeat by Essex at Leyton, hitting fifteen fours and two sixes, and struck six more sixes in his 109 out of 142 in an hour and a half against Notts in a rained-off draw at Blackwell. The extent to which he dominated Derbyshire's first innings of 185 at Leyton is shown by the fact that the next highest score was 23, a personal best for James Handford, a batsman from Hayfield, in his only season of first-class cricket. Gilbert Curgenven's other century was his first at county level – 124 against Surrey at Derby in 1904. Of all Derbyshire's Reptonians, and there have been nearly thirty of them, only Donald Carr and Guy Willatt, captains during seasons of some success through the 1950s into the early 1960s, have scored more runs for the county.

As a public school drawing its pupils from many parts of the country, Repton has supplied an impressive number of cricketers to counties other than Derbyshire – most notably Charles Fry, one of the most accomplished of all-round sportsmen, the Palairet brothers (Richard and the more famous Lionel), Jack Crawford, who was an immediate success with Surrey at the age of seventeen, and Bryan Valentine, a captain of Kent who was also adept at golf, lawn tennis and soccer. Seven members of the Ford family played cricket for Repton – the father and six uncles of Neville Ford, who, unlike them, assisted Derbyshire and was himself educated at Harrow while his father was headmaster there. Three of the brothers, Augustus, Francis, the youngest, and William, played for Middlesex (as also did Neville), and Francis, a left-hand batsman, took part in five Tests.

Neville Ford made only just over thirty appearances for Derbyshire, the first in 1926 and the last in 1934, and achieved little of note beyond three innings in the sixties, but he scored four centuries for Oxford University, winning his Blue in three successive seasons from 1928. He also toured Canada with the MCC two years before joining the Army on the outbreak of the Second World War. He took part in the Norway campaign and was training for D-Day in the south of England in 1944 when, with security at its tightest, he was allowed leave to Northern Ireland for the birth of his second daughter only after he had personally given Field Marshal Montgomery the right reply to the Commander-in-Chief's brusque question: 'Can you keep your trap shut?' After D-Day, Ford's voice was so distinctive in radio communication as he advanced into Belgium in one of the leading armoured cars that a captured German officer inquired if 'the British officer with the foghorn voice' was still alive because they had not heard him lately. Thereafter Ford found the nickname 'Foghorn' inescapable.

In the family context as far as it concerns Derbyshire, the Curgenvens are in good company with the three Dockers and three Popes (of whom more later), but outnumbered by the Eversheds, Slaters and Hill-Woods.

Ludford Charles Docker was the more accomplished of the three Staffordshire-born brothers who played for the county. Powerfully built and more than six feet tall, he was captain in succession to Robert Smith in 1884, the fourth of the six seasons he spent in making almost fifty appearances for Derbyshire. Noted for the freedom of his driving, he headed the county's batting in the first four of those seasons – though that was not saying all that much considering he twice did so with an average only a fraction above eighteen and managed only one century (107 in a three-wicket defeat of Kent at Maidstone in 1881).

After leaving Derbyshire following the 1886 season, Docker scored three centuries in a row. Two of them were for his home club, Smethwick, in cup games, the other for Warwickshire, whom he represented in fewer than a dozen games, but later served as president for some fifteen years up to 1930. He played his other county cricket for Worcestershire before they achieved first-class status, and assisted Handsworth Wood in the Birmingham League. His brothers Frank and Ralph, who both played in just a couple of matches for Derbyshire, were also with Warwickshire while that county was still rated second class.

When two English teams toured Australia in 1887-88, Ludford Docker was in the one taken by Arthur Shrewsbury and Alfred Shaw, who both also played, under the captaincy of C Aubrey Smith, the Cambridge Blue and Sussex player who was known as 'Round the Corner' Smith, because of his run-up to bowl from a deep mid-off position or from behind the umpire, before becoming a well-known film actor in Hollywood. The other team was captained by the Hon M B Hawke (as Lord Hawke then was) and managed by the

Melbourne club. Docker found no place in the England side, chosen from both touring parties, that won the only Test with the Surrey amateur Walter Read as captain after Smith and his fellow skipper George Vernon (appointed when Hawke returned home following the death of his father) had also failed to gain selection. Vernon, a Middlesex batsman who had won one Test cap against Australia several years earlier, also played for England at rugby.

Although the Test call never came for Docker, he had already played for an England XI against the Australians. In 1882, he was with William Mycroft in the strong representative side bearing that title which had the worst of the rained-off draw at Derby with the third touring side from the Antipodes. The Australians, for whom Frederick ('Demon') Spofforth, later to play for Derbyshire, took nine wickets in the match, were only thirty-eight runs from victory, with half their wickets intact, at the enforced finish.

The Slaters supplied Harry and his three sons, Archie, Herbert and George, to Derbyshire cricket, a combined length of service extending from 1882 to 1931, though George, the eldest, played only in the 1900 match with the West Indians that was not rated first-class.

And there were four other Slater sons who acquitted themselves well in club cricket – Harry Junior, Arthur and Sam, who all played for the Creswell Colliery first team, and Stuart, the youngest of the seven, and the only one not to work at that pit, who captained Warsop Main. Sam, a batsman difficult to dislodge, eventually moved to Bentley, in the Doncaster coalfield, and gained further experience in the Yorkshire Council.

In his early days, Harry Senior was in a travelling troupe known as the 'Clown Cricketers' who were a big attraction at galas, fetes and flower shows in combining their comical antics with not a little playing skill. Heanor-born, he lived at Pilsley and Tibshelf before settling down at Creswell, where a new coal mine had been sunk in 1898. That area near the county's eastern border with Yorkshire and Nottinghamshire was a big provider of cricketing talent, dating back to the first appearance for Derbyshire in 1880 of James Stubbings, whose brother Walter played just one game for the county ten years later.

Herbert, the most stylish batsman among the Slaters, also played for Shirebrook and the Oxcroft and Mansfield colliery teams, but he did not take his cricket as seriously as his brothers did. He frequently had to be lured out of 'retirement' when Creswell Colliery were a man short, and it said much for his innate ability that he was still capable of a useful innings even when out of practice. It was therefore left to Archie to achieve the greater success, right from the moment on Whit Tuesday in 1909 when he was the Creswell first team's top scorer against Worksop on his debut at the tender age of fifteen. Admittedly, he made only five runs, but the rest of the side managed one fewer between them.

Not far below Test standard, Archie accumulated almost six thousand runs in a little more than two hundred first-class matches, took exactly five hundred wickets, and held over one hundred catches. A medium-paced bowler who exploited both swing and spin, he profited greatly from the leg theory form of attack, delivering from round the wicket, and made his last county season of 1931 his most successful with the ball in taking 108 wickets at a cost of only just over sixteen runs each. His 8-24 in a West Indian innings at Derby in 1928 and 14-48, including three wickets in four balls, in the match with Somerset at Chesterfield in 1930 have still to be surpassed for Derbyshire against those opponents. He is also a joint holder of the county's record for the number of catches in one game, wicketkeepers apart, with six at Leyton in 1914.

As a batsman, he had to wait sixteen years from his county debut in 1911 for his only first-class century, but that was at least partly due to the fact that he found league cricket a more lucrative outlet for his talent. 'There was,' he freely admitted, 'only one question – a financial one. The terms were too good to refuse.' Consequently, he interrupted his spells with Derbyshire by accepting engagements in the Bradford and Lancashire leagues, helping Bacup to a league and cup double, and in 1931 he was tempted back to the Lancashire League by an offer from the Colne club. Five years later, while Derbyshire were winning the Championship, he was the professional at Rawtenstall.

The season of 1927 in which he made that lone century for Derbyshire, 105 against Warwickshire, was the first of the successive five in which he was a county regular – after missing three figures by only one run in a stand of 191 with Arthur Morton, who was out for 96, against Hampshire at Basingstoke in 1914. That partnership stood as a Derbyshire record for the fifth wicket until exceeded first by Chris Wilkins and Ian Buxton, who added 203 at Old Trafford in 1971, then by John Morris and Dominic Cork, who increased it to 302 at Cheltenham in 1993. In all, the score was raised by 346, from 58 to 404, between the fall of the fourth and fifth wickets in that match with Gloucestershire, which Derbyshire won by seven wickets after both sides had exceeded 500. Matthew Vandrau, Surrey-born but Johannesburg-raised, joined Morris when Cork had to retire because of a hamstring injury and shared in the run feast with a half-century. Morris, a Cheshire-born briefly England batsman who later won other county caps with Durham and Nottinghamshire, completed his first double-century, with 32 fours and three sixes in his 229 (he made an unbeaten 71 in the second innings), and Cork resumed to reach a maiden Championship century with the aid of a runner.

At Edgbaston in 1912, Archie Slater was the unwitting cause of an unusual umpiring error. There was no doubt that he was out – Sydney Santall, whose son Frederick followed him into the Warwickshire side, bowled him with the sixth ball of an over – but the umpire failed to call 'Over' at the fall of that wicket, and Santall sent down five more deliveries before he did so. Strangely enough, another Warwickshire player, Jack Marshall, also had an extended over in the course of taking 5-65 with his leg-breaks and googlies on his debut against Worcestershire at Dudley in 1946.

Four Evershed brothers in the Burton brewing family played for Derbyshire, but one of them, Frank, did so only during the second-class exile. They also had a cousin, Geoffrey Bell, who played a few times for Derbyshire – the first of them while still a Repton student, the others after winning a Blue at Oxford. Bell, later headmaster at Trent College and Highgate School, had little success in first-class cricket, but he scored 159 for the county against Dublin University at Burton in 1921, adding 301 for the fifth wicket with Joe Bowden. In the same year he also played in a two-day game with the West of Scotland that was best remembered for the fact that one of the umpires was so drunk that he had to be replaced. Bell's biggest score at the top level was 64 for the Gentlemen of England against Oxford in the first first-class match to be played after the 1914-18 War, and, though failing as a batsman, he caught the eye in the 1919 Varsity Match by sprinting some thirty yards to hold a great catch in the deep.

Frank Evershed, who scored a century in Derbyshire's innings defeat of Norfolk at Norwich in 1890, attracted some extra, if undesirable, attention in being another of the cricketers whose death has been prematurely reported. He survived for another nine years after *Wisden* had told of his demise 'in London, March 18, 1945.'

The most efficient cricketer among the Evershed brothers, who, like Bell, were all born in Staffordshire, was the eldest, Sydney Herbert Evershed, later Sir Herbert, who made his Derbyshire debut at nineteen in 1880 after doing well as a batsman at Clifton College. He helped the county to regain first-class status in 1895 during his eight years as captain up to 1898, though he had the misfortune to miss most of the 1894 season after being thrown from his trap. It was then that George Walker had a turn as his deputy. Herbert Evershed also served as chairman and president after ending his playing career in the grand manner by reaching a century before lunch, and altogether scoring 123 out of 170 for the first wicket, on the opening day of the last of his 76 first-class matches, his only one of 1901, against Hampshire at Southampton.

The biggest of his four centuries was 153 out of 229 in just under three hours in a drawn game with Warwickshire at Derby in 1898, his most successful season. He had his day as a rarely used bowler at Derby in 1883, when, put on as a last resort, he polished off the MCC's first innings with five wickets at a cost of only nineteen runs in a drawn game curtailed by the weather. On continuing playing with the Burton club, of which he was captain from 1880 until his death at seventy-six in March 1937, he averaged 59, heading the batting averages, in 1913 at the age of fifty-two. He was also an adept rugby player, captaining the Burton club and Midland Counties, twice playing for the North against the South, and once chosen as reserve half-back for England.

Wallis Evershed was a regular member of the Derbyshire side in only one of his three seasons with the county, 1883, during which he hit sixteen boundaries in his highest score of 92, made in 80 minutes, in the bad light of a Friday evening at The Oval. Following on 179 behind, Derbyshire compelled Surrey to bat again in totalling 300, but were beaten by six wickets. The youngest of the Evershed brothers, Edward, played only once for Derbyshire, in an away draw with Warwickshire in 1898, and scored just a single in his one innings.

Herbert Evershed's successor as Derbyshire's captain, from 1899 to 1901, was Samuel Hill-Wood, who had four sons, three of them cricketing Blues, who followed him to Eton and then into the Derbyshire side. Worcestershire were called Fostershire for having seven Foster brothers, but the Hill-Woods, as they became known with a name change in 1910, have supplied the only instance of a father and his four sons all playing first-class cricket for the same county.

Cricket took second place to soccer for Sir Samuel Hill-Wood, as he became while representing the High Peak division of Derbyshire as a Conservative MP from 1910 to 1929. It was through Association football that he rose to prominence in English sport during the first half of the twentieth century. At a personal cost of some £30,000, he helped his home club, Glossop North End, to League status, including one season in the First Division, from 1898 until their resignation after the First World War, then was Arsenal's chairman from 1927 up to his death, aged seventy-six, early in 1949. Even so, he has his special place in the summer game's record books despite having an unimpressive average of slightly over seventeen for his 758 first-class runs. At Lord's in 1900, while playing for Derbyshire against the MCC, he scored ten runs off one hit with the aid of an experimental net system the Marylebone club tried during the early part of that season. It proved too clumsy to be practical, however, and was abandoned after modifications had brought no improvement.

The batsman was credited with two runs when the ball was stopped by a net, some two to three feet in height, that was positioned around the normal boundary, and with three runs when it went over it. The Derbyshire captain's historic hit began with an all-run four, and he also gained the two-run bonus because the ball reached the net. The ball was then overthrown to the opposite net for two more runs, the batsmen crossing for another couple while it was on its way. In the county's same innings there were two sevens in William Storer's unbeaten 175 in a total of 383 that set up a Derbyshire victory by 107 runs. In recording the demise of the net, *Wisden* commented:

'There was something to be said for the plan of having all the hits run out, and perhaps the experiment would have had a better chance if there had been no allowance of two runs when the ball was stopped by the netting. The plan, as adopted, placed brilliant hitting at a discount, and it put such a premium on hits that just reached the ring that it deserved to fail.'

The hapless, and only occasional, bowler who suffered at Wood's hands was one Cuthbert James Burnup. Later captain of Kent, he was a Cambridge Blue at both cricket and soccer who had also been unfortunate in having his controversial choice for one football cap coincide with the ending, by Scotland in Glasgow in 1896, of an England record run of twenty games without defeat.

Only one other batsman has scored ten runs from one stroke in first-class cricket – in his case a gross occurrence not just because it was not a 'net' one. Albert ('Monkey') Hornby, who comes into this Derbyshire story a little later on, made half of his twenty runs, top score in Lancashire's total of 100 at The Oval in 1873, off one delivery from the Surrey fast bowler James Street. What a muddle of overthrows that was. Looking further back into cricket history, there was a chap named Roupell – John Harvey Torrens Roupell, to give him all his names – who needed neither net nor overthrows to score ten runs off one hit, but not in the top class. His obituary in *Wisden* tells us that 'in an innings of 97 for Trinity Hall v Emmanuel College in June 1865, he made clear hits for 10, 9 and 8 ... the tenner travelled about 240 yards.'

Also from the copious pages of *Wisden* can be culled reference to a batsman who 'ran about 250' off one hit. In the obituary for George Edward Hemingway, a Macclesfield-born batsman who played for Gloucestershire against Yorkshire at Sheffield in 1898, it is asserted that he made that prodigious score while his two brothers, against whom he was playing a single-wicket match, quarrelled about which of them should retrieve the ball from a bed of nettles into which he had hit it.

In his book *Talking Cricket,* Ian Peebles, the Middlesex and England spin bowler, told of 'an elderly and deaf member of a famous club' who was posted in the deep field despite having never 'caught anything high enough to clear the umpire's head'. This was how he continued the tale:

'So when, by a titanic fluke, he froze onto a lofty drive his jubilation knew no bounds. He tossed the ball from hand to hand, caressed it, threw it up in the air, and finally pocketed it as he lay down luxuriously to await the next batsman's arrival. The shouts which greeted his feat were to him distant whispers, but his beautiful reverie was disrupted by the arrival of a breathless mid-on. "Throw it in, you old fool," bellowed this emissary. "It's a no-ball, and they've already run seven".'

Samuel Hill Wood was available to lead the side in only four games in 1899, the first of the three seasons of his appointment as captain. His deputy was Thomas Atkinson Higson, who had entered county cricket with Cheshire (he was born at Stockport) at the age of seventeen but was to become most closely connected with Lancashire. From Rossall School, where he captained the cricket and hockey teams and was Fives champion, Tom Higson took an MA degree at Oxford and played for the university at both cricket and Association football, though without gaining a Blue. In first-class cricket his top score and number of wickets both amounted to fewer than fifty, but his career at that level lasted, with some interruptions, from 1899, when he played regularly for Derbyshire, to 1923, when he captained Lancashire to victory against the West

Indian tourists in his final game. After just the one season with Derbyshire he was out of top cricket until assisting MCC (he had been a member since 1897) against the South Africans at Lord's in 1904, then was with Lancashire from 1905 to 1907, played his last four games for Derbyshire in 1909 and 1910, and rejoined Lancashire in 1921.

For almost fifty years Higson, a Manchester solicitor, was a member of the Lancashire committee. After eight years as the club's honorary treasurer, he succeeded the late Sir Edwin Stockton as chairman in 1932, remaining in office until his death in 1949, and from 1931 to 1934 he was also on the MCC selection committee – a responsibility that included the choice of the party for the controversial 'body-line' tour of Australia. One of his sons, also given the forenames of Thomas Atkinson, followed him as a player with both Derbyshire and Lancashire, becoming chairman and president at Old Trafford; his eldest son, Peter, took part in just a few matches for Lancashire, but also had his turn as president.

One of Sir Samuel Hill-Wood's sons, Denis, was a cricket and soccer Blue at Oxford, for whom he opened the batting in the 1928 game against Cambridge during which Charles, the youngest brother, opened the Oxford bowling. Denis succeeded his father as chairman of Arsenal, and since Denis's death in 1982 the family's tradition in that role has been carried on by his own son Peter, who played his one first-class cricket match for the Free Foresters in 1960.

Wilfred, who, along with Basil, the eldest brother, also followed Sir Samuel to a knighthood, was the best cricketer of the five Hill-Woods, though he only just squeezed into the last place for his Blue in his second summer at Cambridge in 1922. He justified that selection with a painstaking 81 in an innings victory, and later that year he was a member of the MCC party led in Australia and New Zealand by Archie MacLaren, the Lancashire captain remembered for his then record 424 in an away match with Somerset. At Melbourne, Hill-Wood staved off defeat in partnership with Old Harrovian Geoffrey Wilson, later a captain of Yorkshire, after Victoria, having dismissed the tourists for 71, had declared at 617 for six. The opening pair batted through the rest of the match in an unbroken stand of 282, Wilson making 142 and Hill-Wood 122.

Wilfred further distinguished himself on his return from that 1922-23 tour by finishing at the top of Derbyshire's batting averages and, with 107, helping Joe Bowden (114) to break the county's first-wicket record with a partnership of 206 against Somerset at Bath. Unfortunately for Derbyshire, that was his only century in the County Championship, and his only season as a regular member of their team. It was unfortunate for England too, several reliable judges having already reckoned him a potential Test player. His style was unattractive because of the crouching stance he adopted to counteract a tendency to move away, but he had a good range of strokes and a sound defence. Still a student at Eton when he first played for Derbyshire in 1919, he was only twenty-two when he ceased to be regularly available. He was among the many amateurs who had to give up serious cricket prematurely to concentrate on their careers outside the game. His last county appearance, his sixty-third at the first-class level, was Derbyshire's first one of their 1936 title season, in which he signed off a dozen runs from a half-century in a drawn match with Hampshire at Southampton. He later served for many years on the MCC committee.

To extend the Hill-Wood connection with first-class cricket still further, Basil had a brother-in-law, David Brand, who played for Cambridge University and the MCC. And David Brand's grandfather Henry, who became the second Viscount Hampden, played for Sussex – as did his brother-in-law Freeman Thomas and his son, also Freeman Thomas, who became the first Lord Willingdon. Even that is not all. Freeman Thomas Senior had a brother-in-law, Earl de la Warr, who turned out twice for Lord Sheffield's XI in matches rated first-class.

5. Expulsion from First-Class

Four disastrous seasons, starting when they lost all ten of their County Championship matches in 1884, and ending with their third finish at the foot of the table, the last two of them in successive years, led to Derbyshire's expulsion from cricket's first-class elite. Mounting defeats had undermined morale, given rise to a serious financial situation, and spread rumours of declining discipline. Tales had become rife of players keeping late hours during matches, and even of turning up the worse for drink.

Derbyshire won only one of their thirty-three fixtures in the Championship during that period from 1884 to 1887, recovering to beat Lancashire by 73 runs at Manchester in 1885 after having only six on the board at the fall of their fifth wicket in a first innings of 54. That was the year in which they rose to sixth out of nine, above Gloucestershire, Middlesex and Sussex, but fulfilled the fewest fixtures – just eight, half as many as Surrey and Yorkshire. The axe fell after they had been beaten in eight of their nine games in 1886 (they had the worst of the other one in a rained-off draw at Old Trafford) and in all six to which they were restricted in 1887.

The wielders of that axe were not the members of the newly formed County Cricket Council, on which Derbyshire were represented. Nor were they those of the MCC, to whom the Council agreed to leave the responsibility for the Laws of the Game and the rules for county qualification – an agreement that left the Council with so little to do that its speedy dissolution became inevitable.

No, with the MCC standing aloof, the decision to cast out Derbyshire originated from London's sports (hardly sporting) Press, the unchallenged self-appointed rulers of the County Championship roost in those early days. And, just as *Wisden* had put the official stamp on Derbyshire's loss of the 1874 title, so the revered cricket almanack was right at the forefront of the county's denigrators in 1887. To quote Will Taylor, Derbyshire's longest-serving secretary, 'Mr Charles F Pardon, then editor of *Wisden*, was a leading protagonist in the move.' The *Lillywhite* annual joined in by saying that the reduction in rank was 'by general consent of the critics'.

In his history of the county club (as far as 1898), Walter J Piper Junior said that it was only after 'a good deal of discussion' that this downgrading answered the outcry which had arisen against Derbyshire's retention of first-class status. Despite that, there was precious little backing for the protesting outcasts, and the demotion was accepted readily enough by the cricketing public as well as by the eight other top-class counties. As Piper put it: 'It was universally admitted that Derbyshire were superior to the then second-class counties, and quite as good as certain of those which were permitted to retain their position in the front rank.' The facts clearly supported that statement. Of the ten matches Derbyshire played against counties outside the Championship during those four seasons, they won eight and lost only one, with the other drawn. They also twice defeated the MCC, forced honourable draws with two of the strongest counties, Nottinghamshire and Yorkshire, and gave a good account of themselves the only time Gloucestershire condescended to meet them.

The chief objection to Derbyshire was that they did not play sufficient matches against first-class teams to entitle them to continue competing in the Championship, and it was made clear that their reinstatement could not be considered until that drawback was overcome. Easier said than done, though. Derbyshire were in what would now be called a Catch 22 situation. Of the counties then in the Championship, only three, Lancashire, Surrey and Yorkshire, deigned to give them games in the 1887 season that brought their banishment. And Surrey and Yorkshire were the only first-class clubs to arrange fixtures with them during their six seasons out in the second-class cold. It was significant that Somerset were promptly elevated to first-class status and a place in the Championship once they were able to arrange the then required twelve matches against other counties at the meeting of county secretaries in December 1890.

Derbyshire's solitary defeat by a second-class side during the four years immediately before their expulsion was inflicted at Derby in 1885 by Essex, a county against which they were successful in their four other meetings over that period. The setback was by 62 runs, but Derbyshire had some excuse in having to contend with a rain-affected pitch after inching ahead on first innings. Four of their batsmen played on as an amateur named Bishop undermined them with seven wickets. When Essex next visited Derby the following year they enforced the follow-on, but were beaten by 46 runs after collapsing for 66 in their second innings in face of what Piper termed 'some sensational bowling' by George Davidson, whose four wickets cost only six runs. Four of the others fell a little more expensively to William Cropper, Derbyshire's top scorer with a half-century. Davidson was again in form with the ball in the return match at Leyton, his 8-48 in Essex's second innings carrying Derbyshire to victory by an innings and 78 runs after century-maker William Chatterton had received the backing of half-centuries by Walter Sugg and Edmund Maynard in a total only seven short of 400.

Charles Bray, who played as an amateur for Essex before becoming the *Daily Herald's* cricket correspondent, described the Leyton ground as 'like a dirty urchin – grimy, lovable, but not lovely', adding that 'there was something in its dirtiness, its ramshackle pavilion, its "cow-shed" along one side and those cold, grim stone terraces which got under your skin'. Chatterton, as has already been noted, and Davidson were certainly among those who enjoyed playing there – as they once more showed in Derbyshire's eight-wicket away win in their last match of the 1887 season. Both scored a half-century and

Davidson snapped up another eight wickets, six of them for 61 runs as Essex were this time the ones forced to follow on.

MCC were also crushed by an innings in 1886, in the match at Lord's that marked George Davidson's debut for Derbyshire and almost another century by Chatterton, stumped in going for a big hit at 97. Davidson was run out that day before getting into double figures, but his 4-33 combined with George Walker's 6-26 to engineer the strong home side's second-innings collapse. Derbyshire's other win at cricket's headquarters during these four seasons under review was by the contrastingly slender margin of seven runs in 1884. Arnold Rylott, a right-hand tail-end batsman and left-arm fast bowler from Grantham who headed the ground staff at Lord's before qualifying for Leicestershire when well into his thirties, did the hat-trick at the expense of Robert Smith and the Sugg brothers as Derbyshire were dismissed for 82 after being 60 ahead on first innings. This set MCC to score 143, and a stand between Cecil Wilson (71) and Harold Ruggles-Brise (33) put them well on the way to getting them until Nottinghamshire-born Joseph Marlow (5-43) mopped up the tail in an exciting finish. Wilson, who played for Kent along with his elder brother Leslie, was a clergyman who became Archdeacon of Adelaide, then Bishop of Bunbury in Western Australia for the last twenty years of his life. Ruggles-Brise, knighted like his brother, was a soldier who rose to the rank of Major-General.

The other Derbyshire victories during their last four seasons before being temporarily reduced to the second class were gained against Hampshire (twice) and Cheshire in 1885, and in their first meeting with Leicestershire two years later. Three Derbyshire records were broken at Southampton – their biggest total, victory and individual score up to that time. Hampshire were thrashed by an innings and 243 runs, and in the visitors' 427 Frank Sugg, going in at the fall of the third wicket, batted without blemish for his 187 as the total was taken from 91 to 405. The catch that ended his brilliant display was held by Francis Lacey, who carried his bat right through Hampshire's first innings for 61 out of 135, but was powerless to prevent their coming a real Cropper in the follow-on as the player of that name finished things off at 49 by completing a hat-trick with his seventh wicket. Lacey, who in 1887 made 323, then the highest individual score in a county match, at the same ground against Norfolk, captained Hampshire before being appointed MCC secretary in 1898 – a post he held until 1926, when he was knighted on retirement.

Hampshire had also been on the receiving end of Derbyshire's previous biggest total of 319 in which Jack Platts scored his century at Derby in 1877. Chatterton was the top scorer with 44 in a low-scoring match when the double was completed over them in 1885 by seven wickets. He also took five wickets for only thirteen runs in the visitors' second innings, but the amateur H H Armstrong, who had claimed Sugg's wicket at Southampton, had a bigger bag with 7-33 in Derbyshire's first innings.

In their two matches with Cheshire that year, Derbyshire had the better of a draw at Stockport after having to follow on, then won at Buxton by 177 runs. Cheshire had the Wright man for the occasion at home, that player scoring 44 and 59 in his two innings without being dismissed, but Derbyshire rallied mainly through Chatterton (70 not out) and William Wood-Sims (60), an opening batsman from Ironville, and at the close Cheshire were more than fifty from victory with only two wickets left. Frank Sugg was again in form in the return, top-scoring with 67.

The defeat of Leicestershire at Derby in 1887 was by 74 runs. This was another match in which Derbyshire had to follow on (despite a fine 60 by Chatterton), and they were still only fifteen runs ahead with six wickets down in their second innings. Harry Slater, run out for 54, then led a strong wagging of the tail, leaving the visitors with a target of 191 they found well beyond them as George Davidson (6-51) was given good support by Joe Hulme (4-35), a left-arm medium-fast bowler from Church Gresley who was a doughty performer for Derbyshire over some dozen seasons despite health problems.

But when it came to facing first-class opposition what a very different story it was. Thirteen times in the four seasons 1884-87 Derbyshire were beaten by an innings; in four other games they lost by ten wickets. In 1884 they were also twice defeated by Sussex, who had finished last in the table in four of the previous seven seasons, did so again in 1885, and were back down there in four of the seven years during which Derbyshire were excluded. In their eight meetings with Sussex before 1884 Derbyshire had only just enjoyed the better of the exchanges in gaining four wins against three, although one of those failures had been by just three runs at Hove after enforcing the follow-on and then being caught on a rain-affected pitch exploited by the left-arm fast bowling of John Juniper, who took 7-61. Juniper overcame the handicap of having sight in only one eye, but three years after that match with Derbyshire he died at the early age of twenty-three from typhoid fever.

More than a hundred years went by before another county recovered to defeat Derbyshire after having to follow on, Somerset winning by 79 runs at Derby in 1995, yet on Derbyshire's very next visit to Hove after their 1882 upset at that ground they were the ones to succeed in similar circumstances. Following-on 113 behind, they improved with half-centuries by Chatterton and Wallis Evershed, then shot out Sussex for 74 to triumph by 29 runs. Joe Marlow, who next season did the hat-trick in the home match with Kent, was the main cause of that collapse, taking 6-27. Almost a hundred years again elapsed before Derbyshire equalled their follow-on to victory feat, beating Lancashire by 15 runs at Buxton in 1976 after being 151 adrift, but they achieved it once more only eight years after that – by 28 runs at Nottingham after trailing by 222 on first innings.

After the double defeat of 1884, Derbyshire would not face Sussex again for twenty years – and then a second-innings century by Maynard Ashcroft, a doctor from Manchester who stood in as Derbyshire's captain around that time, could not avert an innings beating back at Hove that owed much to a double-century by C B Fry. It was in another match with Sussex, at Derby, that Ashcroft was involved in one of cricket's most freakish incidents. This was how he recalled it:

'I was completely beaten and bowled by Albert Relf and was preparing to depart when my partner, L G Wright, called me to run. We ran two. The wicket was spreadeagled, but one bail remained on the off-stump groove and the leg bail lodged part way down the middle and leg stumps. The rule then read: "The bails must be dislodged from the wicket." They actually were not dislodged from the wicket, and I was adjudged not out. I believe C B Fry took a snap of the state of the chaos in my wicket. If he did not secure a snap, he dashed off for a camera for that purpose. I proceeded to collect many more undeserved runs – about 75.'

Ashcroft said that happened in 'about 1905', but it could also have been a year later. In 1905 he scored 73 in both innings of a drawn match – first caught by Relf, then not out – and was in century stands with Wright, who made 149 not out and 51. In the following season, when Derbyshire defeated Sussex at Derby by five wickets, Ashcroft scored 74 (run out) and 100 not out, sharing another century partnership with Wright (96) in the first innings. There were escapes similar to Ashcroft's during two other Derbyshire matches. At Derby in 1935, a bail just turned in its groove instead of falling off when a ball from Worcestershire's Reg Perks hit the wicket and flew into the hands of first slip. At Chesterfield in 1972, Mike Hendrick hit the stumps of Alan Tait and Mushtaq Mohammad (first ball) without dislodging the bails while demolishing Northamptonshire's first innings with a spell of 5-15 in his 8-50.

Tom Goddard, the Gloucestershire and England spinner, almost had the same experience when he bowled Peter Smith, of Essex, at Bristol in 1936. The bails only moved out of their grooves, and did not fall until a photograph was about to be taken of the wicket. In 1902, Jim Iremonger, the Nottingham Forest defender who was capped by England at soccer but missed a Test call despite touring Australia with the MCC, proceeded to a century for Nottinghamshire against the MCC at Lord's after having one of his stumps disturbed. The enamelled stumps then being used had still to dry properly, and, as the cricket writer A A Thomson put it, 'the bail remained faithful'.

There was also the sad case of 'Gubby' Allen, the Middlesex and England all-rounder. The bails stayed on when he played the ball into his wicket during a Services match, also at Lord's, during the Second World War, so, with a great feeling of relief, he picked the ball up and sportingly tossed it back to the bowler. Was that worthy duly grateful? Oh no! He promptly appealed, and Allen was given out for handling the ball.

The heaviest of Derbyshire's defeats during their four barren years from 1884 that temporarily cost them their place in the Championship was the one by an innings and 250 runs by Notts at Derby in 1885 to which reference has already been made. Seven of the others were suffered in eight games against Yorkshire, the exception being the benefit for Jack Platts, earlier in the month of that thrashing by Notts, which was left drawn when Derbyshire were only 16 runs from the 70 they needed for victory in 75 minutes with half their wickets in hand.

As already recalled, Frank Shacklock was the man of that match, with his 8-45 in Yorkshire's first innings of 96 and 13-142 overall, but on the other occasions the bowling honours were monopolised by Yorkshire's Test trio of Ted Peate, Tom Emmett and Billy Bates, who took more than eighty Derbyshire wickets between them during that four-year period. Peate, first of the great slow left-arm bowlers produced by Yorkshire, wreaked most of his havoc in the clubs' first meeting of that 1885 season, at Fartown, Huddersfield, as Yorkshire hustled to an innings win inside two days after rain had prevented play on the first. He took five wickets in each innings at a total cost of only 45 runs, with eight of the others falling to the left-arm pace of Emmett and the remaining two to Bates.

Emmett, described by the 'Grand Old Man' of English cricket, Sir Pelham ('Plum') Warner, as 'a man of inexhaustible good humour and spirit', was one of Yorkshire's most colourful cricketing characters, possessor of a special type of delivery he dubbed his 'sostenuter' before changing to slow-medium as age took its toll. He had his biggest successes against Derbyshire in 1884, when his second-innings figures of 7-20 at Derby and 6-28 at Bradford sealed ten-wicket wins. Bates, known as 'The Duke' because of his smart attire (he was a woollen weaver by trade), took two centuries off Derbyshire and combined both with some highly effective spin bowling. At Holbeck, Leeds, in 1886 he followed his 106 in a total of 161 with a match return of 10-75; at Derby a year later he scored 103 and took 8-74.

Peate, successor to Alfred Shaw as England's slow bowler, dropped out of the Yorkshire side at the beginning of that 1887 season, his career ending at a comparatively young age after putting on too much weight. 'Without using a harsh word,' said *Wisden*, 'it may fairly be said that he would have lasted longer if he had ordered his life more carefully.' It was because of disciplinary action, however, that the curtain came down on his career so abruptly. According to the *Who's Who of Cricketers* brought out by Philip Bailey, Philip Thorn and Peter Wynne-Thomas, 'his sudden departure from county cricket whilst in his prime was caused by Lord Hawke's determination to rid the Yorkshire team of its more unruly elements.'

Exit from the first-class stage also came prematurely for Bates, and in very sad circumstances. On his fifth tour of Australia late in 1887, he was struck in an eye by the ball with such force during net practice in Melbourne that his sight was permanently damaged. With further county cricket out of the question, he became so despondent that he attempted suicide after returning home, but he was eventually able to play in league cricket as professional at Haslingden and Leek in addition to doing some coaching.

Others to excel for Yorkshire against Derbyshire before the Peak county's expulsion most notably included George ('Happy Jack') Ulyett, who at Sheffield in 1887, a season of sun and hard pitches, made the highest score of his outstanding 20-year career, and the biggest against Derbyshire up to that time, in carrying his bat for 199, made in just under six hours, right through a total of 399 that the visitors were 163 runs short of equalling in their two innings. Ulyett, big in both deed and build, was something of a practical joker, and my old friend Keith Farnsworth, in his book about cricket at Bramall Lane, has told of the time he and Peate 'once had the audacity to walk uninvited into one of Gladstone's receptions at No 10 Downing Street, Ulyett pretending to be stone deaf, Peate purporting to be his keeper.'

Another Yorkshireman, besides the already mentioned Billy Bates, was among the scorers of the eighteen centuries conceded by Derbyshire during the fifteen seasons of their first spell as a first-class county, Irwin Grimshaw carrying his bat for 122 at Sheffield, but the glutton among all that run-getting was Walter Read. In the three seasons from 1885 to 1887 he scored four hundreds in successive innings for Surrey against Derbyshire – 123 at Derby, 109 and 115 at The Oval, 145 at Derby. Derbyshire lost each of those matches by an innings. Indeed, after winning their first meeting with Surrey at Derby in 1883, they suffered eighteen consecutive, and mostly heavy, defeats by that southern county before, as will be recalled in more detail in a later chapter, they sensationally ended the sorry sequence by beating the reigning champions while rated second-class.

In the first match between the clubs, Derbyshire restricted Surrey to a first-innings lead of just under 50 despite being dismissed for 80, then set their new visitors to score 178 thanks mainly to a spirited half-century by Ludford Docker. By the resumption of play on the final morning, that target had been reduced to 76 with six wickets still standing, and it was down to 52 for the loss of just one more wicket when the last five crashed without further addition to William Cropper and James Brelsford.

In his second of only eight games for the county, Brelsford, a medium-pace bowler from the Mycrofts' home village of Brimington, followed up his 4-42 on the opening day with 5-31 as Walter Read was left stranded on 55 not out. All but two of Derbyshire's wickets in that match were shared by Edward Barratt and Maurice Read, twelve of them falling to Barratt, an import from the North-East who could impart a prodigious break on his slow left-arm deliveries. Maurice Read's brother was not Walter but Frederick, a railway clerk who also played in first-class cricket for Surrey – just the once. Their uncle, Heathfield Stephenson, later a noted coach at Uppingham School, made more than 250 appearances for that county and captained the first England team in Australia in 1861-62.

Three of Surrey's batsmen went within a few runs of adding to the list of century-makers against Derbyshire before the latter's demotion. All-rounder Bob Henderson made the closest of those approaches in being caught at the wicket two runs short of three figures at The Oval in 1887 after partnering the diminutive and aptly named Bobby Abel, popularly known as 'The Guv'nor', in a stand of 177 as Surrey recovered from a first-innings deficit. With luck Derbyshire might have salvaged a draw, but heavy overnight rain made conditions perfect for Abel's rarely used off-breaks. In just over twenty-four overs, sixteen of which were maidens, he took 6-15 in a paltry total of 42.

In Surrey's first innings of that match, K J Key, an Oxford double Blue who became John Shuter's successor as the county's captain and later rose to be Sir Kingsmill James Key, was bowled by George Walker for 95. At Derby the previous month he had been dismissed for 97 during the innings in which Walter Read made the biggest of his centuries against Derbyshire and Abel fell for 92 – all three victims of George Davidson. That was third time unlucky for Abel, for he had been out in the nineties on Derbyshire's visits to The Oval in the previous two seasons. In 1885 he was also eight short; next time he got to 94 and shared with Shuter an opening stand of 186 that laid the firm foundation for a total only six from 500, then the biggest against Derbyshire. Key, whose death in 1932 was from blood poisoning caused by an insect bite, finally got to a century off Derbyshire in 1890 – but only after being badly missed in the slips at 18 – and Abel did so four years later.

Prominent among the other batsmen who flourished against Derbyshire during those far-off days was Albert Hornby, an England international at rugby as well as cricket who not only played for Lancashire for nearly thirty-three years but also served them up to 1916, first as chairman then president, partly both at the same time. In 1881, the second of his twenty years as the club's captain (a post later also held by his son), he scored 188, the highest individual score in county cricket that season, against Derbyshire at Old Trafford, and 145 in the return game of George Porter's debut. Dismissed for 102, 62, 48 and 59 in those two matches, Derbyshire lost both by an innings.

Seven years later, Hornby, who compensated for his short stature with an excess of energy that earned him the nickname 'Monkey', was at the centre of the dispute that caused Lancashire, once so supportive, to drop their fixtures with then second-class Derbyshire for the four seasons 1889-1892. Incensed by barracking from the Derby crowd, he led his men off the field for a hold-up that lasted some fifteen minutes, and it was with considerable difficulty that he was persuaded to finish the match in which Lancashire completed yet another decisive double. The spectators responsible for that disturbance were showing their displeasure at Lancashire's luring away of Frank Sugg, who on either side of that reappearance at Derby with the opposition helped England to defeat Australia at The Oval and in Manchester for a 2-1 series win. He totalled only 55 runs in his two innings of his only two Tests, but they were sufficient to put him second to John Shuter in England's batting averages for a rubber that had begun with an Australian win in a Lord's match of only 291 runs for its forty wickets – then the lowest aggregate for a Test and not reduced, to 234 for twenty-nine wickets, until Australia trounced South Africa, dismissed for 36 and 45, at Melbourne in 1932.

Ilkestonan Frank Howe Sugg, a brilliant outfielder with a very safe pair of hands in addition to being an enterprising batsman, had an undistinguished first season with Yorkshire in 1883 before demonstrating the strength of his driving and square-leg hitting in three seasons with his native county. He was twice runner-up, and once third, in the Derbyshire batting averages, albeit with modest figures in those times of generally low scoring, but it was during his thirteen seasons with Lancashire, for whom he qualified by residence, that he had his greatest success. The fifteen centuries he made for them in accumulating more than 10,000 runs included his highest score of 220 against Gloucestershire in 1896 and five others of over 150. In 1890 he was one of *Wisden's* Cricketers of the Year.

Sugg, a strapping six-footer, was a man of many sports. Apart from his cricket – at which he also held the distance record for throwing the ball – he played soccer for the Wednesday, Derby County, Burnley and Bolton Wanderers, revelled in long-distance swimming, reached the final of the Liverpool amateur billiards championship, and won prizes for rifle shooting, bowls, putting the shot and weightlifting. Quite a fellow, and, as we shall be coming to later, one matched for versatility by his brother Walter.

Even so, there was no story-book return to Derby for Frank Sugg in that disrupted visit by Lancashire of August 1888. He had made Lancashire's top score of 60 in Derbyshire's innings defeat in Manchester earlier that season, but this time, although again on the winning side (by four wickets) he managed just twenty runs in being bowled twice by Joe Hulme. In Lancashire's total of 182 at Old Trafford that year, Hulme gave the first of his many fine displays for Derbyshire in taking 7-62, but the visitors, below strength and batting in the worst of the conditions after rain in their second innings, truly looked the second-class county they had become in being collapsing for 87 and an abysmal 17. That was the match in which, as recalled in the second chapter, Johnny Briggs took thirteen of the wickets (7-35 and 6-4), but at Derby he was outshone by that man Watson, whose six wickets in Derbyshire's second-innings slump to 56 cost only seventeen runs.

Hulme ended the 1888 season at the head of Derbyshire's bowling averages with sixty wickets for just over tens runs apiece, but the paucity of the batting was so acute that Chatterton needed an average of only seventeen to come out on top. Not only because of Sugg's departure did the decline in Derbyshire's fortunes accelerate. The departure of Shacklock to Nottinghamshire, who had also acquired the promising John Tye, and Docker to Warwickshire were other big blows, and there was also the tragic loss of William

Cropper and Tom Mycroft through their early deaths. William Mycroft's retirement left another huge gap to be filled, but Hulme turned in a number of exceptional performances in going some way towards doing so.

George Davidson, too, was to come through as one of the game's leading all-rounders, and in William Storer Derbyshire were to produce, in their last season before demotion, a player who became, in 1899, their first to be one of *Wisden's* top five of the year. At the time of his death in 1912 the almanack said that 'Derbyshire has perhaps never produced a more remarkable player'. W G Grace also paid his tribute. 'I can't say that his batting style is elegant,' he wrote, 'but it's vigorous and he gets runs with almost unfailing regularity. A more alert and resourceful cricketer is not to be found.'

While Derbyshire's fortunes were at such a low ebb, both on the field and financially, during those years of the 1880s that led to their expulsion from the elite, their search for new talent through the Colts matches they arranged brought out two players who were to serve them especially well for many seasons. At the outset, however, Levi George Wright (always known simply as L G) and Harry Bagshaw did nothing to suggest what a force they were to become. When first given a try-out in the Whit Week of 1883 both were out without scoring in their first innings, and managed only five runs between them in their second.

Wright did not come right to the fore until 1890, when he scored the first of his twenty centuries, but he retired at the end of the 1909 season, in his forty-eighth year, as Derbyshire's record run-getter, and his aggregate of 14,800 runs (15,166 in all his first-class games) has since been exceeded for the county by only six players. *Wisden* said that he was 'probably a better player at the age of 40 than at any other period of his career'.

It took Bagshaw a little longer than Wright to establish himself in the Derbyshire side, but for the best part of a decade he was a free-hitting left-hand batsman well above the average, scorer of more than 7,000 runs (nearly 5,500 of them first-class) that included seven centuries – one of them before lunch on the third day of the match with Yorkshire at Derby in 1896. He was unlucky not to have made at least two more, for in a second-class game against Essex at the same ground three years earlier he was stumped for 96 in the first innings and stranded on 90 in the second when the 160 needed in less than three hours were knocked off in eighty minutes for the loss of only one wicket – Wright's, run out for 57. Bagshaw's biggest achievements with bat and ball came in league cricket with Barnsley: 220 against Crofton Wanderers, all ten wickets in an innings against Wakefield. Five years after playing his last game for Derbyshire in 1902, he turned to umpiring, and he stood in more than two hundred County Championship games up to 1923.

When he died at Crowden, near Glossop, at the age of sixty-seven early in 1927, he was buried, as he had requested, in his umpire's coat with a cricket ball in his hand. His grave is in the churchyard at Eyam, the Derbyshire village where 267 of the 350 inhabitants perished in the plague of the seventeenth century that was not allowed to spread elsewhere because, due mainly to the efforts of the rector, nobody was allowed in or out while it raged. Bagshaw's imposing dark grey headstone shows an umpire's finger pointing to heaven and a set of stumps broken by a ball with the bails falling. It also bears lines from Grantland Rice's famous cricket poem:

> 'For when the one great Scorer comes
> To write against your name
> He writes – not that you won or lost
> But how you played the game.'

Bagshaw was local-born, at Foolow, just down the road from Eyam, whereas Wright made his way to Derby from his home city of Oxford by taking a post at St Anne's School as a 19-year-old in 1881. Wright, who had first played his cricket for Oxford City, soon gave up teaching to work as a clerk for the Midland Railway, and it was his consistent form for the Derby Midland team that caught Derbyshire's attention.

Bagshaw began the 1887 season that was to be Derbyshire's last as a first-class county for six years by again being dismissed twice without scoring in the team's totals of 78 and 36 on his first-team debut in a defeat by the MCC at Lord's, and he was not selected again that year despite taking a couple of wickets cheaply with his medium-paced right-arm bowling. Wright opened the batting in all except the last two of Derbyshire's ten games, but ended a very ordinary fifth in the averages headed by George Davidson and Chatterton, totalling 219 runs at 13.68 with a top score of 32 from his sixteen innings. He temporarily lost his place after being dismissed for a duck by Leicestershire's Dick Pougher, an all-rounder who had been one of Bagshaw's victims, also without scoring, while playing for MCC in the opening match.

Pougher, whose most memorable feat was to take five wickets in fifteen balls without cost in the MCC's rout of the Australians for 18 at Lord's in 1896 (his last victim, Tom McKibbin, was caught by George Davidson), made up for that failure against Derbyshire with several outstanding performances at their expense. He took eight of their wickets in an 1888 match they lost at Leicester by 27 runs when wanting only 87, scored 135 in Leicestershire's innings win at Derby three seasons later, and sent back seven more batsmen in that year's return game – from which, however, Derbyshire emerged worthy winners after having to follow on. The four innings of the 1888 game at Leicester totalled fewer than 250 runs. The home side were all out for 82 and 52, Hulme's seven wickets in their second innings costing a mere eleven runs, but Derbyshire's replies reached only 48 and 59.

Derbyshire's most successful bowlers in the 1887 season that culminated in their reduction in rank were Cropper and George Davidson, who both three times took six wickets in an innings. The county's attack was heavily punished by only Surrey and Yorkshire, but their batting was such a big let-down that Davidson's 75 in the home match with Yorkshire was the highest individual score, and only twice in eighteen innings did Derbyshire get beyond 200. William Storer, in particular, gave no sign of the treats he had in store, only just completing fifty runs in the nine innings of his first season at an average of a little over six.

6. The Demon Spofforth

It was while Derbyshire were cast out into the second-class cold that they acquired one of the most talented and feared cricketers the game then had to offer. *Wisden* called him 'one of the most remarkable players the game has ever known'.

Frederick Robert Spofforth, lean, swarthy, angular, 6ft 3in tall, and with long sideburns and the regulation drooping moustache of his times, was a devastating bowler invariably known as the Demon. He first came across Derbyshire during the second of his five visits to England as a member of an Australian touring side in 1880, when he took thirteen of their wickets for 85 runs as they tumbled to an eight-wicket defeat. Two years later he took ten more for only 57 runs in an innings victory for the tourists. And two years after that he claimed a further twelve for 83 as Derbyshire were again beaten by an innings.

On his next visit in 1886 injury kept him out of the Australian team that played at Derby, but there was to be no respite. Sixteen of the county's wickets fell for 101 runs to George Giffen, an all-rounder dubbed the W G Grace of Australia because of his likeness, in performance if not appearance, to the giant West Country doctor. To his credit still stands the most astounding double feat in a first-class match – 271 runs and sixteen wickets (9-96 and 7-70) for South Australia against Victoria at Adelaide in 1891. Derbyshire were once more emphatically beaten by the Australians in 1886, on that occasion by six wickets. George Walker, run out, was their only batsman not to be dismissed in Giffen's second-innings return of 9-60.

While in England that year, Spofforth married the daughter of Joseph Cadman, a tea merchant, at the village of Breadsall just outside Derby, and went back to Australia with his bride. In 1888 he returned to England not as a Test cricketer but as the Midlands representative of the Star Tea Company, having long forsaken his original job as a clerk in a Sydney bank. This led the following year to his brief association with Derbyshire, who in 1888 were back to losing by an innings to the Australian tourists. They were destroyed largely by Spofforth's successor as his country's premier bowler, Charlie (the Terror) Turner, whose thirteen wickets cost just 46 runs. As when the Demon first dismembered them eight years earlier, Derbyshire mustered a mere 45 runs when they first batted (L G Wright, with 13, alone attained double figures), and they managed only a dozen more when they went in again.

That was but one of a host of triumphs in which Turner (right-arm fast-medium) and his fellow New South Walian John Ferris, a left-arm spinner of variable pace, revelled in tandem that year, one of the wettest on record. Turner, the first to dismiss a hundred batsmen in the first-class matches of an Australian season, ended the tour with 314 wickets; Ferris, who took the seven others at Derby, bagged 220. Ferris fared even better, with 235, when he was among William Chatterton's colleagues with Walter Read's party in South Africa in 1891-92, but he lost form soon after qualifying for Gloucestershire. Disillusioned, he enlisted with the Imperial Light Horse, went back to the Union, and died there from enteric fever during the Boer War.

Turner, who also hit two first-class centuries, took 101 Test wickets at an average cost of 16.53 runs compared with the 94 at 18.41 of Spofforth, whose best with the bat was 56 (against Middlesex). Overall at the first-class level Turner totalled just seven wickets short of a thousand, at 14.25, to Spofforth's 853 at 14.95. After Spofforth's death in Surrey in 1926, at the age of 72, *Wisden's* obituary credited him with 1,146 wickets at an average of 13.55 'in really big cricket, both at home and abroad', but the reassessment of matches worthy of first-class status has since deprived him of reaching the thousand. There was much divergence of opinion as to the merits of the two, though *Wisden* put 'the balance – among English players at any rate – in Spofforth's favour on account of his better head and more varied resources'.

Rick Smith, an Australian authority on the subject, acknowledged that Turner 'must rank as one of the finest of all time', but also pointed to Spofforth's greater variety in referring to his 'cunningly disguised variations of pace', his ability to cut the ball both ways, and his 'armoury more than capable of dismissing the best of batsmen'. Smith described Spofforth as 'the first great Australian bowler and one of the finest in the history of the game', adding: 'Behind a somewhat satanic countenance lurked a finely tuned tactical mind which delighted in setting traps for unwary batsmen.'

Lord Harris also spoke up strongly in favour of Spofforth. In an article in the 1927 edition of *Wisden,* paying tribute after the Australian's death, he wrote:

'I was playing for ten years abroad and at home against those great medium-pace Australian bowlers, Allan, Garrett, Palmer, Giffen, Turner and Ferris, as well as Spofforth, and I have of course also played such great English medium-pace bowlers as Alfred Shaw, Watson, Jim Lillywhite, Lohmann, C T Studd and W G Grace, and I am quite satisfied, and always have been, that Spofforth was the most difficult of them all, because he concealed so well the pace of the ball. What he could have done on the easy wickets of the present day no-one can say, but I am sure he could have adapted his bowling to them; and does it matter? What we must judge performances by are the circumstances and conditions of the time when they were done, and, taking those as the criteria, I do not see how any bowler can be held to be better than was F R Spofforth.

Some years ago, a series of articles in *The Times* named the 100 Greatest Cricketers of all time, a list compiled by John Woodcock, then that newspaper's cricket correspondent and a former editor of *Wisden*. Only three players who have represented Derbyshire were among that elite, and Spofforth was the best-placed of those at thirty-second. Fred Trueman, who briefly assisted the county in only one-day games after ending his career with Yorkshire, came forty-fifth, and Michael Holding, the former West Indies fast bowler, sixty-fifth. Of course, such a list can be no more than a matter of opinion, in Woodcock's words 'inevitably invidious and essentially provocative', and there must have been many, including this writer, who disagreed for a start with Don Bradman being rated runner-up to W G Grace. In *Wisden* itself, Grace has been described as 'the pot-bellied genius who in middle age was far too heavy for any horse to bear', and a 'not particularly attractive man' who was 'notorious for employing, in order to pursue victory or personal achievement, a variety of wiles and tricks that may be thought of as, well, hardly cricket.'

Spofforth was born in the Sydney suburb of Balmain on 9 September 1853, the son of a Yorkshireman who had migrated to Australia twenty-five years earlier, but spent his childhood at Hokianga, near Auckland in New Zealand. He began his cricket by bowling fast under-arm as a schoolboy, but switched to over-arm after seeing George Tarrant in action for George Parr's visiting English team in the 1863-64 Australian season.

Tarrant, a noted member of the Cambridgeshire side in the 1860s, was a relative of Frank Tarrant, the Australian all-rounder who enhanced his formidable reputation with Middlesex during most of the seasons of the twentieth century leading up to the First World War. Spofforth also studied the methods of James Southerton, who in 1870 became the first to take two hundred wickets in a season at the advanced age of forty-two, and Alfred Shaw, the Notts purveyor of what W G Grace called 'good length and unvaried precision'. His aim was to combine the 73 virtues of all three of those role models, and the extent to which he succeeded was dramatically demonstrated in the second match of his first visit to England when he took ten wickets for only twenty runs as a strong MCC team, dismissed for 33 and 19, crashed to a sensational nine-wicket defeat in four and a half hours' play on 27 May 1878 at Lord's. A G (Johnny) Moyes, a player with South Australia and Victoria, team selector for New South Wales, then commentator on the game both on radio and in print, said it was 'a day of destiny for Australian cricket', though one that could hardly have been foreshadowed when the tour opened with an innings thrashing by Nottinghamshire.

In twenty-three balls, Spofforth's 6-4 in the MCC's first innings included one of his career's three hat-tricks (the others against England in Melbourne, the South of England at The Oval). Indicative of his skilful changes of pace, two of his victims were stumped. W G, out without scoring, was among the four batsmen he clean bowled when the MCC went in again after Nottinghamshire's Shaw and Morley had restricted the tourists' reply to 41 with five wickets apiece. As *Punch* put it:

'Our Grace before dinner was very soon done,
And Grace after dinner did not get a run.'

Henry Boyle, whose partnership with Spofforth did so much to establish the reputation of Australian cricket, took nine of the MCC's other wickets, six of them for only three runs in their second innings.

'From that day forward,' said *Wisden,* 'Spofforth was always regarded as a man to be feared, even by the strongest teams.' His bowling was exceptionally fast on that tour, but he subsequently became generally regarded as fast-medium, with well-disguised yorkers usually his quickest deliveries. He placed great reliance on what he called his 'judgment' ball, delivered at medium pace with great variety of flight and a strong break from the off. Many a batsman was deceived by a ball that was much slower than they were given to expect by the intimidating pace at which he tore in to bowl from an oblique approach to the wicket. Experience of English pitches, slower than those in Australia, soon made him realise that he could not rely on sheer speed alone, and it was the skill with which he adapted to those changed conditions that made him such a fearsome adversary.

Spofforth, who could run the 100 yards in eleven seconds, earned his Demon nickname more for his aggressive demeanour and the terrifying aspect of his final bound at the wicket when delivering the ball, long arms whirling from his commanding height. In his *Book of Cricket,* Sir Pelham Warner said Spofforth was so called 'not only because of the fear which his bowling inspired, but also because of a certain Mephistophelian cast of countenance', referring to the evil spirit to whom Faust, in German legend, sold his soul.

There were no Tests on that 1878 tour, in which more minor than major games were played by the Australians, but the Demon had already made up for some lost time after having refused to play in the first-ever match with England, at Melbourne in March 1877, because his New South Wales clubmate Billy Murdoch had not been chosen as wicketkeeper. Spofforth considered that Murdoch, who pulled off those two stumpings in the MCC's eclipse, was the man who could best take his bowling, but he agreed to turn out in the second game against England, also at Melbourne, the following month, even though Murdoch, having been brought into the team, was again not required to keep wicket. Ironically, Spofforth then owed his first Test wicket, that of Alfred Shaw, to the player preferred to Murdoch behind the stumps – the darkly-bearded John McCarthy Blackham, who was to dismiss almost 300 batsmen (181 caught, 118 stumped) in the Australians' first nine tours of Britain and also succeed Murdoch to his country's captaincy.

England were beaten by 45 runs in what was upgraded as the inaugural Test after originally being just a match between an English professional touring team and a combined New South Wales and Victorian side, but they won the second encounter by four wickets. When Spofforth next faced them, again at Melbourne early in 1879 – once more with Blackham behind the wicket and Murdoch in the side as a batsman – he piloted Australia to a ten-wicket win with 6-48, including the first Test hat-trick, and 7-62. Injury kept him out of the only Test Australia played on their 1880 England tour, and out of all but the last of the four matches in their 1881-82 home series, but he was again the match-winner when they gained their first Test success in England in 1882 – the match that prompted the *Sporting Times* to publish its famous obituary notice 'in affectionate remembrance of English cricket, which died at The Oval on 29 August 1882 – deeply lamented by a large circle of sorrowing friends and acquaintances'.

England, 38 ahead on first innings in reply to a total of only 63, were beaten by seven runs after reducing the 85 they required for victory to 34 with three wickets down. Spofforth – venting anger aroused by W G Grace's running-out of Samuel Jones when that batsman, mistakenly thinking the ball was dead, had ventured up the pitch to do some 'gardening' – then switched to the pavilion end and, to quote Moyes again, 'swept through the side like fire through a field of wheat.' He took four of those remaining seven wickets to follow his first-innings 7-46 with 7-44. His match haul of 14-90 was to stand as an Australian Test record for ninety years – until Bob Massie took sixteen for 137 (8-84 and 8-53) on his debut in an eight-wicket defeat of England at Lord's in June 1972. The previous best by a bowler in his first Test was twelve for 102 (6-50 and 6-52) by Fred Martin, of Kent, in England's two-wicket win over Australia at The Oval in August 1890.

In all his matches of 1878 and 1880 Spofforth plundered more than 1,500 wickets, an astounding tally even though the great majority of those games were second-class. Against the Eighteen of Hastings in 1878 he took nine wickets in twenty balls, a deadly spell he was to surpass in 1880 with twelve in eighteen against the Eighteen of Burnley. His 764 (average 6.08) in 1878 comprised 281 during a preliminary tour of Australia and New Zealand in which he three times took 22 wickets against teams of twelve, 326 in England (97 of them first-class), 69 in the United States and Canada, and 88 in a wind-up tour on the return to Australia. In 1880 his overall total was 763 (5.49), including 391 at 5.16 in the tour of Britain – just forty of them during the Australians' first-class programme of only ten games. In fixtures with teams of eighteen players he took twenty wickets in Bradford, nineteen at each of the North-West venues of Hunslet and Werneth, eighteen in Hull, seventeen at Longsight (a district of Manchester), Northampton and Sunderland, and fifteen at Harrogate.

Unlike the first two Australian tours, most of the matches on the 1882 visit were first-class, with only four second-class and none against odds. Spofforth had the biggest bag of first-class wickets among the four tourists who got into three figures, his 158 costing fewer than thirteen runs each. Five times he took at least ten in a match; in seventeen innings he claimed at least five. Added to that, he swept up twenty-five at Leicester and Taunton, where the home counties were still rated second-class. On the 1884 tour, Spofforth's first-class wickets total rose to 205 at 12.50, and he claimed eleven more very cheaply at

Leicester in the only minor match played. Injury reduced his effectiveness on his remaining visit as a member of an Australian team after another two-year interval – he dislocated a finger in attempting to stop a hard drive by Lord Harris while playing against the Gentlemen at Lord's – but he still topped the tourists' bowling averages, if with a diminished tally of 89 wickets at 17.15. That took him to totals for his five trips of 589 first-class wickets and nearly 1,650 overall.

Back in Australia, where he played his senior cricket for New South Wales by birth and for Victoria by residence before settling in England, Spofforth was reputed to have taken all twenty of the opposing side's wickets – each of them bowled, indeed – in an up-country game during the 1881-82 season. Unfortunately, no scorecard of that game has ever been traced to bear out a feat one would expect to find only in schoolboy fiction.

From the mind-boggling authenticated array of Spofforth statistics, it can readily be appreciated what a coup, aided by his marriage to a young lady from the county, was pulled off when Derbyshire acquired the Demon. Excessive though his number of scalps against lesser opposition was, even the best of batsmen were mown down by this human scythe. Quite apart from his Test triumphs, he took fourteen of An England XI's wickets at Birmingham (seven of them for only three runs in the second innings), another fourteen, and also twelve, in games against the Players of England at The Oval, thirteen more when the Players were also well beaten at Sheffield, and a further two dozen in two matches with the South of England. The batting line-ups of such leading counties as Surrey and Yorkshire were others swept aside, and he was only one wicket away from taking all ten in one Lancashire innings.

Derbyshire hoped to persuade the authorities to allow Spofforth to play for them without having the wait for the two years' qualification by residence, and, at the County Cricket Council's meeting at Lord's on 10 December, 1888, their representative, John Smith, moved a resolution that 'if a cricketer, born out of the United Kingdom, comes to England, the county in which his home is situated should, for the purposes of county cricket, be considered the county of his birth'. This, however, was rejected, so Derbyshire decided to ask each of their opponents if they would agree to Spofforth's playing against them in the ensuing season.

After all, the County Championship would not have been involved because Derbyshire were no longer in it, but the response was almost entirely unfavourable. In some quarters the Demon was regarded as an intruder. It was even suggested that in Surrey's case the refusal was an act of spite because he had not agreed to join them. The *Sporting Chronicle* accused the Surrey committee of acting 'with a stupidity and asinine stubbornness of which they have shown a peculiar development this season', pointing out that the authorities at The Oval had not always adhered so rigidly to the rules concerning the qualification of players.

The upshot was that Spofforth was able to play in only one match for Derbyshire in 1889, though it would have been two if the weather had not washed out play in a Bank Holiday fixture at Sheffield before he could either bat or bowl. Yorkshire, with what our old friend Piper called 'an amount of magnanimity which has always characterised them', decided to waive the point about his qualification and were therefore the only county to accept his inclusion against them that year.

To Derbyshire's acute embarrassment, he promptly showed his appreciation by taking fifteen of their wickets for 81 runs at Derby. The last laugh, however, was with Yorkshire, for this was yet another of those games Derbyshire lost despite an exceptional performance on their behalf. Having offset the disadvantage of losing the toss by shooting out their visitors for 132 thanks chiefly to Spofforth's 7-45, they could not cobble together even half that modest total in trailing by 75 runs on first innings. Then they retrieved some of that lost ground as Spofforth stepped up another gear with 8-36 in Yorkshire's dismissal for 92, only to slip up again themselves and fall 55 short of the 168 they were left to get for victory.

The man who countered Spofforth's spectacular start was Bobby Peel, second in the line of the distinguished slow left-arm bowlers – after Edmund Peate and before Wilfred Rhodes and Hedley Verity – who served Yorkshire so nobly over the sixty seasons from 1879 to 1939. He outdid the Australian, slightly on average but not on the number of wickets, by bagging 6-24 and 8-43. Peel, also no mean batsman, had another big match against Derbyshire at Leeds three years later, when his eight wickets cost only 33 runs – five of them for just seven as the bewildered visitors tumbled to a second-innings total of 46 and defeat by an innings and 43. A young man then not far into a celebrated county career spanning forty years, one George Herbert Hirst, was mainly responsible for Derbyshire's dismal showing when they first batted, taking 5-12 on his way to match figures of 8-26.

Hirst, another left-hander, but at a brisk pace with a prodigious swerve, has alone scored 2,000 runs and taken 200 wickets in one season (1906), and he altogether amassed more than 36,000 and 2,700 respectively. Peel did not fare too badly either, with over 11,000 runs and 1,550 wickets, but it was to be regretted that his county career ended, like Peate's, through disciplinary action. He was sent off the field by Lord Hawke during the game with Middlesex at Bramall Lane in August 1897 in circumstances that arose from his thirst for beer. George Hirst found him far from sober at breakfast at the team's lodgings, sent him back to bed, and reported him too ill to play. Lord Hawke therefore brought in his twelfth man, but then found an extra player on the field when Peel, still groggy but clutching the ball determined to bowl, turned up for the start of the day's play. According to one report, Peel first responded to being told to leave by delivering 'an elaborately cunning ball in the direction of the sightscreen'. Another account suggested that he urinated on the field.

Peel always denied both those versions, and claimed that he was ordered off because he twice slipped while fielding. He was told at the end of the match that he would not be required again that season, but he might have been restored to the side the following year if he had made a formal apology. In absolutely refusing to do so, regardless of Hirst's urgent appeals, he was convinced that Yorkshire could not afford to be without him. The coinciding introduction of Wilfred Rhodes into the county's ranks made him very mistaken, and he never played for Yorkshire again. He did, however, turn out for an England XI against Joe Darling's Australian team at Truro two years later, and, in taking five wickets, demonstrated that he still possessed much of the skill with which, as *Wisden* remarked, he had done 'some remarkable things' during his twenty Tests against the Aussies. It is also good to know that he and Lord Hawke bore no ill-feeling towards each other. The cricket writer A A Thomson tells us that 'Lord Hawke was forever sorry that Bobby had to go, and when they met later, at Scarborough and such places, they were the best of friends'.

When a county cricketer was next ordered off the field by his captain, Hampshire's Jack Newman did earn a reprieve by apologising after being banished by the Hon L H (later Lord) Tennyson at Trent Bridge in 1922. Newman had been barracked by the crowd for his delaying tactics while bowling, repeatedly altering his field setting besides showing a general lack of urgency, and he responded in what was euphemistically called 'an offensive manner' when his captain told him to get on with the game. When his lordship accordingly pointed him to the pavilion, he flung the ball to the ground, kicked the stumps flying, and left to a chorus of booing. On having his apology accepted, he went on to complete twenty-five years with Hampshire up to 1930, then put in nine more seasons as a first-class umpire before spending the rest of his life in South Africa.

The third instance of this kind regrettably involved a Derbyshire player. In only his seventh game as the club's captain, and in a match against his home county of Yorkshire, Brian Bolus expelled Alan Ward at Chesterfield in 1973, also for refusing to bowl. Ward began well enough by having Geoffrey Boycott caught by Bolus in his first over as Yorkshire started their reply to Derbyshire's 311, but soon afterwards he lost his rhythm and co-ordination to such an extent that he was no-balled nine times and had nineteen runs hit off him in one over by another England batsman, Jack Hampshire, later of Derbyshire. Ward, off whom Hampshire was dropped before scoring, was rested after conceding 56 runs in nine overs, and it was when Bolus called upon him to re-enter the attack that he refused. Bolus, having first left the field to speak to the Derbyshire secretary, Major Douglas Carr, then made his dismissive gesture.

Ward walked off, and he had left the ground by the time the day's play ended. He apologised for his behaviour the next day, but very soon after that he announced his retirement from first-class cricket, complaining of mental pressure and frustration since his fast bowling had earned him England caps against New Zealand and Pakistan. Less than five months later, however, he changed his mind and returned to the fray, temporarily more relaxed, on a one-year contract that was extended for two seasons, during which he made a one-Test comeback against the West Indies, before his disillusioned departure to Leicestershire. In 1969 he had been Derbyshire's first Young Cricketer of the Year in *Wisden*, to be followed by Mike Hendrick (1973) and Geoff Miller (1976).

Back in 1889, Bobby Peel took half the Derbyshire wickets that fell in the match with Yorkshire at Bramall Lane before rain prevented further play with the score at 164 for six. Spofforth was due to be next man in.

For the following season the Australian was appointed Derbyshire's captain, but he played in only six of their fourteen games that year, and, counting that curtailed game at Sheffield, he was in their team no more than nine times in all – exactly half his number of appearances for Australia – before ending his association with the county after just one match in 1891. His complete bowling record for Derbyshire was:

	O	M	R	W	Average
1889	53	19	81	15	5.40
1890	240.1	66	498	42	11.85
1891	41	10	106	2	53.00
Total	334.1	95	685	59	11.61

His first match of 1890, after completing his qualifying time, was against his fellow countrymen. Rain washed out play on the opening day, the last one of June, and further hold-ups on the two others enabled Derbyshire to emerge with a draw as some small relief from their heavy defeats in each of their five previous meetings with the Australians.

Spofforth, naturally, was their star man. He followed his 3-34 in the tourists' first innings of 108 with 6-42 as they sagged again to 75 for nine. George Davidson (five) and Walter Sugg (four) shared nine of the ten wickets that eluded him, the other being the running-out of Hughie Trumble, an off-spinner who was twice to do the hat-trick in Test cricket. With conditions so much in favour of the bowlers, Derbyshire must have been thankful not to have the opportunity to bat again after Turner (6-16) and Ferris (4-30) had cut them down for 54.

In Derbyshire's next match, Spofforth played the chief supporting role with six wickets to Davidson's eight as Yorkshire were crushed by an innings and 25 runs at Derby. A stand of 114 between L G Wright (80) and Chatterton (66) after the early departure of Walter Sugg was built upon by a half-century from Davidson as Derbyshire batted throughout the first day to reach 295 for the loss of six wickets. Overnight rain made batting more of a lottery, and, after the home innings had closed for the addition of only seventeen more runs, Yorkshire were forced to follow on and beaten inside two days. Those normally formidable visitors were not at full strength, but they still fielded a reasonably representative side – as had also been the case two years earlier when Joe Hulme's match-best of 8-30 and 7-40 had pointed Derbyshire to their first victory over Yorkshire, by seven wickets, since the Mycroft-inspired double success of 1879, ending a run of seventeen games without a win against the county of the White Rose. On each of those occasions Yorkshire's absentees included Ulyett and Peel, but both were in a team lacking only Lord Hawke when Derbyshire, without Spofforth, completed their 1890 double by also winning at Sheffield, by 52 runs. A curious aspect of that game, in which most of Yorkshire's wickets fell to Davidson, Walker and Porter, was that Derbyshire twice totalled 202.

Spofforth was back at his best both immediately before and after missing that Bramall Lane encounter. Leicestershire were defeated at Derby largely due to his fourteen wickets for 114 runs (9-56 in their first innings). Against Norfolk he surprisingly went without a wicket as Walker took five cheaply when the visitors were all out for 91 in their first innings, but his 7-26 did most to demolish them for 49 in their second venture after Derbyshire had gained a lead of 72. That defeat of Norfolk chalked up another double, Derbyshire having also outclassed them by an innings at Norwich with the help of Frank Evershed's century, but they were beaten in both the other matches in which they had Spofforth's assistance that season.

Nottinghamshire were the winners by an innings when they visited Derby, and in their next match, also at home, Derbyshire lost by eight wickets to Essex. The game with Notts was worthy of special mention because of Chatterton's unusual and unlucky dismissal. Struck in the stomach by a sharply rising delivery, he prevented the ball dropping straight to the ground as he doubled up instinctively, then unwisely took hold of it and threw it down. The prompt appeal by the Notts players was frowned upon as unsportsmanlike, but they were quite within the law and Chatterton had to go – out 'handled the ball' with only two runs to his name. *Wisden* overlooked that incident when it stated that Karl Krikken's departure for the same reason in the match with the Indian tourists in 1996 (he handled the ball as it bounced towards the stumps after he had chopped it into the ground) was 'the first such dismissal in Derbyshire's history'. Unwanted as it was, the county's second-class exile did occupy six years of that history.

Whitwell-born Sam Malthouse, a left-hand batsman but right-arm bowler whose son William also played for Derbyshire, was top scorer with 22 in Derbyshire's paltry first-innings total of 62 in that 1890 visit by Nottinghamshire. By the end of the opening day's play those neighbouring rivals had already built up a winning position with 244 runs on the board for the loss of seven wickets – four of them to Spofforth, but at the cost of 111 runs by the time next day when Derbyshire were left to get 222 to save the innings defeat. It was a target that proved 71 beyond them. Most of their wickets in the match fell to Flowers and their former player Shacklock, who was also only one run from a half-century.

In the game with Essex, Spofforth, with just one wicket in each innings, had his thunder stolen by George Walker, whose six for only five runs limited those visitors to a first-innings lead of 41 after Walter Mead, an off-break and occasional leg-break bowler who played once for England, had found the pitch very much to his liking after rain by taking 6-27 in Derbyshire's capitulation for 42. When the home side batted again they folded for 93 despite improving conditions in face of the fast bowling of Henry Pickett, whose 6-40 gave him ten wickets in the match, a total he was to attain in one Leicestershire innings, at Leyton, in Essex's first Championship season of 1895. Pickett, sadly, came to an untimely end. He disappeared late in the September of 1907, and it was not until the end of December that a body discovered on the beach at Aberavon early in October was identified as his from articles found in the clothing.

All the eight Derbyshire matches in which Spofforth took an active part were played at Derby, and he appeared in the last of them against Leicestershire in the county's second fixture of the 1891 season. Sadly, he looked little like a Demon in a weakened team. His two wickets cost 53 runs apiece in a total of 409 as Leicestershire extracted convincing revenge, by an innings and 75 runs, for their double defeat by Derbyshire of the season before. Spofforth did a bit better as a batsman in what was to be his farewell game, compiling his top score of 32 for the county and totalling 42 for once out. Only Chatterton, who hit two half-centuries, made more runs than he did in Derbyshire's second innings.

This was the match in which, as recalled in the previous chapter, Dick Pougher scored a century besides taking six wickets. The backbone of Leicestershire's batting was provided by his partnership with his captain, Charles de Trafford, son of the former owner of the Old Trafford ground, who was only a dozen runs from also getting into three figures when caught off Spofforth. That was a very contrasting experience for de Trafford compared with the one that caused a good deal of unpleasantness when the counties met at Leicester a couple of years later. He was then given out for obstructing the field without getting off the mark in a match Derbyshire won with an outstanding contribution from Joe Hulme – eleven wickets for fewer than eight runs each and scores of 48 and 41.

Disappointing as Spofforth's final game for Derbyshire was, he could by no means be considered a spent force, even at rising thirty-eight. Having found wickets easy to come by in Derby and district club cricket, particularly for Derby Midland and Belper Meadows, he reaped not far off a thousand more, at just over seven runs each, in about fifteen years with the Hampstead club after his job had taken him to the London area. Twice, in away games with Marlow, he took all ten wickets in an innings – for twenty runs in 1893 (17-40 in the match), for fourteen in 1894. In that latter year he claimed 200 at an average under six. He also still played in a few first-class matches, including appearances for the Gentlemen, and in 1896 his twenty-eight wickets at that level for 9.14 runs each gave him the lowest bowling average of the season. In the same year, at the age of forty-two, he took eleven wickets for Wembley Park against the touring Australians.

Spofforth, who was a brother-in-law of Spencer Lyttelton, one of six brothers in a famous cricketing family (away from cricket he was chief private secretary to William Gladstone during that statesman's last spell as Prime Minister from 1892-94), continued to live in England when his cricketing days were finally over, and it was at Ditton Hill, Surbiton, that he died on 4 June, 1926. He left £164,000, a fortune in those days.

7. Seasons in Exile

Those rarities of a double defeat of Yorkshire in 1890 and the shock success the following season against a Surrey side heading for the fifth of six successive titles (the first three of them, one shared in a triple tie, since discounted) were the highlights of Derbyshire's six-year stint in cricket's second class. It was also during that period that they formed the strong nucleus of the team which earned their recall to the upper crust for 1894.

By the time that reprieve was granted, William Chatterton, a regular choice for the five seasons leading up to the loss of status, and George Davidson, an automatic selection for the last two of those seasons from the time of his debut in the first game of 1886, had been joined as established Derbyshire players by Herbert Evershed, the captain, Walter Sugg, L G Wright, William Storer and Harry Bagshaw. In support of that select seven during the temporary exile, the county relied mostly on George Porter, Joe Hulme, George Walker and, to a lesser extent, William Eadie, Walter Hall and Sam Malthouse. Eadie was an amateur from Burton-upon-Trent who, regrettably, too often confined his best form to net practice.

Davidson missed only one of the seventy-eight matches Derbyshire played in those six second-class years, Chatterton just two – one of them, in 1892, because he was at Lord's in a Players team that defeated the Gentlemen (W G Grace and all) by an innings. Chatterton did not make a big contribution to that victory, just fifteen runs and a couple of catches, but in another extra match that year, one that did not coincide with a Derbyshire fixture, he scored 109 at Lord's for MCC against Lancashire, carrying his bat right through a total of 238, in just over 160 five-ball overs, that led to a win by ten wickets.

A promising start was made under Chatterton's captaincy to Derbyshire's first demoted season of 1888, with victories in the opening two games by 45 runs against the MCC at Lord's and by seven wickets against Essex at Leyton, but all but one of the remaining ten were lost – seven of them in succession before the home win over Yorkshire in which Hulme took fifteen wickets was greeted by Walter Piper as 'an oasis in the desert of continued misfortune and disaster'.

Rain prevented a start on the first day of the visit to Lord's, and the pitch was made so favourable for bowlers in consequence that by the close of the second day's play 34 wickets had fallen for 310 runs. Walker, an ever-present that season along with Chatterton, Hulme and the ill-fated Cropper, took 5-31 in the MCC's dismissal for 83 in reply to a total of 92, and Hulme also captured five wickets, but at a cost of only eleven runs, as the home side slipped to 63 on the third day after Derbyshire's second innings had ended one short of three figures. The MCC's most successful bowler, with nine cheap wickets in the match, was James Wootton, the 5ft 6in Kent slow left-arm bowler who was to join Hampshire for their first County Championship season of 1895 after becoming coach at Winchester College. He had already enjoyed himself well enough at Derbyshire's expense, having taken nineteen of their wickets in Kent's wins at Derby and Tunbridge Wells in 1886 and five more in their rout for 36 by the MCC in 1887, but he was never to torment them again. Kent did not renew fixtures with Derbyshire until some years after he had switched counties, and he had lost much of his old skill by the time he faced them in just a couple of his occasional appearances for Hampshire.

Chatterton, with an unbeaten 40 in his only innings and four wickets for a mere eleven runs, shared the individual honours in the away win over Essex with Davidson, whose nine wickets in the match included another remarkably economical return of 6-16 that made a third day's play unnecessary. Like the MCC, Essex twice failed to reach 100; Derbyshire's 99 at Lord's was the biggest of the eight totals in those first two games.

Scoring was also low when Derbyshire's losing sequence then began back at Derby with one of their innings defeats by Surrey, no batsman progressing beyond 18 apart from Walter Read, whose 86 helped the visitors to a first-innings lead of no more than 52 despite Derbyshire's dismissal for an unimpressive 115. Yet that slim advantage proved more than enough. When Derbyshire went in again they were routed for 46, only Storer getting into double figures. He was bowled for 13 by Tom Bowley, a Nottinghamshire man recruited from Northamptonshire who added 4-30 to his first-innings 5-29. The other destroyer was Jack Beaumont, taker of 5-14 in that second-innings slump. Beaumont had done nothing of note for his home county of Yorkshire, but went through several seasons of considerable success after making a startling start with Surrey by claiming 6-11 in Middlesex's collapse for 25.

Beaumont was again a main cause of Derbyshire's discomfort in their final game of the 1888 season, his nine wickets costing only 62 runs as they were hustled out for 89 and 62 at The Oval. His chief ally with six wickets on that occasion, aside from the fact that Derbyshire contributed to their own downfall by having five men run out, was George Lohmann, another of the exceptional talents that made Surrey such a force in that era. 'Plum' Warner, writing early in the twentieth century, described Lohmann as 'probably the greatest medium-paced bowler that ever lived'. Gordon Ross, in his book, *The Surrey Story*, said that 'it was Walter Read and George Lohmann who, more than anyone else, enabled Surrey, under Shuter's leadership, to gain the position of leading county'. In almost 500 first-class games, eighteen of them Tests, Read scored more than 20,000 runs besides taking over one hundred wickets; Lohmann, also eighteen times an England player, accumulated nearly 1,850 wickets.

Twice while in the second class, in 1890 and 1893, Derbyshire outnumbered defeats by gaining their then biggest tally of seven victories in both. In the first of those seasons two of the wins, both by an innings, were registered against Norfolk, new opponents demeaned by Piper as 'really no class'. For the following year Norfolk were replaced by other newcomers, Warwickshire, against whom, after a rain-hit draw at Derby, one of six successes was recorded in Birmingham on a pitch favourable to bowlers which Porter exploited by twice taking 5-34. That was among the five consecutive wins, also including the defeat of Surrey, with which Derbyshire ended a season they had begun with only one in seven games.

As already noted, Derbyshire's double defeat of Yorkshire in 1890 repeated the Mycroft-inspired achievement of 1879, though in the absence of Peel and Ulyett on Test duty at The Oval, but there has yet to be a third instance more than a hundred seasons on. In fact, Derbyshire went without a Championship win over Yorkshire, either home or away, from 1905 until 1950, when they recovered with an unbeaten century by one veteran, Denis Smith, to end that desolate run by 79 runs at Bradford through the cleverly flighted leg-breaks of another, Bert ('Dusty') Rhodes. Set to get 299 in 160 minutes, Yorkshire were given the flying start of an opening stand of 123 in just under the hour by Len Hutton (107) and Frank Lowson (51), only to lose their last eight wickets for 37 runs in 45 minutes as Rhodes added to his first-innings 4-52 with 6-74. Hopes of another, long overdue, double were swiftly dispelled in that year's return game at Chesterfield, however. Yorkshire took a firm grip from the first day and triumphed by seven wickets.

Two years later Derbyshire defeated Yorkshire at Chesterfield for the first time, the Tykes having won sixteen and drawn eleven of their previous meetings there. The jinx was broken by 81 runs, but Derbyshire's chance of at last again getting the better of them twice in one season had already been ruined by an innings beating at Sheffield, where left-hander Vic Wilson had made a career-best 230 after the home team had been put in to bat. Having laid the Chesterfield bogy, Derbyshire were winners there against Yorkshire twice more in the next four seasons. In 1953 they collapsed to defeat at Scarborough after a century by the dependable Arnold Hamer, an import from Yorkshire, had helped them to a ten-wicket victory at Queen's Park, but in 1956, after squeaking home by six runs at Chesterfield, they had real hopes of completing another double until that man Wilson salvaged a draw from a slump at Leeds with a not-out half-century. Between those two other Chesterfield wins Derbyshire were successful at Headingley by six wickets, Hamer scoring another hundred, after holding the initiative for most of a drawn game at Queen's Park.

In 1957, Les Jackson, the most prolific wicket-taker in Derbyshire's long history, dismissed eleven Yorkshire batsmen in his benefit match at Burton-upon-Trent as Derbyshire won by 84 runs after being well beaten at Bradford, but that was to be their last success in this series of matches for twenty-six years – and their last at home against Yorkshire until six more years after that (they won at Chesterfield by three wickets in 1989 after escaping from Leeds with a draw). In 1983 the further sequence of Yorkshire success against Derbyshire was ended by the narrow margin of 22 runs on a Sheffield pitch of uneven bounce that was reported as being sub-standard, but back at Chesterfield that year an undefeated century by England opener Geoffrey Boycott enabled Yorkshire to secure a comfortable draw after being forced to follow on. That elusive third double was closer at Queen's Park in 1986 and 1988. Both those matches, interrupted by rain, ended with Derbyshire only 28 runs from victory – first with seven wickets in hand, then six – after respective victories at Sheffield and Leeds.

Influential as Derbyshire's 1890 double over Yorkshire was in the eventual reconsideration of their worth as a first-class county, the decisive defeat of Surrey's champions a year later had an even more important bearing on their reinstatement. Unfortunately, it proved also to be just an isolated occurrence, but Walter Piper observed that it 'did them a world of good in the eyes of the cricketing public'.

Disappointment at the abandonment without a ball bowled of Surrey's visit to Derby earlier that season because of rain was dispelled in the most emphatic fashion by the ten-wicket triumph gained inside two days at Kennington Oval.

Walter Read, hitherto such a scourge of Derbyshire bowlers, failed with the bat that time, twice bowled by George Porter in totalling only thirteen runs, but he still showed to some advantage by taking 5-31 with his underarm slow deliveries after the Georges Davidson and Porter had bowled unchanged in a Surrey first innings that only just scraped past the hundred mark. For the lead of 83 they gained, Derbyshire were almost wholly reliant on a third-wicket stand between Chatterton (59) and Bagshaw (80), only Storer (15 not out) also getting into double figures. With Porter taking the six-wicket leading role from Davidson in once more sharing with him all those that fell to bowlers (there was one run out) when the home team batted again, Derbyshire were left requiring just 29 runs for their first win over Surrey since the first match between the counties eight years earlier. That ended a sequence of fifteen defeats by Surrey, seven of them by an innings, and Derbyshire were to go through twenty-one more matches with them, all lost (eight more by an innings) except for four draws when rain curtailed play, before chalking up a third victory at their expense – by 111 runs at Chesterfield in 1903.

Fifty years went by after that before Derbyshire gained another landmark victory against Surrey, beating them by an innings and one run at Derby in the second of the seven successive seasons in which the southern county were champions – but that was the only time they defeated them during that record run.

More penetrative bowling by Porter and Davidson, whose respective returns for the two Surrey innings were identical at 6-62, gave Derbyshire some hopes of winning at The Oval for a second consecutive year in 1892, especially while Davidson and Chatterton were going well in a third-wicket stand chasing a target to 189, but their last eight wickets fell for 27 runs to William Lockwood, a fast bowler with a most deceptive slower delivery who became one of the most famous of his generation after Nottinghamshire had let him slip away following an unsuccessful trial. 'Plum' Warner rated Lockwood superior even to the formidable Tom Richardson, whose many outstanding returns included 8-36 in one of Surrey's big wins at Derby, and Ranjitsinhji, the gifted Indian batsman who played for England and Sussex, contended that Lockwood, at his best, was the more difficult of the two to cope with.

Derbyshire lost both their matches with Surrey in each of their six seasons as a second-class county apart from that of 1891, and they took a real caning at The Oval in 1890 when three of their bowlers, Davidson, Chatterton and Malthouse, each conceded more than a hundred runs (Davidson not far off two hundred) as 541 runs were piled up. That pasting came immediately after an MCC orgy of 452 in an innings defeat for Derbyshire at Lord's, where Frank Shacklock chipped in with a half-century against his old county as George Davenport, the Cheshire professional, did most of the plundering with an unbeaten 158. The bowling brunt was borne that day by every member of the Derbyshire team except Bill Storer, who on other occasions broke from his usual wicketkeeping duties sufficiently to tot up 232 first-class wickets with his leg-breaks.

Heavy toll was also taken of Derbyshire's attack in the game at Derby with the Australian tourists of 1893, whose declaration at 494 for the loss of nine wickets was built on a big partnership between two of the smallest men in the team, Alexander Bannerman and Henry Graham. Bannerman, whose older brother Charles scored the first Test century in what later came to be acknowledged as the inaugural match between Australia and England at Melbourne in 1877, varied his steady garnering of runs with stonewalling in the style for which he was so notorious in making 105 before being bowled by Joseph Cupitt, a left-arm medium-pacer from Barrow Hill, near Chesterfield. Graham, 'the Little Dasher,' fell to a return catch by the same bowler – but not until he had scored 219.

That was the sixth and last tour of England on which Alec Bannerman drove both bowlers and crowds to distraction with his extreme patience, but it was back home in Sydney that he most boringly laboured through in an innings of 91 against England for seven and a half hours, spread over three days. He scored off only five of the 204 balls bowled to him by William ('Dick') Attewell, a Nottinghamshire medium-pacer noted for his extreme accuracy, but the barracking turned to praise when that marathon effort led to the clinching of the series. Graham, a contrastingly hard hitter whose nickname derived from his rapid running between the wickets, was on the first of his two visits when he made his double-century against Derbyshire. He topped the tourists' averages that season, but ill health handicapped him on his return in 1896.

Derbyshire's own biggest total while second class was 384 for five against Essex at Leyton in 1889. In six hours Chatterton (168) and Davidson (129) added 293, but the then novelty of a declaration, 397 ahead, did not leave sufficient time to avert a draw, the home side finishing on 136 with half their wickets in hand.

That was the year in which discrepancies in Derbyshire's finances were first made public as the incoming captain, Fred Spofforth, blew the whistle on Sam Richardson by unearthing the embezzlement of funds in both the cricket and soccer sections. It was this astounding news that brought about a change in the cricket club's management. Instead of having an honorary secretary (Arthur Wilson) and an assistant secretary (Richardson), the committee decided to appoint a paid secretary.

The choice fell on William Barclay Delacombe, standing 6ft 5in, who was to hold that office until 1907 and altogether take an active interest in the county's affairs across three decades until shortly before his death in 1911. Even at his exceptional height, he has not remained Derbyshire's tallest player. Dallas Moir, a left-arm spinner born in Malta of Scottish parents who was the county's leading wicket-taker in his first full season of 1982, stood 6ft 8in. Delacombe, who was born at Ascension, that little dot of an island in the Atlantic ocean, often accompanied the team to keep the score and was also a stand-in captain in some of the occasional appearances he made as a player from 1892 to 1900. Useful with both bat and ball, and a reliable outfielder, he had his hour of on-field glory at Dunstable in 1897 when, playing for Incogniti against L C R Thring's XI, he did the hat-trick in taking all ten wickets. He was one of the original members of the Derbyshire Friars team in 1878.

Twice more after their big score against Essex in their second season of demotion Derbyshire exceeded 350 in an innings, both against Leicestershire, while a second-class county. The improving strength of their batting by the time they were restored to the top flight was reflected in the fact that their number of completed innings below 100 was halved in 1889 from the fourteen out of twenty-two the previous year, and then totalled only thirteen more over the four other seasons.

Derbyshire won eight and drew seven of their games against first-class teams during their six seasons as a second-class county, but were beaten in the twenty-eight others. Half those eight victories were gained at the expense of Yorkshire – and they were desperately unlucky not to notch a fifth at Derby in 1893, the season in which Yorkshire, soon to be habitual table-toppers, ended a twenty-year wait for their first title. The belated champions-to-be had to follow on 180 behind after Chatterton (101 not out) and Herbert Evershed (72) had mastered their bowling, and Derbyshire were only 27 runs from victory with eight wickets in hand when rain ended play.

The twenty-eight defeats by a first-class county included one by seven wickets at Derby during 1888 in what was to be Derbyshire's only meeting with Middlesex for more than forty years. The coincidental feature of that brief encounter was that the highest score on both sides was 92 not out – for Derbyshire by William Cropper, for Middlesex by Edward Hadow, youngest of the four of seven brothers who were in the Harrow XI at various times. Not until July 1929 did Derbyshire and Middlesex meet again, and not until the year after that, at the fifth attempt, did Derbyshire defeat them for the first time, winning by seven wickets at Burton-upon-Trent with the help of a century by Leslie Townsend, one of the finest all-rounders of the period between the two world wars. It was also at the fifth attempt that Derbyshire beat Middlesex for the first time at Lord's, in 1933.

Of their thirty-five games with fellow second-class sides from 1888 to 1893, Derbyshire demonstrated their high standing in that sphere by winning twenty-three. Four of the others were drawn and eight lost. Essex, with five wins, were the most successful of their second-class opponents, but Derbyshire also defeated them five times – most notably in 1893 when, at Derby, they were set to get 160 runs in less than three hours and knocked them off in eighty minutes for the loss of only one wicket. That was the match in which, as recalled in an earlier chapter, Harry Bagshaw was twice close to a century.

One of Essex's most successful batsmen on that occasion was Hugh Owen, who had Derbyshire among the three counties for which at one time he was qualified. Bath-born, he could have played for Somerset by birth and for Derbyshire by residence while a master at Trent College, but Essex, the county of his family home, was the only one for which he played – for nearly twenty years, and as their captain from 1895 to 1901. He scored five centuries for Trent College, and in one match against Tibshelf he carried his bat through both their innings, for 27 and 46. He also played for Nottingham Forest Amateurs, with whom four not-outs in his five innings of one season gave him an average of 244.

The three other defeats suffered by Derbyshire by a second-class county while they themselves were in that category were inflicted by Leicestershire – one of them by an innings, but the two others by the slender margins of 27 runs and one wicket. In 1888, Derbyshire folded up for 59 after Joe Hulme's 7-11 in Leicestershire's second innings of 52 had left them needing only 87 (though that would have been the biggest total of the match); in 1892, also at Leicester, Porter (6-20) and Davidson (3-29) only just failed to prevent the home side reaching their meagre target of 78.

Against those defeats, Derbyshire beat Leicestershire seven times during their second-class years, twice by an innings and twice after having to follow on. At Derby in 1892, they recovered so emphatically from having to bat again 115 behind that they declared at 423 for seven, Herbert Evershed and George

Davidson scoring centuries, and then shot Leicestershire out for 98. Hulme's five wickets in the visitors' second innings cost only three runs in seven overs, three of which were maidens.

The other game between these counties while Derbyshire were second class was a rained-off draw in 1889 at Leicester, where Hulme was in form with both bat and ball, top-scoring with 61 not out and backing up Davidson's 6-47 in the home team's first innings with 5-28 in the second. When the weather called a halt Derbyshire were only just over a hundred runs from victory with nine wickets in hand.

In their last two demoted seasons Derbyshire went without a win in ten games against first-class counties (there were only two of those opponents, Surrey and Yorkshire, in 1892), but underlined their superiority against second-class teams with twelve victories to three. Their reinstatement in the top class for 1894, but not into the County Championship until a year later, then began inauspiciously with the customary heavy defeat at The Oval, but a drawn game at Southampton in which L G Wright scored 53 and 171 not out, and Storer 90 and 39 not out, led to a revival in which MCC, Lancashire and Warwickshire were convincingly beaten in succession. Davidson bagged eleven of the MCC's wickets and Hulme took 5-17 in Lancashire's first innings. Further setbacks against Lancashire, Yorkshire and in the return game with Warwickshire followed, with heavy rain saving Derbyshire from another one when they had much the worst of a home draw with Surrey, but even in adversity some outstanding individual displays were given.

At Old Trafford half Lancashire's second-innings wickets were down for only 21 runs, Davidson including a spell of 5-5 in his 7-55, before the tail wagged sufficiently to leave Derbyshire requiring a total that proved only four boundaries beyond them. In the three-wicket defeat by Yorkshire at Derby, Davidson scored 81 and 72 not out, and Hulme took 6-94 and 4-61. And Davidson captured five more wickets in a Surrey score of more than 300 in reply to which Derbyshire could muster only 89 before the weather brought merciful relief.

In the next two matches, Derbyshire emerged with much credit from a drawn first meeting with a South African touring side, and then decisively avenged their defeat by Yorkshire with a nine-wicket win at Sheffield. It was not a particularly pleasant first visit to the British Isles for the Springboks. Their hastily and badly arranged itinerary was not granted first-class status, and they failed to attract the public to such a degree that their gross gate receipts amounted to less than £500. Indeed, it was for financial reasons that they were almost left stranded in Ireland. At Derby, their captain, Herbert Castens, put the county in to bat and a team differing in only two respects (the amateurs S H Wood and J P Ward for Bagshaw and Malthouse) from the one routed for 39 at Edgbaston the previous day rallied from losing L G Wright without scoring to make 325.

The backbone of that total was provided by Walter Sugg, the first to score a century for Derbyshire in a match outside the County Championship. There were to be three more hundreds in his aggregate of just over 5,000 runs (all but some 1,500 first-class) during a career with the county that lasted from 1884 to 1902 except for the 1885 season. To quote *Wisden* again, 'although not built on such generous lines as his more famous brother Frank, and while not so successful, he had a good eye and flexible wrists, and generally looked to be the better batsman.' Against the South Africans, straight from twice being bowled for nought in the match with Warwickshire in Birmingham, he made 121 before being run out – a fate that also befell Storer, who missed a half-century by only one run, and Davidson. The next highest scorer, with 53, was Chatterton, who went five better without being dismissed in Derbyshire's second innings of 197.

The South Africans' first innings of 300 was also monopolised by one man, and to a greater degree than Derbyshire's. Four of Cyril Sewell's colleagues got into the thirties, but he left them all well behind with a skilful 128 before being the first victim of a Hulme hat-trick. Sewell, then only 19, also scored a century, 170, against Somerset at Taunton, and he finished as the tourists' leading scorer with a little more than a thousand runs at an average of 30. On returning the following year to settle in England, he assisted Gloucestershire intermittently until as late as 1919, succeeding the big-hitter Gilbert Jessop as both captain and secretary of that county.

Walter Sugg scored two of his other centuries against Leicestershire – run out for 104 in an innings win at Derby in 1889, and not out for the same score in a victory at Leicester during Derbyshire's first season back in the Championship in 1895. When he again reached three figures, for the second time in a first-class match, he did so before lunch on the third day of the drawn game with Worcestershire at Derby in 1899. He was unbeaten on 102 at the break, but added only five more runs before being bowled by the visitors' captain, Harry Foster, the eldest of the seven brothers who played for that county at various times. Two of those other brothers, Reginald (compiler of the then record Test score of 287 against Australia at Sydney in 1903) and Wilfred, were also in the Worcestershire team in that match, and Reginald had to take over behind the stumps when wicketkeeper Tom Straw was knocked unconscious by the ball while practising before the game began. Although Straw, a Nottinghamshire man, recovered and wanted to play, it was not thought advisable.

Leicestershire looked on the way to winning when they ended the first day of the 1895 match at Grace Road at 143 for the loss of only two wickets in response to the 211 Derbyshire made after being put in, but next day George Walker snapped up the remaining eight for fewer than twenty runs. That provided him with his best figures of 9-68, the only wicket to elude him being that of opener and captain Charles de Trafford, caught behind by Storer off the bowling of George Porter. Sugg's century then helped Derbyshire to extend their lead beyond 300 and Walker, also scorer of 63 runs for once out, increased his match haul to thirteen wickets as outplayed Leicestershire lost by 127 runs.

In common with his younger brother, Walter Sugg was born at Ilkeston, educated at Sheffield Grammar School, worked outside cricket as a solicitor's clerk (their father was a Sheffield solicitor), turned out for Yorkshire (in his case just the one match) before joining their home county, played professional football and was a fine billiards player. In being as versatile a sportsman as his brother, he was a scratch scratch golfer too, and he also found time to be a professional cricketer with Durham City, Burnley and Rochdale besides playing for a number of other clubs either on a match basis or as an amateur. The brothers opened two sports shops in Liverpool, and for a dozen years, 1894 to 1905, issued *Sugg's Cricket Annual*. In 1933 they died within eight days of each other, Walter at Dore in Yorkshire on May 21, Frank at Waterloo, Liverpool, on May 29.

Derbyshire's revenge victory over Yorkshire at Bramall Lane in 1894, by the comfortable margin of nine wickets, was down to yet another prime example of the potency of the Davidson-Hulme partnership. Bowling unchanged, they routed the home side for 81 and 50, Davidson taking 8-33 in the first innings, Hulme 9-27 in the second. Four years later, Yorkshire's opening pair, the short but strongly built John Brown and the 6ft 2in John Tunnicliffe ('Long John of Pudsey'), were to make cricketing history with a world record stand of 554 in Walter Sugg's benefit match at Chesterfield, but in this game they managed only 22 runs between them in the first innings and were both out without scoring in the second.

From the high of that convincing away win against Yorkshire, Derbyshire went straight to another low with a home defeat by Hampshire, but then ended the season, and their brief banishment from the County Championship, by beating Leicestershire home and away – by an innings and 36 runs at Leicester, where Porter had match figures of 9-37, and by eight wickets at Derby, where Davidson took 5-39 and 5-45. Walter Sugg was again in form with the bat in scoring 77 against Hampshire after being run out for 27 in the first innings, and he made 70 before being run out again in his only innings at Leicester. He was also the second highest scorer, with 40, to Storer, who was unbeaten on 78, in the final game.

George Davidson ended that season only one short of his 1892 total of 91 wickets for Derbyshire, again at an average cost of just over twelve runs each, and in the following one his personal best in all matches of 138 at just under seventeen apiece included his top tally for the county of 93. One of his finest all-round performances during that first year back in the Championship was given at The Oval, where he scored 67 and 62, and took 5-72, before rain washed out play when Derbyshire were 346 runs ahead with four wickets in hand. In the return game at Derby just over a week later, however, Surrey's supremacy was restored by a thumping victory in a match umpired by Dick Barlow and George Ulyett. Tom Richardson, a man of remarkable stamina despite his intimidating long run-up, and Lohmann bowled unchanged as Derbyshire were hurried out for 63 and 57. Richardson had overall figures of 11-60, Lohmann 8-59.

Davidson headed both the batting and bowling averages for Derbyshire that year. He was to go on to even greater deeds until the devastating, unexpected news that broke on the morning of Wednesday, the eighth of February in 1899.

WILL TAYLOR – THE LONGEST-SERVING COUNTY SECRETARY

William Thomas Taylor was Derbyshire's secretary, appointed from a short list of five, for a record 51 years and 149 days from 4 August 1908 until 31 December 1959. This beat by seventeen months the time in office of the previous longest-serving county secretary, A J Lancaster, who was with Kent from 18 May 1885 until 21 June 1936 after succeeding his father in the post.

When Taylor was appointed, the *Derbyshire Cricket Guide* described him as 'an enthusiastic worker of a firm but courteous disposition who is likely to prove a successful official, combining the advantages of a good business training with an intimate knowledge of cricket and cricketers'. It was a spot-on prediction. During his half-century at the helm, Derbyshire were often in a most precarious situation because of their extreme financial difficulties, and Capt G R Jackson, the club's former captain who was chairman of the committee which agreed to Taylor's request to retire with 'the greatest regret', said that it was 'quite possible that without Mr Taylor's great administrative ability, his personal charm, and his capacity for hard work, county cricket in Derbyshire would have ceased to exist'.

Taylor took over from R S T Cochrane, who held the post for only seven months in succession to W B Delacombe before leaving for a better-paid job with a London brewery. In common with Delacombe, who, according to an article John Grainger wrote for the *Derbyshire Year Book*, burnt all the club's scorebooks and various other records on being asked to resign after eighteen years in office, Taylor also played for the county – in one match at Trent Bridge in 1905, another, against the West Indies tourists at Derby, in 1906 and two more, also at Derby, against Kent and Surrey, in 1910. He had a top score of only eleven, scoring 53 runs at an average of 7.57, and his two wickets cost 28 runs each. He also held two catches. His younger brother Francis also played for Derbyshire, but in only eight games from 1908 to 1911, and also with no great success.

Like Delacombe too, Will Taylor frequently travelled with the team to away matches in his early years as secretary, acting as scorer or twelfth man. He was the oldest surviving former Derbyshire player until his death, in his ninety-second year, at the village of Breadsall, just outside Derby, on 17 August 1976. He was offered the Lancashire secretaryship during the 1920s, but, in *Wisden's* words, 'Derbyshire was always his county.'

In club cricket, Taylor played for Wirksworth, where he was born on 14 April 1885. His father became a member of that club and his three other sons, two of whom died in the First World War, also played for the team.

Taylor, who bore on his forehead the deep groove left by the bullet that badly wounded him while in the Army during the 1914-18 war (he reached the rank of captain), retained his connection with the Derbyshire club to the very end, for he was made an honorary life member as well as a vice-president after handing over the secretarial duties to Donald Carr, who undertook them for the last three years of his captaincy before leaving to join the administrative staff at Lord's. In addition, Taylor was Derbyshire's honorary secretary from 1962 to 1972, and a member of the committee from 1960 to 1973. He also succeeded Lord Hives as president of the Supporters' Club, which has provided the parent club with such crucial financial assistance since its formation in 1952.

On the eve of the 1958 season, Taylor, then seventy-three, was made an honorary life member of the MCC for his services to cricket. And to mark the fiftieth anniversary of his appointment as Derbyshire's secretary he was treated to a small private lunch during the county's match with Nottinghamshire at Trent Bridge in the July of that year.

The players' viewpoint of the respect in which he was held was summed up by George Dawkes, Derbyshire's wicketkeeper at the time of the secretary's retirement. 'He has always been very helpful to professional cricketers,' said Dawkes, 'particularly in the way he handled matters relating to terms and contracts. But he was always something more … a real friend to every one of us.' Ronnie Aird, secretary of the MCC when Taylor retired, said that 'a more considerate and kind-hearted man it would be difficult to find'.

The Supporters' Club was formed at a special meeting at the St James's Salerooms in Derby on 18 July 1952 with the main objects of helping the county club to raise funds and increase membership. Its first officers were: President, Lord Hives; secretary, F G Peach (who held the post until his death in 1996); treasurer, F Tatlow; committee, A H Collard, N Cholerton, R Magnall, E A Hooper, A West.

8. Death of a Record Breaker

The shock premature death, in his thirty-third year, of George Arthur Davidson deprived Derbyshire of a player who for some years had been their best all-rounder, of even greater value to the team than the admirable Chatterton because of his superior bowling. In his obituary, *Wisden* declared that, up to that time, 'with the exception of William Storer, the county has never produced a player of finer powers.'

Of medium height, but long on both strength and stamina, Davidson was in his prime when he ended his thirteenth Derbyshire season of 1898 with a career total of not far off 8,000 runs, 5,546 of them in first-class matches, nearly one thousand wickets, 621 first-class, and in the region of 150 catches. Yet just over five months later, on the eighth day of February, came the shattering news of his death from pneumonia that developed out of influenza.

Davidson missed only three Derbyshire matches in those thirteen seasons – at Leicester in 1888, when he bounced straight back with 94 runs for once out against Middlesex, at home to Yorkshire in 1895 when he was away at Lord's in the Players team that defeated the Gentlemen, and again at Leicester in 1898 when he and Chatterton, also very rarely an absentee, were out injured.

The 1895 season was Davidson's best statistically. For Derbyshire he scored 760 runs and took his highest annual county total of 93 wickets, but with the addition of a dozen other matches he became the only player in the country to complete the cricketer's double that season. He ended it with 1,296 runs at an average of 28, and 138 wickets at a cost of fewer than seventeen runs each. It was a distinguished company he joined, for the feat had previously been achieved by only four players: W G Grace, Charles Studd, the youngest and most famous of three brothers who all played for Eton, Cambridge University and Middlesex, the Notts all-rounder Wilfred Flowers, and George Giffen, who was also the first Australian to score 1,000 runs and take 100 wickets in Tests.

Most of Davidson's extra first-class appearances in 1895 were with the MCC, for whom he hit half-centuries against Essex, Lancashire and Cambridge University besides twice taking five or more wickets in an innings. He also played twice for the North against the South, for the Players against the Gentlemen, and for a Rest of England XI at the Hastings Festival against a team assembled by A E Stoddart, one of the few to play for England at both cricket and rugby.

Stoddart also had the distinction of making the biggest individual score in a game of any description, 485 for the Hampstead club against the Stoics in 1886, until Arthur Collins compiled his 628 not out, spread over five days, in a junior house match at Clifton College in 1899. Stoddart was to make a most fitting farewell to the first-class cricketing scene with his highest first-class score of 221, against Somerset, in his last match for Middlesex in 1890, but both he and Collins came to a tragically premature end. Collins, a lieutenant in the Royal Engineers, was killed in action soon after the outbreak of the 1914-18 war, and Stoddart committed suicide, shooting himself in the head, in the spring of 1915.

Davidson did nothing of note in the Players' defeat of the Gentlemen at Lord's in 1895, but the Derbyshire representation was upheld in typically assured style by Storer, who missed a century by only seven runs and shared a seventh-wicket stand just four short of three figures with Yorkshireman Bobby Peel. Storer was to follow Chatterton as an England player with appearances in all five Tests in Australia in 1897-98 and another at Trent Bridge in 1899, but that honour was denied Davidson. *Wisden* suggested that Davidson 'might have enjoyed a still more brilliant career had he been associated with a stronger county, the fact of being so often on the beaten side having naturally a somewhat depressing effect on his cricket'. The same might also have been said of Storer but for the fact that he developed into a batsman of such reliability, coupled with his excellent wicketkeeping and additional ability as a bowler in spells when he handed over the gloves to Chatterton or Wright, that his international claims just could not be ignored.

Wisden also said of Davidson: 'It is a fair criticism to say that, though never quite the cricketer one would choose for England against Australia, he fell only a little below the highest class.' Outside Tests, appearances for an England XI were among those Davidson made against the Aussies apart from Derbyshire matches, but his best figures in those games, 3-36, were upstaged at Crystal Palace in 1888 by his county clubmate Joe Hulme's 7-14 in a 78-run win for a team that also included Chatterton and Cropper. Hulme again outdid Davidson (and George Porter) with 6-54 in helping the Midland Counties to defeat the 1896 Australian tourists by four wickets at Edgbaston. It was for the Hurst Park club, at their ground at East Molesley in 1890, that Davidson gave his best performance against the Australians excluding Derbyshire matches, though that was only as a bowler. Sharing the attack unchanged with Lancashire's Arthur Mold (6-57), he took 4-31 in a total of 101. Although again finishing on the winning side, he failed as a batsman, twice out without scoring.

On the Australians' visits to Derby, Davidson did best as a bowler with five wickets in the rain-curtailed drawn match of 1890, and made his top score of 60 in 1896 when the tourists left themselves with insufficient time to gain victory by keeping Derbyshire in the field for more than nine hours in piling up a total of 625 to which three players, Harry Donnan, Clem Hill and Harry Trott contributed centuries. Every player in the Derbyshire team except Wright, who took over from Storer behind the stumps, joined in the flayed attack from which Walter Sugg emerged with most credit by taking four wickets at a cost of only just over fifteen runs apiece.

It was the Australians' biggest total of that tour, and well ahead of the previous biggest by any team against Derbyshire. As far as first-class matches were concerned, that had been 512 by Surrey at Derby at the start of the same season, when Tom Hayward had profited from a few lives to make an unbeaten double-century, though Derbyshire had been punished for 541 at The Oval six years earlier during their second-class exile. It took only two years for the Australian record to be broken, in a match in which Derbyshire suffered their heaviest defeat. More about that in due course.

The other teams for which George Davidson played away from Derbyshire included the Second-Class Counties (against the Australians) and a side assembled under the name of Charles Thornton, a batsman who specialised in dispatching the ball great distances. Chatterton and Storer frequently accompanied Davidson to his various representative matches, mixing in the exalted company of such men as W G Grace, Lord Hawke, Archie MacLaren, William Gunn, Albert Hornby and Jack Hearne. Davidson was seen at his best as an all-rounder in those games when he followed five cheap wickets for the MCC in a Cambridge University XII innings with an adventurous knock of 93. In one of his appearances for the North, at Scarborough in 1895, his five wickets included that of his former Derbyshire colleague Fred Spofforth, who, however, gained swift revenge by also dismissing him cheaply. A year later, Spofforth was among his MCC team-mates at the same ground against Yorkshire, but Davidson went without a wicket in a rained-off draw while the Australian took 8-74.

In ten seasons Davidson was Derbyshire's top wicket-taker. Two of those seasons were his first two, and the only exception in his last nine was that of 1896, when he finished second with twelve fewer than Joe Hulme's 86. Twice he headed the county's bowling averages, and on four other occasions he was the runner-up – twice to Cropper, twice to Hulme. His best figures for one innings, the 9-39 in a home win against Warwickshire in 1895 that so narrowly improved upon his 9-42 in the 1886 defeat by Gloucestershire at Derby, helped him to one of his four match hauls of eleven wickets. He also took ten wickets in a match four times, twelve and thirteen once each, but his biggest bag of fifteen came in 1898, emphasising his undiminished accuracy of length in what was to be his final season.

Incredible as it may seem, Walter Piper assures us that 'he bowled the first hour and a half of the game [against Essex at Leyton] without a run being obtained off him'. Thirty of Davidson's five-ball overs in the home side's first innings were indeed maidens, though the fact that Derbyshire still managed to lose by 129 runs might well be regarded as even more incredible. The 42 runs he conceded for his seven wickets were taken off his sixteen other overs and three balls. With eight more wickets added for 74 runs when Essex batted again, his fifteen altogether cost 116, still the best figures against that county for Derbyshire.

Davidson had also taken eight wickets in an innings, for 48 runs, on his first visit to Leyton in 1886. And Derbyshire had made no mistake that time, winning by an innings and 78 runs after Essex had followed on almost 200 behind a total of 393 that was based on a century by Chatterton with sound support from Edmund Maynard and Walter Sugg. Davidson's most economical eight wickets in one innings, for 25 runs in 1895, included the first of his two hat-tricks (the other came in an innings victory over the MCC at Lord's in 1898) and restricted Lancashire's first-innings lead after they had overhauled Derbyshire's total with only three men out.

That was the game in which George Porter, as recalled in the second chapter, caused the visitors' second-innings collapse to defeat following a Derbyshire batting recovery led by a Storer century. Lancashire might also have been beaten by Derbyshire earlier in that month of August at Old Trafford, where Davidson completed his season's double of 1,000 runs and 100 wickets in only his 20th match, scoring 77 and taking 4-68 and 6-68. A heavy storm prevented further play when Derbyshire, with one wicket down, required only 118 on a pitch that had been playing easily. Eight wickets in an innings also fell to Davidson for 33 runs against Yorkshire at Sheffield in 1894, and for 70 runs against Warwickshire at Edgbaston in 1896. Yorkshire, all out for 81 and 50, were beaten by nine wickets, Joe Hulme outdoing Davidson with 9-27 in their second innings, but there was time only for Warwickshire to be dismissed for 166 before the weather called a halt. It was also against Warwickshire that Davidson achieved one of his finest all-round performances, coupling his eleven of their wickets at Derby in 1895 with an innings of 79.

Derbyshire's team in that first season back in the Championship was their strongest up to that time. They finished fifth out of fourteen behind Surrey, Lancashire, Yorkshire and Gloucestershire, then the game's acknowledged elite, and lost only four of their sixteen matches. Seven of the others were drawn, and they might have had more than five wins but for being rained off when in favourable positions against Surrey and Lancashire. At The Oval they had a lead of almost 350 with four wickets in hand after Davidson, who also took five wickets, Bagshaw and Chatterton had been the leading scorers in both their innings, but the champions reasserted their authority in no uncertain manner in the return game at Derby a week later. Demoralised by Richardson (11-60) and Lohmann (8-59), Derbyshire slumped to totals of 63 and 57 as Surrey's modest 173 proved sufficient for an innings victory with 53 runs to spare.

In only one other match that year, however, were Derbyshire so outplayed, and they then fielded a weakened team in also losing by an innings to Hampshire at Southampton. Facing a total of 294 compiled on a fast pitch, they were dismissed twice on the second day by the pace of Nottinghamshire-born Tom Soar (11-113) and the off-breaks of the portly Harry Baldwin (8-93), who shared the attack unchanged throughout. Baldwin's son, christened Herbert but also known as Harry, played his county cricket for Surrey, but became best known as the umpire of Test standard who no-balled Ernie McCormick, the Australian fast bowler, nineteen times in three overs in the opening match of the 1938 tour at Worcester.

As a batsman, George Davidson touched his heights in 1896 when he not only, with Chatterton, followed Storer to doing what no Derbyshire player had done before – score a thousand runs for the county in one season – but also hit his club record 274 against Lancashire at Old Trafford (see p.332). His stay of 435 minutes was ended by a catch at long-off by no other than his former team-mate Frank Sugg, off the bowling of Johnny Briggs. After openers Wright and Bagshaw had gone with only 26 runs on the board, Davidson added 208 for the third wicket with Chatterton, who was bowled by Albert Hallam, a future *Wisden* Cricketer of the Year, for 104, and 308 for the fourth with Storer, who won the race to being the first to reach 1,000 runs in a season for Derbyshire in making 116 before becoming another of the six victims Briggs claimed at the high cost of 185 runs in ninety five-ball overs. It was the first time three centuries had been scored for Derbyshire in one innings, and the partnership between Davidson and Storer, the most productive of all those for Derbyshire up to that time, remained the county's record for the fourth wicket until Pat Vaulkhard and Denis Smith added 328 against Nottinghamshire at Trent Bridge in 1946.

The 264 with which Vaulkhard, an amateur who had played a few times for Notts before the Second World War, made the closest approach to breaking Davidson's record was his only three-figure score in 122 first-class innings. It was the biggest of that season, and the third highest by a player who never made another century (behind Pervez Akhtar's 337 not out for Railways against Dera Ismail Khan in Pakistan's Ayub zonal tournament in 1964 and Cecil Maxwell's 268 for Notts against Leicestershire at Nottingham in 1935).

In the match at Manchester in 1896 Derbyshire piled up 553 before their fifth wicket fell, but lost the remaining five for the addition of only 24 runs as the tail made little attempt to wag with the intention of getting at Lancashire's batsmen in the last hour or so of the second day's play. The law allowing a captain to declare his innings closed was not introduced until three years later, and not until two years after that was it possible to do so before the second day's lunch interval. Prior to that amendment, a captain could declare whenever he pleased in a one-day match, but only on the last day of a game arranged for more than one day.

The introduction of the declaration was made in an attempt not only to reduce the number of drawn matches but also to avoid the throwing away of wickets such as Derbyshire had indulged in. As an experimental measure in the first season after the 1939-45 war, captains were allowed to declare on the first day if a score of 300 had been made, and from 1951 a first-day declaration was allowed irrespective of the score – an alteration that was not extended to Test matches until 1957, since when declarations in all first-class matches have been authorised at any time.

Lancashire were unable to escape the follow-on in reply to Derbyshire's huge 1896 total, but the pitch was too good to permit their dismissal twice in the time available. Frank Sugg was fittingly their top scorer against his former county in a first-innings total of 278, stumped for 96 by Wright off Storer, who had handed over the wicketkeeping duties to become the fifth bowler tried, and he was unbeaten on 26 when the match ended with Lancashire at 63 for the loss of three wickets.

The total of 577 did not last long as a Derbyshire record. On Tuesday, 2 August 1898 the county's last wicket fell to the first ball of the 191st over of the innings against Hampshire at Derby with 645 runs on the board (see p.332). They were given a flying start the previous day by an opening stand of 134 between L G Wright and skipper Evershed, and after Bagshaw's departure forty runs later Storer helped to add 123 before Wright was out for 134, made in three hours and a quarter. Storer's stay of just one hour less ended at exactly 100, and Chatterton also completed a century, with Davidson as his new partner, shortly before the close of the first day's play at 477 for four.

The fifth-wicket stand, by then worth 101, became the biggest of the innings, altogether worth 176, before Chatterton gave a return catch with his score on 142, made in three hours, and Davidson became the record-equalling fourth century-maker of the innings in taking two hours, fifty minutes over his 108. The remaining wickets then fell cheaply – mainly to Francis Quinton, an Army captain who rose to the rank of Brigadier-General. He emerged from the wreckage of Hampshire's bowling with the creditable figures of 5-93, and, although caught for a duck as the chastened visitors lost half their first-innings wickets for a paltry 31 runs, ended as the sixth to make a hundred in that historic match by being unbeaten on 101 when, midway through the third day's play, rain ensured a draw at 232 for four in the follow-on that began 405 behind.

The other player to get into three figures was also an Army man, and also one who became a Brigadier-General. He was Robert Poore, then a major, who led Hampshire's recovery from that demoralising start to their first innings with an unbeaten 121 in their total of 240. Poore, whose sixth-wicket partnership with Oxford Blue Edward Lee realised 110 runs, was in his first season of county cricket at the age of 32. He had returned to England only that year from service abroad, though three years earlier he had played in three Tests for South Africa while stationed in that country. England had won each of those matches convincingly, routing the Springboks in the first one at Port Elizabeth for a total of 30 that remained a Test record (equalled by South Africa at Edgbaston in 1924) until New Zealand were shot out for 26 by England at Auckland in 1955.

Poore averaged only 12.66 in the short 1895-96 series, with a top score of

20 in his six innings, but in his second Hampshire season of 1899 this strapping soldier – he stood 6ft 4in – had a top score of 304 among his seven centuries, sharing in a stand of 411 against Somerset that was then the second highest for any wicket, and headed the English batting list with an average of 91.23 that was not bettered until Herbert Sutcliffe's 96.96 in 1931. Unfortunately for Hampshire, but no doubt to the relief of many an opposing bowler, Army duties restricted his subsequent appearances.

The brothers Davidson were Derbyshire's most successful bowlers in the 1898 match with Hampshire at Derby, George following up his century with six wickets for 42 runs in the visitors' first innings and Frank taking three of the four that fell in the second at the same cost.

Although John Hancock, a left-arm medium-pace bowler from Old Tupton, a Derbyshire village near Clay Cross, went without a wicket in that match, he had made a creditable entry into the county team the previous season when, tried in the absence of Hulme through illness, he had taken just over fifty, only seven fewer than George Davidson's top tally for the club that year. Hancock left Derbyshire after the 1900 season and played for Scotland in the last of nearly fifty first-class matches in 1906, finishing only six short of a century of wickets in all.

Not for ninety-seven years were Derbyshire again to make as many as six hundred runs in an innings, and ten more years went by after that before their record total was raised to the dizzy heights of 707 for seven declared in their final match of the 2005 season against Somerset at Taunton.

In their opening County Championship game of 1995 they declared at 603 for six against Sussex with their biggest-ever first-innings lead of 492, and went on to triumph by their record margin of an innings and 379 runs. They had inflicted the previous heaviest defeat by an innings and 250 in 1902 against Warwickshire. But for the declaration against Sussex there might again have been four Derbyshire century- makers, for it left Dominic Cork on 84 not out. Those who did get into three figures were Kim Barnett (164), Chris Adams (111) and the South African Test player Daryll Cullinan, whose 134 made him the first to score a century on his debut for Derbyshire in a Championship match. Seven years earlier Peter Bowler, scorer of 100 not out on his debut for Leicestershire in 1986, had completed a unique double in making 155, also unbeaten, in his first innings for Derbyshire, but that had been in a match outside the Championship, against Cambridge University at Fenner's.

Only a few days before his century against Sussex, Cullinan had profited from an early life to make an unbeaten hundred in a Benson and Hedges Cup group game with Scotland in Glasgow, and he scored a third century in the next Championship fixture at Nottingham. A broken finger on a Chesterfield pitch of uneven bounce then checked his progress in the following match against Yorkshire, but he still ended what was to be his only season with Derbyshire at the top of the county's batting averages.

It is also worth mentioning here a culinary note Cullinan introduced into cricket after his return home. He caused one of the game's most bizarre incidents while batting for Border against Boland, fried calamari (squid) stopping play when his hit for six landed the ball in a frying pan. About ten minutes elapsed before it was cool enough for the umpires to remove the grease, and even then it had to be replaced because it could not be gripped properly for bowling.

The breaking of Derbyshire's long-standing record total on 23 September 2005 put even the flightiest fancies of schoolboy fiction to shame. The county went into that match in the West Country already condemned to finishing last in the Second Division for the third time in five seasons since their relegation as wooden spoonists in the First Division's inaugural year of 2000. And the innings victory that resulted, against the team immediately above them in the table, was their first for fourteen months after ten draws and eleven defeats. At home they had gone twenty-nine matches without a win.

In soaring to 707 in their 2,563rd first-class match, they were indebted to a second-wicket stand of 283 between Steve Stubbings (151) and Hassan Adnan (191), whose scores were career-bests, half-centuries by Graeme Welch, Ant Botha, Jon Moss and Luke Sutton, the captain they were losing to Lancashire, plus a near-50 by Chris Bassano, who was ending a Championship career with the county he had begun uniquely four years before by scoring a century in both innings of a home game against Gloucestershire.

Behind the fact that the unlucky Welch's unbeaten and under-stated half-century was only one run from being a full one lies the sorry tale of a declaration that, unknowingly at the time, deprived him of the chance to win the Walter Lawrence Trophy for the fastest first-class hundred of the season. A single off the next delivery he faced would have put Welch in line for the prize with a century off 72 balls, but it had already been agreed to declare at the fall of the next wicket to afford a reasonable chance of dismissing Somerset again – and that wicket just happened to be the captain's. Instead, and ironically, the trophy was secured in Somerset's second innings by the Chesterfield-born Ian Blackwell, a former Derbyshire player, who, in a lost cause, raced to three figures off 67 balls. It all also made for quite an eventful exit from top-level cricket for umpire David Shepherd, the former Gloucestershire player who had spent 25 seasons on the first-class list and stood in 92 Tests.

Daryll Cullinan's three centuries in 1995 came in his first four innings for Derbyshire, but back in the late nineteenth century the county possessed a batsman who scored four in five innings. In 1896, William Storer began his purple patch with 100 and 100 not out against Yorkshire at Derby, where Derbyshire had to follow on but forced a draw after declaring at 450 about an hour before the close with Storer and Hulme (51 not out) together in an unbroken partnership for the ninth wicket. Storer thus became the first professional to hit two hundreds in one match, this having previously been done only by three amateurs, the inevitable W G Grace, A E Stoddart and George Brann, of Sussex. Harry Bagshaw also hit a hundred in that Derbyshire second innings, sharing a second-wicket stand with his captain, Herbert Evershed, who made 85.

Storer followed his two centuries against Yorkshire with an unbeaten 142 in his only innings of a big win at Leicester. Next, after being dismissed for 16 in his first innings of the return match with Yorkshire at Sheffield, he made 122 out of 164 in the follow-on, but Evershed, Wright, Bagshaw, Chatterton and Davidson could muster only 30 runs between them as Derbyshire folded to a nine-wicket defeat. Storer kept in the runs groove with 52 in his only innings of the next match – although Bagshaw (121) and Davidson (88) were mainly responsible for the strong position gained before time lost through rain helped Leicestershire to salvage a draw at Derby in the follow-on – and in successive games he twice went close to a fifth century of the season, with 92 against Essex at Leyton and 98 off Hampshire at Derby, before completing it in Davidson's Match at Old Trafford. After all that, it was scarcely surprising that he was the first Derbyshire batsman to finish a season with an average of more than fifty. These were the top three positions for the county's matches:

* = not out	Inns	NO	Total	HS	Avg
W Storer	25	3	1125	*142	51.13
G A Davidson	27	2	1033	274	41.32
W Chatterton	29	4	1019	111	40.76

Storer's biggest score in his innings for other teams that season was 62, the top one for a Players team, also including Chatterton and Davidson, that was soundly beaten by the Australians at Leyton. The Derbyshire trio's other extra appearances were with the MCC, Chatterton scoring a not-out century against Glamorgan, and Davidson taking eight of the Welsh county's wickets.

Storer was within a fraction of again averaging fifty in 1898, when, for the first of four consecutive seasons, he also exceeded 1,000 runs, and although he was by then one of the best wicketkeepers in the game, it was for his batting alone that he was chosen that year for the Players against the Gentlemen at Lord's. With A A ('Dick') Lilley, of Warwickshire, behind the stumps in that match, Storer justified the fifth of his seven selections for the Players with scores of 59 and 73. He had first come right to the fore as a wicketkeeper in 1893. Chosen to play for the MCC in their second match with the Australian tourists that season, he caused quite a stir by the competent manner in which he kept to the fearsome deliveries of Essex's Charles Kortright, generally acknowledged as the fastest bowler then in English cricket.

It was as the first-choice wicketkeeper that Storer went to Australia in 1897-98 with the team captained by A E Stoddart. In playing in all five Tests he held nearly a dozen catches, scored just over two hundred runs, including one half-century and close approaches to two others, and further demonstrated his versatility by taking time off from his wicketkeeping to break a couple of stubborn partnerships as a bowler. In Melbourne, where Australia gained the first of their four successive victories in that series after England had won the opening match in Sydney, he bowled opener Charlie McLeod for 112; in the fourth Test, again in Melbourne, he had Hugh Trumble caught to end a century stand with Clem Hill. Unfortunately for Storer, he did not do himself justice when he made his other England appearance in the drawn first game of the following rubber, at Nottingham in 1899, and lost his place to Lilley. That was the year in which five Tests were first played in England during an Australian tour. Three of the others were also drawn, but Australia won at Lord's to retain the Ashes.

Butterley-born Storer was the first Derbyshire player to be among *Wisden's* Five Cricketers of the Year. That was in the edition for 1899, the year in which he hit the highest of his seventeen first-class centuries (fifteen of them for the county) by carrying his bat for 216 against Leicestershire at Chesterfield. He ended the following season with his top aggregate of 1,255 runs, averaging nearly forty, and when he retired in 1905 he had 9,887 runs to his name in 351 innings for Derbyshire at an average of just over thirty. For the whole of his first-class career his total of runs was only thirty-four from 13,000. He took 260 catches for the county and made two dozen stumpings (378 and 53 respectively all told) and took 214 wickets (232 in all) for about thirty-four runs apiece.

Soccer came second to his cricket. The reverse was the case for his younger brother Harry, who played in only half-a-dozen games for Derbyshire – all during their first season back in the County Championship in 1895, when he scored just 92 runs for an average a fraction over ten – but made almost 200 appearances as a goalkeeper in League football. Harry, who was born at Ripley, became Woolwich Arsenal's first player to gain senior representative honours (for the Football League against the Scottish League in Glasgow) before helping Liverpool to win the Second Division title and then finish runners-up in Division One.

Both brothers started out as footballers with Derby Midland, and both also had spells with Derby County and Loughborough Town. Derby fielded Bill Storer, who rounded off his senior soccer career with Glossop North End, in all five forward positions in giving him limited opportunities, but Harry, who played the last of his 102 League games for Liverpool in a narrow defeat at the Baseball Ground on Christmas Day 1899, did not get a first-team chance during the season he spent on Derby's books after the Midland's merger with the Rams. Harry's son, also Harry, of whom more later, combined long and rewarding service as a Derbyshire cricketer with a football career in which he was a 'fire and brimstone' type of player with Grimsby, Derby and Burnley, winning two England caps besides helping the Rams back to the League's top division, and then, as a manager, guiding Coventry, Birmingham and Derby to promotion.

Like George Davidson, the Storer brothers died comparatively young – Harry three months before his thirty-eighth birthday in April 1908, William a month after his forty-fifth in February 1912.

9. Bestwick's All-10 Comeback

After making an encouraging return to the County Championship by finishing fifth in the table in 1895 and seventh in 1896, Derbyshire never again ended in the top half throughout the remaining eighteen seasons before the First World War put the competition in limbo for four years from 1915. Their highest final position over that period was ninth out of fourteen in 1898. Five times they came last, in 1897, 1899, 1901, 1906 and 1907. Twice they were next to last, four times third from the foot.

Yet their team during that lean phase included four men who played for England, and another who was to do so after leaving the club. They also possessed an opening batsman whose aggregate of runs for a season and a career, plus his number of centuries, broke the county's records, and an opening bowler who was to retire as their most prolific taker of wickets. From that era, too, there still stands to Derbyshire's credit a world-record partnership for the ninth wicket, and one of the most astounding victories in the whole history of the game, gained despite the highest individual score ever made against them. Plus, as already recalled, the total that has only in recent years been superseded as the biggest in the club's history.

The opening batsman L G Wright never had the chance to show his mastery of the cut for England, but by the time he retired after the 1909 season he had succeeded William Storer as the county's leading run-getter, if with an average of not much more than twenty-six, and also overtaken him with twenty centuries.

His 577 innings were spread over two dozen seasons from 1883 (excluding those of 1885 and 1886), but it was not until 1899, when he had attained the advanced age for first-class cricket of thirty-seven, that he exceeded one thousand runs in a season for the first time. He then again did so in five of the next seven seasons, scaling a peak that was not to be surpassed for thirty years by a Derbyshire player in totalling 1,716 runs at 42.90 (1,855 altogether) in his forty-fourth year of 1905.

That was the season in which he also equalled Storer's achievement of making three successive centuries and earned a place among *Wisden's* Five. Against Northamptonshire at Derby he edged two runs past the previous highest score of 193 he had taken off Nottinghamshire, also at Derby, in 1901, then punished Warwickshire for 176 and 122 at Edgbaston. On five other occasions for the county he exceeded 140. The last four of his centuries were all hit off Warwickshire, the final one, 111 in the follow-on to a ten-wicket defeat at Derby, in 1908. Three times he carried his bat through a completed innings – twice against Essex at Leyton (59 out of 112 in 1899, 58 out of 136 in 1903), and in 1906 at Leicester, where he completed another unbeaten half-century just before the last wicket fell at 104.

Although enjoying his most prosperous seasons too late to be a serious contender for a Test cap, Wright was not short of representative cricket. He played four times for the Gentlemen against the Players and was also selected for the North and Rest of England teams. Having learned the game before hooking and pulling came into vogue, he played forward a lot and scored chiefly on the off side. *Wisden* said that 'he displayed a good deal of enterprise considering that during the whole of his career he so regularly found himself battling for a side that was nearly always struggling'. A E Lawton, his captain for several seasons, considered he was at his best against fast bowling, and reckoned that he rarely failed to get runs when he was heard to be humming *When We Are Married,* the catchy melody from the musical *The Belle of New York,* just before going in to bat.

But, as Lawton also recalled, Wright's team-mates probably derived particular inspiration from his superb fielding at point, where he not only stopped hard hits but also held some of the most amazing catches while standing only six or seven yards from the bat – with shin guards his only concession to protective gear. He habitually celebrated his catches by immediately jerking the ball high into the air behind his back. E M Grace, brother of the famous doctor, used to relate how on one occasion when a batsman kept poking at the ball and cocking it up, Wright crept in closer and closer until he was only a yard or so away. Soon he saw his chance of a catch, but the crowd cheered prematurely. It was the bat, not the ball, that he grabbed.

One catch of Wright's that Albert Lawton remembered with special relish sent back Hampshire's hard-hitting Arthur Hill at Southampton off a quick half-volley, just wide of the off stump, which the bowler, Arnold Warren, had intended as a yorker. This was how Lawton described it:

'Across went "Brownie" Hill's left leg, and down went his bat to time it perfectly. It went like a bullet, but, to the utter amazement of us all, L G snapped it up ankle high, and into the air it went behind his back. It was a few seconds before Hill realised he was out, and off he went to the pavilion muttering. R B (Reggie) Rickman, who was fielding on the boundary at deep third man, just by the pavilion, reported to us that as Hill walked through the gate he hadn't nearly come to the end of his remarks about his bad luck!'

A similar exceptional effort, again off Warren's bowling, accounted for another Hampshire batsman, Arthur Webb, in an August Bank Holiday match at Derby, but there was also a game at Leyton in which Essex's Alfred Lucas was given an equally astonishing let-off by Wright. The first ball of that encounter, sent down by Bill Bestwick, the burly opening bowler Wright had brought to Derbyshire's attention, lobbed gently into L G's hands off the shoulder of the bat, but slipped through them to the ground. Lucas went on to hit a century.

Wright, who was also an adept soccer and rugby player, was bitten by the bowls bug after laying down his bat, and, remarkably active for his age, he played regularly at the Arboretum club in Derby until his late eighties in addition to rarely missing watching the cricket at the County Ground. He was only four days from his ninety-first birthday when he died on 11 January, 1953.

Arnold Warren, who scored two goals in eight League games for Derby County in the 1901-02 season, was one of Derbyshire's Test players in the early part of the twentieth century, and Bill Bestwick the bowler whose 1,452 wickets set a Derbyshire record that survived for more than thirty years. By just one year Warren, a six-footer from Codnor who was one of the fastest right-arm bowlers of his time, beat Bestwick, a tall and heavily built miner, to the distinction of being the first to take a hundred wickets in one season for the county. In 1904 his 124 cost a fraction under twenty-one runs each; in 1905 Bestwick took 104 at just under 22 runs apiece.

Warren had two other 100-plus tallies, but only one of them for Derbyshire – 105 in 1908. His 101 in 1906 included other first-class matches. In 1909 he stuck on 99. For his biggest number of victims in one match he looked back fondly on 1904. Of the eighteen Nottinghamshire wickets that fell on a soft pitch at Welbeck, he claimed fifteen for 112 runs (8-69 and 7-43). He took eight in an innings on two other occasions, but considered his best performance to be his 7-52 on an unhelpful track at Ashby-de-la-Zouch in 1912 when Leicestershire, needing 180 to win, were all out for 97. In a career that lasted from 1897 to 1920, he took 918 wickets for Derbyshire at 24.57, and 939 in all.

As a batsman, Warren was regarded as little more than useful, but he did score one century – and that, fourteen fours in his 123, came in the world record ninth-wicket stand of 283 in five minutes under three hours that he shared against Warwickshire at the Miners' Welfare Ground at Blackwell in 1910 with John Chapman, Lawton's successor as Derbyshire's captain (see p.333). Chapman was reputed to have scored forty centuries in club cricket, in which he played frequently for Sheffield Collegiate and also for Barnsley before joining Derbyshire, but his 165 (two sixes, 19 fours) in that match-saving partnership was only his second, and last, in the top flight. The other, 198 (two sixes, 29 fours) at Coventry in 1909, was made against the same county in the sixth match of his first season with Derbyshire, for whom he qualified by residence on moving to live at Unstone, near Dronfield.

Derbyshire followed on 242 runs behind Warwickshire's declared total of 504 for seven, in which Crowther Charlesworth made a career-best 216 (30 fours and six sixes) out of 338 in three hours, forty minutes, and they started the final day's play at 51 for one, still 191 in arrears. In the first 75 minutes seven more wickets fell for the addition of eighty runs, so when Chapman was joined by Warren at ten minutes to one o'clock the requirement, at 131 for eight, to avoid the innings defeat was 111. Playing with increasing freedom and confidence, they added 81 in the 40 minutes before lunch, cleared the deficit soon afterwards, and dispelled all danger of defeat before Warren, by then handicapped by lameness, was snapped up in the slips with the total on 414. Joe Humphries finally helped to raise it to 430, the innings ending when Chapman was bowled, and the game petered out as a draw with Warwickshire 63 for two in their second innings at the close. This was how Will Taylor, then in his third year of his record reign as Derbyshire's secretary, recalled the occasion:

'At lunch-time on the last day Warwickshire looked certain of a comfortable win. Derbyshire, with eight wickets down, were a long way behind Warwickshire's first-innings score, and, well as Chapman and Warren were batting, few Derbyshire folk could hope that defeat would be avoided. In view of their strong position, Warwickshire, I knew, were hoping to catch an early-afternoon train, and in conversation during the interval I remarked to their fast bowler, Frank Field: "You look like catching your train all right, Frank." The reply was "I'm not so sure about that, Mr Taylor. These chaps are pretty good bats, you know." How right he was.'

The record Chapman and Warren broke was the 232 achieved by Clem Hill and Edwin Walkley, for South Australia against New South Wales at Adelaide in 1900. Until John Commins and Nicky Boje added 268 for the South Africa 'A' team's ninth wicket against Mashonaland at Harare in the 1994-95 Zimbabwe season, the closest approach to the Derbyshire pair's record was made against Derbyshire by Johnny Douglas and S N Hare, who were in a stand of 251 for Essex at Leyton in 1921. Stericker Norman Hare, CBE, a club cricketer with Ilford and captain of Chigwell in 1918, played in only three first-class matches for Essex, all of them in that year, and his 98 at No 10 in his big partnership with Douglas was made in his first innings for the county. Douglas was left unbeaten on 210, and, as if that was not enough, he also took nine wickets for 47 runs in Derbyshire's first innings, then rounded off their crushing defeat by taking their last two without cost in the only five balls he bowled when they batted again.

Arnold Warren's Test call-up came in 1905, for the third match of the series against Australia at Leeds, but there was not to be another one despite the fact that he did so well on his debut that the ball he used in the tourists' first innings was mounted, suitably inscribed, and presented to him, becoming one of his most treasured possessions. He earned that lone England appearance with match figures of twelve for 126 (7-57 and 5-69) in a shock defeat of Yorkshire, though that season's champions were weakened by the absence of Stanley Jackson, Schofield Haigh and Wilfred Rhodes on England duty in the second Test at Lord's. Replying at Headingley to an England total of 301 in which Jackson set a captain's example with an unbeaten 144, Australia were all out for 195, and half their wickets fell to Warren for 57 runs. Four of the top six in the order were among those he dismissed – Victor Trumper, Monty Noble, Warwick Armstrong and skipper Joe Darling. And in Australia's second innings he got rid of the great Trumper again – for a duck.

The other Derbyshire player who, in the early years of the twentieth century, followed Chatterton and Storer to Test standard was Stonebroom-born Joe Humphries, who joined the county as Storer's wicketkeeping understudy in 1899 and three years later succeeded him as first choice for the remaining seasons before the 1914-18 war intervened. In a first-class career of 302 games, Humphries held 565 catches, seven of them in a match on six occasions, made 110 stumpings, scored almost 5,500 runs, and also took three wickets as a bowler – one of them when every member of the team bowled at Worcester in 1902. His most successful season of 1906, in which he achieved 81 dismissals (75 for Derbyshire) and impressed particularly with his slick stumpings, led to his selection for the MCC's 1907-08 tour of Australia.

It proved an ill-fated venture for the team – and initially for Humphries too, though he came through as one of the successes. Pneumonia kept the captain, Arthur Jones of Notts, out of the first three Tests, and Australia won the series 4-1 to regain the Ashes. The Sussex amateur Richard Young, who wore spectacles, was preferred to Humphries as wicketkeeper for the first Test in Sydney, where the home side won by two wickets, but the Derbyshire man was brought in for the next match in Melbourne and played a prominent part as batsman as well as wicketkeeper in an England victory by one wicket. Seventy-three runs were still required when he joined Sydney Barnes, but he helped the famous spin bowler to tip the balance the tourists' way in a crucial ninth-wicket stand.

Humphries also efficiently justified his retention for the following two Tests, only to be replaced by Young for the final one. Like Warren, he was most unfortunate to be never chosen for his country again. Young, also an amateur football international, won the vote at the start and finish of the series on the supposed superiority of his batting, at which he had excelled at Repton and Cambridge University, yet he mustered only 27 runs in his four innings for an average of 6.75. Humphries totalled 44 in six innings at 8.80.

The Derbyshire player of that period who turned out for England after moving to another county was Fred Root. Derbyshire-born, but originally on Leicestershire's ground staff, he was an orthodox type of bowler while with his home county, but changed his style after moving to Worcestershire in 1921. Bowling fast-medium inswingers on the leg stump with five fieldsmen close in on the leg side, he became a leading exponent of the leg-theory tactics that caused such a furore when exploited by Harold Larwood and company under Douglas Jardine's captaincy on the 1932-33 'body-line' Test series in Australia. Another Worcestershire player, William Burns, the fairness of whose delivery was often questioned, had the dubious distinction of being the first to try that method in county cricket – against Middlesex at Lord's four years before the 1914-18 war, during which he was killed in action.

The switch to leg theory proved so successful for Root that he took more than one hundred wickets in each of nine consecutive seasons from 1923, broke a Worcestershire record with 219 victims (average 17.21) in 1925, and was chosen for three of England's matches in the 1926 home series – though he had no chance to take part in the opening one at Nottingham which was washed out after Jack Hobbs and Herbert Sutcliffe had scored 32 in 50 minutes without being separated, and was omitted from the final one at The Oval, where England won to reclaim the Ashes after a lapse of fourteen years.

While Root was with Derbyshire the county's reserve wicketkeeper was George Beet, who had only the first post-war season of 1919 as first choice after Humphries' retirement. The juxtaposition of those surnames offered what some might consider a tasty form of dismissal, but there was just the one instance of 'caught Beet bowled Root' in the scorebook – that of Herbert Chaplin, the Sussex captain, at Derby in 1913. And even then it was not as a wicketkeeper that Beet held the catch. Humphries was then still behind the stumps, Beet justifying his inclusion as a batsman with a half-century in a drawn game.

George Beet, whose son Hector and grandson Gordon (Hector's nephew) also played for Derbyshire, regularly umpired in matches at Lord's during the First World War along with Archie Fowler, who served Middlesex as slow left-arm bowler, head coach and scorer in more than half a century's connection with cricket's headquarters. Beet, who also coached in South Africa, was appointed to the list of first-class umpires in 1929, four years after ending his county career. In the first season after another world war he realised his ambition to stand in a Test, the second match of the 1946 series in which India escaped with a draw at Old Trafford after wicketkeeper Paul Gibb had twice missed the chance to part the tourists' last-wicket pair. Beet was taken seriously ill on his train journey back home after that game, and he had to be rushed to the Derbyshire Royal Infirmary for an operation. He never fully recovered, and he died, aged sixty, shortly before the end of the year.

Before leaving the Beets, it is worth mentioning that although Gordon, a right-hand batsman but left-arm bowler, played in only half-a-dozen first-class games for Derbyshire he has an unusual place in the county's annals. Gordon, whose father Leslie also used to be on the club's ground staff, was Derbyshire's twelfth man when he fielded as a substitute for Gloucestershire in a match at Derby in 1959 – for Martin Young in the home first innings, for Tom Graveney in the second – and caught four of his clubmates. Three of those catches were held as Derbyshire faded to a 48-run defeat with half-an-hour to spare, one of them sending back top scorer John Kelly, and afterwards there was a surprise present for young Beet. He was handed £4, a pound for each of his catches, by Graveney, the Gloucestershire captain, for whom victory was the perfect antidote after the pain of an arm cut he had to have stitched after falling down stairs at his hotel on the morning of the final day's play.

In common with George Beet, Big Bill Bestwick, one of a miner's fourteen children, played his last match for Derbyshire in 1925, but whereas Beet took part in just under fifty first-class games, Bestwick totalled 323 — all but two of them for the county — after having trials with Leicestershire and Warwickshire. Bestwick was one of the bowlers, along with Joe Hulme, who so upset W G Grace with the lbw decisions they gained in the 1900 match with London County that was recalled in Chapter Four.

And Bestwick it was who set the wickets record since beaten for Derbyshire by only Cliff Gladwin and Les Jackson, one of the game's greatest opening bowling partnerships.

From 1898 to 1909 a Derbyshire team without Bestwick was a rarity, but, after three times taking more than a hundred wickets in a season, he ended his first spell with the club in acrimonious circumstances. Drink was his big problem. He worked hard (down the pit, where he started at the age of eleven) and he played hard, developing a thirst for beer that too often took too much quenching. When he had not indulged he was an ideal team man, always ready to give help and advice to newcomers to the side, but after sinking several pints he could be awkward and difficult to handle, with violent mood swings. Even Guy Jackson, the disciplinarian who was one of his captains, found him difficult to deal with at times.

Life, however, put Bestwick at the centre of two tragedies that could have driven many other strong characters to drink. He was left with a seven-year-old son to look after when his wife died in the summer of 1906, so they both moved to live with his parents. Then, early the following year, he was charged with manslaughter when a man died from a knife wound during a struggle at Heanor in which Bestwick himself was injured, but he was released after an inquest jury found that he had acted in self-defence.

Bestwick got the wrong side of the Derbyshire committee when he failed to turn up for a match with Northamptonshire at Derby in August 1909. With no explanation forthcoming, he was first suspended for the rest of that season, then not offered terms for the following one. By that time in his mid-thirties, he played for Shirebrook and in the Lancashire League before moving in 1912 to South Wales, where he obtained work at Merthyr Tydfil and became the professional with the Llanelly (as it was then spelt) club. Soon afterwards he joined Neath, where he met his second wife, and qualified by residence for Glamorgan, for whom he made his Minor Counties debut against Durham at Swansea in 1914.

When war broke out he returned to live in his home county and was regularly among the wickets for Heanor in the Derbyshire Alliance. He did the hat-trick in his 7-20 against Jacksdale after sleeping off the effects of drink while Heanor batted, took all ten in a Swanwick innings, seven of them bowled, and 9-40 at Riddings. Though continuing to play for Heanor, he rejoined Derbyshire at the age of forty-four in the first post-war season of 1919 and showed much of his old form in heading their bowling averages with 89 wickets at just over eighteen runs each.

In the following appalling season for Derbyshire, Bestwick made only one county appearance, taking 7-97 in the match at Leicester, before again departing after failing to agree terms. He rejoined Neath as professional and also played again for Glamorgan, but instead of continuing with the Welsh county when they were brought into the County Championship for 1921 he went back to Derbyshire, lured by their better offer and the promise of some coaching. And what a comeback that turned out to be.

Most remarkably, for a man of his heavy build and at the age of forty-six, he enjoyed the most successful of his eighteen county seasons in taking 147 wickets – exactly as many as the ten other Derbyshire bowlers managed between them – for just fewer than seventeen runs apiece in twenty matches, during which he delivered 935.3 overs. And against Glamorgan he bagged all ten in an innings, seven of them clean bowled, for 40 runs in Cardiff – in nineteen overs, two of them maidens, before lunch, a feat without parallel in first-class cricket (see p.334). It was typical of the man that he performed that feat after heavy drinking with some friends from Neath the previous evening.

William James Vincent Tomlinson headed the batting and bowling averages when captain of Felsted School in 1920. He took 5-53 in his first match for Derbyshire, at Hove that August, but failed to sustain that form and played few further matches for the county after winning his Blue at Cambridge in 1923. He died in Norfolk in 1984, aged 82. Walter Reader-Blackton also played only a few matches for Derbyshire. He was born in the county at Shirland in 1895 and died at Derby in 1976.

Bestwick bowled unchanged as the Welshmen were dismissed for 106 after leading by 85 on first innings, and Derbyshire knocked off the 192 they required for the loss of eight wickets, winning inside two days. It was a close call, though. Routed for 83 when they first batted, Derbyshire were in danger of defeat until their ninth-wicket pair, Wilf Carter and Harry Elliott, came together in an unbroken stand of 77. Carter, who was born in Nottinghamshire but brought up in Derbyshire at Bolsover, combined his cricket with soccer as a Watford wing-half and played in the first match at that club's Vicarage Road ground. Elliott developed into one of the best wicket-keepers in the country as successor to George Beet, and, although his early promise as a batsman never matured, this was one of those occasions when he showed himself to be an excellent man to have in a tight corner.

During that 1921 season Bestwick took five or more wickets in an innings a club record seventeen times, with 9-65 against Warwickshire at Edgbaston the next best to his Cardiff haul. It was in the following year's match with Warwickshire at Derby that he and his son Robert, three of whose five Championship appearances were made against that county, provided another of cricket's curios. They opened the attack together, and for six overs there was the unique sight of the Bestwicks bowling while another father and son, Willie and Bernard Quaife, were batting. Willie completed a century before being bowled by Robert, and although his son was rather less successful Warwickshire were comfortable winners after twice dispatching Derbyshire cheaply. Willie Quaife retired in 1927 at the age of fifty-six, but in the following year he was invited back for one final match – against Derbyshire. And he ended as he had begun, with a century. On his debut for Warwickshire in 1893 he had taken an unbeaten 102 off Durham. Against Derbyshire he scored 115, making him, at 56 years and 140 days, the oldest century-maker in county cricket.

On five occasions in 1921 Bill Bestwick took ten or more wickets in a match (twenty-seven times in his career). He owed his exceptional strength and durability to his work as a miner, capable of bowling at full speed for long spells because he came off a short run-up. The power of his right arm and body produced the pace and lift that so bothered batsmen. He was in his fiftieth year when he bowled for Derbyshire for the last time in the drawn Bank Holiday match with Warwickshire in August 1925.

He took part in only seven Championship games that season, spending most of his time in charge of the young players on the ground staff, but he departed at the top of the county's bowling averages, and in one of his last appearances took seven Leicestershire wickets for only twenty runs at Burton-upon-Trent. That exactly equalled his figures in the rout of Surrey for 68 when Derbyshire had gained one of their rare victories against that county at Chesterfield in 1903.

Test cricket eluded Bestwick, but in one of his two first-class matches away from Derbyshire he played for an England XI against the 1902 Australians at Eastbourne, and in the tourists' first innings claimed the prized wickets of Vic Trumper, Clem Hill, Syd Gregory and skipper Joe Darling for just thirty runs. Derbyshire gained one of their most momentous victories in his other first-class absence from their ranks in 1919 – he was at Lord's assisting the Players against the Gentlemen – but more about that in its turn.

After finishing as a player with a truly grand total of 1,457 wickets behind him at an average of 21.28 (Gladwin reached 1,653 at 18.30, Jackson 1,733 at 17.36), Bestwick remained a familiar figure on the field as an umpire. He stood in three Tests, and more than two hundred Championship games, until illness compelled his retirement the year before his death at Nottingham General Hospital in the early May of 1938, at the age of sixty-two.

One of the matches in which he umpired coincided with Denis Compton's Championship debut for Middlesex against Sussex at Lord's in May 1936. The future England batsman, who was eighteen that month, went in at No 11 and helped Gubby Allen to gain a slender first-innings lead before being controversially given out lbw by Bestwick. When Allen afterwards protested to the bluff Derbyshire man that he had made a mistake Big Bill promptly agreed, but blithely told him: 'Well, you had your first-innings lead, and I was dying to spend a penny' (or words to that effect).

Of all the matches in which he bowled, Bestwick had to toil hardest and longest at Chesterfield in July, 1904. That was the game which made victory incredible for leaving Essex's Percy ('Peter' to his friends) Perrin on the losing side after scoring an undefeated triple century containing sixty-eight fours – six more than the record set by Archie MacLaren in his 424 at Taunton in 1895.

Not until West Indian Brian Lara hit sixty-two fours and ten sixes in his record first-class score of 501 not out for Warwickshire against Durham at Edgbaston in 1994 were more boundaries hit by a batsman in one innings, but a dozen or more of Perrin's fours would have been sixes if hits clearing the boundary had then earned an extra two runs. Even Albert Trott was credited with only four runs when he deposited the ball onto the roof of the pavilion at Lord's in 1899. It was not until 1910 that the counties' advisory committee passed a resolution that six runs should be awarded for all hits that 'drop over and clear of the boundary line or fence'.

A West Indian was mainly responsible for Essex's failure to capitalise on the first-innings total of 597 they built on Perrin's 343 not out in 345 minutes at Queen's Park (see p.335). Charles Augustus Ollivierre, whose birthplace of Kingstown in St Vincent is not to be confused with Kingston in Jamaica, countered with 229 (one five, thirty-seven fours) in 225 minutes in Derbyshire's reply of 548, then piloted them to an extraordinary nine-wicket win by carrying his bat for 92 after the visitors had lost their first seven wickets for only 33 runs, and been whisked all out for 97, in their second venture. William Storer, whose 48 gave him a match total of 92 for once out, shared in an unbroken second-wicket stand of 138 following the early loss of L G Wright, who in the first innings had made 68 in an opening partnership of 191 with Ollivierre that stood as a Derbyshire record for nearly twenty years.

The opening day's play ended with Essex on 524 for the loss of eight wickets, and Perrin just five from 300 after receiving most support from opener and captain Frederick Fane (63), Johnny Douglas (47) and Frank Gillingham (43). Gillingham was born in Tokyo, but came to England at an early age and qualified for Essex after being ordained and becoming a curate at Leyton. Appointed chaplain to the King in 1939, he rose to be a canon.

Wicketkeeper Edward Russell, whose brother and nephew also kept wicket for Essex ('Tich' Freeman, the Kent and England leg-break and googly bowler was their cousin), helped to take the Essex total to 586 on the second day before he was ninth out. Then Bestwick brought welcome relief for himself and eight other Derbyshire bowlers by trapping last man Claude Buckenham, later a coach at Repton, lbw with the first ball of his forty-third over for his third wicket at a cost of 160 runs. His opening partner Warren also paid a high price, 143 runs, for his three wickets, but both were chiefly responsible for Essex's second-innings collapse, Warren taking 4-42 and Bestwick 3-34, after a draw had seemed inevitable when both teams had completed one innings for a combined total of 1,145 runs.

There had been only two previous instances of a side scoring more than 550 and being beaten, both in Australia. At Sydney in 1894 England had won by ten runs after facing a total of 586, and at Adelaide in 1903 South Australia had defeated Lord Hawke's XI by 97 runs after those tourists had made 553. On both those occasions, however, play had lasted for more than three days and victory had been gained after following on. Moreover, in the Sydney Test Australia had been caught on a rain-affected pitch in their second innings. In those circumstances Derbyshire's astonishing feat was the more praiseworthy, as *Wisden* agreed with this comment:

'It was the more creditable as there was nothing flukey about the way in which the triumph was gained, for it was not a case of following on and so tiring out the opposing bowlers. The result was simply due to the wonderful way in which the eleven set about an apparently hopeless task and surmounted their difficulties.'

Ollivierre's personal best double-century ended when he was bowled by Bill Reeves, who conceded almost forty runs for each of his five wickets. Three years earlier, Reeves had taken Derbyshire's last five for no runs in eleven balls on a Leyton pitch renowned for favouring batsmen. Subsequent generations knew him as one of the most respected of the first-class umpires, noted for his caustic wit. It was he who told a protesting batsman to look in the next morning's paper to see that he was indeed out.

Ninety-two years went by before another batsman finished on the losing side after scoring a triple-century in a County Championship match – and that was also against Derbyshire – though there were two other cases abroad in the meantime.

During the last week of 1931 Roger Blunt hit 41 fours in his unbeaten 338, then the highest score by a New Zealander, for Otago in their Plunket Shield match with Canterbury, who won by three wickets, at Christ-church, and in 1943, Vijay Hazare, who nine years later skippered India to their first Test victory, against England in Madras, scored 309 in a total of 387 as The Rest followed on against the Hindus, who won by an innings. Hazare's brother Vivek made only 21 in their stand of 300.

The man who shared Perrin's fate in England was an Australian, Jason Gallian, whose 312 for Lancashire against Derbyshire in July 1996 was not only the biggest individual score ever made at Old Trafford but also the longest innings in Championship history. He faced 583 balls in batting for 670 minutes, hitting four sixes and 33 fours. Bobby Simpson's 311 for Australia against England in 1964 was the previous highest at the Manchester ground. For duration, Darren Bicknell's 235 not out for Surrey at Nottingham in 1994 was surpassed by thirty-two minutes.

Derbyshire's match in Manchester in 1996 differed, however, in one important respect from that at Chesterfield in 1904, for, unlike Essex, Lancashire were not bowled out in their second innings. They declared with three wickets down, setting a two-session target of 289 that Derbyshire reached with their ninth pair together after losing five wickets for twenty runs in the wake of a stand of 198 between Kim Barnett (92) and his successor as captain, Dean Jones (107).

For the maker of a double-century who was on the beaten side against Derbyshire, I well remember Cyril Poole, the Nottinghamshire left-hander, who hit three sixes and 33 fours in his 219 against Derbyshire, who won by an innings and 93 runs, at Ilkeston in 1952. As a footballer, Poole was Mansfield Town's youngest player at fifteen, but he did not enter first-class cricket until he was twenty-seven. His team-mates once tried to break him of his habit of using any bat he found lying about in the dressing room by making available a trick bat that was just a shell filled with sawdust. Apparently, he never noticed and scored a half-century with it.

In 1912, Essex made an even bigger score against Derbyshire than their 587 at Chesterfield, declaring at 609-4 at Leyton and going on to win by an innings. Perrin was again the plunderer-in-chief, scoring 245 and partnering Charles McGahey (150) in a third-wicket stand of 312 that lasted only about three hours. Perrin, then thirty-six, and McGahey, forty-one, were known as the 'Essex Twins', and a lofty pair they were – Perrin at 6ft 3in, McGahey 6ft 2in. It was also at Leyton, and also against Derbyshire, that McGahey made his highest score of 277 in 1905. He was another of those cricketers who met a most untimely end. Septic poisoning set in fatally when he damaged a finger in slipping on a greasy pavement on Christmas Day in 1934.

Derbyshire brought off a real coup in making Charles Ollivierre their second acquisition from overseas after Spofforth. Acknowledged as among the best batsmen of his time, he came from a well-known Kingstown cricketing family, his three brothers also successfully following their father into the game. Two of them, Helon and Richard, also played in first-class cricket.

Having headed the averages, on 32.70, and been the heaviest scorer, with 883 runs, for the first West Indian team to tour England in 1900 (Richard was in the second one in 1906), Charles Ollivierre decided to stay on and qualify for Derbyshire, who readily recognised his talent even though he was overshadowed by members of two other families of distinguished Caribbean cricketers when he played against them during that inaugural visit.

At Derby the tourists were best served by Percy Goodman, the leading all-rounder among the four Goodmans who were prominent players in Barbados, and Lebrun Constantine, whose son Learie became one of the most exciting and gifted players ever to come out of the West Indies. Goodman carried his bat for 104 and was in a fifth-wicket stand of 103 in just over an hour with Constantine Senior (62), who had already hit the first century for a West Indies team in England by taking 113 off the Gentlemen of the MCC's attack at Lord's. Charles Ollivierre made only three runs when he first batted against Derbyshire, one of the six victims Hulme claimed at a cost of 76, but he was

23 not out in his second innings as the rain-curtailed match petered out in a draw. Defeat for Derbyshire had looked likely when they had been only eight runs ahead with half their side out during the final day's play.

With strokes all round the wicket, and particularly strong in cutting and playing to leg, Ollivierre was likened to the great Ranjitsinhji by 'Plum' Warner, who partnered him in an opening stand of 238 against Leicestershire. Warner scored 113 in his only game for the tourists, who were captained by his elder brother Aucher. Ollivierre's 159 was one of the best innings seen anywhere that season. The Warner brothers were born fourteen years apart in Trinidad, where their father was Attorney General for many years, but 'Plum' travelled to England in his early teens, studied at Rugby and Oxford, and had a prosperous career with Middlesex and England, both of whom he captained, before serving with distinction behind the scenes as Test selector, tour manager and, ultimately, president of MCC. Not for nothing was he dubbed the 'Grand Old Man' of English cricket.

Before briefly 'guesting' as Ollivierre's partner, Warner had been out of action for a few weeks after being struck on the shin by a ball from Arthur Mold while batting for Middlesex against Lancashire, and he was again laid up when struck on the same shin by Leicestershire's Arthur Woodcock, who was almost as fast as Mold. Ten years later, Woodcock was another of the cricketers who committed suicide.

Ollivierre continued in fine form after becoming eligible for Derbyshire, though he came in for some criticism because of his erratic running between the wickets. Warner, in one of his many authoritative writings on the game, observed that this was a common fault among the 1900 visitors from the Caribbean. In the early part of the tour he considered them, both individually and as a team, the worst judges of a run he had ever seen – with Ollivierre one of the main offenders.

That, however, was a fault this popular West Indian soon rectified in smartly settling down to become a valued member of the Derbyshire team. In his first season with the county, 1902, his 167 helped them to a defeat of Warwickshire at Derby by an innings and 250 runs that stood as their biggest winning margin until Sussex were beaten by an innings and 379 at the same ground in 1995, but he is still best remembered for his 321 for once out in that extraordinary game against Essex at Chesterfield. He last appeared for Derbyshire in 1907, when eye trouble compelled his retirement from first-class cricket, in which he scored nearly five thousand runs in just over two hundred innings, but he played on in club cricket for Darley Dale, and also in Yorkshire. From 1924 until the outbreak of war in 1939 he went to Holland each year to coach schoolboys. He died at Pontefract in March 1949. At seventy-two, he was the age Spofforth reached.

10. Chesterfield Run Feast

The frequently feeble form that set in after Derbyshire's encouraging return to the County Championship in 1895, leading them into years of being firmly among the also-rans before the resurgence swept them which to their lone undisputed title success of 1936, was demonstrated with chilling clarity by the inconsistent manner in which they finished the 1898 season. Failure, indeed, was the only really consistent feature of their play in many of the years during that depressing period.

After home defeats by an innings at the hands of Surrey and Essex in 1898, they had much the better of drawn games with Notts, Warwickshire and Yorkshire. Then they ran up the total of 645 against Hampshire that survived as the county's highest for more than a hundred years, but suffered another innings reverse in their next match at Leicester before their remaining two games brought the biggest beating in their history and the rain-assisted escape to another draw. The number of runs they conceded in those last three matches of the season after their own run glut against Hampshire amounted to 1,554.

The thrashing that is still a record for Derbyshire was by an innings and 387 runs at Chesterfield by a Yorkshire side that differed in only one respect (schoolmaster Ernest Smith for Ted Wainwright, the county's beneficiary that year) from the one that only the month before had been grateful for a draw at Harrogate, after Derbyshire, set to get 336 in 190 minutes, had finished 117 short with seven wickets in hand and century-maker Bagshaw going well. In the return game, however, Derbyshire were never in the hunt right from the moment Yorkshire, that year's champions, won the toss and the Johns, Brown and Tunnicliffe, on a good fast pitch, settled into an opening partnership that reached 554 on the second day before Tunnicliffe was caught for 243 by Frank Davidson off the bowling of Bill Storer, who had handed over the wicket-keeping to Chatterton (see p.336).

Just over a year previously, this first-wicket pair had established a record for top-class cricket by starting with a stand of 378 against Sussex at Sheffield (Brown 311, Tunnicliffe 147) that had eclipsed the 346 made in 1892 at Taunton for Somerset against Yorkshire by Bert Hewitt (201) and Lionel Palairet (146). In his book, *Bramall Lane Before & After,* this was how my former colleague Keith Farnsworth told of the amusing scene that the Rev R S Holmes, a Yorkshire cricket historian, had recalled seeing on the pavilion balcony during that Brown-Tunnicliffe partnership:

'When Brown and Tunnicliffe had made their first hundred, two of Holmes' neighbours celebrated with a visit to the bar, and both agreed to drink a further pint for every 50 added to the stand. By the time the batsmen had made 350 these two spectators were somewhat intoxicated, and one of them, looking at his dwindling funds, said: "If this goes on much longer I'll be ruined!"

Within a few weeks of wresting the record from the Somerset pair, Brown and Tunnicliffe lost it, by just one run, as Surrey's Bobby Abel and Bill Brockwell took toll of Hampshire's attack at The Oval. Abel, who made 173, had scored 215 in the previous match at the ground, at Yorkshire's expense. Against Hampshire, Brockwell himself hit a double-century, a career-best 225. In regaining the record for Yorkshire to Derbyshire's discomfort, Brown and Tunnicliffe not only surpassed that Surrey onslaught but also the 472 by Stanley Colman and Percy Coles, for Devonshire Park against G W Morrison's XI at Eastbourne in 1892, which had been the biggest stand for any wicket in all grades of cricket.

Yorkshire very nearly had to yield another distinction to Surrey the season after reclaiming the first-wicket record. In 1896, a then eighth-wicket top stand of 292 by Lord Hawke and Bobby Peel had boosted them to a total of 887 against Warwickshire in Birmingham, beating the 843 by the Australians against the Universities Past and Present XI, at Portsmouth in 1893, and the 801 county best by Lancashire, against Somerset at Taunton in 1895, that included Archie MacLaren's 424. In 1899, Somerset were again on the receiving end as Abel most emphatically again lived up to his name by carrying his bat for 357 right through a Surrey innings of 811 at The Oval. And in the same year, at the same ground, Abel (193) joined forces with Tom Hayward (273) to raise their record fourth-wicket stand from the 334 achieved against Somerset that May to 448 against Yorkshire in August – then second only in first-class cricket to the mammoth Brown-Tunnicliffe stand in Walter Sugg's benefit match of 1898.

Derbyshire suffered a serious blow in that epic encounter at Chesterfield with just three runs on the board – all scored off the only over George Davidson, with difficulty, was able to deliver as he opened the attack. Overworked for much of that season, as he also had been for much of the previous one, after Joe Hulme's absence through ill health had weakened his bowling support, he broke down with the recurrence of a leg injury. And that was destined to be the last over he ever sent down. Despite his handicap, he was top scorer with 36 in Derbyshire's first innings of 118, and he stayed in the team as a batsman for the following final match of the season in Manchester. Chatterton put up most resistance in the follow-on against Yorkshire, giving a return catch to Wilfred Rhodes shortly after getting to his half-century.

Against Derbyshire's weary and depleted attack (depleted in strength but not in numbers, as all but Chatterton bowled), Brown and Tunnicliffe, who each hit forty-eight fours, survived several chances – four difficult ones offered by Brown, his partner just one – in taking the total to 503 by the end of the first day's play. They altogether batted for five minutes over five hours before being parted, and Brown left five minutes later when, having completed his third century, he followed instructions by deliberately playing his bat into his stumps to present Storer with one of his three wickets, the top three in the order. The previous biggest stand in a first-class match, irrespective of wicket, had been the 398 by Arthur Shrewsbury (267) and William Gunn (196) for the Notts second wicket against Sussex at Trent Bridge in 1890.

Alfred Charlesworth, an amateur from Simmondley, near Glossop, made his seventh and last County Championship appearance for Derbyshire, all of them in 1898, in that game with Yorkshire, though he had first played for the county ten years before – in the first of their second-class seasons. It was indeed an unhappy exit for him, not only because he was in a side so soundly trounced. He also finished on the injured list with George Davidson.

Many years later, Lord Hawke. Yorkshire's captain, recalled in *Wisden* how he came to be the one who had to sit waiting to go in to bat while his opening pair indulged themselves. Stanley Jackson, widely known as 'Jacker', was to have gone in first wicket down, but, to quote his lordship, 'though he had just taken seven for 42 against Middlesex somebody had run him out for a song and he did not seem keen to play in the next match at Chesterfield.' Lord Hawke continued:

"'Why," I argued with him, "you've just got seven of 'em out at six apiece! You must come." So he came all right. Next day, as I was writing out the order I asked him where he'd like to go in, so he said, "Oh, don't know. Treat me as a bowler." So I was No 3 that day in Jackson's place. As Brown and Tunnicliffe walked out to bat I put on my pads. I took them off for the lunch interval; I put them on again and took them off again for the tea interval. Again I put them on and sat for another couple of hours. Such is cricket!'"

Derbyshire also had good reason, but of a very different kind, to remember their match with Yorkshire at Dewsbury the following year. When the final day's play in that game began on 10 June 1899, the professionals in their team had to take the field in their everyday attire because their cricketing clothes and boots were unfit for use through a thorough soaking. The taps above their dressing room had been left open overnight, and it was flooded when the water was turned on again at the mains that morning.

The equipment of the amateurs Tom Higson and L G Wright escaped the deluge in their separate dressing room, so, as the only members of the side left with spiked boots, it was they who had to share the bowling when Brown and Tunnicliffe went in to bat needing only 32 runs for victory. The runs were hit off in twenty minutes for the loss of one wicket – that of Brown, who was bowled by Higson with a dozen still required. Brown's opening partnership with Tunnicliffe did not last long in the first innings of that match either, but half-centuries by Stanley Jackson and George Hirst, plus near-ones by Tunnicliffe and Wainwright, helped Yorkshire to a total of almost 350 that was sufficiently out of Derbyshire's reach to compel the follow-on despite a determined innings of 96 by Storer. That redoubtable pair Hirst and Rhodes shared Yorkshire's bowling honours. Derbyshire's most successful man with the ball was John Berwick, a Northamptonshire-born left-arm fast-medium bowler whose five wickets cost just over sixteen runs each.

Yorkshire's total of 662 in 1898 set a record against Derbyshire that Nottinghamshire were just two runs from beating at Derby only three years later. In more than a hundred seasons since then the next closest approach has been made by Northamptonshire, who declared at 647 with five wickets down, also at Derby, in 2003 as soon as David Sales completed the fifth double-century of his career off only 217 balls. The 273 Billy Gunn made for Notts in the 1901 match at the County Ground was his eighth double-century, and his third against Derbyshire (there were also four single ones). His nephew John (84) and Arthur Shrewsbury (99), both caught at the wicket by Storer, gave him most support, but Derbyshire comfortably managed a draw despite having to follow on just over two hundred runs behind. L G Wright dominated their first innings with his 193, batting for the same length of time as Gunn (330 minutes), and his opening stand with Bill Locker (76) realised 140 runs. Locker, like Gunn, played football for Notts County. He was in their team that lost to Blackburn Rovers in the 1891 F A Cup final – the Saturday after scoring one of their goals in a 7-1 League win at Blackburn.

Nottinghamshire were also involved in a big form reversal the month before taking 661 off Derbyshire. From scoring 642 for seven in Sussex they went straight to capitulating for 13, the lowest-ever total in a county match, against Yorkshire at Trent Bridge with a team that showed just one change – former skipper John Dixon for the injured Arthur Shrewsbury. Dixon, like Gunn and Locker, played soccer for Notts County, and, again like Gunn (an international at both cricket and soccer), also for England.

Yorkshire's record total against Derbyshire might well have been even bigger, even exceeding the 887, the first one to include four individual centuries, that they amassed at Edgbaston in 1896, if some of their other batsmen, notably George Hirst and Wilfred Rhodes, had not followed Brown's example by giving their wickets away. That 887 still stands as an inter-county record, second only in England to the 903 at which England declared with three wickets in hand against Australia at The Oval in 1938, but there have been a number even greater in games abroad – headed by a couple in excess of a thousand by Victoria at Melbourne in the 1920s.

The Brown-Tunnicliffe partnership at Chesterfield remained a record for the first wicket until Herbert Sutcliffe (313) and Percy Holmes (224 not out) kept it for Yorkshire against Essex at Leyton in 1932. They batted for seven and a half hours before Sutcliffe, who had not given a chance, also got out on purpose, clean bowled in taking a terrific wipe at a ball from Laurie Eastman, after the score had been taken just one run past the 554 of 1898. The pair were posing for their photograph in front of the scoreboard when, to their absolute consternation, the total was suddenly changed to 554, and there was much agonising before a further inspection of the scorebook providentially unearthed a no-ball that had been overlooked. In those days the scorers used to sit directly under the scoreboard, and could not easily see when it went wrong. Charles Bray, who was the Essex captain, later recalled in his *Wisden* history of the county's cricket:

'A very worried Charles McGahey, the Essex scorer, came to me in the dressing room. Would I agree to the total being changed? The umpires (what accommodating people they are) said a no-ball had not been recorded. There was no doubt in Charles's mind an extra run was being "found". I told him I thought the two batsmen had put up a magnificent performance and it would be cruel luck if they were to be deprived of the honour of breaking the record because our scoreboard had gone wrong. If the umpires said a no-ball had not been recorded it was OK with me. Charles went away happy.'

The reinstated total of 555 was not exceeded until 1977, when the Pakistanis Waheed Mirza (324) and Mansoor Akhtar (224 not out) scored 561 together for Karachi Whites against Quetta at Karachi.

Both those big opening stands for Yorkshire were achieved despite one of the batsmen involved being under some physical handicap. Tunnicliffe chose to sit up the previous night rather than risk what he considered to be unsatisfactory hotel accommodation, and he batted throughout the next day with only a sandwich to sustain him because of catering confusion at the ground. At Leyton, the 44-year-old Holmes, suffering from lumbago, was in obvious pain for much of his long innings.

After their mauling by Yorkshire, Derbyshire were most fortunate not to end the 1898 season with another resounding defeat, for the weather intervened at Old Trafford after they had struggled to 77 for the loss of eight wickets, still requiring 350 to avoid following on in face of Lancashire's 546. Their destroyer that time was the dapper John Thomas Tyldesley, who was caught by Walker off Storer for exactly 200 – the first of his thirteen double-centuries in first-class cricket. It was also against Derbyshire that he was to score the last of them. His 272 at Chesterfield in 1919 was second only for size to his 295 not out against Kent at Manchester in 1906.

In the *Manchester Guardian*, Neville Cardus, that doyen of cricket writers, said that 'if a maiden over were bowled at him, JTT would gnaw a glove at the end of it. He had no patience with a good attack; he felt the necessity of falling on it and demolishing it without delay.' Well, Derbyshire's attack that late August day was certainly not of the best, and Tyldesley took full advantage of its shortcomings on a pitch that was firm and true. So did Frank Sugg, the next highest home scorer with 64, and three others who also hit a half-century – Willis Cuttell, George Baker and Johnny Briggs. When it came Derbyshire's turn to bat the pitch had been enlivened by rain, and they promptly rain into more trouble against Cuttell and Briggs. Cuttell, who, like Baker, had played briefly for his home county of Yorkshire before joining Lancashire on a residential qualification, took five of their wickets for 48 runs, the Nottinghamshire-born Briggs the three others that fell for 27.

Johnny Tyldesley, whose younger brother Ernest followed him as a Lancashire and England batsman, stayed on at Old Trafford as coach until the end of the 1930 season after ending his playing career, but ill health had dogged him for some time, and on a November morning that year he suffered a fatal collapse while putting on his boots as he prepared to leave home to go to his business in the Deansgate area of Manchester. He was only fifty-seven.

Derbyshire concluded their eventful 1898 season ninth out of fourteen in the Championship, and although they had only two wins to set against six defeats and seven draws it could not fail to be an improvement on what had gone before. In 1897 they had been winless through seventeen matches, their bleakest season up to that time. They were to finish at the bottom of the heap on four other occasions before ending as high as ninth again in the first post-war season of 1919. And, as we shall be coming to, very much worse was soon to follow.

For 1899, another of the years in which Derbyshire pitched up at the foot of the table, there was a change of captaincy. Herbert Evershed stood down after eight years in office and Samuel Hill-Wood took over until the appointment for 1902 of Albert Lawton, who had deputised as skipper the previous year when Wood had been available for only five matches. After only two seasons, Lawton shared the post for the next two with Maynard Ashcroft, then dramatically resigned in 1906 because of what he regarded as a gratuitous insult by a member of the committee. This referred to a telegram he received before a match at Leicester, requesting him not to 'monkey' with the bowling – as he was supposed to have done at Derby the previous day, when Lancashire, threatened with defeat, had started the season by getting away with a victory.

After that game with Leicestershire, who also won, Lawton vowed never to play for Derbyshire again, but a belated apology by the county's committee cleared up what was termed 'little more than a petty misunderstanding' the following year. As *Wisden* remarked, however, 'the loss of their most dangerous hitter, and certainly one of their best fieldsmen, proved irreparable' during the remainder of the 1906 season as Derbyshire faded away to finish last again. They won only two of their twenty matches, losing seventeen, and had a minus percentage of 78.94 in contrast to the 77.77 plus percentage of champions Kent. Ironically, this was Joe Humphries' best season for dismissals (69 caught, six stumped), and L G Wright, in scoring 50 out of 104 at Leicester, also earned a special mention for carrying his bat through a completed innings for the third time.

Hereabouts Wright was in the best form of his career. In 1905 his 1,716 runs at an average of 42.90 set a club record that lasted thirty years and included centuries in three successive innings – two of them in the match with Warwickshire at Edgbaston after his highest score of 195 against Northamptonshire at Derby. During that year he also made fifteen half-centuries, the most for the club in one season (equalled by Donald Carr, Kim Barnett and John Morris) until the seventeen of Mohammad Azharuddin, the Indian Test captain, in 1991, and Peter Bowler in 1992.

It was Wright who recommended Lawton to Derbyshire after receiving a tip-off about him and making a special journey to see him play for Cromford. And, as Lawton was quick to acknowledge, it was 'thanks to good old L G' that he was given an early chance to redeem himself after scoring only one run in the two innings of his debut against Lancashire at Old Trafford in 1900. He was promptly omitted, but soon afterwards Wright also dropped out, through injury, and badgered the committee into sending Lawton a telegram, telling him to report at Lord's to play against the MCC. As Lawton modestly remembered it, 'luck was then all my way, and I duly became a regular member of the side.'

One of his best displays in that first season with the club was given at The Oval, where he scored a half-century in the biggest stand of Derbyshire's first innings of 325 with Samuel Wood (later Sir Samuel Hill-Wood). All was overshadowed in that match, however, by the home side's opening partnership of 364 in 247 minutes between Bobby Abel (193) and his captain D L A Jephson (213), an all-rounder already out of the ordinary with his Christian names of Digby Loder Armroid. It was only fifteen runs short of the Surrey record Abel had set with Bill Brockwell against Hampshire at the same ground three years earlier (raised to 428 by Jack Hobbs and Andy Sandham against Oxford University in 1926), and remained the second biggest for the first wicket against Derbyshire until Barry Dudleston (202) and John Steele (187) set up Leicestershire's record of 390 at Leicester in 1979.

Surrey were 523 for five at the second day's close, but rain prevented further play, saving Derbyshire from the prospect of another heavy defeat at the hands of that county. Jephson's double-century, which included two fives and 26 fours, was his biggest score at the top level, but he three times exceeded it in club cricket and had a career-best of 301 not out for Wanderers against Norwood. He found further distinction as a bowler by abandoning his fast over-arm style to become a leading exponent of the ancient art of lobbed deliveries with which he twice took all ten wickets in an innings. In 1898 his match haul of 9-55 helped Surrey to their innings win at Chesterfield; at the same ground the following year he rounded off another huge victory by taking 5-12 in Derbyshire's second innings after Tom Hayward, the first batsman after W G Grace to make a hundred centuries, had done the hat-trick in the first. That success completed an emphatic winning double for Surrey, a century before lunch by Brockwell having helped then to a ten-wicket win at The Oval.

Jephson expressed himself particularly fond of the underhand leg-break, otherwise referred to as the 'lob' or 'grub'. He observed that he and his kind were called 'one ball one nut artists in the garbled language of the fair', adding that 'when on many a ground throughout the country there has arisen on every side the gentle sound of "Take him orf!", were it not that the side ever comes before oneself I would bowl, and bowl, and bowl until at eventide the cows come home.'

After Albert Lawton's brush with Derbyshire's committee, the reconciliation came too late to enable him to play in no more than four games in 1907. He celebrated his comeback with 106 in the follow-on against Leicestershire, winners by nine wickets at Derby. That was the first century of the season for Derbyshire, and in their next game Lawton hit another, 112 not out, as they gained their first win at home, against Northamptonshire. Having been second top scorer with 44 behind Ollivierre's 53 in Derbyshire's first innings, he helped Wright (98) to pave the way to a declaration with an opening century stand. Then Fred Bracey, whose left-arm spinners could be expensive at other times, completed Northants' discomfiture with his career-best match figures of eleven for 45 (5-9 and 6-36).

Although Lawton was so smartly off the mark in showing Derbyshire what they had been missing, and his average of 62.66 over seven innings put him well clear at the head of their batting averages, they were powerless to prevent another last-place finish – with depressing statistics identical in every respect to those of the previous year. Without him after that rare victory, they slipped back into their losing rut in being routed for 44 and 72 at Glossop by Yorkshire's peerless combination of Hirst (11-44) and Rhodes (8-71). It was the third occasion that season on which a pair of bowlers shared the attack unchanged throughout heavy defeats for Derbyshire. Jack Crawford (6-52), one of the many graduates to county cricket from Repton, and 'Razor' Smith (11-65) did so for Surrey at Derby, Tom Wass (10-67) and Albert Hallam (8-84) for champions Notts at Chesterfield.

Three years earlier, 'Topsy' Wass had bowled unchanged with John Gunn in Derbyshire's dismissal for 32 at Queen's Park. And two years later he took 10-87, and Hallam 10-63, when Notts again needed no other bowlers to sweep their neighbours aside at Nottingham. Wass also took eight wickets in an innings against Derbyshire, for only 13 runs, at Welbeck in 1901, and nine, for 67, at Blackwell in 1911.

He retired in 1920 with a Notts record of 1,679 wickets, yet never played for England. No great shakes as a batsman, or as a fielder for that matter, he still also caused Derbyshire a lot of trouble with the only half-century of his career, aided by four missed catches, in a ninth-wicket stand of 98 with John Day that led to a ten-wicket win for Notts at Derby in 1906.

Wright took over the captaincy in the absence that year of Lawton, and retained it for the following season. Lawton shared it with Reggie Rickman in

1908 but then had it on his own again for one more season. He last played for Derbyshire the year after that, and when his connection with the cotton industry took him to Manchester he assisted Lancashire from 1912 until war intervened – supposedly on a birth qualification, though he once said he was born in a house, at Dukinfield, not many yards on the Cheshire side of the border with Lancashire. It was in Manchester, at a nursing home, that Lawton died on Christmas Day in 1955, aged seventy-six.

In all, he scored 7,509 runs in first-class cricket, 5,554 of them in 226 innings for Derbyshire, at an average of almost 25. He also took 113 wickets, though at a cost of nearly 32 runs each, held 125 catches, and made one stumping. Eight of his eleven centuries were made for Derbyshire, three of them in the 1902 season in which he completed a thousand runs for the second successive year – 149 against a London County side captained by W G Grace, 146 against Hampshire, and 126 against Warwickshire, all at Derby.

On the only occasion he opposed Derbyshire while with Lancashire, at Old Trafford in 1914, he failed with the bat, but claimed four second-innings wickets cheaply in helping his new county to a victory by 35 runs. He was twice bowled, for nought and 26, by Tom Forester, a left-hand batsman and right-arm bowler from Clay Cross who first played for Warwickshire, but he gained some measure of revenge by having him among his victims, trapped lbw. Forester (or Forrester, as he was also known) had a peculiar bowling action that at times made him appear to deliver the ball with his right foot in front, but he could make the ball swerve or spin appreciably. He took five wickets in both Lancashire innings of that match.

Lawton was followed as captain by John Chapman, who came from a Cheshire family on his father's side but was born at Frocester Court, near Gloucester, the home of his mother's family. It was said he received his earliest cricket advice from E M Grace, which would account for his powerful and unorthodox hitting that was so typical of W G's brother. Chapman subsequently lived in Yorkshire, and he played half-a-dozen times for that county's second team, twice as captain, after his attractive batting had first caught attention while a student at Uppingham. His team-mates there included Tom Taylor, who went on to win his Blue at Cambridge and play for Yorkshire, the county he also served as president from 1948 until his death in 1960.

Chapman went to Oxford University from Uppingham, but although he did well as a batsman for Oriel College he never had a trial for either the Freshmen or the Seniors. In 1901 business took him to Russia for a couple of years, and on his return he prospered in club cricket, often with Sheffield Collegiate. According to the *Derbyshire Cricket Guide* he scored no fewer than forty centuries in that sphere before qualifying for Derbyshire in 1909 by residence on moving to live at Unstone, near Dronfield.

His most successful year for Derbyshire was 1911, the middle one of his first spell as captain. In thirty-three innings he totalled 854 runs for an average of 30, with a top score of 96 against Leicestershire at Chesterfield. Like Lawton, he was always eager to attack, and a most entertaining batsman when in form. A fierce driver, he struck one of his most spectacular sixes by depositing a delivery from Johnny Douglas straight over the sightscreen at the Nottingham Road end of the Derby ground. He preceded his century in the world record ninth-wicket stand with Arnold Warren by making his top score of 198 (two sixes, 29 fours) in about three and a half hours at Coventry in 1909 – still Derbyshire's highest individual innings against Warwickshire – but in 1912 he was hampered by injury and suffered an acute loss of form. This led him to resign from the captaincy at the end of that season, but he played on, and after serving with the Remount Department during the 1914-18 war he had further spells as skipper in 1919 and 1920 before another depressing sequence of low scores prompted his retirement from the county game.

He made his final appearance for Derbyshire at Weston-super-Mare against Somerset, off whom he had made 76 in the first match between the counties at Taunton seven years earlier. An unusual feature of the 1920 Weston match was that Derbyshire fielded as many as seven amateurs, and Somerset nine. The most successful of the sixteen was John Daniell, the home captain, who scored a swift century, the first 50 out of 53 in less than half-an-hour, in his team's ten-wicket win. He repeatedly swept deliveries from Arthur Morton to the leg boundary.

After Chapman's death at his home, Carlecotes Hall, near Sheffield, in 1956, his old friend Major Llewellyn Eardley-Simpson, who was Derbyshire's honorary secretary and treasurer during almost fifty years' service to the county, recalled that he was 'a cheerful companion, but inclined to be too easily depressed by any failures of his own'.

Richard Romer Claude Baggallay, Chapman's successor as captain in 1913, was a Londoner who first played for Derbyshire the previous year against the Australians and Northamptonshire, under a residential qualification. The outbreak of war, during which he was awarded the Distinguished Service Order and Military Cross, brought his recall to his regiment as Adjutant of Yeomanry in the South Notts Hussars, and although he resumed the Derbyshire captaincy in 1919 he had taken part in only three matches when his appointment as military secretary to the Viceroy of Ireland, Lord Ypres, created the vacancy that restored Chapman to the leadership of the county side.

Baggallay went on to attain the rank of Lieutenant-Colonel, finally serving with the Irish Guards. For just three weeks he was the last surviving county cricket captain of the years before the First World War until he died after a short illness, in his ninety-second year, on 12 December, 1975.

Tom Manning, Northamptonshire's captain from 1908-10, who made his top score of 57 against Derbyshire, died at ninety-one the month before. Baggallay's best score was 88, against Somerset at Derby in 1913. He averaged only just under twelve for his sixty innings in first-class cricket, with an aggregate approaching 700. He was also a wicketkeeper, though not for the county, and not to the same standard as his brother who wore the gloves for Cambridge University. One of their cousins played for Surrey.

In 1920, the captaincy passed from Chapman to Leonard Oliver, a forcing left-hand batsman but (occasional) right-arm medium-pace bowler from Glossop whose career with the county produced more than six thousand runs, if at an average barely above twenty, in 174 matches from 1908 to 1924. His most successful season was 1913, when he got within 43 runs of 1,000, but it was not until seven years later that he made the biggest of his six centuries, 170 (two sixes, 18 fours) against Nottinghamshire at Trent Bridge. That was one of the very few bright spots in the most deplorable season Derbyshire have ever had to endure, but more about that in the next chapter. Oliver continued in club cricket after leaving Derbyshire, and as late as 1931, in his forty-fifth year, he headed the Lancashire and Cheshire League batting averages. He was one of Derbyshire's vice-presidents at the time of his sudden death back at Glossop early in 1948.

11. From Glory to Gloom

The first two cricket seasons after the First World War took Derbyshire from a moment of rare national glory to the deepest of a funereal gloom that threatened to plunge them into extinction.

In 1919 they were the only county side to defeat the Australian Imperial Forces XI (see p.337). In 1920 they plummeted back to the Championship's depths without even one point out of the 85 they could have obtained. The only one of their eighteen matches they did not lose was the Chesterfield clash with Nottinghamshire, scheduled for Joe Humphries' benefit, that was rained off without a ball being bowled.

For the first post-war season games were of two days' duration instead of three, with longer playing hours (11.30am to 7.30pm on the first day, 11am to 7.30 on the second). It was an experiment both unpopular and impracticable, and was promptly discarded. With fine weather favouring batsmen, the number of drawn matches became unacceptably high, and disagreement over the extended playing time each day precipitated an early change in the captaincy of the Australian team.

The tourists had fulfilled only six fixtures when the displeased Charles Kelleway stood down in favour of Herbie Collins, a fellow New South Walian widely known as 'Horseshoe' because of his good fortune in horseracing as a bookmaker and in winning the toss at cricket. Collins, possessor of extreme patience and an exceptionally sound defence, was to earn unwelcome notoriety two years later for spending nearly five hours over 40 runs in the Test at Old Trafford after time lost through rain had left Australia with only a draw to play for, but he set a splendid example to his men on that Forces tour of 1919 by doing the double. His 1,615 runs at an average near forty included six centuries; the 106 wickets he took with his left-arm spinners cost fewer than seventeen runs each.

An impressive cricket team had been formed during the war from the ranks of the Australian Forces serving in Europe, and in that first year of restored peace it was still of sufficient strength to win twelve of twenty-eight first-class games, with only four defeats, after it had been agreed to make a tour of England before the players returned home for demobilisation. That season's champions, Yorkshire, were among the beaten counties, if by the nerve-jangling margin of just one wicket.

No more than five of the seventeen tourists of 1919 were back in England with the full Australian party two years on, but although the AIF squad was not as powerful as it might have been wished, it contained, in addition to Collins, three batsmen who also exceeded a thousand runs (Carl Willis, 'Nip' Pellew and John Taylor), two who went very near to doing so (Bill Trenerry and Jack Gregory), and another bowler besides Collins (Gregory) who took more than a hundred wickets. The man they missed most was Charlie Macartney, the 'Governor General', who was one of the most entertaining batsmen ever to come out of Australia – scorer of the most runs in one day when he raced to 345 out of 540 in 235 minutes against Nottinghamshire at Trent Bridge in 1921, hitting 47 fours and four sixes. He went back home before the 1919 season started.

Of the players left to undertake that year's tour, those who became the best-known apart from Collins and Kellaway included three others from New South Wales: Taylor, a polished batsman and brilliant cover point; Gregory, a fearsome fast bowler also capable of scoring Test centuries (one of them the swiftest for time at that level in 70 minutes against South Africa in Johannesburg); and Bert Oldfield, the neat and skilful wicketkeeper whose 52 stumpings set a Test record. That trio, plus the original AIF captain and his successor, were the five who came back under Warwick Armstrong's abrasively adept captaincy at the next opportunity. Oldfield, promoted from the AIF second team when Ted Long was injured, went desperately close to losing his life in the war. While serving as a corporal in an ambulance brigade, he was buried for several hours during the heavy bombardment of Polygon Wood in 1918, and was barely alive when rescued.

Gregory took nine wickets, Collins five, in that historic match at Derby. Oldfield stumped three batsmen in a row, and held three catches. The Australians' three other defeats – by the Gentlemen of England at Lord's, the South of England at Hastings, and C I Thornton's XI at Scarborough – were suffered against representative sides that were expected to give them a testing time. Derbyshire, on the other hand, were experiencing their customary season of struggle, and their victory, by 36 runs, was the big turn-up of the tour – especially as they were without their main strike bowler. Bill Bestwick was at Lord's with the Players against the Gentlemen, though he had little chance to shine in a drawn game and was allowed only three overs during a first innings in which Lancashire's Cecil Parkin and Alec Kennedy, of Hampshire, mopped up the wickets.

In Bestwick's absence, the home attack was shared, apart from eleven deliveries, to devastating effect by James Horsley and Arthur Morton, who, with Leonard Oliver, were the only three members of the side to have played in the county's last game in 1914 against Lancashire. Those eleven balls were bowled by Derby-born George Ratcliffe, whose only first-class match for Derbyshire that was, in the Forces' second innings. Horsley and Morton both sent down nineteen overs as the tourists were dismissed for 125 in reply to 181. Horsley did the hat-trick (one bowled, two lbw) in his six for 55; Morton took four for 66. Gregory (6-65) and Collins (4-39) then limited the extension of the home lead to 168 in also bowling unchanged, but the Australians were all out for 132 when they batted again. Horsley took 6-62, and Morton 3-54, in forty-three overs between them before Ratcliffe, taking over after Horsley had sprained an ankle, ended a stubborn last-wicket stand with the aid of a stumping by George Beet off the fifth ball of his second over.

Unfortunately, the match aroused some bad feeling, with talk of faulty decisions by the local umpires. Two Australians were given out lbw in their first innings, and one in the second, but Horsley, last out in the home second innings, was the only Derbyshire player to be dismissed in that manner. Although Derbyshire's wretched form in 1920 was said to have cost them a fixture with the Australians in 1921, not a few people attributed it to some of the questionable umpiring of 1919. Whatever the reason, the fact remains that in each AIF innings five batsmen had no cause to quibble. They were comprehensively bowled.

This remained the last victory by an English county against an Australian team until 1956, when Surrey, champions that year for the fifth of seven successive seasons, beat Ian Johnson's tourists by ten wickets at The Oval. But because the AIF side lacked official standing it was Hampshire's eight-wicket win at Southampton in 1912 to which the records referred back for the last previous instance before The Oval match in which Jim Laker took all ten wickets in an innings – a feat the Surrey off-spinner repeated in his astounding haul of nineteen in the fourth Test triumph at Old Trafford that ensured England's retention of the Ashes in the same season.

Derbyshire went without another win against an Australian touring team until 1997, when they scrambled home by one wicket on a bland pitch at Derby. Their pursuit of their biggest fourth-innings total of 371, with 69 overs available, got off to an explosive start with 91 from 76 balls by Chris Adams, whose argument with umpire Van Holder over his controversial lbw dismissal in his first innings was to cost him a £750 club fine, but there were only three balls to spare when their last pair, Paul Aldred and Kevin Dean, reached the target.

It was a particularly satisfying victory for Derbyshire's captain, Dean Jones, who had been discarded from the Australian Test team, but there was a woeful sequel. Derbyshire were well beaten by Hampshire at Chesterfield in their next game, and within a week Jones walked out as dressing-room tensions boiled over. More about that in the last chapter.

Jim Horsley, like his relation John Young, who played for Derbyshire around the turn into the twentieth century, was born just inside the county's southern boundary at Melbourne, but he first attracted attention as a fast-medium bowler while living in Nottingham. It was therefore with Notts that he entered county cricket, though he did little of note in his three games for them in 1913 before becoming an immediate success on switching to play for Derbyshire the following year. He not only headed his home county's bowling averages in the last pre-war season, finishing fourth in the national list with 56 wickets at 16.33, but also partnered Joe Humphries in a stand of 93, against Lancashire at Derby, that survived as a record for Derbyshire's last wicket for seventy-two years. Humphries had also had a share in the previous best, 87 with Tom Forester against Warwickshire at Edgbaston in 1910.

Derbyshire became the last of the then seventeen first-class counties to have a final partnership worth a hundred or more runs when Alan Hill, whose 172 not out was a career-best, and Martin Jean-Jacques (73), an all-rounder from Dominica who was making his debut after being spotted playing for Buckinghamshire and the Shepherd's Bush club in London, added 132 against Yorkshire at Abbeydale Park in 1986. The Humphries-Horsley stand has also been overtaken since then by Geoff Miller (47 not out) and Simon Base (58), who added 107 for the last wicket, again against Yorkshire, at Chesterfield in 1990, and by Mo Sheikh (22 not out) and Nick Walker (80), with 103 against Somerset at Derby in 2004. Walker's score, in which three of his four sixes came in one over, replaced Martin-Jacques' 73 as the biggest ever made by a last man for Derbyshire.

In Derbyshire's limited programme of fourteen County Championship matches in 1919, Horsley took only twice as many wickets as his dozen in that shock defeat of the Australian Imperial Forces team, but even with that modest return, at a cost of almost 23 runs each, he was second in the county's averages to Bill Bestwick, who took ten wickets in a match on three occasions in totalling 89, plus one for the Players, at an average under nineteen on his return to first-class cricket after an absence of nine years. It was indeed fortunate for Derbyshire that Bestwick was enticed back for that first post-war season. His number of wickets exceeded the combined aggregate of Derbyshire's eleven other bowlers, so without him the county's final position would have been even lower than tenth out of fifteen.

This was forcibly driven home when Bestwick, and Horsley too, played in only one match during the county's appallingly sterile season that followed. Bestwick, as recalled earlier, had not yet finished with Derbyshire, however – and neither had Horsley. After going into league cricket with Burnley, Horsley returned to Derbyshire in 1923 and took 170 wickets for them in three seasons before again re-entering league cricket in Lancashire and then spending two summers with Aberdeenshire. After that he was the professional of several clubs in Northern Ireland up to the outbreak of another world war in 1939. He was eighty-six when he died at Derby in February 1976.

No fewer than thirty-nine players were tried as Derbyshire desperately attempted to stem the flood of defeats in their deplorable season of 1920, and it was surprising in those unhappy circumstances that in two respects some improvement was shown. Whereas in 1919 no Derbyshire player had managed a century (Leonard Oliver failed by one run and George Beet was unbeaten on 92), two of them did so in what still ranks as the county's blackest season despite the other woeful campaigns they have since had to endure. And instead of having the bowling so heavily reliant upon one man, there were two who each attained a half-century of wickets. Arthur Morton matched Bestwick's 89 of the previous year; Sam Cadman collected 58 – both at an average under twenty-one.

The century-makers were Oliver and Morton. Oliver, who, in Chapman's absence, had captained the team that toppled the AIF, hit two sixes and eighteen fours in his 170 at Nottingham. Morton carried his bat through a completed innings for the second time in scoring 105 out of 204 in the match with Leicestershire at Derby, having first done so with 28 when Derbyshire were skittled out for 62 by Yorkshire at Bradford ten years earlier. In common with Chapman, Morton had a career total of six centuries, but, unlike him, four of them were taken off Essex at Leyton (shades of Chatterton) in consecutive seasons from 1922.

This stockily-built all-rounder, also like Chapman from Glossop, was one of Derbyshire's most durable performers. He gained a regular place in 1904, the year after his debut, and continued playing for the county until 1926, totalling 350 appearances. In all first-class cricket he garnered 10,957 runs, with a top score of 131 but an average below twenty, and took 981 wickets for 22.77 runs each. Three times he had eight wickets in an innings, with best figures of 9-71 against Notts at Blackwell in 1911. His most successful season as a bowler was that of 1910, when his off-breaks claimed 116 victims for Derbyshire at 22.67, and he bagged exactly 100 at 17.24 twelve years later. As an all-rounder he had his best year in 1914, heading the county's batting averages with 1,023 runs and taking fifty wickets.

When he died, aged only fifty-one after a long illness, at Stockport shortly before Christmas in 1935, Morton's name was still on the list of first-class umpires for the ensuing season – the one that Derbyshire were to end as genuine champions – even though he had been compelled by ill health to relinquish appointments in 1935. In addition to one Test, he stood in 171 Championship matches, having cause to remember one of them in particular. This was how R C Robertson-Glasgow (the former Oxford University and Somerset player who acquired the nicknamed 'Crusoe' after Charles McGahey, the Essex and England batsman, had been dismissed first ball by what he called 'a chap named Robinson Crusoe') told of it in his other occupation as a journalist:

'He called several no-balls against a certain West Indies fast bowler. The excitable victim, resenting these attentions, revenged himself by running towards the wicket, knocking Morton flat on his face, and shouting: "Was *that* a no-ball then?" Apologies were made; Morton straightened his teeth and scraped the grass from his eyebrows, and the game proceeded.'

Morton was only seventeen when first tried by Derbyshire, and, by an outlandish coincidence, the county had another Arthur Morton who made his debut at eighteen, against Warwickshire in Birmingham, in 1901. This Morton, however, played in just that one match, in which he took no wickets (he was given only three overs) or catches, and was twice bowled without scoring.

Though born in Salford, he spent much of his life at Bakewell and captained the local club, of which he was later president. He was a successful right-arm fast bowler in club cricket, with hat-tricks and an all-ten (for eleven runs against Chatsworth) to his credit, and in 1933, when fifty years old, he took seven Matlock wickets for only four runs. No mean batsman at that level either, he shared an unbroken double-century stand while with Darley Dale, another Derbyshire club he captained. He also played for Broughton in the Manchester Alliance League before ending his years in Sheffield. It was in hospital there that he died early in 1970, just a few weeks from his eighty-seventh birthday.

Of the others who have played just the one first-team match for Derbyshire, Charles Ernest Nornable is also worth a special mention. A right-hand batsman and fast-medium bowler who was with Sheffield United CC as both player (for twenty-two years) and coach, he was invited to turn out again for the county against the Australians the month after taking 5-72 on his debut against Sussex at Derby in 1909, but was taken ill with appendicitis. Then his employers, Sheffield Corporation, declined to release him when he was offered a place on the Derbyshire staff for 1911.

A A Milne, the author of children's books that included *Winnie-the-Pooh*, penned this limerick about him:

> 'There was – or there wasn't – a Nornable
>   Who mayn't have been born, but was bornable
> Did he walk upon stilts?
>   Or play cricket for Wilts?
> Or was he a bird – like a horner-bill?'

The fact that Derbyshire's lamentable showing in the 1920 season put them in real danger of going out of business was underlined by Major Eardley-Simpson, who for so many years had to contend with severe financial constraints as the club's honorary treasurer. In his booklet *The Rise of Derbyshire Cricket, 1919-35*, he described it as 'a horrible experience, unrelieved by one gleam of hope', adding that 'the selection committee had about as many meetings as there were matches, and on more than one occasion it was not easy to find a full eleven'. He continued:

'As the end of the season approached it became a question of whether it was worthwhile trying any longer to keep the county flag flying, and I often wonder what would have been the end had not one bright gleam appeared in the darkness in which the year ended. This was the offer of Captain G M Buckston to lead the side for one season as the last effort to stave off the approaching collapse.'

There was a real element of risk in George Buckston's appointment. Not only had he been out of county cricket for fourteen years, having last played for Derbyshire in 1907, he had also turned forty and contracted malaria while on active service in the Army during the war. In the event, however, he proved just the man for the job. He quickly restored morale as what had been a disorganised, dispirited bunch of individuals began pulling together as a team, and, although the recovery was not exceptional – a rise of six places up the table, with five victories to offset a dozen defeats – it was seen as a definite turning point. And they might have finished still higher but for bad luck with the weather in August.

As already recalled, their highlight of that season was the taking of all ten Glamorgan wickets in Cardiff by Bill Bestwick. In two of the heaviest defeats, however, Yorkshire seriously exposed the brittle batting by routing Derbyshire for 23 at Hull and 37 at Chesterfield. Harry Elliott, run out for nine, was the top scorer in the humiliation of the away game, in which George Macaulay, who was so soon to mark his Test debut in South Africa by taking a wicket with his first ball and then making the winning hit, had this remarkable analysis: 7-4-3-6. Macaulay did not get to bowl in Derbyshire's first innings at Queen's Park, where Emmott Robinson (5-16) and Abram Waddington (4-13) shared the attack unchanged, but he ensured another innings victory with 6-32 when they batted again.

In addition to doing such a good job as captain, George Buckston, who had been a late choice for Cambridge in the University Match of 1903, three years after playing for Eton against Harrow, fared better than could have been expected with the bat on his return to the Derbyshire team after such a long absence and at such an advanced age for a first-class cricketer. He had an aggregate of just one run fewer than 300, with a top score of 71 in a win at Worcester, though Major Eardley-Simpson observed that 'he would have been well worth his place had he never scored a run'. His biggest innings in county cricket, in his second Derbyshire season of 1906 (he played in only a couple of games the previous year) was 96 against Hampshire at Southampton. It gave him a match total of 149, but still not enough to avert defeat. Along with his colleagues, he found the going increasingly difficult the following season as Derbyshire finished at the foot of the table for the second successive year, and dropped out of the side.

Buckston, whose son Robin also captained Derbyshire (for the last three seasons before the 1939-45 war) could not be persuaded to carry on leading the team for a second year in 1922, but he gave the county further service as chairman of the committee – another post in which his son was to follow him. George Buckston's successor as captain, Guy Jackson, a fellow former Derbyshire Yeomanry officer, was also Robin Buckston's immediate predecessor as chairman. This Old Harrovian left-hand batsman, who had first played for Derbyshire in 1919, was to be the county's longest-reigning captain, for the nine seasons from 1922 to 1930, until overtaken by Kim Barnett in 1992. The Staffordshire-born Barnett, who, at not quite 23, became the club's youngest in that role when he took over after Barry Wood, the former Lancashire and England all-rounder, had resigned a few weeks into the 1983 season, stood down after thirteen years and 271 first-class matches, but continued as a Derbyshire player for three more seasons before leaving to complete his county career with Gloucestershire. He departed as Derbyshire's most prolific batsman, scorer of 23,854 runs at an average of 41.12, and with a total of 53 centuries that put him twenty ahead of runner-up John Morris. In all, also including four Test appearances, Barnett retired with 28,593 first-class runs and 61 centuries to his name.

Guy Jackson, whose brother Geoffrey preceded him as a Derbyshire player but was killed during the 1914-18 war, also continued to turn out for the county, though not regularly, after giving up the captaincy. It was not until 1936 that he played his last game, his only one of that year – not in the Championship-winning side, but against the Indian tourists. His availability during those final seasons was restricted because more of his attention was required at the family iron and steel business at Clay Cross, where he became joint managing director, but he still found time to be chairman of Derbyshire's general committee from 1943 to 1960 and was also a member of the MCC committee for the five years up to 1938.

Jackson, who died in a Chesterfield hospital early in 1966, at the age of sixty-nine, could look back on his nine years at the Derbyshire helm with the great satisfaction of knowing that the county, as *Wisden* said, had been transformed during that time from having their 'fortunes at a very low ebb' to being 'well established among the leading teams of the day'. As befitted a man who, as also a captain in the Army, had twice been mentioned in dispatches, awarded the Military Cross, the *Legion d'Honneur* and a Greek decoration during the First World War, Jackson, though a stern disciplinarian, soon gained the full confidence and respect of his team. He was a natural leader, a fine fieldsman, and one of the best amateur batsmen ever to represent Derbyshire. He exceeded a thousand runs in a season four times, made 10,291 in all first-class cricket – 9,741 of them in 438 innings for the county – for an average in the mid-twenties, and held 110 catches.

Seven times while with Derbyshire he was out in the nineties, but he still managed to make nine centuries. The biggest, and last, of them, 140, came in a stand of 132 with Charles Clarke for the ninth wicket against Kent at Ilkeston in 1930. Clarke, a Burton-born batsman who was in the team at Repton, played in twenty-five first-class games for Derbyshire from 1929 to 1933, and three for Sussex in 1947, but never surpassed the unbeaten 35 he made in that partnership.

From 1935 until the war, in which he became a captain in the RASC, he was with Staffordshire. In club cricket he was known as the Conjuror because of his brilliance in the field. For a time he was player-coach at Kendal, and he later he managed a white-elephant shop. He was at a nursing home at

Carnforth, in Lancashire, when he died towards the end of 1997, the month before his eighty-seventh birthday.

At the outset there was some criticism of Guy Jackson's handling of the bowling, but that evaporated as he quickly gained in experience. To quote Eardley-Simpson again:

'Apart from the usual duties of leadership there was one important point which, perhaps, did more to raise Derbyshire in the opinion of cricketers generally than mere success; no-one could ever imagine Guy Jackson departing by a millionth of an inch from the strictest sportsmanship. Not only were opponents sure of the game being played according to the rules, but they knew they were going to "play cricket" in the widest sense of that term. What that meant it is impossible to define in words, but it meant everything to the success of the side.'

Steady progress was made in Jackson's first two seasons as captain. In 1922, although the batting was often disappointing and undid some of the good work of the bowlers, the number of wins went up to six, the defeats dropped to ten, and there was a rise of one further place in the table to eleventh. In 1923, when Horsley topped the bowling averages on returning from his three seasons with Burnley in league cricket, only four victories were gained, but the defeats were cut to seven and the final position was tenth.

It was in that second year of his captaincy that Jackson hit the first two of his centuries and was chosen for the North v South Test trial at Old Trafford, but in the company of Jack Hobbs, Herbert Sutcliffe, Frank Woolley and Percy Chapman he failed to trouble the scorers in either of his innings. In the following year he also encountered the one big setback of his county regime.

Derbyshire ended the 1924 season back at the bottom of the table with a record (thirteen defeats and no wins in two dozen games) little better than that of 1920. The only match they raised hopes of winning was lost to Gloucestershire at Derby by eight runs after they had trailed by only five on first innings and had then recovered from a century stand by the visitors' opening pair to face a reasonable target of 167. There was still a chance when they went to lunch on the last day needing 26 with two wickets left, but that disappeared as Horsley ran himself out.

Bestwick (65 wickets), Morton (62) and Horsley (55) did themselves some justice during that wretched season, but much of the batting was abysmal. Apart from John Crommelin-Brown (33.66) and Wilfred Hill-Wood (27.66), who played a mere nine innings between them, only Jackson (24.42) and Cadman (23.82) averaged over twenty. Crommelin-Brown, who made irregular appearances from 1922 to 1926, rejoined Derbyshire as honorary secretary in 1945, staying until 1949, while in his final years as a housemaster at Repton. He was on the school's staff for nearly forty years, many of them in charge of cricket. In his younger days he also played football for the Corinthians and was no mean performer at billiards.

For the remaining six seasons with Guy Jackson as captain, Derbyshire improved steadily from fourteenth in 1925 to eleventh in 1926 (despite the departure of Bestwick and Horsley), fifth in 1927, then slipped to tenth in 1928 but rose to seventh in 1929 before another slight decline to ninth in 1930. Jackson set a captain's example in 1925 by scoring three centuries and heading the county's batting averages with the first of his four seasonal aggregates of more than a thousand runs. The only other Derbyshire player to get into four figures that year – he and Jackson were the first to do so for the county since the war – was Garnet Lee, an experienced newcomer who was to play a prominent part in the rise from the depths of 1920 and 1924 by scoring not far off ten thousand runs in his nine Derbyshire seasons before retiring after the 1933 campaign, at the age of forty-six, with the team on the brink of the dramatic rise to the top.

Garnet Morley Lee, a sound right-hand batsman and bowler of leg-breaks and googlies, joined the Nottinghamshire staff in 1905 (he was born at the village of Calverton, a few miles from Nottingham), but had to wait five years for his debut in the County Championship.

His first opponents were Sussex, against whom he was involved in a piece of cricketing history at Hove during the following 1911 season. That was the match in which Ted Alletson had his one big day of glory in scoring 189 out of 227 in ninety minutes, hitting three of his eight sixes, and four of his 23 fours, in one over from Ernest Killick that included two no-balls. Lee helped him to add 73 in forty minutes.

Two years later, Lee made his highest score, 200 not out in five hours, against Leicestershire at Trent Bridge, partnering Arthur Carr (169), who was to captain Notts from 1919 to 1934, in a second-wicket stand of 333 that lasted just over three hours. That 1913 season, however, was the only one in which Lee completed a thousand runs for his home county, and he spent two years qualifying for Derbyshire after losing his place in 1922 to William Whysall, a future England batsman who was only forty-three when, on Remembrance Day in 1930, he died from blood poisoning after injuring an elbow in a fall on a dance floor.

Lee's impact with Derbyshire was immediate. Though second to Guy Jackson in the county's batting averages in 1925, he exceeded his captain's aggregate of runs by 58 with 1,238. They both scored a century in sharing a third-wicket partnership of 162 at Weston-super-Mare, where Somerset, six runs behind on first innings, were beaten by three wickets with three minutes to spare. In 1926, Lee made his biggest score for Derbyshire, 191 against Kent at Derby, and in the next year, when he topped the county's bowling averages with 72 wickets at 17.61 each (he was sixth in the national list), he produced his best all-round display in scoring 100 not out, taking twelve wickets for 143 runs (5-65 and 7-78) and holding two catches in a nine-wicket victory at Northampton. He also took three Glamorgan wickets in four balls at Swansea that season, but was relieved of regular bowling when Tommy Mitchell, of whom more in another chapter, arrived on the scene.

Early in 1928 Lee toured Jamaica with Lionel Tennyson's team, and later that year played for the North against the South at Bournemouth. The next main highlights of his second career occurred in 1931, when Northamptonshire again suffered heavily at his hands. At Derby, he punished them for 173; at Northampton he scored an unbeaten 141 in a declared total of 217 for six, hitting V W C Jupp for eight sixes – three of them off consecutive deliveries. Vallance William Crisp Jupp, who also played for Sussex, was not normally an adversary to be trifled with. He was a Test player who ten times did the double, five times performed the hat-trick, once took all ten wickets in an innings, and altogether claimed more than 1,600. It was just not his day. Lee and Albert Alderman, who made only 39 of the 156 they added in almost two and a half hours, were both missed off Jupp's bowling before getting into double figures, and Lee had another escape at 36. The other key man in that match – of whom, with Alderman, also more later – was Leslie Townsend, who did the hat-trick. He took 8-45 and 4-10 as Northants collapsed for 90 and 56.

There were two other centuries at Northampton – 155 in 1928 and 128 in 1933 – among the sixteen Lee scored for Derbyshire (twenty-two in all first-class cricket). He showed a liking for Essex's bowling too, and his third hundred off their attack, 130 at Chesterfield in 1932, came in the club's record sixth-wicket stand of 212 with Stan Worthington (another featured more prominently in subsequent chapters), who missed a century by seven runs. Lee's partnership of 170 with Alf Pope against Leicestershire at Chesterfield in 1933 also broke the county's record, but is now down to fourth place.

Lee became Longton's professional and coach in the Staffordshire League after finally leaving the top-class game with 14,858 runs (9,652 of them in 386 innings for Derbyshire) at an average of nearly twenty-six, 397 wickets (313 for Derbyshire) costing a fraction over twenty-eight runs each, and 156 catches (87 for Derbyshire). He was an umpire in 177 County Championship matches from 1935 to 1949, when he resigned due to his wife's illness, and he coached at Repton for several years during the Second World War while L B Blaxland, another former Derbyshire player, was in one of his two spells in charge of cricket there. Lee was in his eighty-ninth year when he died at Newark in February, 1976.

It was under the guidance of Blaxland and Lee that Donald Carr developed into one of the best schoolboy all-rounders of his day and went on to become the scorer of most runs in a season for Derbyshire (2,165 at 48.11 in 1959) during his eight seasons as the county's captain. Blaxland, christened Lionel Bruce but known as 'Bill', was a master at Repton from 1922 to 1958, when he retired to take holy orders and become rector of Tansley, then vicar at Doveridge. He made the first of his intermittent appearances, just nineteen, for Derbyshire as an amateur in 1925, and the last one in 1947 when he captained the side against the South Africans in the match at Derby in which Ian Smith, a leg-break bowler who was the tourists' youngest player at twenty-one, achieved a feat then unique in English first-class cricket. In four overs and five balls, Smith took six wickets for only one run as Derbyshire's last seven wickets fell while the score staggered from 30 to 32, polishing off their second innings with a hat-trick. Even then the Springboks had to struggle for a three-wicket victory after losing half their side for 39.

The previous cheapest six wickets in a Derbyshire innings had been claimed at a cost of three runs by Lancashire's Dick Barlow (including a hat-trick) at Derby in 1881, and by George Macaulay, of Yorkshire, at Hull in 1921. A chap named Cossick had taken 6-1 for Victoria against Tasmania at Melbourne in the 1868-69 Australian season, but he had required 85 deliveries to do it, as against Smith's 29, and in a very dubious first-class match. The only other case of a bowling average as low as 0.16 being recorded for a single innings in a first-class game occurred at Bahawalpur in February 1958, when Israr Ali's 6-1, coupled with Raizmood's 3-5, skittled Dacca University for 39, the smallest total in Pakistan that season, in a Quaid-I-Azam Trophy semi-final. Bahawalpur went on to win the trophy for the second time in four years.

Ian Smith's deadly spell against Derbyshire was surpassed when Tony Merrick, of Warwickshire, did the hat-trick in taking six wickets in ten balls without having a run scored off him at Derby in 1988, but they altogether cost him 29. Rain stopped play shortly after Derbyshire's fourth wicket had fallen at 161; within three and a half overs of the resumption they were all out for 166. Devon Malcolm countered with six wickets for Derbyshire, four of them in seven deliveries, and in the home side's second innings New Zealander John Wright's twenty-seventh and last century for the county did most to earn a draw despite the loss of Kim Barnett with an injury, suffered in an intervening Sunday game, that delayed his Test debut.

Warwickshire were also the opposition when, in 1933, 'Bill' Blaxland, who hailed from Shrewsbury, made his top score of 64 in first-class cricket. He played mostly for good club teams, notably the Friars, before losing an eye while playing for the Cryptics in Portugal. At football, he turned out at wing-half (midfield in modern terminology) for Oxford University in the 1920-21 season, and for the Corinthians. He was seventy-eight when he died in Kent in 1976.

12. Talent from the Nursery

The best thing Derbyshire did as they sought to rise above the also-rans and climb onto the title trail was to form a nursery for the development of new talent.

This was originally established shortly before the First World War under the coaching of Henry Blacklidge, a former Surrey left-hander, but he was killed on active service in Mesopotamia in May, 1917. Special subscriptions were raised to restart the nursery soon after the war, and for two years Sam Cadman supervised it while also continuing to play for the county. That, however, was not an ideal arrangement because he obviously could not devote his full attention to it, so for the next three years it was put under the control of Fred Tate, the former Sussex and England bowler who had been coaching at Trent College.

Tate had many fine performances to his credit during a first-class playing career that lasted from 1888 to 1905, but he has been best remembered for his involvement in one of the most dramatic of Test finishes in the match between England and Australia at Old Trafford in 1902. Not a happy involvement, though that was his most successful season for his county. Already a controversial late choice to the exclusion of George Hirst, he dropped a crucial catch given by Joe Darling, the Australian captain, straight after being moved to field in the deep, a position entirely foreign to him because he usually stood in the slips. This move was as a result of a request to England's captain, Archie MacLaren, by Len Braund, who was bowling at the time and wanted his Somerset colleague Lionel Palairet to cross over to square-leg when Darling, a left-hander, and Syd Gregory changed ends in taking a single.

The runs the Australian fourth-wicket pair added after that lapse were to prove decisive, for they alone got into double figures in a total of 86 which left England needing only 124 for victory – but on a treacherous pitch with rain threatening. More wickets fell cheaply in the anxiety to press on before the storm broke, and the ninth one went down with just eight runs required. At that point the weather did hold up play – for threequarters of an hour before Wilfred Rhodes was joined by Tate, who had taken two wickets for only seven runs in the five overs allowed him during Australia's second-innings collapse. Tate snicked the first ball he received for four, blocked the second, let the third go by, but was bowled by the next to give the tourists victory – and the rubber – by three runs. A few minutes later the rain returned with an intensity that would have made further play impossible.

Fred Tate had two sons who followed him into county cricket. Maurice, also of Sussex and England, was one of the game's greatest-hearted bowlers, taker of 2,784 wickets at an average cost of just over eighteen from 1912 to 1937. 'Chubby,' as he was known to his many friends and admirers, revealed that he fulfilled his father's greatest ambition when he was also chosen for England, for it gave him the opportunity, which he took in such splendid style, to offset the costly mistakes Fred had made in Manchester. The other son, the lesser-known Cecil, a left-hand batsman and slow left-arm bowler, played in four matches for Derbyshire in 1928, then in seven more for Warwickshire before becoming the Sidmouth club's professional in Devon for the last few pre-war years. He was afterwards the licensee at several public houses in Derby and Burton, following his father at the White Lion in the brewery town.

When Fred Tate retired from coaching at the Derbyshire nursery, Bill Bestwick took charge for a year, after which Cadman was reappointed direct from ending his playing career. Cadman was in his fiftieth year, like Bestwick, when he took part in his last match – his only appearance of 1926, against Kent at Chatham. Inevitably, considering the differing views there are to be had on coaching, Cadman's methods did not satisfy everyone, but he achieved such excellent results that Major Eardley-Simpson, writing on the eve of the 1936 title season, commented: 'With the exception of Elliott and Storer, all the present professionals have come via the nursery since Cadman has been in control, and there are more still in reserve.' He added:

'The nursery has been the finest investment ever made by the county committee, and one trembles to think where we should have been now without it. The county has owed more than I can ever express to two men for their work in this direction. In the first place, Captain Evelyn Wright has used all his great influence in the county in getting financial support. In every way his assistance has been always at the service of the club, and his enthusiasm has never flagged. And then we have had the great good fortune to have the Reverend Henry Ellison to lead our Second XI and Club and Ground sides for many years. What he had done is quite beyond my power to tell. A great leader himself, he has the flair for spotting a good player almost at sight, and his advice has been even more important than his leadership on the field.'

After giving up playing in first-class cricket, Samuel William Anthony Cadman combined his coaching – part of which took him to the Wanderers club in Johannesburg – with assisting his local club, Glossop, in the Lancashire and Cheshire League. He turned out for their second team at the age of seventy, only five years before his death, which was announced while Derbyshire were opening their 1952 season against Middlesex at Lord's. His service with Derbyshire dated back to the first year of the twentieth century. He gained a regular place in the first team four years after being taken onto the staff, and held it until 1925.

A steady, often dependable batsman, he totalled 14,078 runs, at an average in the early twenties, and his medium-pace bowling brought him 807 wickets at just over twenty-five runs each. As also holder of nearly three hundred catches, he was an all-rounder essential to the county's cause during some of their most difficult years. At the time he retired he had played in more games for Derbyshire than anybody else, twenty-five ahead of Arthur Morton at 375, but he is now well down a list headed by Derek Morgan with 540.

His most successful seasons were those of 1908, when he was second in Derbyshire's batting averages with 942 runs at 26.91 and top of the bowling with 55 wickets at 19.29 runs apiece; 1909, when he exceeded a thousand runs for the first time; 1910, when he had his biggest seasonal tally of 67 wickets (23.67); and 1911, when he headed the county's batting with his best aggregate of 1,036 runs at 29.60 and represented the Players against the Gentlemen at Scarborough.

In 1905, he was largely responsible for the fright Derbyshire gave Joe Darling's Australian team. He took 5-94 in the tourists' first innings of 253, then top-scored with 66 in the county's second innings. Set 337 to win by a declaration, Derbyshire had 200 on the board for the loss of only four wickets, but the remaining six fell with a clatter for the addition of 31 mainly to the pace of Bert Cotter (6-63). In 1913, Cadman dismissed seven Essex batsmen for 39 runs at Derby, the last five of them for 19, and rounded off his best all-round match performance with innings of 66 and 76. A year later, he captured three Somerset wickets in four balls at Taunton. He hit seven of his eight centuries before the 1914-18 war. The last one, 125 not out, was scored during the bleak season of 1924 at Northampton, where four years earlier he had taken his biggest number of wickets in one match, fourteen for 104 runs.

Harry Elliott and Harry Storer Junior, the two members of the team that rose to become champions who did not graduate through the nursery, both had the misfortune to be brought into the Derbyshire side in the literally pointless season of 1920 that *Wisden* cautiously described as 'perhaps the most dismal record of any county since the Championship came into existence'. Perhaps? No doubt about it. Such was the poverty-stricken state of the batting, Elliott's 299 runs in twenty-eight innings, with a top score of 42 not out and an average of under sixteen, hoisted him to the exalted position of third in the county's list behind Oliver (546 at 22.75) and Cadman (527 at 15.96). Storer was down to seventeenth, averaging 6.68 with 147 runs in twenty-four innings and a top score of 32.

Elliott was recommended to Derbyshire by Sir Archibald White, who had captained Yorkshire to the 1912 county title, while working for Sir Joseph Laycock at Wiseton Hall in Nottinghamshire. He acquitted himself well as wicketkeeper, and was not out in both his innings, when he made his debut against Essex, but Derbyshire were defeated by six wickets. Johnny Douglas turned in one of the best bowling displays seen at Derby that season when the home team were whisked out for 103 in a little over two hours, his 8-39 surpassed only by Arthur Morton's 8-37 against Somerset.

From that personally creditable entry onto the county scene until the end of the 1939 season, the last one before another world war, Elliott averaged about sixty dismissals a year, creating in 1933 a club record of 87 (66 caught,

21 stumped) that he improved by three (68 caught, 22 stumped) in 1935. When he finally retired in 1947 he had 1,202 dismissals (898 caught, 304 stumped) to his name – a total that had then been exceeded by only four other wicket-keepers. Those ahead of him, with totals, like Elliott's, as amended with the reassessments of matches rated first-class, were Herbert Strudwick (Surrey), 1,497; Surrey-born Fred Huish (Kent's predecessor to Les Ames, 'Hopper' Levett, Godfrey Evans and Alan Knott) 1,310; David Hunter, Yorkshire's successor to his brother Joseph, 1,253; and Harry Butt (Sussex), 1,228.

Of Elliott's truly grand total of victims, 1,179 were gobbled up for Derbyshire (883 caught, 296 stumped). That made him the county's leading wicketkeeper until 1,304 (1,157 caught, 147 stumped) were accumulated by Bob Taylor, whose overall tally of 1,649 (1,473 caught, 176 stumped), which includes fifty-seven Tests, has made him the current world leader ahead of the 1,527 (1,270; 257) of John Murray (Middlesex and England) and Strudwick.

The word 'finally' has to be used when referring to Elliott's retirement because he originally hung up his pads and gloves to become an umpire for the first post-war season of 1946, but he increased his number of appearances for Derbyshire to 520 (a total only Morgan has overhauled) by making a four-game comeback in an emergency after rejoining the county as coach. At that time, in 1947, he was said to be fifty-one, but it transpired twenty years later that he had actually been almost fifty-six – to be exact, 55 years and 276 days old on the last day of his final match, against Warwickshire at Derby. That took from Bill Bestwick (50 years, 161 days) the distinction of being the oldest player to appear for the county. In 1967, at a reunion of the 1936 champions, Elliott disclosed that he had been born – at Scarcliffe, near Bolsover – not in 1895, as hitherto publicised, but in 1891.

Elliott held the last seven of his catches, and made his final stumping, during that temporary return during the late July and early August of 1947. In the first of his four matches Derbyshire defeated Nottinghamshire by only fifteen runs at Ilkeston with the help of a George Pope hat-trick. In the others they lost to Surrey at The Oval, beat Northamptonshire at Rushden, and drew at home with Warwickshire. His nephew Charlie Elliott kept wicket when he missed a defeat at Leicester between the last two of those matches.

Harry Elliott, who owned a sports outfitting business at 44, Osmaston Road, opposite the well-known Derby landmark known as The Spot, in partnership with Sammy Crooks, the Derby County and England winger, returned to the umpires' list in 1952 and he had stood in 203 County Championship matches by the time he left it after the 1963 season. A man of great integrity, he made a most courageous decision when he changed his mind after giving Gilbert Parkhouse out for 99 in response to a loud appeal by Fred Titmus, the Middlesex and England spinner, for a catch at the wicket. Realising on second thought that the Glamorgan batsman had hit the ground and not the ball, Elliott recalled him, and Parkhouse progressed to his then top score of 182 before wicketkeeper Leslie Compton was definitely adjudged to have caught him off Titmus. It was the first century by a Glamorgan player at Lord's for twenty-one years – and the Welsh county went on to win by twenty-two runs.

Another H Elliott was on the first-class umpires' list at the same time as his Derbyshire namesake. He was Harold Elliott, of Lancashire, who, by a quirk of coincidence, was one of the officials in the first and last games of Harry's playing comeback. Harold had been on Lancashire's playing staff from 1927 to 1938, also as a wicketkeeper, but, with Test player George Duckworth and his deputy Bill Farrimond gaining preference, he had been restricted to one Championship appearance, against Surrey at Old Trafford in 1930. While still a Lancashire player, in his last two seasons at Old Trafford, he had umpired in Minor Counties matches before being appointed to the first-class list in 1939.

Three times between the two world wars Harry Elliott equalled the six dismissals in an innings Tommy Foster had made in his first game as Derbyshire's wicketkeeper at The Oval in 1883 – a then record for the county, but subsequently raised to seven by Bob Taylor – and on one of those occasions, against Lancashire in Manchester in 1935, he set the club record of ten in a match (eight caught, two stumped) which Taylor was to share. His other innings of six dismissals were at Worcester in 1931, and against Middlesex at Derby in 1932. He claimed five victims in an innings ten times. Twice he had eight in a match, and there were ten games in which he achieved the seven dismissals that had been the club record created by Jim Disney in 1882 (when only thirteen Yorkshire wickets fell) and equalled five times by Joe Humphries.

When Elliott first sent back six batsmen in an innings only two wicketkeepers, 'Tiger' Smith, for Warwickshire against Derbyshire at Edgbaston in 1926, and Lancashire's Farrimond, had accounted for as many as seven. More than forty others have done so since then. The world record was boosted to eight (all caught) by Wally Grout, the Australian Test player, for Queensland in 1960. It was equalled by David East (Essex) and Steve Marsh (Kent) – then by the Australian Tim Zoehrer, against Surrey, after Pakistani Tahir Rashid had increased it to nine (eight caught) while playing for Habib Bank in late 1992. When Wayne James, the Matabeleland captain, caught seven and stumped two in the Mashonaland Country Districts first innings in the Lonrho Logan Cup final at Bulawayo in 1996, he went on to break the world record for wicketkeeping victims in one match with four more catches that took him one dismissal ahead of the twelve claimed as far back as 1888 by Ted Pooley, for Surrey against Sussex at The Oval, and equalled by Australians Don Tallon and Brian Taber. Not content with all that, James scored 99 runs in both Matabeleland innings – caught on the brink of a century first time, then left unbeaten one short when his team won by six wickets.

At Test level, Bob Taylor equalled the record of seven (all caught) dismissals in an innings set by Wasim Bari, of Pakistan – and since also matched by New Zealander Ian Smith and Ridley Jacobs, of the West Indies – on his way to a record ten in the Golden Jubilee Test with India at Bombay in 1980. Adam Gilchrist also took ten catches twenty years later, for Australia against New Zealand at Hamilton, but by then Gloucestershire's 'Jack' Russell, watched by Taylor, had held on to eleven (all but three of them off the bowling of a Derbyshire pair, Devon Malcolm and Dominic Cork) in England's 1995 match with South Africa in Johannesburg.

Harry Elliott's first selection for an MCC tour was also to South Africa, in 1927-28. It brought him an unhappy experience similar to that encountered by Humphries when Joe toured Australia. Guy Jackson, Elliott's county captain, was invited to lead the team, but shortly before the departure date he had to drop out through illness. If he had made the trip Will Taylor, Derbyshire's secretary, would have accompanied him as manager. Unfortunately for Elliott, the replacement for Jackson was also a wicketkeeper – Yorkshireman Ronald Stanyforth, an Army officer who had recently toured South America under the captaincy of 'Plum' Warner. As a result, the Derbyshire man's Test debut was delayed until the final match of the series in Durban – and he would also have missed that one if Stanyforth had not been injured. Elliott took his belated chance well, conceding only four byes while just over 400 runs were scored, but South Africa won comfortably to square the rubber after having been two down. Elliott could be miserly indeed when it came to byes. He did not concede even one in twenty-five completed innings in the title year of 1936.

In the 1933 season that preceded the tour of South Africa, Elliott provided some inspiration for an innings victory by also allowing no byes in the match with Leicestershire at Loughborough, but his main contribution on that occasion was to make his highest score of 94. Captaining the side for the first time, he promoted himself in the batting order as night-watchman and partnered Leslie Townsend, who made his own top score of 233, in a stand of 222 that was then the biggest for the county's third wicket. Elliott lacked style as a batsman, specialising in his 'cow' shot to leg, but he was dogged and valued performer, often difficult to dismiss.

Back home a few months after his return from South Africa, Elliott was kept out of the first Test against the West Indies by Harry Smith, of Gloucestershire, but he was recalled for the next match at Old Trafford. That broke his sequence of 185 games for Derbyshire since his debut, but, after also missing the final match of that 1928 season, against Lancashire at Burton-upon-Trent, because of a finger injury suffered at Blackpool, his admirable consistency enabled him to put together a further run of 226 appearances before injury caused another interruption in 1937. Although playing in that 226th consecutive match, Elliott had to hand over the wicketkeeping to a rarely-required deputy, Albert Alderman, after damaging a hand while batting.

So, if that England game were allowed to count in his sequence, it could be said that only the last match of 1928 interrupted what would otherwise have been 413 successive appearances from 1920 to 1937, a truly remarkable record. Jimmy Binks, the Yorkshire wicketkeeper, had an unbroken run of 412 Championship games before announcing his retirement after the 1969 season. In the same year, Ken Suttle, the Sussex all-rounder who had been Bob Taylor's first victim in top-class cricket, reached 423 consecutive Championship appearances before he was omitted from the match with Surrey at the beginning of August.

Having won both the first two games against the West Indies in 1928 by an innings, England called upon another wicketkeeper, the vociferous Lancastrian George Duckworth, for the third and final Test at The Oval, where another innings victory was England's biggest of the series. Though not selected again by his country at home, Elliott completed his international career by playing in two of the three Tests during the 1933-34 tour of India, on which he was accompanied by his county clubmate Leslie Townsend.

Derbyshire were indeed fortunate to have five players of such excellence as William Storer, Joe Humphries, Harry Elliott, George Dawkes and Bob Taylor to be their main wicketkeepers from the beginning of the 1890s to the mid-1980s. Of that select group, only Dawkes did not also keep wicket for England, though he almost certainly would have done so but for a world war and a chap down in Kent named Godfrey Evans. Ironically, another Kent wicketkeeper was also in the way before Taylor was given his long-overdue chance of an extended run in the England side, the vacancy opening up when Alan Knott was among the players who accepted lucrative contracts with the Australian tycoon Kerry Packer.

Dawkes did, however, play in an unofficial Test. With his cap hopes dashed when Yorkshire's Don Brennan was surprisingly preferred as rival to Evans, who had been showing some signs of staleness, for a Test trial at Edgbaston, he had to settle for taking part in the Commonwealth team's 1949-50 tour of India, Pakistan and Ceylon (now Sri Lanka), for which George Pope was also chosen. Even then he found his opportunities limited – partly due to a back injury, but mainly because Australian Jock Livingston, the Northants left-hand batsman who captained the side, kept wicket so soundly in addition to completing a thousand runs on the tour. As a result, Dawkes played in only just over half of the first-class games, and in only the fifth and last of the unofficial Tests, which India won in Madras to clinch a series from which the MCC had opted out. He totalled only a dozen runs and made one stumping.

Acquired from Leicestershire, with whom he had entered county cricket against Notts at Worksop in 1937 as surely the youngest wicketkeeper in that grade when not quite seventeen, Dawkes joined Derbyshire too late in life to get near the number of games played for the county by Elliott and Taylor (third in the list with 514), but he made 289 of his 392 appearances in succession before a knee injury, for which he had to have a cartilage operation, forced him out during his final season of 1961. That sequence was twice broken as far as wicketkeeping was concerned, however, for against Surrey at

Derby in 1954 and Yorkshire at Bradford in 1957 he could not take his place behind the stumps because of injuries received while batting. Gerry Wyatt, who, with Bob Taylor following Dawkes, had fewer than a dozen first-team opportunities, took over on the first of those occasions, having been included in the side as a batsman, and Laurie Johnson, a Barbados-born batsman, deputised on the second.

Dawkes was forced to miss all but five of Derbyshire's remaining twenty-two fixtures after breaking down late on the first day of the match with Lancashire at Old Trafford early in June 1961, but he made a most fitting farewell against Surrey at Chesterfield that August. Though in considerable pain when his injury recurred, he held six typically brilliant catches as the fading former champions of a record seven successive seasons (1952-58), who were without Peter May, Ken Barrington and Tony Lock on Test duty, were beaten by Derbyshire for the first time in eight years. There was also a catch for Bob Taylor in that match – a superb one at mid-off when he fielded as a substitute for Harold Rhodes.

With Leicestershire, Dawkes was both preceded and succeeded as wicket-keeper by 'Paddy' Corrall, who was later to be among the newcomers to the list of first-class umpires when Harry Elliott rejoined it. Having become the regular choice in preference to Corrall in 1938, Dawkes kept his place for the last pre-war season, but service in the RAF made him unavailable when county cricket was resumed in 1946, and the veteran Corrall promptly snapped up the chance to re-establish himself. Although Leicestershire wanted him back as a batsman, Dawkes was determined to keep on keeping wicket, so when he was demobilised he readily accepted Derbyshire's invitation to answer the pressing problem that had provoked Harry Elliott's temporary recall, with Walter Fullwood, Pat Vaulkhard and Denis Smith having in turn shouldered that responsibility.

As a batsman, Dawkes was the heaviest scorer among Derbyshire wicket-keepers since William Storer. He backed up his career total of 895 catches and 147 stumpings (770 and 105 for Derbyshire) with almost ten thousand runs for the county and nearly 11,500 in all, if at an average of under twenty. A few days before making his debut for Derbyshire against Yorkshire at Scarborough in August 1947, he scored 102 and 53 not out in a Services game at Lord's against the Royal Navy, who were beaten by seven wickets. He scored just one century for Derbyshire, 143 against Hampshire at Burton in 1954, but he might have had another the following year – and the fastest of the season at that.

He admitted he never gave a thought to the 100-guinea prize for the quickest hundred as he smote 86, including three sixes and eight fours, in 66 minutes against his former county at Ashby-de-la-Zouch. 'I just kept having a slash and enjoying myself,' he said after falling to a well-taken catch on the boundary by the bespectacled Mike Smith, the Oxford Blue and double international (cricket and rugby) who later played for Warwickshire, captained England, and became one the game's influential backroom figures. The time Dawkes needed to beat was 92 minutes, by George Emmett, the Gloucestershire captain, but Ray Smith, of Essex, later lowered it to 73 minutes.

It was in that match with Leicestershire that Dawkes, besides being in the long line of distinguished Derbyshire wicketkeepers, had something else in common with William Storer, Joe Humphries, Harry Elliott and Bob Taylor by shedding his pads and gloves to do a bit of bowling. With only five minutes left for play, and a draw inevitable, he became Derbyshire's eleventh bowler when the field was solemnly rearranged for him to deliver an over that cost nine runs. Only once before had all the Derbyshire players bowled in one innings – in 1902 at Worcester, where Humphries, who bowled a batsman out on two other occasions, delivered five overs for nineteen runs in taking one of the seven wickets that fell as the home side batted throughout the third day's play for 463 after the first two had been rained off. Fred Bowley and the brothers Harry and Reginald Foster each scored a century.

Harry Elliott and Bob Taylor were also far from rivalling Bill Storer as a bowler, but, if considerably stretching a point, Elliott could claim to have bowled unchanged through one innings. Yorkshire needed just four runs for victory at Scarborough in 1935, and Arthur Wood and Hedley Verity obtained them off three balls from Elliott. On several occasions, Bob Taylor was put on to open the bowling for Derbyshire when the opposition wanted only a few runs to win, and he was even given a couple of overs at his unpretentious medium pace as the Test of 1982 with India in Madras petered out into a draw. At Portsmouth in 1973, he conceded Hampshire's winning four off the only ball that was necessary in their second innings – and the player who struck it was none other than Derby-born Bob Stephenson, the wicketkeeper who had changed counties after finding his path to a regular Derbyshire place barred by Taylor.

In 1984, the last of his two dozen seasons with Derbyshire, Stoke-born Taylor took his one wicket as a bowler at Gloucester. Brought into the attack while the home side were being fed runs to hurry a declaration, he had Andy Stovold caught near the boundary as the opening batsman was aiming to hit a four for his century. Derbyshire just managed to hold out for a draw after being set to get 270 in 85 minutes.

For turning the arm over, William Storer was more closely approached by his nephew Harry, who, by a most remarkable coincidence, took exactly the same number of first-class wickets as a bowler, 232, as he did – and at a slightly better average, 32.43 to 33.89. At medium pace, Harry had his match to remember at Chesterfield in 1922, when his best return of 7-26 included a hat-trick and inspired a 53-run defeat of Northamptonshire, but it was as a batsman that he was of most value to the county – after, that is, he had shown the strength of character to battle back into favour from the utter collapse of his game in Derbyshire's deplorable season of 1924. Of the team's many individual batting failures that year, none were more acute than those of Storer and fellow footballing cricketer Wilfred Carter. Major Eardley Simpson described Carter as 'a complete failure', and declared Storer to be 'even worse'.

Carter had been Derbyshire's most successful batsman two seasons earlier, when he had made his highest score of 145 at Leicester in raising the county's eighth-wicket record to 182 (beaten in 1996 when Dominic Cork and Karl Krikken added 198 at Old Trafford) in association with A H M Jackson (75), later Sir Anthony Mather-Jackson.

Carter scored 100 not out against Northamptonshire at Chesterfield the next season, when he was runner-up to Wilfred Hill-Wood in the averages, but in the wholesale decline of 1924 he slumped to sixteenth with fewer than three hundred runs in twenty-five innings (highest score 57; average a fraction over twelve). He left the staff after that season, and although he returned in 1926 he did nothing in his five matches to warrant being kept on. He ended the 1920s as coach at Repton, and also spent a few years in Scotland as the Drumpellier club's professional.

If, as the good major maintained, anybody could be worse than a complete failure, then it would be difficult to imagine that a player of normally high-class ability ever managed that seeming impossibility to a greater degree than did the hapless Harry Storer in 1924. Here was the man who in the previous few seasons had overcome the considerable handicap of being pitchforked into the 1920 maelstrom by showing encouraging signs – including, besides his hat-trick, a maiden century (126) against Warwickshire at Derby – of upholding the high family traditions set by his father and uncle. Here, too, was the man who was to retire at the end of the 1936 title season as the scorer of 13,513 first-class runs and with a total of eighteen centuries that had then been exceeded for the county by only Leslie Townsend (19) and L G Wright (20). Yet in 1924 Storer had a wretched top score of only eighteen in twenty-six innings, scraping together 178 runs for a pitiable average of 6.84.

Compare that with his most productive season of 1929, when he averaged 36.71 from a total of 1,652, emulated uncle William by hitting two hundreds in one match (119 and 100 against Sussex at Derby), and, in scoring the first of his two double-centuries (28 fours in his 209), helped to boost the county's first-wicket record to the still-existing 322, in five minutes over four hours, against Essex at Derby. The steady Joe Bowden, Wilfred Hill-Wood's partner in the county's previous largest opening stand of 206 at Bath in 1923, progressed from 94 when Storer was out to 120, the biggest of his four Derbyshire centuries, before treading on his wicket. It contained a dozen fours.

Bowden made his debut for Derbyshire in 1909, but left to play in the Central Lancashire League before rejoining the county in 1921. He altogether scored 7,613 first-class runs at an average of 20.57 up to his retirement in

1930, playing his last match in Bristol when almost into his forty-seventh year. He afterwards coached at Felstead School. In its 1927 edition, the *Derbyshire Cricket Guide* stated:

'Bowden is of the stolid, painstaking type of opening batsman, well calculated to take the edge off the bowling be it ever so good. He is a very difficult man to dismiss, for he never believes in taking risks at the outset of an innings. On many occasions on a difficult wicket he has kept his end up whilst the majority of the side have made a hurried exit, but he has also shown enterprising qualities when the occasion warranted freedom.'

Harry Storer, whose big scores of 1929 also included 176 at Trent Bridge, headed Derbyshire's batting averages in seven years out of nine from 1926 and finished second in the two others. He twice averaged more than forty, and it was in one of the seasons, 1933, in which he was the runner-up (narrowly behind Leslie Townsend) that he achieved his best of 44.36. That was also the year in which, particularly strong on the leg side, he became the first to score a second double-century for Derbyshire, again against Essex at Derby. And to his 232, which contained twenty boundaries and lasted for more than five hours, he added an unbeaten 58 out of 135 in the second innings for a match aggregate of 290 as Derbyshire won by eight wickets with fifteen minutes of the extra half-hour to spare.

Six times Storer exceeded a thousand runs in a season, doing so in four successive years from 1928. In 1926, when his final batting average of 36.54 was the highest by a Derbyshire regular for more than twenty summers, he gave one of his finest all-round performances by scoring 132 against Somerset at Derby, partnering Jim Hutchinson (81) in a stand of 206 after the first three wickets had toppled for 48, and then taking 6-48 in the visitors' dismissal for 129. He did not bat again in that match, nor did he repeat his destruction with the ball, but he still had a crucial part to play. Derbyshire, having declined to enforce the follow-on, declared nearly 400 ahead following an opening century stand by Bowden (73 not out) and Garnet Lee (60), but Somerset's defiant last-wicket pair, Guy Earle (43) and Jim Bridges (15 not out) threatened to deny them victory. Stan Worthington bowled the final over, and off the second delivery Storer held the slip catch that ended Earle's resistance.

There were 213 other catches in the Storer repertoire, and he even pulled off a stumping on one of the rare occasions when Harry Elliott was not in his customary place.

All those runs, wickets and catches added up to quite an imposing record after the miseries of 1924 that caused him to be restricted to three innings – none notable and one runless – for Derbyshire in 1925 as he spent most of that season rebuilding his form and confidence in league cricket. It was the type of comeback that was only to be expected of an abrasive, combative character not renowned for his tolerance of the flagging spirit. Nor for nothing did Will Taylor rate him the best batsman he had seen play for the county during his long connection with it. Storer, he said, was 'good on any type of pitch, and with terrific determination'.

James Metcalf Hutchinson, Storer's partner in that recovery stand against Somerset, also has a special place in Derbyshire cricket history as arguably the finest of the county's cover-points; certainly one of the very best. And on top of that he achieved something special as far as the whole of first-class cricket is concerned, attaining a life century to cap his five with the bat. In August 1999, he overtook Rupert de Smidt, a former Western Province fast bowler who had died in 1986 at 103, to become the longest-lived former player, and he was only twenty-two days short of his 104th birthday when he died in Doncaster Royal Infirmary on 7 November, 2000. He had become the oldest living former county cricketer on 3 December, 1991 with the death, only a few days into his 100th year, of Willis Walker, a batsman who played for Nottinghamshire from 1913 to 1937. When Walker died Hutchinson had just turned 95, the year of his November 29 birthdate having been amended from 1897 to 1896 in the 1981 edition of *Wisden*, and in 1996 he became only the eighth former first-class cricketer, and the fourth English, known to have reached the age of 100.

Hutchinson was then living in the village of Thurnscoe, between Barnsley and Rotherham, having moved to South Yorkshire on ending his career with Derbyshire in 1931. That career began in the county's awful year of 1920, which he survived as a Derbyshire player – unlike no fewer than twenty-one of the record thirty-nine men called upon – to become what *Wisden* termed 'a gifted, if not always disciplined, batsman best known for his athleticism in the field'. He was introduced to the club by Joe Humphries after playing impressively for Bulcroft Colliery against a team the wicketkeeper took to play in a charity match in Yorkshire. The first of his five centuries with the bat was also the biggest – 143 against Leicestershire at Chesterfield in 1924, the year in which he made his one first-class appearance away from Derbyshire. It was for the Players against the Gentlemen at Stanley Park in Blackpool. He was unbeaten on 13 in a total of 200, but did not get the chance to bat again as the five runs the Players needed for victory in their second innings were knocked off in only one over, with only one wicket down.

For ten successive seasons Hutchinson was a regular member of the Derbyshire team despite form that in most of them was no more than ordinary with the bat and costly with his infrequently used off-breaks. His superb fielding was often his saving grace. He was at his best in 1927, when he scored two of his other centuries and had his top average of just over 27, and 1928, when he got within 67 runs of completing 1,000 for what would have been the only time. His 110 off Glamorgan at Chesterfield in 1927 came in a stand of 153 with Worthington (98) that set a record for any Derbyshire wicket against the Welsh county that stood for more than 30 years. The last of his first-class hundreds was his 138 against Somerset at Burton-upon-Trent in 1929. After that his output fell away sharply, and in his final season he cobbled together only 218 runs in fourteen innings at an average below seventeen.

One of seven children, Hutchinson came from a mining family. His brother Ben was decorated for his rescue work down the pit, and their father was under-manager at the Oxcroft colliery near Chesterfield when Jim went to work there full-time underground at the age of only fourteen. Jim was studying mining engineering when he received a telegram asking him to play against Sussex at Chesterfield. That was the first of the 255 first-class appearances for Derbyshire in which he scored just over seven thousand runs in the middle of the order at an average of nearly nineteen, took 31 wickets that cost over 40 runs each, held 96 catches, and made two stumpings as an emergency wicketkeeper. After retiring from first-class cricket he returned to mining, but continued playing for the Thurnscoe club until he was 66. He was involved in the opening of a new colliery at Markham Main, and later became safety manager at Hickleton Main near Rotherham – but then came the decline in the industry that so deeply saddened him.

He drove a car until his late nineties, attributing his longevity to ignoring all advice about avoiding fatty foods. He had bacon and eggs for breakfast, ate plenty of red meat, and had a particular liking for pork chops and onion rings.

13. Cricketing Footballers

Of the nineteen men who have played cricket for Derbyshire and Association football for Derby County, Harry Storer (the son, not the father) achieved most success at both games.

With the Rams, he was a promotion winner as both player and manager; with Derbyshire, he bowed out of county cricket after his seventeenth season of 1936 in which they were champions. At soccer he was capped twice by England, piloted Coventry City and Birmingham City to promotion before completing the treble with Derby, and took Birmingham to the League South title in the transitional season of 1945-46. He was also in charge when Birmingham reached the last four of the FA Cup in 1946 before losing to Derby, of all teams, after extra-time in a replay at Maine Road, Manchester, under the handicap of being reduced to ten men by injury to a key defender.

Although born (on 2 February 1898) not at Derby but West Derby, in that district of Liverpool while his father was a goalkeeper there for the Anfield club, Harry Storer firmly regarded himself as having Derbyshire roots. Both his parents were born in the county, and they took him to live at Holloway, near Matlock, when he was only four years old, then to Ripley at the age of ten. 'So,' he said, 'my whole background is in Derbyshire, and I would claim that, except for a freak of birth, I am a Derbyshire man.' He played soccer for Ripley Town and Eastwood before signing amateur forms for Notts County, then entered League football as Grimsby Town's centre-forward in a home defeat by Stockport County on the first day of the 1919-20 season.

That setback set the tone for one of the worst seasons in the Grimsby club's history. By the end of January they had won a mere four of 25 games and they gained only six more in finishing two points adrift at the foot of the Second Division. Storer played in all but six of their 42 matches and was their top scorer with a dozen of their paltry 34 goals. Then came the blackest season for Derbyshire cricket into which he was introduced the following summer. Few, if any, sportsmen can have had such a dismal entry into two spheres of professional sport, yet how triumphantly Storer emerged from the wreckage.

A reprieve for Grimsby was at hand. There was no room for them in the Second Division of 1920-21, nor for Lincoln City, the club that had finished immediately above them. But whereas Lincoln were cast out of the League, replaced by Cardiff City from the Southern League, Grimsby were admitted to the new Third Division with the rest of the clubs from Division One of the Southern League. Officially, the additional section was known as Division Three (South) despite the inclusion of Grimsby from an area even further north than Manchester, but that anomaly was done away with when the Mariners, with George Fraser, a former Lincoln player and manager, in charge, were switched to the Third Division (North) that came into existence for 1921-22. Lincoln City were brought back into the fold as another of its founder members.

By then, Harry Storer had been transferred to Derby County, helping to ease Grimsby's financial problems. The fee has been reported as £4,500, but while I was on the sports staff of the *Derby Evening Telegraph* I had access to a list that purported to give the correct amounts paid and received by the Rams for players during the inter-war period. This gave the figure as £2,500. Storer spent most of his playing days with the Rams in the wing-half position he had filled as a hard-working strong tackler for much of his last season with Grimsby, but for 1923-24 he returned to the forward line, at what was then known as inside-left, and was Derby's leading scorer. His two dozen goals in the League, plus three more in an FA Cup run that ended only after a third replay with Newcastle United, included four in succession in 39 minutes in the County's record 8-0 away win against Bristol City (the week after losing to them at home) and four more in a 6-0 Boxing Day defeat of Nelson (the day after losing away to that Lancashire club, who lost League membership to Chester seven years later).

A fortnight after the bitter disappointment of ending that season by being in the team that missed regaining First Division status by a fraction of a goal, Storer was in Paris making a scoring debut for England in a 3-1 victory over France. His Derby clubmate George Thornewell was in the same forward line, on the right wing, and another County colleague, full-back Tommy Cooper, was with him when he won his second cap, at left-half, in a 2-0 defeat by Ireland in Belfast three years later.

Derby's desperately narrow failure to get out of the Second Division in 1924 left them in third place with a goal average of 1.785 to the 1.800 that enabled Bury to squeeze into the second promotion place behind Leeds United – a difference of 0.015 of a goal. The Rams, with Storer one of the scorers, were 4-0 up against Leicester City at the Baseball Ground with the second half of their final match of the season barely twenty minutes old but there was no further scoring as, try as they might, they could not get that vital fifth goal.

Derby again finished third, but two points adrift of runners-up Manchester United, when Leicester were Division Two champions the following season, but it was third time lucky for them the next year under the new management of Geordie George Jobey, who was to be the club's most successful manager until Brian Clough stormed in from the North-East. They claimed the second spot three points behind the Wednesday, whom they twice defeated 4-1, and five clear of third-placed Chelsea. Storer, who had had to endure a three-month lay-off through injury the previous season, was an ever-present in that run towards promotion until another injury, on the day the Rams completed the double over their Sheffield rivals, kept him out of the last dozen games.

But for injury, which three years earlier had caused him to miss the FA Cup run that took the club to the brink of the first Wembley final (they conceded five goals to West Ham in the semi-final at Stamford Bridge after not letting in any in the previous four rounds), Storer would have joined the select band who have played more than 300 games for the County. As it was, he made 274 appearances, scoring 63 goals. He did get to the third century of matches for Derbyshire, totalling 302, and there would also have been more if football had not taken him away from his cricket. It could be said that he might well have had a better chance of also playing for England at cricket if, apart from the strong competition, his soccer had not intervened at crucial times. Otherwise he could have seriously come into the reckoning for an overseas tour during an English winter. Even a Test batsman as established as Denis Compton had to forgo a trip to South Africa because Arsenal had first claim on his services.

From Derby County, Storer moved to Burnley for £4,250 in February 1929 and helped them to shake off the threat of relegation from the First Division with his typically resolute displays in their last dozen games of that season. Having escaped the drop by only one point the year before, the Lancashire club improved to finish seven clear of Bury, who went down with Cardiff City, but the warning signs were all too evident. They had the worst defensive record in the top two divisions, leaking 103 goals, and that unenviable distinction was repeated as they let in 97 when they sank into Division Two with Everton the following season. The Goodison club bounced straight back, completing a prime treble by going on to win the First Division title and FA Cup in the next two seasons, but Burnley had to wait seventeen years for their return to the top flight.

By one of the freaks of fixture lists, Derby County were the visitors for Burnley's First Division farewell in April 1930 and also for the first game at Turf Moor after promotion in August 1947. Storer, whose wholehearted style had again made him injury prone, was restored to the attack against the Rams for only his third first-team appearance of that 1929-30 season, and he played his usual energetic part in a too-late 6-2 victory over the League's runners-up to Sheffield Wednesday. Derby again scored twice when they went back there on the first Tuesday evening of the second post-war season, but on that occasion they kept their defence intact to douse Burnley expectations of a happy home return to the top flight heightened by a win at Portsmouth on the opening day.

As at Derby, Harry Storer remained a first choice at Burnley right up to his departure. In April 1933, aged thirty-three, he embarked upon his career in management with the first of the two spells he spent at Coventry each side of his three and a half years with Birmingham. Only one full season after leaving Coventry for the second time, he obtained his release from a cricket coaching appointment at a Clacton holiday camp to make his football comeback with County in 1955, chosen from more than forty applicants, and at the second attempt led them out of the Third Division (North) into which they had fallen for the first time in their history. In those days when a club had to be champions to get out of either the North or South sections of Division Three, the Rams went close as runners-up the year before, and in both those seasons they broke the club's scoring record with three-figure totals. Storer was unable to take them any further, but by the time he retired in May 1962 he had the added satisfaction of having cut their overdraft to nearly a third of the £60,000 at which he had found them. He died in Derby five years later, on the first day of September in 1967, at the age of sixty-nine.

Storer was one of three Derbyshire cricketers and Derby County footballers who were capped by England at soccer, but the two others played in only five cricket games for the county between them – John Goodall in two, Horatio Stratton Carter in three. Soccer, however, was the strong suit for that distinguished pair, who, like Storer, both captained the Rams. Goodall, one of the Invincibles of Preston North End, who in 1888-89 were the first champions of the Football League without losing a match and winners of the FA Cup without conceding a goal, played fourteen times for England and 238 for Derby County.

Raich Carter, a pre-war League champion and Cup winner with Sunderland and Cup winner again with Derby in the first post-war final, made thirty appearances for England (thirteen of them in full internationals) and 149 for Derby (83 of them in League or Cup) after 279 games and 130 goals for Sunderland. Goodall scored 85 goals for the Rams, Carter 107 (57 of them in 66 games as a war-time guest).

Goodall, who later played for Hertfordshire after finding his way from Derby to Watford, where he was player and manager, via New Brighton and Glossop, scored all but two of his 38 runs for Derbyshire on his debut in the defeat of Yorkshire at Leeds in 1895, and although he failed on his second appearance, against Warwickshire at Derby the following season, he was again on the winning side.

Carter, a right-hand batsman but slow left-arm bowler, totalled only eight runs in four innings during matches at Stourbridge, Northampton and The Oval in the June of 1946, but took the wickets of Worcestershire's top scorers, Eddie Cooper (80) and Ronald Bird (47), both bowled. Worcestershire won by an innings, but the two other games in which Carter played were drawn – with Northants mainly because of time lost to rain; with Surrey, who finished five runs short at 179-8, following a hold-up just before the close when Walter Fullwood, the Derbyshire wicketkeeper, needed attention after being struck on the body by a ball from Cliff Gladwin.

The sight of the Surrey captain, Nigel Bennett, rushing out to the crease with about a minute to go, only to be promptly bowled by Gladwin, was one of the two main memories Carter carried from his county cricket farewell. The other concerned his own captain, Denis Smith, who was standing in for

Gilbert Hodgkinson while Stan Worthington, the senior professional, was also absent. For Smith it was a painful and most unpleasant memory. A waitress tripped in serving lunch and upset a plate of hot soup over him.

Carter's introduction to top cricket came too late. He admitted he was 'no match for the wiles of the first-class bowler who used his brains, and at thirty I was too old to start learning'. But he was a real force as a batsman in his youth, so much so that he was known as 'the Gilbert Jessop of Durham cricket.' In one match he raced to a half-century in thirteen minutes. In another, playing for the Hendon club in his home district of Sunderland, he scored 106 of his 135 in twenty-five hits, smashing four windows in the houses of an adjoining street. He graduated to the Durham first team after making an impressive start for the second XI against a Yorkshire side that included a promising young opening batsman named Len Hutton, and what he termed 'undoubtedly the highlight of my cricket career' came when he played at Sunderland against the Australian tourists of 1934, though it was not a personal success. He drove the first ball he received from 'Chuck' Fleetwood-Smith to the boundary, but was bowled by the next – deceived by the left-arm spinner's googly.

Carter was left to wonder if he might have entered first-class cricket with Leicestershire had he not been turned down by Leicester City at the outset of his football career before joining Sunderland, for at that time he was as keen on the summer game as football. He did admit, however, that his enthusiasm for cricket could no doubt have been dampened if his attacking style of play had been curbed by the demands at top level. He also made two observations that were quite illuminating in comparing the two sports. For someone who maintained such a high standard in withstanding the rigours of League and war-time football for the best part of twenty years, up to the age of almost forty with Hull City (and finally in the League of Ireland with Cork City), it was somewhat surprising to hear him say that the long periods in the field during his three games for Derbyshire 'were a great strain and tired me out completely'. And, considering how dispassionate he was as a footballer, how remarkable was this recollection of a cricket cup-tie in which his 91 not out did most to snatch a dramatic victory:

'We were greeted with wild cheering as we came off the field. When I reached the dressing room in the pavilion the tension snapped and the reaction set in. I broke down and cried. It is a thing I have never done, or been near doing, in football. I feel the tension of cricket to a much greater extent, and it has a far more emotional reaction upon me.'

Colin Boulton, the goalkeeper who alone played in all eighty-four matches of Derby County's two title-winning teams of the 1970s, has told me that he, too, found county cricket more taxing than football. He was never a signed Derbyshire player, but, as with Carter, he found the ball constantly coming in his direction, though just out of reach so that he had to do a lot of chasing which led to his limping off with a pulled muscle when he fielded as a substitute during an opening partnership of 256 for Kent by Brian Luckhurst and Graham Johnson at Derby in 1973. It beat by one run the previous highest for Kent against Derbyshire, by Frank Woolley and 'Wally' Hardinge (one of the select band who played for England at both cricket and football) at Chesterfield in 1929, and was only 27 short of the county's record stand for the first wicket that Arthur Fagg established with Peter Sunnucks in the second innings of the match with Essex at Colchester in 1938. That was the occasion on which Fagg became the only player to have scored two double-centuries in one game.

The first Derbyshire cricketers to play for Derby County were William Chatterton, Percy Exham and Frank Sugg, who were in the side thrashed 0-7 by Walsall Town in the Rams' first match, an FA Cup-tie on 8 November 1884. Sugg, like Exham, was not called upon again, but he went on to play ten times for Everton in the League and three for Burnley in the Cup. Chatterton played in five further matches, all in the first Football League season of 1888-89, and scored one goal – in a 4-2 home defeat by Everton.

Haydn Morley, the first player signed by Derby County after his father, a member of the Derbyshire CCC committee, and brother William, a Midland Railway clerk, had been instrumental in its formation as an offshoot of the cricket club, also took part in that game, but he did not make what was to be his only appearance for Derbyshire until the opening fixture of the 1891 season, during their second-class exile. He was twice dismissed cheaply in a ten-wicket defeat at Nottingham while opening the batting with L G Wright, who played four times for the Rams in their first League season of 1888-89. Wright, who also played for Derby Midland and Derby Junction, made a scoring debut in the first of his two games at centre-half – in a 2-3 home defeat by John Goodall's Preston North End – and then moved to full-back before bowing out at centre-forward in another home reverse, by 0-2 against Blackburn Rovers.

Morley, a full-back, captained the Wednesday to the 1890 FA Cup final after making a few more appearances for the Rams, and at the finish fans of the Sheffield club carried him shoulder-high from the field at Kennington Oval in recognition of his plucky display against overwhelming odds. Blackburn Rovers' 6-1 victory was the biggest for the final until injury-hit Derby County were Bury'd 0-6 in 1903, and it took a timely intervention by Morley to deny them a seventh goal after sections of the crowd had caused a delay of several minutes by spilling onto the pitch as time was running out. In club cricket, Morley was a successful batsman with Belper Meadows, whom he captained in succession to the 'Demon' Spofforth. Not until his nineties did he retire from his work as a solicitor – and even then it was forced on him when he lost a leg as a scratch on a foot became infected. He had another big F A Cup disappointment a few years before his death at ninety-two in 1953.

He wanted to attend the all-ticket semi-final between Derby County and Manchester United at Sheffield Wednesday's ground, but failed with his written application.

William Cropper, William Storer and Arnold Warren were other Derby County players whose cricket careers with Derbyshire began in the late nineteenth century, though all three also had only a brief connection with the Rams. Cropper played for them just the once, at centre-forward in an F A Cup defeat at home to Mitchell St George's in 1886. Warren was given eight successive League games at outside-right in the 1901-02 season, scoring twice, before leaving for Brentford. Storer, who was later with Loughborough Town and Glossop N E, played in fewer than thirty first-team matches for the Rams, yet appeared in all five forward positions of the standard 2-3-5 formation.

Regrettably, Warren's stay with Brentford, also short, was tarnished by his involvement in a public-house brawl that resulted in his serving a prison sentence after being convicted of assault. Soon after his release, in April 1903, he rejoined Ripley Town, with whom he had three spells. Heanor Town, Ripley Athletic and Glossop North End were other clubs for which he played.

The link between Derbyshire and Derby County was also slender for Jack Davis, Tom Fletcher and Stuart McMillan. 'Pimmy' Davis, for thirty-five years a miner, and later a boilermaker, from Ironville, inherited the family nickname as the eldest of five brothers. He was a lively winger, on either flank of the attack, for the best part of five seasons in the first decade of the twentieth century, making more than 150 appearances before leaving for Ilkeston United in the autumn of 1910, but he had the misfortune to play his one game for Derbyshire, against Essex at Southend, during their barren season of 1920. This free-scoring batsman with the Codnor Park and the Swanwick and Loscoe colliery teams managed just nine runs in his two innings for the county, yet in the Border League he played many good innings.

Fletcher, born at Heanor, not far from Davis's birthplace, also had only one opportunity with Derbyshire – in the 1906 match with the West Indians that the county won by six wickets largely due to the unbeaten half-century Charles Ollivierre took off his compatriots. For Derby County, Fletcher held a regular first-team place for the second half of the 1904-05 season and part of the next. Like William Storer, he filled all five positions in the forward line.

McMillan, son of a former Derby winger who scored five goals in the first of the club's record 9-0 League wins (against Wolves in 1891), played just once in the Rams' senior side, in a home draw with Glossop on the second day of 1915, and four times for Derbyshire in the early 1920s. All but six of the 30 runs he scored in six innings came in one knock; in the few overs he bowled he conceded fourteen runs without taking a wicket. The six other football clubs for which he played after leaving the Rams and seeing war service with the Derbyshire Yeomanry included Gillingham, where his father was manager, and Wolves, whom he helped out of the Third (North) in 1923-24 under the guidance of George Jobey, the manager who was also to lead Derby County to promotion, returning them to the First Division, with the team that contained Harry Storer. But it was back with the Rams that McMillan was to achieve what has stubbornly remained his unique place in soccer history – as manager of the FA Cup winners in the first post-war final of 1946. Since then Derby have been nearest to repeating that long overdue success as twice losing semi-finalists.

Of the Derby County players who scored most runs for Derbyshire, third place behind L G Wright and Harry Storer Junior is held by Albert Edward Alderman. In 529 innings for the county this opening batsman, born in the Alvaston suburb of Derby, accumulated 12,376 runs at an average of almost 26 in a first-class career that lasted from 1928 to 1948 apart from the war years. A product of the nursery, where he changed his batting style under Sam Cadman to become a dour opener ('he may at times have been prosaic and almost anonymous at the crease', said *Wisden*), he was an established member of the pre-war side from the 1931 season in which he scored the first of his dozen centuries, 113 not out, at The Oval and was again unbeaten with 50 in the second innings.

It was also at Surrey's headquarters that, in the title-winning season of 1936, Alderman pulled off one of the most remarkable catches ever seen at that ground, one that *Wisden* declared 'should live in the memories of all those who were present'. A six seemed certain when Tom Barling swept a ball from Bill Copson high to leg, but Alderman sprinted fully thirty yards round the boundary and held the ball with his outstretched right hand just above the palings. Although not an exact replica, some idea of how spectacular that brilliant effort was can be derived from the one-handed catch that India's Sachin Tendulkar took, after a dash over a similar distance, to dismiss Allan Lamb in the Lord's Test of 1990 in which John Morris, of Derbyshire, made his England debut.

No wonder that when Albert Alderman died – at the age of eighty-two only the month before that Tendulkar piece of magic – *Wisden* said in his obituary that 'in the deep field he was a star of the first magnitude'. He saved many runs with his excellent fielding, and at Trent Bridge in 1938 he even came up with another wonderful catch to rival his Oval masterpiece. Running at full tilt, he again held the ball in his outstretched right hand – right in front of the astonished Nottinghamshire members sitting in the pavilion. His victim that time was George Heane, the Notts captain. There were two hundred other Alderman catches besides those two extraordinary ones. He also made two stumpings as an emergency wicketkeeper.

Alderman twice narrowly failed to complete a thousand runs in a season before he did so, comfortably, each year from 1934 to 1939. Handicapped by injury and illness, he never got properly into his stride again after the war, but in his final season he showed much of his old reliability with the last of his centuries, 114, in a second-wicket stand of 209 with Denis Smith (96) that put Derbyshire on course for a defeat of Leicestershire at Ashby-de-la-Zouch after they had trailed on first innings.

He was also in a double-century partnership with Smith against Leicestershire, for the first wicket, when he made his biggest score of 175 (one six, seventeen fours) at Chesterfield in his most successful season of 1937 (1,509 runs at 33.53). In three hours they took the score to 233, and after Smith's dismissal for 121 – it was the third time both Derbyshire openers had scored a century in the same innings – Alderman was joined by Stan Worthington in a stand of 149. Derbyshire went on to defeat a side that included George Dawkes by an innings and 199 runs after declaring at 470 for six. The most memorable of Alderman's other centuries were a chanceless 124 when he carried his bat right through an innings of 291 that lasted for five and a half hours as Derbyshire battled to avert defeat in the follow-on against Hampshire at Portsmouth in 1934, an equally determined 112 in the defeat of the 1937 New Zealand tourists at Derby (after being out for a duck in the first innings), and 125 in a third-wicket stand of 215 with Leslie Townsend (167 not out) against Sussex at Eastbourne in 1938. Only one of his other hundreds was made at Derby – 115 against Northants in 1934.

For three seasons in the 1960s Alderman umpired in almost sixty County Championship matches. His other big contribution to the game was as a coach. While still with Derbyshire he escaped some English winters to give young players the benefit of his experience in New Zealand, and after his retirement he coached at Repton School and the Royal Military Academy at Sandhurst. When Martin Donnelly, one of cricket's finest left-hand batsmen, visited England with the New Zealand tourists in 1937 he paid this tribute to Alderman's expertise: 'I have been playing cricket ever since I can remember, but I owe whatever skill I now have to the coaching of Albert Alderman. He coached me very carefully, and I learned a tremendous amount from him.'

With Derby County, Alderman was a speedy, but mainly reserve, winger or inside-forward, restricted to twenty-one First Division games and three FA Cup-ties, before following the Storer path to Burnley, priced at all of £200. He made nineteen more League appearances for the Lancashire club, adding two goals to the half-dozen he had scored for Derby's first team.

The last four to do the Derby County-Derbyshire double were the post-war quartet of George Robert ('Bob') Stephenson, Ian Hall, Ray Swallow and Ian Buxton. Spinner Fred Swarbrook was also with the Rams, but played only in their junior team.

Stephenson, the wicketkeeper who, because of Bob Taylor's tight hold on that position in the Derbyshire team, departed on a special registration to fill the Hampshire vacancy left by Brian Timms' retirement, came from a footballing family. His father, George, won two of his three England caps while with Derby County (the other with Sheffield Wednesday) after being on Aston

Villa's books as the same time as his two elder brothers, Clem and Jimmy, and two of Bob's other uncles played in non-League soccer. Clem and Jimmy were team-mates several times in the Villa forward line, but not George. Like Clem before him, he was loaned out to Stourbridge to gain experience, and shortly before his return Clem was transferred to Huddersfield Town, whom he captained to their three successive First Division titles in the 1920s, and Jimmy left for Sunderland. Clem and George both later managed Huddersfield.

Bob Stephenson, who was born at Derby, joined the Rams from the local side Derwent Sports and played fourteen senior games in their forward line, scoring one goal in a defeat of Bristol Rovers towards the end of the 1961-62 season, before dropping into the Third Division with Shrewsbury Town, then the Fourth with Rochdale. After that he wound up out of the Football League with Lockheed Leamington, Worcester City and Buxton.

With Derbyshire, he was confined to nine County Championship appearances, seven of them in succession at the end of the 1967 season while Taylor was out injured. He made his top first-team score for the county, 64 in 80 minutes, on his debut in a drawn home match with Middlesex, and hit his one century (100 not out) for Hampshire, whom he captained in 1979, against Somerset at Taunton, where the result was also a draw, in 1976. One of the most competent keepers in the country in a career that lasted until 1980, he claimed 910 victims – 661 (584 caught, 77 stumped) in first-class games, the rest in one-day fixtures. His aggregate of runs fell not far short of 5,000, but at an average just under seventeen.

Ian Hall, an England schoolboy and youth soccer international, was born at Sutton Scarsdale, near Bolsover, but family moves took him to other parts of the county, at Glapwell, Ashover and Tansley, before he followed up his promising form as a schoolboy cricketer by scoring the first century made in the Central Derbyshire League at the age of just fifteen. That was for the Matlock club, with which his father, a schoolmaster, was captain, but soon afterwards he joined Cromford Meadows and graduated to the Derbyshire Juniors team.

His prowess as a footballer was also catching attention, and he was an amateur with Wolverhampton Wanderers before he signed professional forms for Derby County in the same year, 1959, that he was called upon at short notice to make his senior debut for Derbyshire at Lord's as deputy for opener John Kelly, formerly of Lancashire, who had injured a hand in the previous game at Swansea. In his ninth innings Hall scored 113 in more than five hours against Hampshire at Derby, becoming, at nineteen, the youngest player to hit a century for the county's first team.

Six years later, he scored two in the same match, both 101, against Kent at Folkestone. There were six more in his final aggregate of 11,666, at an average of nearly twenty-six, with a top score of 136 that he made twice – against Northants at Derby in 1963, and, undefeated, Oxford University in the Parks in 1972, on the only occasion he captained the side. In five seasons he exceeded a thousand runs, during the period from 1960 to his penultimate year of 1971. Also adept as a wicketkeeper, he held four of his 189 catches in his occasional stints behind the stumps as deputy for Dawkes or Taylor, and had a match best of six against Warwickshire at Coventry.

Hall, a creative midfielder, scored sixteen goals in fifty-one first-team games for Derby County before being signed by Raich Carter for Mansfield Town, whom he helped to promotion from the Fourth Division in 1962-63, but his double career was checked by a severed Achilles tendon, suffered during the 1966-67 season. While still with Derby County his opening partner in several Derbyshire matches – one of more than a dozen he had with the county – was his fellow Rams forward and former schoolboy international Ray Swallow, a Londoner signed by Harry Storer from Arsenal the year after making his debut in first-class cricket for the MCC against Scotland at Aberdeen.

Swallow, scorer of twenty-two goals in 128 senior appearances for the County before leaving the League for Poole Town, averaged almost 47 in scoring more than 1,300 runs, including five centuries, for the Derbyshire second XI and Club and Ground side in 1959. Two years later he scored 131 not out and 101 in a draw with Lancashire's second team at Derby, and in the first innings of the next game he hit four sixes and fifteen fours in a rapid 119 at Northampton – despite which Derbyshire II were beaten with only five minutes to spare.

Swallow headed the second team's batting averages that season with nearly 450 runs in ten innings at 48.44, but played in only half-a-dozen Championship games mainly because of a severe attack of influenza in Whit Week. His opening partnership with Hall began promisingly in 1960 with stands of 103 and 71 against Somerset at Chesterfield, and another of 75 in the second innings of the next match at Northampton, but it then faded away to finish dismally against Essex at Romford in 1963. Only one of their other partnerships, which realised 74 against Somerset at the Imperial ground in Bristol, got beyond the mid-thirties before they were parted. Swallow's only first-class hundred was scored against Oxford University.

To Ian Buxton fell the distinction of being the last to play for both Derby County and Derbyshire. He scored hundreds of runs for his home club Cromford before joining the Derbyshire ground staff in 1959, and he gathered 11,803 more, averaging a fraction under twenty-four, before leaving the first-class game in 1973. He captained the team for three of those fifteen seasons, also making a big contribution as a bowler, with 483 wickets at 26.38, and as a fielder with 199 catches. Five times he exceeded a thousand runs, sharing what was then the county's record fifth-wicket stand of 203 with the South African Chris Wilkins against Lancashire at Old Trafford in 1971. He twice took ten wickets in a match, and did the hat-trick against Oxford University at Derby in his first match as captain.

For Derby County he scored forty-three goals in 158 League and Cup appearances before being swept out with the arrival as manager of Brian Clough, who regarded him as little more than a part-timer because he had a clause in his contract that allowed him a holiday at the end of the cricket season. Off he went to Luton Town, and promptly won a Fourth Division title medal. Then he moved to Port Vale after a short stay with Notts County and also helped them into Division Three.

So the number of Derby County footballers and Derbyshire cricketers has stuck at nineteen, but it could have been increased to a nice round number if my step father, George Richards, had been able to accept an invitation to be in the Derbyshire party for three consecutive matches in the South of England. He had to say he was ineligible by both birth and residence, having been born in Nottinghamshire, at Bulwell, and then lived in Leicestershire, at Castle Donington. While with the Rams during most of the years of the twentieth century leading up to the 1914-18 war, he shared his cricket among several clubs, notably taking part in two unbroken double-century opening partnershjps for Darley Dale – one with Charles Ollivierre, the other with one of Will Taylor's brothers.

Two Derbyshire cricketers whose soccer careers overlapped that of George Richards, but who did not play for Derby County, were Ernest Needham and Willie Foulke, both of Sheffield United. Foulke, a goalkeeper whose massive bulk – his weight approached 26st while he was with Bradford City after also playing for Chelsea – earned him such nicknames as Fatty and Big Bill, turned out in only four games for Derbyshire, all in 1900, but Needham was a left-hand batsman, with a sound defence if not a graceful style, who scored more than 6,500 runs in nearly 350 innings for the county from 1901 to 1912. Needham, who came from the Newbold district of Chesterfield, scored a half-century on his debut at the late age of twenty-eight against the South African tourists, and made two of his seven first-class centuries in one match with Essex at Leyton in 1908 – the month after also reaching three figures against that county in the home game.

With 1,178 runs at 28.73, that season of 1908 was Needham's most successful with Derbyshire. During it, he also twice carried his bat through a completed innings, scoring 58 out of 11 against Surrey at Derby and 107 out of 195 at Leyton. His 104 in the second innings of that away game with Essex came in a total of 204 for four.

Known as the 'Prince of Half-Backs', and also nicknamed 'Nudger' for his solid shoulder charging, Needham made some 550 senior appearances for Sheffield United, whom he joined at eighteen in the summer of 1891 after being in Staveley's Midland League side for a couple of seasons. The outstanding member of one of the smallest half-back lines with Rab Howell and Tom Morren (all three under 5ft 6in), he helped the Blades to win the First Division title in 1897-98 and reach three FA Cup finals – twice as winners, on the first occasion against Derby County. England called on him sixteen times, and he captained them in a 1901 game against Wales at Newcastle in which he scored one of his three international goals. The Rams' sharpshooter Steve Bloomer netted four of the others in a 6-0 win.

Foulke, who was born in Shropshire but grew up in Derbyshire at Blackwell, also played for England at soccer, but just the once. He fell on hard times after ending his playing career, and eked out a precarious living as an 'Aunt Sally' in facing penalty-kicks at fairgrounds and on the sands at Blackpool. He was only forty-two when he died in 1916 after catching a chill at the seaside. Needham died twenty years later, aged sixty-three, after an operation in Chesterfield hospital.

Nowadays, with the seasons overlapping more and more, and the demands on cricketers and footballers at the top level so heavy, the age when those who could combine both games professionally is long past. After Ian Buxton, Chris Marples was a goalkeeper with Chesterfield when he had a short run as Derbyshire's wicketkeeper in the mid-1980s, and Derby County paid Middlesbrough £150,000 in 1980 for a centre-half, Alan Ramage, who was also a fine fast-bowling prospect with Yorkshire until his dual career was ended by a knee injury.

Other Derbyshire cricketers who were with Football League clubs, but not Derby County, included Wilf Carter (Watford), Charlie Elliott (Coventry City), George Dawkes (Leicester City), Arnold Hamer (York City) and Bob Taylor (Port Vale). Mention must also be made of Donald Carr, the Old Reptonian who became the only Derbyshire player to captain England at cricket when he deputised for Lancashire's Nigel Howard, who had pleurisy, in the Madras match of 1952 that unhappily coincided with India's first Test victory at the twenty-fifth attempt.

Carr was an Oxford soccer Blue who twice helped Pegasus, an Oxbridge combination, to win the Amateur Cup. A left-winger in the 1949 Varsity soccer match against Cambridge, he played at inside-left (to use the terminology of the day) when Pegasus first won the trophy in 1951 by beating Bishop Auckland 2-1, and he and Derby-born defender Ken Shearwood, twice an Oxford soccer Blue and once a Derbyshire wicketkeeper (at Bristol in 1949) were among the five members of that team who also took part in the record 6-0 defeat of Harwich and Parkeston in the 1953 final at Wembley. On that day, in front of a crowd of 100,000, Carr played at inside-right and scored twice.

Cricket, however, was foremost for Carr, who limited his football after Pegasus to a few games for Aston-on-Trent, where he lived, the Derbyshire amateur side Old Reptonians (with Dick Sale, another Derbyshire player, among his team-mates, and an FA XI he captained against the UAU at Nottingham Forest's ground. He also signed amateur forms for Burton Albion, but did not play for them in the Birmingham League.

Jack Lee, a centre-forward capped by England soon after joining Derby County from Leicester City, played in only one County Championship match for Leicestershire, at Cardiff in 1947, and delivered just four overs, but he did have Glamorgan opener Arnold Dyson caught off the first ball he bowled.

In more recent times Derbyshire's only top-soccer connection has been in name only. Roger Finney was a right-hand batsman and left-arm bowler from Darley Dale, Ole Mortensen a fast bowler who became the first Dane to make good in county cricket.

14. Townsend and Worthington

The first two prime products of Derbyshire's nursery system were Leslie Fletcher Townsend and Thomas Stanley Worthington. Both made their debut before new talent again came under Sam Cadman's care – Townsend in 1922, Worthington in 1924 – but it was not until a few years later, under the Glossop man's renewed guidance, that they really started to develop to the degree that made them Test players and *Wisden* Cricketers of the Year.

A major influence on Townsend, however, was exercised by George Gunn, the England batsman who was such a force with Derbyshire's Nottinghamshire neighbours. Townsend did not play cricket at the council school he attended, but he travelled regularly to Trent Bridge from his Long Eaton home and was so impressed by Gunn's methods that he resolved to emulate them.

His initial progress was slow, but his subsequent steady improvement, along with Worthington's, made Derbyshire fortunate indeed to have two players of their calibre to fill the gaps left by Cadman and Jim Horsley, who had dropped out of their team at around the same time as Bill Bestwick. Townsend became one of the finest all-rounders of the inter-war years, and Worthington, though he came to be mainly regarded as a batsman, was not one to be underrated as a bowler either.

From his first representative selection, for the North against the South in 1927, Townsend advanced to being chosen for the Players in 1929, and for the tour of the West Indies which the MCC undertook in 1929-30 under the captaincy of the Hon F S (Freddie) Calthorpe, the Cambridge Blue and Warwickshire captain who had been one of the best all-rounders of his time at Repton.

In opting to rest at home, several of England's leading players – Jack Hobbs, Herbert Sutcliffe, Walter Hammond and Harold Larwood prominently among them – missed both that tour and the contemporary one led to Australia and New Zealand by Harold Gilligan, youngest brother of the more famous Arthur. Even so, the MCC were still able to assemble two parties of some strength. Townsend's companions included his unwitting guide, George Gunn, who was then in his fifty-first year, Yorkshire's Wilfred Rhodes, two years Gunn's senior, 'Patsy' Hendren, the Middlesex batsman whose tour average of 126.14 set a record for a season in the West Indies, Leslie Ames, the Kent wicketkeeper, Surrey opening batsman Andy Sandham, Jack O'Connor of Essex, and Bill Voce, Larwood's partner in the Notts speed attack.

Jack O'Connor's father, John, was a Pinxton-born all-rounder who played in nine matches for Derbyshire in 1900 and also assisted Cambridgeshire. John was the brother-in-law of another prominent Essex player, Hubert Carpenter, whose father, Robert, was one of the leading batsmen in England in the 1860s.

The three games the MCC played against the West Indies on that 1929-30 tour were originally described in *Wisden* as 'representative matches', but were later raised to Test status even though England fielded what was little more than an 'A' team. Townsend played in the third of those encounters, at Georgetown, but without doing anything special (two dozen runs and four wickets). His debut at that level unfortunately coincided with the West Indies first-ever victory – by the convincing margin of 289 runs after their main batsman, George Headley, had scored a century in both innings, though only a quarter of an hour was left for play when the tourists' last wicket fell. Headley was run out for 114 in his first innings, caught by Townsend off the bowling of Middlesex's Nigel Haig for two runs fewer in the second.

With the teams level at 1-1 (the first game had been drawn), the final match, at Kingston, was intended to be played to a finish, but it had to be given up as a draw after rain had washed out play on the eighth and ninth days. England piled up what became, with the later Test recognition, their biggest total of 849 until the 903 for seven declared in which Len Hutton made his record 364 against the Australians at The Oval in 1938. At Kingston, the 325 that Andy Sandham compiled in ten hours supplanted Reginald Foster's 287 at Sydney in 1903 as the highest individual score for England, but it was Walter Hammond's unbeaten 336 against New Zealand at Auckland in 1933 that Hutton exceeded.

Townsend played in his three other Tests during the 1933-34 tour of India, on which he was accompanied by Harry Elliott. England won that series 2-0, with the middle match drawn, but his contribution was again muted, and towards the end of the trip he had the added misfortune to suffer salmonella poisoning. The food generally did not agree with him out there, and it was through feeling ill that he had to retire only seven runs from a century in a drawn game with the Southern Punjab at Amritsar. In the Tests he had a top score of 40 and took just two wickets, but he played several useful innings in other matches besides his 97, and headed the tour bowling averages with 43 wickets at 14.13 runs apiece. In an innings victory at Ajmer he took 5-16 in the Rajputana first innings of 32, bowling with six men on the leg side, and had match figures of 12-38. At Rajkot, his 7-16 in the dismissal of Western India States for 64 led to another victory, by four wickets.

After that tour Townsend convalesced in New Zealand. This led to his paying several return visits out of the English season during the 1930s, and in one of his appearances for Auckland he scored 44 and 90 not out, and took 5-89 and 7-25, in a match with Wellington. New Zealand was so much to his liking that he emigrated there with his wife and son after spending three seasons with Northumberland following the 1939-45 war, during which he played in the Bradford League. He worked as a joiner and cabinet maker until he was persuaded to become cricket coach at Nelson on South Island in 1954, and he turned that city into one of New Zealand's thriving cricketing centres, with a good number of Test players produced from its ranks. After his death on 17 February 1993, at the grand old age of eighty-nine, *Wisden* observed that:

'He was remembered there as a strict coach who dressed in MCC sweater and beautifully pressed flannels, and expected equally high standards from his pupils. He was especially keen on youngsters driving through the V, with their left elbow high, which is how spectators may best remember him.'

A teetotaller and non-smoker, Townsend was also described in *Wisden* as 'an admirable type of the present-day professional' when he was named as one of the almanack's Five Cricketers of the Year after completing the double of 2,000 runs and 100 wickets in 1933, despite being unable to bowl through August because of a shoulder injury suffered when he was a passenger in a car that overturned. He hit six hundreds that year, then a record for Derbyshire – and narrowly missed another, and two in one match, in scoring 99 and 106 against Northants at Chesterfield. On five other occasions in his career he was out in the nineties, yet he is still fifth in Derbyshire's list of century-makers with a total of twenty-two. Another of his hundreds, 142, was also taken off Northants during the return match of 1933 at Northampton in which Denis Smith made 129 not out, and Garnet Lee 128, in the same innings.

Townsend's other centuries in that peak year were his personal-best 233 at Loughborough to which reference has already been made, 172 not out against Warwickshire at Derby, 151 off Essex at Leyton, and 100 against Yorkshire at Chesterfield. He beat L G Wright's 1905 Derbyshire record of 1,716 runs in a season by getting 1,966 of his 2,268 runs for the county, at an average, like Wright's, of nearly 43. That put him at the top of the county's batting, and he also headed their bowling averages that year by taking 87 of his 100 wickets in the Championship at 16.91 runs each. His aggregate of runs remained a Derbyshire record for one season until Donald Carr totalled 2,165 at 48.11 in 1959. It has since also been passed by Mohammad Azharuddin with 2,016 at 59.29 in 1991, and by Peter Bowler with 2,044 at 65.93 in 1992.

In his other games of 1933 Townsend scored 49 not out for an England XI in a draw with the West Indies at Folkestone, and followed up an undefeated 44 with 4-87 for the Rest of England against Yorkshire, the champion county, at The Oval.

He achieved the first of his three cricketer's doubles in 1928, scoring 1,001 runs at 29.44 and taking 104 wickets at 16.78 each. He did the double in Championship matches alone in 1932 (1,373 runs at 29.84 and 113 wickets at 18.15) and went near selection for the 1932-33 tour of Australia after Maurice Tate had dropped out of the reckoning through injury.

At the outset of his career, Townsend looked a promising prospect more for his bowling than his batting. In 1927, his accurate off-breaks, delivered at a fairly brisk pace, put him seventh in the national averages, one place behind Garnet Lee, with 70 wickets at 19.38, but his batting at that time was criticised for some recklessness as he was inclined to get out to rash strokes and averaged below twenty. He then set about tightening it up, however, and it reached its full maturity in 1930, making him a genuine all-rounder, when he hit four hundreds – three of them in four matches in May and June – and finished a close second to Harry Storer in the county's averages in completing a thousand runs in a season's Derbyshire matches for the first of eight times. Sound in defence and hard-hitting in attack, he was at his best against spin bowling.

One of his best all-round performances for Derbyshire scuppered Somerset in 1934, when he scored 106 not out and had match figures of eleven for 130 in an innings victory at Weston-super-Mare. He took ten or more wickets in a game on fifteen other occasions, with a best return of fourteen for 90 against Gloucestershire at Chesterfield in 1933 that is also still the best by a Derbyshire player against that county. Three times he took three wickets in four balls – against Sussex at Chesterfield in 1928, Kent at Canterbury in 1931, Lancashire at Buxton in 1932 – and he did the hat-trick at Northampton in 1931. Herbert Sutcliffe described him as a spot bowler, one who could consistently pitch the ball on a chosen spot.

A stomach ulcer that compelled him to postpone his wedding curtailed his cricket towards the end of the 1937 season. Fit again, he had another successful season the following year, but his form fell away in 1939 and at the beginning of August he lost his place to his young brother Arnold. With the outbreak of war then bringing his first-class career of 493 matches to a close, he finished with a total of 19,555 runs, 17,667 of them for Derbyshire, at an average just over 27, 1,088 wickets, 969 for the county, at a cost of 21 runs each, and 241 catches, 212 for Derbyshire.

Arnold Townsend, who died the year after Leslie – almost to the day, on 27 February 1994 – was a painstaking, some might well say plodding, batsman who was with Derbyshire from 1934 to 1950 (less the war years). It was not until after the war that he found his best form, making more than a thousand runs in both 1946 and 1947, and scoring three centuries. As *Wisden* put it: 'Overall, his record – 4,327 runs at 23.13 with five centuries – was not impressive, but he was batting at a time when Derbyshire habitually played on greentops, and he was the epitome of their patient, watchful batting.' An eye injury suffered while fielding at short-leg in 1949 seriously impaired his ability to focus properly and forced his retirement after a comeback that lasted for only two matches the following year.

As with Leslie Townsend, it was chiefly for bowling that the sturdily built, but agile, Stan Worthington found his way onto the Derbyshire staff, though it was as a batsman than he earned his selection for nine Tests. He was seen at his best against fast bowling, strongest with pulls on the leg side but also a fine timer of driving on either side of the wicket. Born at Bolsover in August 1905, he obtained a job as an electrician at the colliery there at the age of seventeen, and it was not long before he caught attention with his bowling, of good length at medium pace, for their cricket team in the Bassetlaw League. Fred Tate spotted him on one of his scouting missions, and he made his County Championship debut for Derbyshire against Nottinghamshire in August 1924.

In what was to be his only first-team appearance that season, he took 3-98 in 28 overs and, batting at No 9, scored twelve runs in his second innings after being dismissed for a duck in the first. He again did little worth talking about in the only three Championship games he was given in 1925, but he then began to make his presence felt under Sam Cadman's guidance and first emerged, along with Townsend, as a notable all-rounder with a top score of 84 (in a match with Kent in which he also took 5-74) and 56 wickets in 1926. A year later he missed a maiden century by only two runs, but that came in 1928 – the first of twenty-seven for the county and thirty-one in all – when he reached three figures as a run-a-minute in making a glorious 133 (four sixes, twelve fours) against Essex at Chesterfield. With another hundred, 121 at Loughborough, soon following, and his completion of a thousand runs for the first of ten seasons – eight of them in a row from 1932 – he advanced a strong claim for the representative recognition that came with his inclusion in the MCC party Harold Gilligan led to Australia and New Zealand in 1929-30.

As with the tour of the West Indies in which Les Townsend took part at the same time, the squad, though not of front rank, was of some strength – stronger, indeed, than the previous three sent to New Zealand. Gilligan, whose only first-class century (143 for Sussex at Hove in 1929) was made against Derbyshire, had mainly fellow amateurs to call upon, but one of them was the gifted Indian prince Kumar Duleepsinhji, nephew of the great Ranjitsinhji, and among the six professionals was Frank Woolley, the stylish Kent left-hander.

With New Zealand newly elevated to Test match status, Worthington was one of those who played in England's first game against them in an official series, at Christchurch on 10-13 January 1930. England, for whom another Test newcomer, Surrey's Maurice Allom, took four wickets in five balls, including a hat-trick, won it by eight wickets. Worthington failed to score in his only innings, but took three wickets cheaply. The only runs he obtained in the four-match rubber were his 32, with the help of a life, in the drawn second Test at Wellington. He did not have the chance to bat in the rain-ruined third game in Auckland, and he was again dismissed without scoring at the same ground in his only innings of the final encounter, which was a late addition to the programme in an attempt to make up for the weather, but was also drawn.

Worthington, whose seven wickets in the series cost a fraction over twenty-six runs each, had better luck with the bat on his other appearance at Auckland, scoring a faultless 125 in a drawn match with a powerful Auckland XI that included four Test players. He also had two big successes as a bowler, taking 7-31 against Wairapa and 7-35 against Rangitiki. For the New Zealand section of the tour, which came after five fixtures in Australia, he totalled 454 runs for an average of almost 35 and took 47 wickets for a fraction over fifteen runs each. He played in all the matches in Australia, but had a very lean time with the bat until he made the top score of 66 in the MCC's second innings in the last of the five, lost to Queensland in Brisbane, and his eight wickets cost nearly 350 runs. His particular disappointment was to score only seven runs in a high-scoring draw with New South Wales in Sydney, where there were three century-makers for the home side – the inevitable Don Bradman among them – and nearly a fourth, plus two for the tourists, one of them a double-century by Woolley.

Only three matches, and no Tests, were played on Worthington's second visit to New Zealand in March 1937, but in one of them, drawn with a combined Canterbury and Otago team at Wellington, he partnered Bob Wyatt, who left Warwickshire for Worcestershire after the war, in a first-wicket stand of 165.

By that time Worthington was well established as a front-line batsman, having been able to concentrate on that aspect of his game in not being required to do so much bowling for Derbyshire. He twice took ten wickets in a match before continuing to show his worth as a change bowler, often capable of breaking a troublesome partnership. Fielding was his other strong point, either at short-leg or deeper. In batting, he rose up the order to No 3 (mainly) or No 4 for the county, but it was also as an opener that he went in for England in the three of the five Tests in which he played during the preceding Australian part of the MCC's 1936-37 tour. England, captained by the Australian-born 'Gubby' Allen, of Middlesex, won the first two games of that series with the Aussies, but lost the remaining three.

Worthington was omitted after being caught at the wicket off the first ball of the opening match in Brisbane and then again falling victim to Bert Oldfield, stumped, for only eight runs in his second innings. He was left out once more following another duck in Melbourne, and accumulated just 74 runs in his six innings – 44 of them when he first batted in the final Test back in Melbourne – for an depressing average of 12.33. He also failed with the ball in Tests, his fruitless ten overs costing 78 runs, but he did have the considerable satisfaction of breaking a century stand by bowling Bradman (for 63) in the drawn match with an Australian XI in Sydney. That was a case of history repeating itself, for in 1929 Worthington had also bowled the great man in the match with New South Wales at the same ground. On that occasion Bradman had made 157, one of three century-makers in a total of more than 600.

In the state matches on the 1936-37 tour of Australia, Worthington had his days of most success at Perth, where he hit 89 in a century stand with Walter Hammond against a Western Australia Combined XI, and Launceston, where he made his next highest score of 50 against Tasmania. His big moment of glory in connection with that tour came back home at Lord's towards the end of May in 1937, in the second match of the MCC's 150th Anniversary Week. Opening for the MCC Australian Touring Team against the Rest of England, he carried his bat right through an innings of 376 for an immaculate 156 that provided a sound foundation for victory (see p.338). The next highest scorer was Walter Robins, of Middlesex, with 58 at No 9. In his second innings Worthington was caught for twelve, one of Surrey fast bowler Alf Gover's seven victims (five of them for five runs in fourteen balls), but the men who had toured Australia won by 69 runs.

Despite Worthington's excellent display in making that century at cricket's headquarters, the 1936-37 series Down Under closed the curtain on his nine-match Test career – an especially sad end to it in the light of his achievements against the Indian tourists during the 1936 season, in which he also headed Derbyshire's batting averages as their leading run-getter on their path to the County Championship title. He was not chosen for the first of the three games with India, which England won by nine wickets at Lord's, and he would not have played in the drawn second one, at Old Trafford, if Maurice Leyland, the Yorkshire left-hander, had not dropped out through injury.

He was the obvious replacement after taking a brilliant 135 off Yorkshire, the champions Derbyshire were to displace, at Sheffield, and he grasped his opportunity in splendid style by partnering Wally Hammond (167) and Joe Hardstaff (94) in stands of 127 and 86 for the third and fifth wickets before being brilliantly caught at extra cover for a flawless 87. And in the final game at The Oval he did even better, becoming the first, and still only, Derbyshire player to score a Test century (128) and helping Hammond (217) to add 266 for the fourth wicket as England cruised to another nine-wicket win. That remained an England record for any wicket against India until Graham Gooch and Allan Lamb put on 308 for the third at Lord's in 1990.

In reporting the Hammond-Worthington stand in *The Daily Telegraph*, Howard Marshall, who was also well-known as the BBC's cricket commentator, deplored the fact that the pitch at The Oval was 'as perfect as man could make it'. He added: 'I have no use for these perfect wickets. They damp down the fires of cricket. They whittle away the subtle arts of the game.' Yet the breaking of the partnership began a spell in which five wickets fell for 49 runs before a declaration, and in India's two innings Jim Sims and 'Gubby' Allen, both of Middlesex, had respective figures of 5-73 and 7-80.

Although not required again for an official Test after the match in Melbourne which Australia won by an innings and 200 runs to clinch the 1936-37 series, Worthington also escaped the following home winter, this time in company with George Pope, as a visitor to India with the first English touring team not to be sponsored by the MCC for nearly forty years. Percy Chapman, Tom Goddard and Wally Hammond declined invitations to make the trip, and the Yorkshire committee refused Maurice Leyland permission to go, but Lord Tennyson, the captain who made all the arrangements, had some justification for claiming that his squad was 'probably the strongest ever to visit India'. It also included Bill Edrich and Ian Peebles (Middlesex), Alf Gover (Surrey), Joe Hardstaff (Notts), Jim Parks and James Langridge (Sussex), and Paul Gibb and Norman Yardley (Yorkshire).

Unfortunately, however, it was bedevilled by illness and injury, the consequent depletion of forces contributing at least in some part to defeat in five of the two dozen matches, though the tourists won three of the five unofficial Tests. George Pope was among those stricken, but, as will be referred to more fully in a later chapter in which he features prominently, he still managed to turn in several excellent displays with both bat and ball. Suffice to say for the moment, one of them was given in association with Worthington, who scored 68, and Pope 49, in a second-innings stand that set up his lordship's team for a victory by 156 runs in the final 'Test' at Bombay which brought the tour to a close.

Worthington also played a crucial role in the second match of the series at the same ground, scoring 49 in an unbroken partnership of 98 with Edrich that clinched a six-wicket win. He made his biggest score of the tour, 82, in the game against the Nawab of Moin-ud-Dowlah's XI at Secunderabad, adding 112 for the fifth wicket with Neil McCorkell, the Hampshire wicket-keeper, but that time it was not enough to avert defeat.

The other 'Test' win for the tourists was gained by nine wickets at the start of the series at Lahore, where cricket was given a new reason for a hold-up in play. A brief, but severe, earthquake shock caused a short stoppage on the second day.

In the English season of 1937 that preceded that tour, Stan Worthington made 238 not out, the highest score of his career and the biggest by a Derbyshire player against Sussex, at Derby. A year later he hit two hundreds (103 and an unbeaten 110) against Nottinghamshire at Ilkeston. Cramp in the match with Sussex cost him the chance of overhauling George Davidson's record score for Derbyshire after he had surged past his not-out 200, made at Chesterfield in 1933, that has still to be exceeded for the county against Worcestershire. The cramp seized him as he got within a dozen runs of 250 with his twenty-ninth boundary, on-driven off Jim Parks, and he had to be assisted from the field. Derbyshire, who declared at 485 for eight in reply to Sussex's 219 after Alan Skinner (82) and George Pope (41) had given Worthington most support in stands of 171 and 135, were left to get only 46 for the win they gained by nine wickets.

Skinner, whose younger brother David captained Derbyshire in 1949, just failed to gain his Blue at Cambridge after captaining the Leys School side of 1931, but in his third year at the university, 1934, he made 1,019 first-class runs at an average of 27.54 and hit his only century in the top grade, 102 for Derbyshire at Gloucester. Although his opportunities to play for the county became more limited due to his business interests, he played several useful innings, and fielded smartly at slip, during his time with Derbyshire, which lasted for just over eighty matches from 1931 to 1938. After the 1939-45 war his first-class cricket was confined to one match for Northamptonshire, captaining them against the New Zealand tourists at Northampton in 1949 – the month before David skippered Derbyshire on the same ground. Alan, who had also been Derbyshire's captain, in a deputy role, was later clerk to the West Suffolk County Council for many years, and it was in the West Suffolk Hospital that he died in 1982, aged sixty-eight.

The one man out in Derbyshire's second innings of the 1937 game with Sussex, in which Stan Worthington made his biggest score. was Denis Smith, who in the previous match, at Trent Bridge, had also hit his second double-century, 202 not out, thereby equalling L G Wright's record of twenty-one three-figure innings for the county (one of them while they were rated second class).

Smith's was again the one wicket to fall when Worthington's second century of the match with Notts hastened Derbyshire to victory with the assistance of an undefeated 80 from Albert Alderman. Only 135 of the near-180 minutes available were needed to reach a target of 205. Worthington, whose son was born a few days earlier, was the fifth player to score two centuries for Derbyshire in one game, following Wright, Ernest Needham and William and Harry Storer. There have been seven more since then.

Nottinghamshire were also the opposition, and Ilkeston the venue, when, in July 1933, Worthington scored a century in sixty minutes that stood as the fastest for Derbyshire until Chris Adams hit 101 in 57 minutes – but in contrived circumstances – on his way to 140 not out in 72 minutes at Worcester 59 years later. Adams, spoon-fed on a farcical last day in the unsuccessful attempt to fashion a result, struck six sixes and twenty fours, twice taking twenty-four runs off an over, and eighteen off another. Derbyshire's declaration set Worcestershire to score 266, but the chase was abandoned at 162 for three with eleven of the stipulated fifty-one overs left. A result was achieved when Worthington cut loose, but not in Derbyshire's favour. Having gone in at the fall of the sixth wicket at 90, he spent only twenty minutes over his second fifty and altogether smote four sixes and fourteen fours before Bill Voce bowled him for 108, made out of 117 in 70 minutes. The tail, however, failed to wag, and Derbyshire, all out for 255 in just under three hours, were beaten by 57 runs.

Although Denis Smith took only an hour to hit 100 of his personal-best 225 against Hampshire at Chesterfield in 1935, he did not do so from the start of his innings. Before Worthington, the county's fastest hundred was made in a little over the hour by Albert Lawton, against Hampshire at Derby in 1902. He and Gilbert Curgenven added 139 in sixty minutes for the sixth wicket.

During the Second World War, in which he served with REME and rose to the rank of captain, Worthington played in a number of charity matches from which he steadfastly refused to take any expenses. He was well into his forty-first year when, as vice-captain, he resumed his county career in the grand manner with a century against Leicestershire at Derby on the very first day of Derbyshire's first post-war Championship season of 1946. Virtually an opener because a young amateur named Tilley held a return catch off his first ball in top-class cricket to send back Alderman at the start of the second over, Worthington was still there, just three runs off 150 after giving only one chance, when a hat-trick by Australian all-rounder Vic Jackson abruptly ended the home innings at 276 some three and a half hours later. Leicestershire trailed 92 behind that total, Worthington breaking a stubborn last-wicket partnership, but an opening stand of 190 by Les Berry and George Watson in their second innings piloted them to victory by seven wickets.

Worthington, who in his career was out eight times in the nineties, compiled the last two of his thirty-one first-class centuries in 1947, scoring 104 against Worcestershire at Derby, and 130 against Leicestershire at Ilkeston, in matches Derbyshire won by an innings. He gave the county's batting a much-needed touch of class before being dogged by injuries that caused him to miss almost half of that season's programme, and, as *Wisden* stated, 'the committee's decision to dispense with him after over twenty years of highly capable service was one of the less happy incidents in an enjoyable summer.'

It was entirely inappropriate that because of that decision Worthington departed the county scene with two successive ducks. Consequently, his total of runs for Derbyshire in 648 innings, 54 of them not out, stuck at exactly 17,000, at an average of 28.61. In all first-class matches he had an aggregate of 19,221 at 29.07, his four centuries away from Derbyshire also including one of 129 for the Players against the Gentlemen. His bowling brought him 682 wickets, 624 of them for Derbyshire, at around twenty-nine runs each, and he held 307 of his 340 catches for the county.

With Derbyshire failing to find a place for him on their coaching staff, he turned briefly to playing for Northumberland, where he followed Les Townsend, and in Lancashire League cricket before being appointed as Lancashire's coaching assistant to Harry Makepeace at the beginning of 1950. He succeeded George Duckworth, the former Lancashire and England wicketkeeper, who at that time was in India as manager of the Commonwealth party that included George Pope and George Dawkes.

Makepeace, one of the select band capped by England at both football and cricket, and an FA Cup winner in the first of his two consecutive finals with Everton, retired two years later, ending an association with Lancashire that had lasted for forty-six years. Worthington took over as chief coach for the next ten years. Just over another ten went by before his death in hospital on the first day of September in 1973, while on holiday at King's Lynn. He was sixty-eight.

For a lighthearted tailpiece to this chapter, I turn to a recollection of Gerald Mortimer, a former Sports Editor of the *Derby Evening Telegraph* who for many years reported on Derby County and Derbyshire CCC, and who has regularly reviewed the county cricket club's season for *Wisden*.

Several times during his last two, post-war, seasons with Derbyshire, Worthington's team-mates included his nephew Eric Marsh, a slow left-arm bowler and left-hand batsman who, like his uncle, started out with the Bolsover Colliery cricket team after obtaining his first job there. Marsh, a survivor of the Markham Colliery explosion of 1938 in which seventy-nine died, was a popular coach at Repton School for thirty years after his four seasons with Derbyshire. In one match with the county, he failed to hold a catch off Worthington's bowling, and his plaintive cry of 'Sorry, uncle Stanley', carried clearly to the spectators.

A Derbyshire get together c.1950. Back row (left to right): R.H.R.Buckston, C.S.Elliott MBE. Second row: Harry Elliott, G.H.Pope, G.M.Lee, J.Horsley, James M.Hutchinson, H.Storer, jun, G.J.Burnham. Third row: Denis Smith, T.S.Worthington, W.H.Copson, A.F.Skinner, W.T.Taylor, Harry Watson-Smith. Front row: R.Sale, A.W.Richardson, Guy R Jackson, E.J.Gothard, J.D.Eggar, Capt P.Vaulkhard.

The original grandstand at the County Ground, Derby, in about 1900
(courtesy of Derek Palmer)

The original Grandstand, pictured circa 1900.

Derbyshire v. Hampshire at Derby, 1908. Standing—R. S. T. Cochrane (Secretary), W. Bestwick, S. Cadman, L. G. Wright, L. Oliver, E. Needham. Seated—A. R. Warren, R. Sale, A. E. Lawton (Capt.), R. B. Rickman, A. Morton, J. Humphries

The three Pope brothers (from left, George, Alf and Harold) who all appeared for Derbyshire against the West Indians at Derby in 1939, pictured here during that game

Les Jackson and Cliff Gladwin, the most prolific wicket-takers in Derbyshire's history, pictured in front of the Chesterfield scoreboard after the dismissal of Middlesex for 29 at Chesterfield in 1957. Gladwin took 5-18, Jackson 3-7
(Raymonds Photographic Agency)

176   THE DERBYSHIRE CHRONICLES

The recently demolished Grandstand ablaze in 1940, apparently without any help from the Luftwaffe!

(Courtesy of Derek Palmer)

Champions of 1936. Back row (left to right): H Elliott, L F Townsend, W H Copson, J Bennett (masseur), H Parker (scorer), A V Pope, D Smith, C S Elliott. Front row: H Storer, T S Worthington, A W Richardson (capt), T B Mitchell, A E Alderman

Jimmy Hutchinson, pictured on reaching his 100th birthday. He died on 7 November 2000, twenty-two days short of 104, and 80 years and 62 days after his debut for Derbyshire
(Derby Evening Telegraph)

DERBYSHIRE 1877

Derbyshire players of 1877. Standing (left to right): R P Smith (capt), J Smith, W Mycroft, A Hind, W Hickton, J Horsley (umpire). Seated: L Jackson, T Foster, W Rigley, A Smith, J T B D Platts, G Frost

The original turnstile entrance to the County Ground. It was demolished in the early 1950s
(courtesy of Derek Palmer)

Derbyshire v. Warwickshire, 1919. *Standing*—A. Morton, J. Horsley, W. Bestwick, T. F. Revill, H. Wild, G. Beet. *Seated*—J. Chapman, T. Forester, R. R. Baggallay, L. Oliver, L. E. Flint.

The Derbyshire XI v. Surrey in the first Championship match at Queen's Park, Chesterfield in 1898.
Standing—J. Wheeler (*Umpire*), W. Storer, J. Wright, W. B. Delacombe (*Secretary*), J. Hancock, W. J. Piper (*Hon. Scorer*), H. Bagshaw, W. Bestwick, M. Sherwin (*Umpire*).
Seated—G. Davidson, W. Sugg, W. Chatterton, S. H. Evershed (*Captain*), W. Boden (*President*), G. G. Walker, L. G. Wright.

F R Spofforth, the Demon bowler from Australia
(courtesy of E Hawkins & Co, Brighton)

15. The Rise of Denis Smith

Denis Smith, the tall, elegant left-hander from Somercotes who, to quote again from *Wisden*, 'approached the artistry of Frank Woolley, though not possessing the fluency of the Kent player,' became, in 1935, the first Derbyshire player to be chosen for England on the strength of his batting alone since William Chatterton made his one Test appearance in Cape Town in 1892.

And Smith was more mainly a batsman than Chatterton, who had a career total of over two hundred wickets in top cricket. Smith only occasionally bowled, at right-arm medium pace, though he took five of his twenty first-class wickets (average 36.75) for 37 runs in one innings. That was in his old pal Joe Hardstaff's benefit match at Trent Bridge in 1948 – and Hardstaff was one of his victims, bowled when needing only three runs for a century, though Notts finished the winners by an innings and 45 runs. Like Chatterton, Smith also did some wicketkeeping. Having taken it up while playing in the Bradford League during the 1939-45 war, he afterwards helped to fill the gap left by Harry Elliott with Derbyshire until the arrival of George Dawkes.

Also in common with Chatterton, it was against South Africa that Smith played his Test cricket. The call for him first came for the opening match of the 1935 series at Trent Bridge, but he had to withdraw because of a cracked rib, an absence which, plus dropped catches, influenced Derbyshire's defeat by Warwickshire at Edgbaston. Smith's first-innings 61 was the biggest individual score in a bowlers' match, and but for his injury he could reasonably have been expected to have made more than the eleven runs he painfully added, unbeaten, down the order as Derbyshire's dismissal for 75 set up the home side for their six-wicket win.

After also missing the second Test at Lord's, where the Springboks followed their rain-assisted draw in Nottingham by gaining their first away victory over England, Smith, fit again, made his international debut when injury kept Herbert Sutcliffe out of the third match on the Yorkshire opener's home turf at Leeds. Smith was given his first chance in company with Joe Hardstaff, who had been one of his schoolmates, and whose father, Joseph Senior, had also played for Notts and England.

Smith created a good impression with scores of 36 and 57, sharing in stands of 52 and 128 with two Yorkshiremen who were also new to the Test arena. Wilf Barber was his partner in the first innings, Arthur Mitchell in the second – and thereby hangs one of those tales that add so much to the charm of cricket. Little more than an hour before the start of play, a desperate search for Mitchell, as hopefully the nearest replacement, had to be made by car when Maurice Leyland was suddenly laid low with lumbago, and he had been hurried to Headingley on being found working in his garden. With skipper Bob Wyatt having won the toss, it was not long before Mitchell was walking out to the wicket, and, though so unprepared for such a demanding task, he responded with a determined innings of 58 that occupied more than three hours. And when England batted again he was sent in to open with Smith, this time helping towards a declaration with a sound 72. South Africa were set to get 340 at about 75 an hour, but after hold-ups through rain and bad light they settled for the draw that came with five wickets down, 146 runs from their target. At the lighthearted end Barber and Mitchell were doing the bowling – and it was Barber who claimed that fifth wicket by having the normally big-hitting Horace ('Jock') Cameron stumped in seeking the runs that would have given him his half-century.

The remaining Tests at Old Trafford and The Oval were also drawn, giving South Africa victory in the series. Denis Smith made what was to be his second and last appearance for England in the Manchester match, losing his place after being missed twice in contributing 35 to a first-wicket stand of 71, then falling lbw without scoring in his second innings. The man preferred to him was the recalled Mitchell, who got near another dour half-century in his only knock – and then, and in the final game of the tour, showed he had more than defensive qualities by scoring 103 in two hours for Leveson-Gower's XI at Scarborough.

Smith's opening partner in Manchester was 'Fred' Bakewell, the Northamptonshire batsman whose career was ended by a tragic road accident while he was on his way home from his county's final match, at Chesterfield, of the following season. The car in which he and fellow opener Reg Northway were travelling overturned near Kibworth in Leicestershire. Northway, who had qualified for Northants only that year after having started out with Somerset, was found dead in a ditch by the roadside. Bakewell so damaged his right arm that he was unable to play county cricket again.

The last first-class innings Bakewell played was one of his most magnificent, but not his biggest. Northants recovered from trailing Derbyshire by 65 runs on first innings to have the reigning champions hanging on for a draw largely due to Bakewell's undefeated 241 in a declared total of 411 for six. Two years earlier he had set a Northants record with 246 against Nottinghamshire in an innings regarded by many as the finest seen on the Northampton ground, only to beat it in the very next game with 257 off the Glamorgan attack at Swansea. Against Derbyshire, he hit nineteen fours in a stay of six hours and ten minutes without giving a chance, and his fourth-wicket stand of 211 with Dennis Brookes transformed the game. Brookes, who made 81, was to be a mainstay of the Northants batting for many years after having slipped through the net of his native Yorkshire, but he had the misfortune to chip a finger bone in his only Test (five fewer than Bakewell) in the West Indies in 1947.

Denis Smith was twice on the losing side against the South Africans in the 1935 season – first with Derbyshire, for whom he was out in the thirties in both innings during a defeat by 209 runs at Ilkeston, then with an England XI that lost by an innings and 109 runs at Folkestone. He again failed to live up to his growing reputation in that representative game, but was far from alone in totals of 96 and 106. At least he had the consolation of knowing that his score of 32 was the biggest in that only slightly improved second venture.

Within a few weeks of the end of that season, Smith and Hardstaff went on their first overseas tour together as members of the MCC party that visited Australasia under the captaincy of Surrey's Errol Holmes. Half the six matches played in Australia were won by the tourists, two drawn, and one lost – by ten wickets to New South Wales. Hardstaff made the highest score of the tour, an undefeated 230, in the defeat of a strong Australian XI by 203 runs, totalling 293 in the match for once out, and Smith scored 109 in a stand of 204 with Wilf Barber against Queensland, who were beaten by an innings. The eighteen New Zealand fixtures included four unofficial Tests, all drawn, for which Smith warmed up against Otago at Dunedin by scoring 165 in partnerships of 239 with Jim Parks and 144 with Hardstaff in a total of 472 that was comfortably enough for another innings victory. Smith's four innings in Australia and fourteen in New Zealand produced just over 700 runs at an average not far off fifty.

The only defeat in New Zealand was inflicted by Wellington. Four more wins were gained in the other games, and there were eight draws – one of them in a rain-affected match with a strong Auckland team in which Smith's Derbyshire clubmate Les Townsend was among its seven Test players. Townsend, making his habitual escape from the English winter, scored an unbeaten half-century.

The steady, if brief, rise Denis Smith made to Test recognition was demonstrable testimony to the value of Sam Cadman's painstaking coaching. *Wisden* underlined this in stating:

'When Smith first came under Cadman's notice he could hit the ball hard, but he did not have many strokes. Under Cadman's tuition the weakness was gradually eradicated, and, going to Derby for a trial during 1926, Smith began his career in county cricket the following year. Since then his form has been variable, and his style has changed considerably. He played at odd times from 1927 to 1929, and the perseverance of the Derbyshire authorities was rewarded in 1930, when Smith established his place as an opening batsman.'

It was during that 1930 season that Smith scored the first of his thirty Derbyshire centuries which remained a record for the county until Kim Barnett came along. Barnett now heads the list with 53 (he made 61 in all), and John Morris, later of Durham and Nottinghamshire, has also moved above Smith with 33 of his 52 first-class hundreds completed for Derbyshire. Smith, having established himself as an attractive opening batsman who scored at a good rate and was severe on bowlers who over-pitched, especially on middle or leg stump, made the breakthrough by following a first-innings 83 with 105 against Nottinghamshire at Trent Bridge in the benefit game for Wilfred Payton, who had helped those Derbyshire neighbours to their 1907 and 1929 titles. And in the very next match Smith did it again, his 107 at The Oval paving the way to Derbyshire's first defeat of Surrey for twenty-six years. Payton's son, a Cambridge Blue, also played for Notts – and against them, at Whitsun 1940, for Derbyshire, whom he assisted in a couple of Championship games in 1949. He was one of the dwindling band of cricketing clergymen, his posts including that of an honorary chaplain to the Queen.

Smith also scored a couple of centuries in 1931, when he topped a thousand runs for the first of the twelve times that set another Derbyshire record broken by Barnett, who reached four figures in fifteen seasons until his departure to Gloucestershire. Only three times in fifteen consecutive peacetime seasons as a regular choice did Smith fail to get to the thousand – and in those exceptions he was very near that number with 975 in 1930, 941 in 1933 and 952 in 1947. He stepped up his century count to three in 1932 and four in 1934 before playing the innings that he considered marked the real turning point in his career. It was his first in his most prolific season of 1935. He scored 189 of the 379 runs Derbyshire plundered off the full Yorkshire attack on the opening day at Chesterfield – only to see the match peter out into a draw, leaving Derbyshire with five points instead of the full fifteen, amid the rain and snow of the final day. He went on to be selected that year for the Players against the Gentlemen at both Lord's and Folkestone, and for The Rest against the champion county at The Oval in addition to his two Test appearances.

For the Players at Lord's he scored 69 runs for once out in their nine-wicket victory; at Folkestone he was out for six in the first innings, then made 22 in the second before being dismissed by 'Tuppy' Owen-Smith, the South African Test all-rounder who played for Middlesex after winning his Blue at Oxford and also excelled at rugby, in which he captained England, and boxing. Owen-Smith did the hat-trick in cheaply taking all four wickets that fell before a declaration. In The Rest's second innings against Yorkshire, who won by 149 runs, Smith scored 78 out of 112 when nobody else got into double figures. This was the last such match to be played until 1947, denying Smith the distinction of playing for both sides in successive years when Derbyshire won the title in 1936.

Wisden made Smith one of its Five Cricketers of the Year after he had finished the 1935 season with 2,175 runs (1,767 for Derbyshire) at an average just under forty. That personal best aggregate included the first of his double-centuries, his highest score of 225 (four sixes, 31 fours) in four hours, after being missed at 156, in a winning total of 378 for nine declared against Hampshire, also at Queen's Park. The other, 202 not out two years later when he had his biggest season's total for Derbyshire of 1,914, was made at Trent Bridge, where in 1946 he touched another peak with his 146 in the stand of 328 with Pat Vaulkhard that broke the county's fourth-wicket record. Notts fell short of

Derbyshire's declared total of 529 for nine by exactly the number of runs Vaulkhard took off them, and they were again in difficulties in the follow-on until rain enabled them to salvage a draw.

As already recalled, Smith's double-century at Nottingham put him level with L G Wright's record of twenty-one hundreds for Derbyshire, but it took him into the lead as far as first-class matches were concerned because one of Wright's centuries, 122 against Surrey at The Oval in 1890, was made while the county were in the second class.

Hampshire once more found Smith a redoubtable opponent when they revisited Chesterfield in 1937. In scoring one of his five centuries that year, 140 out of 265, he carried his bat right through a completed innings, a feat he was to repeat with an unbeaten 57 in a total of 112 against Kent at Ilkeston in the last pre-war season of 1939.

In 1948, Smith's second-innings 88 at Derby, made in twenty minutes under four hours, was then Derbyshire's highest individual score against an Australian touring team, beating the 81 by L G Wright in 1896. West Indian Laurie Johnson exceeded it in 1964 with 101 not out, and after South African Chris Wilkins had become the second to take a century off the Aussies for Derbyshire eight years later with exactly 100, and also not out, New Zealander John Wright took the record up to 144 in 1981.

The last of Smith's centuries was scored in 1950. His unbeaten 122 (two sixes, twelve fours) out of 176 led to a recovery from a bad start at Bradford, and led to Derbyshire's first victory over Yorkshire (by 79 runs) since 1905. For their last previous win in Yorkshire they had to go back a further ten years, and 1895 was also the last year until 1950 in which they defeated both Yorkshire and Lancashire in the same season.

With a testimonial of almost £2,000 behind him, Smith gave up thoughts of retiring when a coaching appointment in South Africa offered the chance to keep fit away from the English winter of 1950-51, but he played in only a dozen games the following summer before succeeding Harry Elliott as Derbyshire's coach. He earned a reputation for being hard to please and dauntingly blunt in that post, which he held until eight years before his sudden death at the age of seventy-two in 1979, but any recipient of praise from him could be sure it was truly deserved. He had also been an uncompromising captain when occasionally given that responsibility inn the absence of both the appointed captain and the usual deputy.

Smith played in his 420th and final county match, his only one of 1952, in a rain-spoiled draw with Leicestershire at Derby. At the age of 45 years and 117 days when that game ended, he was the ninth oldest to represent Derbyshire, following Harry Elliott, Bill Bestwick, Sam Cadman, 'Bill' Blaxland, L G Wright, the Hon W M Jervis, Garnet Lee and Joe Bowden, in that order, with Arnold Warren next, just one day younger than Smith. Fittingly, for someone so consistently eager to attack the bowling, Smith was stumped (for ten) in his farewell innings. He bowed out with 21,843 runs to his name, a then record 20,516 of them for Derbyshire at 31.41, and as the only Derbyshire player to have averaged more than thirty (31.65) over his whole career. William Storer averaged 30.70 for Derbyshire, but 28.87 overall. Six players have since averaged forty-plus for Derbyshire alone, with Kim Barnett depriving Smith of yet another county record with his aggregate of 23,854.

So Smith lost his Derbyshire records for runs scored, centuries made, and seasonal totals of four-figure aggregates to a player he was instrumental in bringing to the county's attention. Barnett was to recall: 'Denis and Frank Rasmussen, who was later Derbyshire's scorer, saw me playing for Leek against Great Chell. Denis knew I could bat a bit, but I was originally taken on as a leg-spinner.'

Another Derbyshire record with which Smith retired, but has also since lost, was for the number of catches he held, not counting wicketkeepers. There were 313 of them, mainly at first slip. With the inclusion of those he took while keeping wicket (plus five stumpings), his full total for the county was 361, and 382 in all his first-class games. He is now third in the list, behind Derek Morgan, who held 563 for Derbyshire and ten more in other matches, and Donald Carr (404; 500). Behind Smith come Alan Revill (327; 396), whose father Tom, a left-handed batsman, took part in Derbyshire's famous win over the Australian Imperial Forces team in 1919, and Stan Worthington (307; 340).

By the time Guy Jackson gave up the Derbyshire captaincy after the 1930 season, Denis Smith was one of seven established members of the team who were to play an important part in the winning of the County Championship in 1936. The others were Albert Alderman, Harry Elliott, Tommy Mitchell, Leslie Townsend, Harry Storer and Stan Worthington, though Storer's opportunities in the title year were limited chiefly because of his soccer commitments. It was a very strong nucleus for the new captain, Arthur Richardson, to inherit. To it as regular or frequent choices, in addition to Richardson himself, were added Bill Copson, who features with Mitchell in the next chapter, Charlie Elliott, Alf Pope and Alan Skinner. Another name on that list would have been that of George Pope but for injury. More about him and his brothers later.

Charles Standish Elliott first played in Derbyshire's first team in 1932 after being in the Bassetlaw League with Bolsover Colliery, but he averaged under fourteen with the bat that season and made only occasional appearances in each of the next three years before missing just ten of the county's twenty-eight Championship matches when the title was won in 1936. He gained a regular place that season after Sam Hunt, a batsman from Doe Lea, had failed to fill the middle-order vacancy caused by Carrington's loss of form, but still had a struggle to get to 500 runs at an average of just under twenty-one – and that only with taking into account his 77, top score in a total of 160, in the drawn game against the Indian tourists. Consequently, he was released the following year, and went into league cricket. After the war, however, he was re-engaged, and this time he made good to such an extent, as a stubborn but dependable opener, that by the time he finally retired as a player after Leicestershire's visit to Derby in mid-August 1953 he had exceeded a thousand runs in the six consecutive seasons from 1947 in mustering 11,965 runs in 468 innings for Derbyshire at an average of 27.25.

Elliott scored the first of his nine centuries, against Essex at Ilford in 1946, ten years after missing that maiden hundred by only three runs at Edgbaston in the season Derbyshire at last became undisputed champions. The last one came against Northamptonshire at Chesterfield the month before his departure, when he batted throughout the second day of a drawn game for 132 not out in a typically sound defensive display. And he held the last of his 209 catches in dismissing Yorkshire's captain, Norman Yardley, off Les Jackson's bowling in his penultimate match, a defeat at Scarborough. He also pulled off one stumping – off the bowling of Bert Rhodes at the expense of Leicestershire's Maurice Tompkin, while standing in for his uncle Harry in 1947.

It was in that year that Charlie Elliott made his top score, 215 in six hours, in a stand of 349 with John Eggar, a master at Repton, against Nottinghamshire at Trent Bridge. In not only breaking the county's record for the second wicket, set up when L G Wright and E M Ashcroft added 210 against Sussex at Derby in 1905, they also exceeded the biggest partnership for any Derbyshire wicket – the 328 by Denis Smith and Pat Vaulkhard at the same ground in 1946. Not until 1997 were both those records taken over by Kim Barnett and Tim Tweats, who put on 417 against Yorkshire at Derby.

When Elliott partnered Eggar in their big stand he was still a year away from ending a professional footballing career with Coventry City that he had begun in 1931, after a spell in the background on the books of Sheffield Wednesday, as a 19-year-old signing from Chesterfield by Harry Storer, the then manager at Highfield Road who was to be one of his Derbyshire teammates. For Coventry, Elliott proved a sound deputy in either full-back position, and on one occasion as a scoring stand-in centre-forward, before excelling at centre-half when skipper George Mason had to miss the last two games of the 1935-36 season in which City clinched the Third Division (South) title.

After playing more frequently during the war despite service in the Royal Navy, Elliott was a regular member of Coventry's defence in the transitional League South of 1945-46, and he then made twenty-eight appearances, his highest number for a Football League season, when the club resumed in the Second Division. A few years after retiring with 101 League and Cup games behind him, he rejoined Coventry as chief scout, and when Jack Fairbrother, the former Newcastle goalkeeper, resigned as manager in October 1954, after the death of his wife in an accident at home, he took over in a caretaker capacity until Jesse Carver, a pre-war wing-half with Blackburn, Newcastle and Bury, was appointed the following June.

Elliott then reverted to being chief scout, but, in those troubled times for relegated Coventry, he resigned in the autumn of 1955, shortly before Carver also left the club to return to Italian football. With his county cricket playing career by then also at an end, Elliott took over a hotel at West Bridgford, near the Trent Bridge ground in Nottingham, and from 1956 until 1974 he rendered the summer game further admirable service as an umpire – one who, besides all the usual umpiring equipment, invariably kept a big cigar in his top pocket. He rose to the very top in that role, for in addition to standing in 335 County Championship games he officiated in forty-two Tests – a number previously exceeded only by the legendary Frank Chester's forty-eight – and two matches between England and the Rest of the World in 1970. When Bob Taylor, Derbyshire's wicketkeeper, made his Test debut in the first match of the 1971 series with New Zealand in Christchurch, Elliott, who was out there on a Churchill Fellowship, accepted an invitation from the New Zealand Cricket Council to be one of the umpires.

A few weeks before that game, Elliott also had the distinction of being the adjudicator of the Man of the Match award in the first one-day international, which was hastily arranged to appease the public on the final day of the rain-curtailed Test between Australia and England at Melbourne. His choice, in a match won by Australia, was John Edrich, the Surrey left-hand opening batsman, who scored 82.

The first Test in which Elliott umpired was the first to be staged at Edgbaston for nearly thirty years. It was the one in which England were brought back from the brink of defeat by a record fourth-wicket stand of 411 between Peter May and Colin Cowdrey. He last stood in a Test when Pakistan drew at Lord's in 1974, after which *Wisden* observed that he 'always carried out his duties in a dignified manner'. Bob Taylor said he was 'one of the old school of umpires, and all the players had a lot of respect for him'.

And that was far from the end of the Charlie Elliott cricketing story. In his seven years up to 1981 as an England selector he earned the tribute from Alec Bedser, the former Surrey and England bowler who was the chairman, that he was 'a great fellow, very reliable, and a sound judge of a player'. Later he was on the Derbyshire committee, including a spells as chairman and president. On being succeeded by Guy Willatt after his year as president, he remarked:

'I first came on this [Derby] ground for two weeks in the nets in 1928, and I joined the ground staff in 1929. Now I'm retiring as president in 1995. I'm quite proud of that.'

He had every reason to be. In his ninetieth year he was still running his guesthouse, liberally festooned with memorabilia, at West Bridgford. He died on New Year's Day 2004, almost four months short of his ninety-second birthday.

Of the players only rarely called upon by Derbyshire in the title year, most appearances – just seven in the Championship, plus two others against Oxford

University and the Indian tourists – were made by Elijah Carrington, a Blackwell-born miner who was an attacking right-hand batsman with Blackwell, Glapwell Colliery and Teversal Welfare in the Bassetlaw League. He made his highest first-class score in the 1934 season of his county debut at Portsmouth, scoring 80 against Worcestershire at Chesterfield in a match that was rained off with Derbyshire on course for victory after leading by 250 on first innings. In the following year he was only six short of that figure at the same ground in helping Denis Smith (189) to add 202 in two hours for the fourth wicket against Yorkshire, but he faded after beginning the 1936 campaign with 72 at Southampton and was released at the end of the next season.

The Bassetlaw League featured prominently in the cricketing life of another player who assisted Derbyshire only a few times in their Championship-winning year. This was George Langdale, a left-hand batsman and right-arm off-break bowler from Thornaby-on-Tees in Yorkshire whose opportunities at first-class level were curtailed by his business commitments. After playing in the Bassetlaw League for Worksop during the 1939-45 war, in which he also turned out for Hull in the Yorkshire League and Kidderminster in the Birmingham League, he wrote *A History of the Bassetlaw and District Cricket League, 1904-1978,* and was its president in 1985. He was a 20-year-old student at Nottingham University when he made his debut for Derbyshire in a drawn game with Notts at Worksop in the middle of August in 1936, but he played only twice more that year, and just once in 1937, all without doing anything of note, before dropping in the Minor Counties with Norfolk for the last pre-war season.

After Army service, he returned to the County Championship with Somerset and made an immediate impact by taking 5-30 on his first appearance against Warwickshire at Edgbaston, then scoring 146 against Yorkshire in his first game at Taunton and 69 not out against Glamorgan at Weston-super-Mare. Such was the power of his driving, cutting and pulling that he hit two sixes and twenty fours in a stay of two and threequarter hours in the drawn match with Yorkshire, and a six and eleven fours in fifty minutes in a light-hearted finish to the Welshmen's visit after a rain-delayed start had made another draw inevitable. Somerset's total of 508 was the biggest made that season against Yorkshire, though those champions-to-be were without two of their main bowlers, Bill Bowes and Arthur Booth – and also Len Hutton.

Booth's 84 wickets at 11.90 runs each in his comeback to first-class cricket with his home county that year were, as *Wisden* said, 'surely without parallel at the age of 43.' Unwanted when first tried by Yorkshire fifteen years earlier, and allowed to slip off to Northamptonshire, he was recalled to fill the yawning gap left by Hedley Verity, the England left-arm spinner whose death on active service with the Green Howards in Italy had been reported on the first day of September in 1943 – exactly four years after his last match for Yorkshire in which he had taken seven wickets for nine runs in a Sussex innings at Hove two days before war broke out.

Three years after playing the last of his twenty games for Somerset in 1949, George Langdale joined Berkshire and topped the Minor Counties bowling averages with 57 wickets at 11.21 in the first of his dozen seasons with that county. In the following year, when Berkshire won the title for the third time, he took all ten wickets for 25 runs in a Dorset innings at Reading and became the first to do the double of 500 runs and 50 wickets at that level since 1927. No other Minor Counties player achieved that feat until Parvez Mir, a Pakistani who scored an unbeaten half-century against Oxford University in his one match for Derbyshire in 1975, did so with Norfolk in 1984.

Langdale made his last first-class appearance in 1953, for the Minor Counties against the Australians at Stoke-on-Trent. It was not an auspicious occasion for either himself or his colleagues. A team that also included Charlie Lee, a Yorkshireman who was to play for, and captain, Derbyshire, collapsed for totals of 56 and 62 on a pitch of doubtful quality and lost by an innings and 171 runs inside two days.

There were four others who played for Derbyshire in the County Championship in 1936, but they totalled only half-a-dozen games between them. Tommy Armstrong, a slow left-arm bowler from Clay Cross, deputised in the last two matches for Mitchell, who had injured a thumb; Arnold Townsend was also called upon twice; and, in Arthur Richardson's absence, the team was captained in the opening fixture by Wilfred Hill-Wood, then in the second match by Capt Niel Walker.

Armstrong, like Townsend, was not to play in his last first-class game for the county until 1950, though his intermittent appearances, dating back to 1929, numbered just fewer than sixty, in which he took 133 wickets at 24.35, over that long period. For the two amateurs it was their Derbyshire farewell, but Hill-Wood played twice more for the MCC at Lord's – against the universities of Cambridge (1938) and Oxford (1939). Niel Alexander McDonald Walker was an Army man, born in Poona (now Pune), who played in two first-class matches for the Europeans in India, against the Hindus in the Lahore tournament of 1923-24, and the MCC at Karachi in 1926, then in just two more for Derbyshire. Five years before leading the team in a defeat by Kent at Gravesend immediately before Richardson took over, he made his county debut against the New Zealanders at Derby.

Arthur Walker Richardson proved an admirable successor to Jackson as captain. He had been in the Winchester XI of 1925, and had shared a second-wicket stand of 295 in scoring 117 against Harrow. As a batsman, slightly ungainly and heavily reliant for his runs on the leg side, he naturally found first-class cricket much more demanding, but, as *Wisden* stated, 'by determination and courage, and keeping sensibly within his own limitations, he played many useful innings.' As a captain, he maintained the high standards set by his predecessor during his six seasons in charge until he retired to concentrate on his family business in the wake of the county's greatest triumph. His enthusiasm and warm personality were key ingredients in the steady climb to the pinnacle. Talk of the major decisions being made for him by the experienced Harry Elliott was soon found to be groundless.

When Richardson first played for Derbyshire in 1928 it was said that his father, in the hope of giving him the boost of having something to aim for, had promised him £1 for every run he scored that season. If that was indeed the case, he would have earned twice the then current pay of a professional, for he ended with a total of 531 runs, with a top score of 70 not out, for an average in the early twenties. His best year, by far, was 1932, in which, as mainly an opener, he averaged almost thirty in gathering 1,258 runs and made his highest county score of 90, against Nottinghamshire at Ilkeston.

That, however, was the most disappointing season of his captaincy in terms of the team's performance, with a fall to tenth place in the final table, though there was an encouraging improvement after losing early ground largely due to the extremely bad weather which caused streets in Derby itself to be flooded. The club's finances were desperately hard hit as torrential rain allowed only one day's play in three home matches during May, and the consequent loss of momentum was then exacerbated by five successive defeats. The revival began in late June with the first win against Nottinghamshire since 1921 in which Richardson got so close to a maiden first-class century, and Smith, Townsend and Worthington went on to join their skipper in exceeding one thousand runs.

Derbyshire rose to sixth in 1933, but illness and injury caused Richardson to miss two-thirds of their matches that year, and, with Skinner capably stepping into the captaincy breach in the meantime, it was not until 1935 that he was again able to play regularly. This resulted in a loss of form he eventually regained only during the closing weeks of the championship-winning season, during which he scored fewer than four hundred runs at an average of only just over twelve. After that he did not appear in a Derbyshire first team again, but he continued to give the club valuable service behind the scenes. He was seventy-six when he died at an Ednaston nursing home in July 1983.

The eldest of his two sons, George William Richardson, also attended Winchester School, where he was in the team in 1956, and also played for Derbyshire. A hard-hitting right-hand batsman and fast left-arm bowler, the well-built William was appointed captain of the second team for 1959, but he led it only a couple of times before being promoted to the senior side as the replacement when Harold Rhodes was chosen to play for the MCC against the Indian tourists at Lord's (but had to drop out through injury). On his debut young Richardson had match figures of seven wickets for 74 runs in a nine-wicket defeat of Worcestershire at Chesterfield, and in his second match he struck three sixes and thirteen fours in an innings of 91 against Glamorgan at

Swansea, scoring 75 of the 81 added for the ninth wicket. That, however, was not enough to bring another victory, the Welsh county winning by three wickets. Neither was Richardson, whose bowling was inclined to be erratic, able to sustain that impressive start, which also included his best return of 8-54, on only his fourth appearance, in Kent's first innings as Derbyshire progressed to a convincing win at Chesterfield. He left first-class cricket with almost 1,500 runs at an average of just under sixteen, and nearly 150 wickets that cost a little below twenty-eight runs apiece.

This Richardson family's connection with the Derbyshire club stretched to a third generation – but only just. William's son Alistair consistently took wickets for the county's second team, but although he made an encouraging first-class debut against Glamorgan in 1992 he was inclined to be expensive and was given only one further senior opportunity before his contract was not renewed for 1995.

16. *Copson and Mitchell*

But for the General Strike of 1926 Derbyshire almost certainly would never have fielded the two bowlers whose speed and spin sparked their title triumph ten years later.

In that peak season of 1936 for the Peakites, the pace of William Henry Copson gobbled up 140 wickets in the Championship at a cost of only 12.8 runs each. The potent mixture of leg-breaks, off-breaks, top-spinners and googlies impishly served up by the bespectacled Thomas Bignall Mitchell accounted for 116 at 20.45.

With the inclusion of Derbyshire's games against Oxford University and the Indian touring team, Copson's total reached 153, and he had an overall tally of 160 at 13.34 when his appearances in three other first-class matches were taken into account – for the Players against the Gentlemen and the North versus the South, both at Lord's, and for the MCC Australian Touring Team against H D G Leveson-Gower's XI at Scarborough. Mitchell's wickets in Derbyshire's two extra fixtures took him to 121 in all at 21.42.

Copson's best return in the three games he played away from the county, all drawn, was 4-29 in the Gents' first innings, and he held the catch off Alf Gover's bowling that sent back Freddie Brown, the top scorer with 55. He also caught Maurice Turnbull, the South's main run-getter on 106, off Hedley Verity, and snapped up Denis Smith off Kenneth Farnes after his Derbyshire team-mate had made 22 for Leveson-Gower's side.

Yet Copson showed no interest in cricket until fellow miners at the Morton Colliery near Chesterfield persuaded him to join in the matches they played on the local recreation ground to help while away their idle hours during the strike that lasted for some ten days early in the May of 1926. And the Creswell-born Mitchell, a faceworker at Creswell Colliery who as a nine-year-old had sung *Oh, for the Wings of a Dove* before King George V and Queen Mary, needed an exceptional amount of cajoling out of his apathy towards the national summer game after his extraordinary ability to apply spin to a ball had entertained miners in the neighbourhood clubs during their pit dispute.

The ball Mitchell manipulated so mesmerisingly was not a cricket ball but a billiard ball. G H Simpson-Hayward, the Worcestershire and England spinner who was one of the last of the underarm bowlers in first-class cricket, got his idea of bowling lobs from spinning a billiard ball. 'In my young days,' he wrote, 'I was very fond of playing with small tops which you spin with your fingers on a tray, and this made my fingers very strong, which is a great help in bowling lobs. It struck me that if I could spin an ivory ball why not a cricket ball?' So he got down to serious practice, and, after a great deal of trial and effort, made the ball 'fizz' off the pitch at a surprising pace in addition to spinning it prodigiously. The cricketing possibilities of Mitchell's phenomenal skill with the billiard ball were readily appreciated by Herbert Slater, one of the three brothers from Creswell who followed their father into the Derbyshire team, but he found it a far more difficult job than he had bargained for in trying to make this obstinate young man share his enthusiasm.

Having failed to make even the slightest dent in Mitchell's stubborn aversion to anything to do with cricket, Slater sought the support of the secretary of the Bassetlaw League, one E Topham, of Worksop. Their combined efforts were also futile at the outset, but they kept at it, and eventually their reluctant protege came to realise the benefits he might gain from harnessing the natural talent he had developed to the expert coaching on length and flight that could turn him into a top-class bowler.

Herbert Slater was joined by his eldest brother, George, in giving that instruction under the auspices of the Creswell club, and all concerned had immediate encouragement as Mitchell bowled his team to victory in an inter-departmental competition the colliers had organised to occupy some of their strike-bound hours. A step up to the colliery's second team brought further successes that earned his rapid promotion to the senior side in the Bassetlaw League, where he promptly became the biggest scourge of batsmen since Harold Larwood had blazed his path to Nottinghamshire and England fame in the same sphere three years earlier.

Mitchell was taken on by Derbyshire after impressing Guy Jackson when the county's captain took a team to play at the colliery, but again he was a hard man to persuade. The original offer of £3 a week had to be stepped up by another pound before he would sign. Within five years of entering first-class cricket in 1928 he was helping England to beat Australia in the blistering heat of Brisbane. By the time his first-class career ended with the outbreak of war in 1939, he had taken more wickets than any other Derbyshire bowler (1,483 at 20.59) – ten or more of them in a match a Derbyshire record twenty-nine times (thirty in all) – broken the county's record for dismissals in a season (168 at 19.54 in 1935), and become their only player to equal Bill Bestwick's feat of capturing all ten wickets in one innings (for 64 runs at Leicester in 1935).

For Derbyshire matches alone, Mitchell, with 1,417 wickets at 20.20, is now fourth in the list behind Les Jackson, Cliff Gladwin and Bestwick, but his seasonal aggregate record still stands – most closely challenged by Bill Copson's 153 at 12.54 in the 1936 year of the champions.

Mitchell, who was in his ninety-fourth year when he died after a long illness at Hickleton Hall, the Sue Ryder Home near Doncaster, on 27 January 1996, made a deceptively subdued entry into Derbyshire's senior ranks at the age of twenty-five, his seventeen wickets in his dozen games of 1928 costing almost 44 runs apiece. But from the first innings of the opening game of the following season, in which he took 5-34 against Lancashire, wickets topped to him in abundance – a hundred or more of them in each of ten successive years from 1929 to 1938. In the early post-war seasons Les Jackson equalled that number, and Cliff Gladwin raised the county record to twelve, but neither of them did so consecutively. Mitchell finished the 1929 season at the head of Derbyshire's bowling averages with 103 Championship wickets (111 in all) at an average cost of just over nineteen. More than half of them came in the club's first eight matches, and three times he claimed at least ten in one game. That rapid rise to the forefront earned this renowned wag and leg-puller a place in The Rest XI against England at Lord's, and after taking part in another Test trial at Old Trafford in 1932 he was in the MCC party that sailed out to Australia aboard the liner *Orantes* that autumn. On 10 February the next year, with England 2-1 up in the series, listeners to Alan Fairfax's crackling commentary on the opening day of the fourth Test in Brisbane heard the dramatic news that he had bowled Bill Woodfull, the Australian captain known as the Unbowlable, on what former Test spinner Arthur Mailey called 'a heartbreaking wicket' for bowlers.

That was the match in which Eddie Paynter, the little Lancashire left-hander, was taken ill with tonsillitis but twice left his sick bed at a nearby nursing home in the course of playing one of the most courageous innings in Test history. Batting down the order, he stemmed an England collapse with his plucky innings of 83, made in nearly four hours without recourse to Woodfull's generous offer of a runner, and when he went in again on the sixth and final day it was entirely fitting that he should strike the winning six that regained the Ashes.

That was also the match in which the flags around the ground flew at half-mast because of the death, at the tragically early age of twenty-three, of Scottish-born Archie Jackson, the gifted New South Wales and Australia batsman who had been hailed as the second Victor Trumper.

Tommy Mitchell captured Woodfull's wicket again (caught by Wally Hammond) in Australia's second innings, but his Test debut match figures of 3-60 in a six-wicket victory were not sufficient to keep him in the team for the final Test in Sydney. In a controversial series dominated by the leg theory of England's pace attack, he was brought in at Brisbane because the pitch used there in the MCC's recent match with Queensland had not favoured fast bowlers – although, in any case, Bill Voce, Harold Larwood's opening speed partner, was unavailable for the fourth Test and Bill Bowes, of Yorkshire, was out of favour. In his book *And Then Came Larwood,* Arthur Mailey wrote:

'The Englishmen were naturally perturbed about the character of the wicket. Jardine [the England captain] illustrated his anxiety on two occasions. During the progress of the recent match [with Queensland] he suggested that the cover should be taken off the Test wicket, which at the time was being prepared. The cover was used to protect the Test wicket against the footmarks of the fieldsmen. Jardine probably thought that a sun-baked wicket would be faster than one which had been sweated under canvas. When the Queensland match had finished, and the crowd had drifted away, Jardine took Mitchell, the slow bowler, out to the ground and tried him out on the worn wicket, in order to see whether he could turn the ball. Both these incidents were significant ... I do not remember such precautionary methods as these being taken before a cricket match.'

On what he saw of Mitchell during that tour, Mailey also provided an interesting Australian viewpoint in regarding the Derbyshire man as 'a keen but irresponsible bowler ... too volatile, impatient, unsettled and highly strung to be a consistently great slow bowler.' He added:

'A little more mellowness, deliberation and patience would have improved his bowling 50 per cent at least. As far as I could see, he seemed to give little thought to the general placing of his field. His tendency was to wave his arms around and alter it after every ball unless he obtained a wicket. When this happened the amusing Tom was satisfied that no field had been so perfectly placed.'

Despite doing nothing extraordinary in the Brisbane Test (England's opening bowlers, Larwood and 'Gubby' Allen, shared most of the Australian wickets after all), Mitchell did have his moments in other games on the tour – notably with 7-77 against Southern Districts at Wagga Wagga, and 5-74 against Tasmania in Launceston. In the MCC's second match with New South Wales in Sydney he also did what Stan Worthington was to do for a second time by bowling Don Bradman, on that occasion for only a single. It was a feat achieved by another Derbyshire player, Eddie Gothard, who, in the last of his two seasons as the county's captain, dismissed Bradman for 62 when the Australians visited Derby in 1948.

Mitchell, with only one wicket at a cost of 49 runs, also had to take a back seat on his second England appearance in one of the two three-day Tests played in the New Zealand section of the 1932-33 tour. But he was not alone. Walter Hammond commandeered that short series with scores of 227 and the then Test record of 336.

Although his career average was unusually low for a spin bowler, Mitchell's eight wickets in Test cricket cost him more than 60 runs each. He admitted that he 'strained too hard' at international level. After taking only one wicket for 108 runs in England's defeat by Australia at Nottingham in the first match of the 1934 series, and none at all for 117 in the tourists' only innings of the drawn fourth match in which Bradman made his second triple century at Leeds, he was awarded what was to be his fifth and final cap in controversial circumstances against South Africa at Lord's in 1935.

P F Warner, a selector that year with Percy Perrin, Tom Higson and Bob Wyatt, who was co-opted as captain, recalled in his book *Cricket Between Two Wars* that 'the choice of this team involved the longest selection meeting of my experience.' He continued:

'It began at 11 o'clock in the morning and did not end until nearly seven. The point at issue was whether Robins [Walter Robins, the Middlesex all-rounder] or Mitchell should play. The selectors were unanimous in urging the claims of Robins, and Wyatt, for his part, was emphatic in urging Mitchell. We pointed out that Mitchell, good bowler as he was, had been a complete failure against the Australians the previous summer, and that in no sense could he be compared with Robins either as batsman or fieldsman [though Mitchell, in fact, was often brilliant in the field, especially at cover point].

'1935 was the year of the leatherjacket – the larvae of the daddy-longlegs as it was officially described – which had descended on Lord's and caused it to look like the sand on the sea shore, and Wyatt was of the opinion that Mitchell would win the match for us on the leatherjacket wicket. He had recently played against Mitchell in the Warwickshire v Derbyshire match at Birmingham, and had been impressed by his bowling [Mitchell had bowled him for a duck in match figures of 7-82].

'Finally, we said to him, 'If you don't have Mitchell, you would feel that you had not been given the team you, as captain, wish?' He said, 'Yes, I would.' Now the captain has a casting vote – and great weight must obviously be given to his views. No argument, no comparison of previous performances, however, could convince him, and in the end we gave way. None of us can escape responsibility; it was a committee decision. Dearly we were to pay for it.'

They paid for it with South Africa's first Test victory in England. In a comparatively low-scoring match (South Africa 228 and 278-7 declared; England 198 and 151) Mitchell conceded 164 runs in taking three wickets in 53 overs. He made a good start by bowling opener Ivan Siedle with only 27 runs on the board – and he had the same batsman caught at the wicket when the total was 32 in South Africa's second innings – but his namesake Bruce Mitchell shared century stands with Eric Rowan and Arthur ('Chud') Langton in carrying his bat for 161. That was only fifteen runs short of the then biggest score by a Springbok against England, made by Herby Taylor in Johannesburg in 1923. The declaration set a target of 309 in 285 minutes that proved well out of reach under the handicap of Herbert Sutcliffe and Leslie Ames both having the employ a runner because of strains.

In a county match, Walter Robins, the player the selectors wanted in preference to Mitchell, was also a victim of the Derbyshire player in another sense, heightened by a prank played by his impish Middlesex colleague 'Patsy' Hendren. He was batting with Hendren against Derbyshire on a damp day at Lord's when he failed to make contact with the ball in running out to try to drive Mitchell, so he kept straight on for the pavilion without looking back, convinced that he would be stumped. 'Look out,' cried Hendren. 'He's missed it.' Robins promptly wheeled round, dived full length, and just managed to get his bat over the crease with his arm at full stretch. Bespattered with mud, he looked up in relief, only to see Harry Elliott chatting with first slip after having had ample time to break the wicket while Robins was well out of his ground.

Any chance of the Test door reopening for Tommy Mitchell after being slammed shut on him following his disputed selection against the Springboks was blighted by his getting the wrong side of the man who had championed his cause. He fell into an argument with Bob Wyatt during that Lord's match, reputedly telling him: 'You couldn't captain a box of bloody lead soldiers.'

For his county, however, and for all his faults, Mitchell, the mercurial Creswell conjurer, was undoubtedly one of cricket's most consistent performers and genuine characters throughout the 1930s. When 'Crusoe' Robertson-Glasgow, who wrote so entertainingly and authoritatively on the game, drew up his list of nearly a hundred batsmen and bowlers of the years 1920-40 in his book *Cricket Prints,* Mitchell was the only Derbyshire player to feature. Not that it was all glowing praise, though. Indeed, 'Crusoe' thought there was 'something of Donald Duck about him', adding: 'No cricketer so conveys to the spectators the perplexities and frustration of a man at the mercy of malignant fate … He is the comedian of tragedy.'

'Crusoe,' however, acknowledged Mitchell as 'one of the great bowlers, an artist of spin and deception, a master of flight and variety – but … only when he feels like it. His brain, shrewd and calculating, is of the North, but his temperament is torrid, of the far South'. Robertson-Glasgow continued:

'His overs are rapid and impatient. Very short of leg, strangely long in body, with sleeves flapping, he pivots into the attack and astonishes the batsman with a sharp burst of leg-breaks, top-spinners, googlies and old-fashioned off-breaks. A ghastly long-hop is hooked whizzingly past short-leg's head. He stands, arms akimbo, reproving the invisible, then flicks up the returned ball from boot to hand. Next ball, he emits a shattering appeal, and his very spectacles flash disagreement with the answer. But on his red-letter days, when all the tricks are going right, he is the master; and then he looks as if he might break into song or execute a rhumba.'

Of those red-letter days, Mitchell served up some of his most magical at Chesterfield in 1931, Derby and Stourbridge in 1934, and Leicester in 1935. On the first of those occasions he took twelve Sussex wickets for thirty runs (6-11 and 6-10); on each of the next two he tweaked out thirteen batsmen in matches with Middlesex and Worcestershire; on the other he had an analysis of 19.1-4-64-10 in a Leicestershire total of 123 (see p.339).

His 6-56 in Middlesex's first innings at Derby included a seven-ball spell in which he took four wickets without cost. Victory was assured with his second-innings 7-57 that completed the best match figures by a Derbyshire bowler against that county. At Stourbridge, he took 8-22 in 36 balls as Worcestershire were spun out for 48, the lowest total of the season, in just over an hour after tea. Then, backed up by Leslie Townsend (5-48), he bagged 5-66 as the home county followed on to an innings defeat. The all-ten feat (twelve in the match), despite which Leicestershire salvaged a draw, came in Mitchell's most successful season, during which he broke Bill Bestwick's club record of 147 wickets.

Four years later, Bestwick's career total also went by the board, though he still headed Mitchell for Derbyshire games alone.

In matches with touring teams, Mitchell returned Derbyshire's best match figures of 10-49 against the Indians at Ilkeston in 1932, and 10-176 against the New Zealanders at Derby in 1937. At Chesterfield in 1934 he took 7-105 in one Australian innings.

Mitchell, whose son (also Tom, and also a leg-spin bowler) had a spell on Derbyshire's nursery staff in the mid-1950s but without getting into the first team, preceded his personal best year of 1935 with 111 wickets in 1929, 138 in 1930, 110 in 1931, 212 in 1932, 142 in 1933 and 145 in 1934. After it, he took 121 in 1936, 129 in 1937 and 131 in 1938 before, in the last pre-war season, falling below the century mark for the first time since his debut year. In 1939 he was eighteen short. As a batsman, he was a typical No 11, reaching a half-century just once with 57 against Lancashire at Old Trafford in 1937, though he took part in four last-wicket stands of more than fifty.

On failing to agree terms with Derbyshire after the war, he returned to mining, and for almost ten seasons he continued his wicketful way well into his fifties with Hickleton Main, helping them to win both Yorkshire Council league and cup before a severe injury to his right hand compelled him to give up the game. In one match with Heckmondwike, he took 4-22 in forming a winning ex-Derbyshire combination with Jim Hutchinson (6-7).

The Derbyshire career of Bill Copson, who was nearly seven years Mitchell's junior, stretched into a thirteenth first-class season (one more than Mitchell) when, in 1950, shortly after his forty-first birthday, he was recalled from his professional post with Lidget Green in the Bradford League for one final appearance at Leicester. He was suddenly required in the absence of Cliff Gladwin, who had tonsillitis, and Les Jackson, who was playing for The Rest against England in the Test trial at Bradford in which Jim Laker, Surrey's Yorkshire-born off-spinner, exploited conditions that did not favour fast bowling by returning the astonishing analysis of 14-12-2-8 in The Rest's first innings. Eric Hollies, the Warwickshire spinner, took 6-28 when a side that included another Derbyshire player, Donald Carr, sagged a second time to an innings defeat; Bob Berry, a slow bowler then with Lancashire who won his third county cap with Derbyshire after also assisting Worcestershire, was The Rest's most successful bowler with 5-73.

Derbyshire were also beaten in Bill Copson's surprise farewell game, despite a century by Alan Revill against the county he was to join, but the veteran fast bowler still managed to make a praiseworthy exit with the wickets of two of Leicestershire's best batsmen, the long-serving Gerry Lester and their new secretary-captain from Worcestershire, Charles Palmer. Those wickets took him to a total of 1,033 for Derbyshire at 18.76 each, and 1,094 overall. At that time only Bestwick and Mitchell had got into four figures for the county, though Leslie Townsend had done so in all his first-class games.

Copson's thousandth victim was Brunton Smith, caught by George Dawkes in the New Zealanders' second innings at Derby in 1949. His first, seventeen years earlier, caused quite a sensation. Off the very first ball he bowled in the County Championship, Charlie Elliott held the catch that sent back Andy Sandham, amasser of more than 40,000 runs and a century of centuries during nearly a score of peacetime seasons with Surrey. Henry Curgenven had been the first to take a wicket with his first ball Derbyshire, dismissing Essex's Frederick Fane, later an England captain, at Leyton in 1896. In 1958, F C ('Jim') Brailsford, who played in only three first-team matches in his two seasons on the ground staff, became the third, dismissing Ted Dexter, another future England skipper, in Sussex's second innings at Derby.

There was a fourth instance, but outside the Championship, at Chesterfield in 1980, when New Zealander John Wright was given a rare bowl after a hat-trick by Mike Hendrick had been offset by a Derbyshire second-innings collapse that had left the West Indian tourists needing only a few runs for victory. Wright, whose 96 in the county's first innings is still their highest individual score against a West Indian team, promptly had Faoud Bacchus caught by South African Peter Kirsten, but then conceded the winning boundary off his fourth delivery.

To his immediate illustrious first 'scalp' at The Oval in 1932, Bill Copson smartly added two others of Test calibre, Douglas Jardine and Percy Fender, and another consistent scorer who went very close to international selection, Tom Shepherd, at a personal cost of 43 runs – only for Surrey to hit back to win by 199.

Sandham's fate was no new experience for the Stonebroom-born Copson. As a lanky youth of seventeen, he found he was a born fast bowler from the moment he grasped a cricket ball for the very first time after one of his mates had urged him to join in as he stood watching the striking miners at play during the early summer of 1926. 'It'll help pass the time he was told,' so he shyly agreed. He ran in, hurled the ball down as fast as he could, and wrecked the wicket off a perfect length before the startled batsman could attempt a stroke. There were guffaws all round and talk of 'a fluke' and 'beginner's luck', but Bill was soon to show how misguided that reaction was.

His appetite whetted, he was given a place in the Morton Colliery second XI when the strike was over, then quickly gained promotion to the first team in which he was regularly among the wickets before stepping up to the Derbyshire League with Clay Cross in 1931. Again there were suggestions that he would now be 'found out', but he answered them in the most emphatic manner by taking all ten Staveley wickets for five runs – an achievement that led to his successful trial with Derbyshire after Fred Marsh, secretary of the Morton Colliery club, had put in a strong recommendation to the county.

After his eventful start against Surrey, Copson played in fifteen further matches in the 1932 season and finished it with 46 wickets at a shade under 27 runs each. From there he progressed to 90 at 21.34 in 1933 (including 7-62 in a Gloucestershire innings at Cheltenham) and 91 at 17.61 in 1934, but missed an increasing number of games in taking 71 at 16.53 in 1935. Those absences raised some serious doubts about his health and fitness. Derbyshire's officials, indeed, were so concerned about his breakdowns that they sent him to Skegness for a bracing holiday. They also had him examined by specialists, and eventually it was found that he had strained the sacroiliac joint at the base of his back. As part of the treatment to remedy this, the carroty-haired Copson was sent off to train with Chesterfield's footballers during the winter of 1935-36.

When the time came round to prepare for the new cricket season, he reported back to Derbyshire a new man – in physique (he put on nearly a stone in weight) if not in demeanour, for his long face still registered little emotion even when he swept to success after success in spearheading Derbyshire's drive to the title as his most productive season placed him, with Stan Worthington, among *Wisden's* Five Cricketers of the Year. In its review of the 1936 season, the almanack observed:

'Copson developed in a way which more than justified the remarks of those who saw in him the makings of one of England's best bowlers of his type for years. His fiery bowling at the beginning of an innings frequently gave Derbyshire the whiphand, and his exceptional "nip" off the pitch, swing and swerve, allied to a good length, demoralised many batsman before they gained a proper sight of the ball.'

In truth, Copson's length was not always as immaculate as *Wisden* made out – some critics considered he was inclined to bowl a little too short – but there was no denying his ability to extract electrifying life from even docile surfaces with an economical free action that made him look deceptively lacking in pace through the air. This, coupled with his vicious and late movement of the ball either way made him almost unplayable when in full cry.

His impressive form of 1936 earned him selection for the Players against the Gentlemen at Lord's, where his 4-29 combined with 6-41 by Surrey's Alf Gover to hustle out the amateurs for 130 after the first six wickets had tumbled for 22 runs in the opening hour. Both were ultimately overshadowed in a drawn game by Jack Stephenson, the ebullient Essex all-rounder, who took 9-46 in the Players' first innings and then claimed a tenth consecutive wicket in the second, but when the MCC party was announced for the forthcoming tour of Australia and New Zealand Copson was in it (with Worthington) and Gover and Stephenson were not. Copson set out as the only uncapped player among the seventeen – and he still was when he came back.

With 'Gubby' Allen, Kenneth Farnes and Bill Voce also chosen, the squad was so overloaded with fast bowlers that there was no room for the Derbyshire man in the Test series England lost after winning the first two of the five matches.

Copson made up for that disappointment by heading the bowling averages for the tour with twenty-seven wickets for 19.81 runs each in other games. He took seven of them for only sixteen runs in a two-day match with Southern Districts of New South Wales in Canberra, then, after the first two of the three fixtures in New Zealand had been drawn, wound up by sharing the bowling honours with Hedley Verity in a seven-wicket victory over Auckland.

When Copson did get into the England team, his three Test appearances were all made in England – the first two during the 1939 series against the West Indies. In his first encounter with those tourists he took their first four second-innings wickets in four overs for only thirteen runs as they chased a modest target of 150 against Derbyshire, only for a hold-up through rain to undermine the county's potentially winning position. The weather intervened on all three days of a drawn match in which the West Indians dismissed Derbyshire for 104 after trailing by 45 runs on first innings. The 40-minute delay after Copson's deadly burst was followed by some stern defensive batting by Ivan Barrow, who six years earlier had been his country's first century-maker in a Test in England, and skipper Rolph Grant, but at the close the tourists were still 96 behind with only four wickets left. Rolph Grant, a Cambridge Blue at both cricket and soccer, and an amateur international goalkeeper, was the younger brother of George ('Jackie') Grant, who captained the West Indies in their 1934-35 home series against England.

Copson's part in the West Indians' near-downfall helped to earn his Test debut in the opening game at Lord's, and he got off to an excellent start in taking 5-85 and 4-67. One of his first-innings five was the West Indies' star batsman George Headley, who equalled Herbert Sutcliffe's feat of hitting two centuries in a match for the second time. Headley was also the first to score a couple in a Test at Lord's, where he had made 129 on his first appearance there against a strong MCC team six years earlier.

Copson could be considered unfortunate to lose his place for the third and final match of the 1939 series at The Oval – a drawn encounter that was to be the last Test for seven years as war loomed – after being limited to a dozen overs and three wickets at a cost of only 33 runs in a rained-off draw at Old Trafford, but he did have the satisfaction of having twice dismissed Headley, in those two appearances.

Arthur Wood, the Yorkshire wicketkeeper, held the catch off Copson's bowling that got rid of Headley in the tourists' first innings at Lord's. But that was not until after he had scored 106 – and when they batted again he made 107 before being caught by Len Hutton off Kent's Doug Wright. Although Headley thus became the only player to make two hundreds in one match with England for the second time (the first at Georgetown in 1930), he still finished on the losing side – and by the wide margin of eight wickets at that. Headley's only cheap dismissal of the series, in which he averaged nearly 67, was down to Wally Hammond's smart reaction in the West Indies second innings in

Manchester. This time Wood was unable to cling on to a sharp snick off Copson, but the England captain clutched the ball from the rebound for his hundredth catch in Tests.

Copson was in his thirty-ninth year, past his best but still capable of beating the best, when he was recalled to England's ranks to replace the injured Harold Butler of Notts – another veteran for Test pace bowling at 34 – for The Oval finale to the 1947 series in which the 'Middlesex twins', Denis Compton and Bill Edrich, gorged themselves off South Africa's bowling. Again he picked up just three wickets, all in the first innings at a cost of 46 runs, and again his victims included a batsman, Bruce Mitchell, who hit a couple of hundreds in the match. Copson altogether delivered almost sixty overs, demonstrating stamina to belie both his age and uncertain health.

In the following year he took 3-39 in a Test trial at Edgbaston, dismissing two of England's top batsmen, Compton and Cyril Washbrook, and the captain, Norman Yardley. The year after that, having raised Derbyshire's testimonial record from Denis Smith's £1,970 to £2,500, this originally reluctant cricketer reluctantly announced his retirement from first-class cricket. He marked it with a spell of 4-10 in the North's four-wicket defeat of the South at Kingston after the completion of Derbyshire's programme – a distinct improvement on his untypical 1-103 in the corresponding match of his 1936 heyday. Though that unexpected recall at Leicester was to come, it seemed appropriate at the time that his final away game in the County Championship should be at Lord's. Having taken 4-50 in the home side's first innings, he helped to reduce them to 36 for five in their second before Denis Compton, with an unbeaten 97, led the recovery to a three-wicket victory that made Middlesex sure of sharing the title with Yorkshire.

And it also looked the perfect finish to an admirable career when, in Derbyshire's next and final match of the season, Copson had overall figures of 6-29 in a big win over Essex at Burton-upon-Trent. That took his total of wickets in his last full Championship season to 63 at an average cost of nearly 27. With four more against the tourists from New Zealand, and the other four for the North in Surrey, his complete tally was 71.

Of all the thousand and more he had claimed since that startling debut in Surrey, the ones for which is best remembered were those that shattered Warwickshire at Derby on 17 July, 1937 (see p.340). Knee trouble which kept him out for two months that season denied him the chance of a three-figure haul of wickets to which he returned with 101 in 1938 (at 19.75) and 146 in 1939 (15.36), but on that day of high summer he was at his most lethal since five of Essex's best, Cutmore, Pearce, O'Connor, Nichols and Bray, had fallen to him for no cost at Brentwood two years before.

Warwickshire were routed for 28 in their first innings. That was a dozen more than their lowest-ever first-class total, against Kent at Tonbridge in 1913, but it was the lowest against Derbyshire since the 25 by both Lancashire (1871) and Kent (1874). There has since been one still lower, Hampshire having been shot out for 23 by Les Jackson and Harold Rhodes in losing at Burton-upon-Trent in 1958 at a time when they were pacemakers for the title that became Surrey's for the seventh season in succession. Hampshire faded to only one win in their last eight games, finishing with another defeat by Derbyshire as Jackson again found wickets plentiful at Bournemouth.

In 1937, Copson finished Warwickshire off by becoming the first Derbyshire player to take four wickets with consecutive deliveries. He had a full analysis of 8.2-2-11-8, the last seven falling in 23 balls, the last four all clean bowled. Then, after hitting seven fours in his 30 not out as Derbyshire replied with 227, he made it five wickets in six balls, and six in eleven, by striking again with his second and seventh deliveries in Warwickshire's second innings. His ten wickets on the day, which the visitors ended at 81 for two, were taken in 53 balls. He gained only one further success in the match, his three second-innings wickets costing 82 runs, but, although Aubrey Hill (105) and 'Tom' Dollery (98) were in a stand of 213, Warwickshire were beaten by five wickets.

In 1972, even Copson's magnificent effort was surpassed by 'Pat' Pocock. The Surrey and England spinner took six wickets in nine balls, and seven in eleven, at Eastbourne as Sussex, needing 18 runs to win at 187 for one with three overs to go, finished three short at 202 for nine. In the first of those overs, Pocock, who up to then had conceded 63 runs and taken no wickets, struck with his first, third and sixth deliveries. Then, after eleven runs had been taken off the next over, bowled by Robin Jackman, without further success, Pocock began the final over with a hat-trick and took another wicket with his fifth ball. And, to cap it all, last man Joshi was run out off the last one to create a first-class record of five wickets falling in one six-ball over.

Warwickshire gave Derbyshire a taste of their 'Copson medicine', also at Derby, in 1988. Tony Merrick took six wickets in ten balls without conceding a run after a hold-up through rain, the score subsiding from 161 for four to 166 all out, but Derbyshire comfortably negotiated a draw. Devon Malcolm took four wickets in seven balls as Warwickshire were limited to a lead of 119, and the 27th and last of New Zealander John Wright's centuries for Derbyshire, in the course of which he had to retire hurt after being struck on the knee by Merrick, led to play ending with a second-innings declaration at 428 for seven.

Lancashire were another club to feel the force of a Copson hat-trick in the 1937 season, at Burton, and he performed that feat for a third time, taking four wickets in five balls, in following his first-innings 5-12 with 5-9 as Oxford University tumbled to defeat in the Parks in 1939. Bert Rhodes has since overtaken him with four for Derbyshire, and five in all, but, as with Copson, only two of them – at Colchester in 1948 and against Sussex at Derby in 1951 – were in the Championship. Only Kent's Doug Wright, with seven, and the

Gloucestershire spinners Charlie Parker and Tom Goddard, with six, have performed the feat more times than Rhodes in first-class cricket.

The other havoc Copson wrought included three wickets in four balls in Gloucestershire's first innings, three in five (the same batsmen) in the second, at Burton in 1935, and another three in four against Leicestershire at Derby in 1936. He twice took twelve wickets in a match: 5-33 and 7-19 against Surrey at Derby, 5-38 and 7-16 against Worcestershire at Worcester, both in the title year. He had eleven once, ten three times, nine fourteen times, and on eight occasions collected eight. Five or more toppled to him in a single innings 64 times – thirteen of them in 1936.

As a confirmed No 11, Bill Copson had no pretensions to being a batsman, with a top score of 43, at Blackpool, and an average below seven. In a tribute to him in one of the *Studies in Greatness* in *Wisden,* Basil Easterbrook, a Kemsley newspaper journalist I remember regaling the press box at the County Ground in Derby, made reference to 'an hilarious knock' of 28 against Sussex at Worthing in which Bill was dropped five times. Easterbrook continued:

'He came in to a thunder of applause, for everyone loves a bowler who has briefly tried to be the Prince of Denmark, and he had gone through the pavilion gate before he realised he had not acknowledged it. Suddenly he loped back onto the field and raised his bat in salute. Naturally, he was twitted about this in the dressing room, and I think it was the only time in his life Bill gave a sheepish grin. "Well lads," he said, "I forgot the drill – you see, I'm a bit out of practice acknowledging applause for my batting".'

In his familiar role, Copson helped Saltaire to the Bradford League title during the Second World War, and in the same league he enjoyed one his last big hauls four years after finally stepping off the first-class stage, taking 8-21 in Idle's dismissal for 66 as Lidget Green romped to victory by nine wickets. Then, in 1958, he reappeared on the county scene for a ten-year stint as an umpire until more ill health drove him into his final retirement. He died at the age of sixty-two as the 1971 season also closed.

17. The Pope Brothers

One brother compensated for the misfortune of another on Derbyshire's path to their undisputed title of 1936. George Pope was out for the rest of the season after injuring a knee in the county's fifth match, against Gloucestershire in Bristol towards the end of May, and had to undergo a cartilage operation. That meant more bowling than he had expected for Alf Pope, seventeen months George's senior, and he responded by making that landmark year for the club the most successful of his career.

In giving Bill Copson and Tommy Mitchell their staunchest support, Alfred Vardy Pope bowled more overs than either of those two main matchwinners and finished only one wicket short of following them to one hundred. 'I like bowling, skipper,' was his ready reply when Arthur Richardson warned him that he might have to keep turning his arm over until the close of play.

There were three other cricketing Pope brothers, one of whom, Harold, also played for Derbyshire – but not very often. Whereas Alf and George both took part in more than two hundred first-class matches, Harold, a leg-break bowler, played in just ten. One of them was the only occasion in which all three were in the same senior Derbyshire team, for the drawn game with the West Indians in the last season before the 1939-45 war. Another was also against a touring side in the first full season after the war, in the match with the Indians in 1946 that produced one of the most exciting finishes seen at the Chesterfield ground. And Harold Pope, the only representative of his family that time, was directly involved in it, for 'Lala' Amarnath sealed Derbyshire's defeat by bowling him with the second ball of the last over.

After service throughout the war as a navigator in the RAF, during which he survived being shot down and also a crash, Harold, generally known as 'Bill,' enjoyed his biggest success with Derbyshire during their restricted programme of 1945, the year before the County Championship was resumed. A Hinckley Grammar School boy named Abbott was the only batsman to reach double figures in well-beaten Leicestershire's totals of 58 and 68 at Derby as Pope took nine wickets for only 34 runs, six of them for twelve in the visitors' first innings. His spinners proved so expensive, however, in the more demanding season that followed, his nine wickets costing more than 46 runs each, that he was released and joined West Bromwich Dartmouth in the Birmingham League.

In 1947, he finished fractionally above brother Alf, who was then with Mitchell's and Butler's, in the league's bowling averages, and although his team ended runners-up to Alf's for the title they were champions themselves the next year. Harold also played in the Durham League before going back as captain to his home Chesterfield club with which he had started out, and for which his brothers George, Eric and Jack had also played around the time when their father, Fred, was the groundsman there – duties he later carried out at Edgbaston. Harold also had a spell as coach at Repton School, and for almost twenty years he was secretary of the Bassetlaw League, then its president. He was eighty-one when he died at Chesterfield during the summer of 2000.

Alf Pope, who, like George, was born at Tibshelf, a village near Alfreton, began work as a coal miner at fourteen, but gave that up during the General Strike of 1926 and two years later was taken onto the Derbyshire ground staff in Sam Cadman's nursery at the County Ground. From a quiet start of just thirteen wickets in four appearances in his first two seasons in the first team, 1930-31, and a total of 50 wickets over the next two that included his career-best 7-84 against Sussex at Hove, he improved to 51 in 1934, 87 in 1935, and then to the 99 at 18.13 runs apiece that put him eleventh in the national averages. Copson (13.34) ended that 1936 season third behind Harold Larwood (12.97) and Hedley Verity (13.18). Mitchell (21.42) was not in the top twenty.

After slipping back to 70 wickets in 1937, Alf Pope again went close to that elusive century in each of the last two pre-war seasons, with 91 in 1938 and 94 in 1939. Those totals took him to 555 in all, 542 of them for Derbyshire, at an average cost of a few decimal points above twenty-two. With the bat he averaged only eighteen, but he did have his moments in getting to within thirty-seven runs of a career aggregate of five thousand. He scored the first of his seventeen half-centuries in an innings defeat of Northamptonshire at Chesterfield in 1932, the year in which, at Ilkeston, he helped Derbyshire to beat Nottinghamshire for the first time since 1921 on the first of the three occasions he took ten wickets in a match.

The 103 he scored when promoted to No 4 against Warwickshire at Edgbaston in 1938 was Alf's only first-class century. That was the match in which he was involved in one of his four century partnerships, adding 103 for the seventh wicket with Robin Buckston. The biggest of them, 170 for the same wicket with Garnet Lee against Leicestershire at Chesterfield in 1933, exceeded by two runs the stand by George Davidson and Maynard Ashcroft at Nottingham in 1897, and remained the county's record for that wicket until brother George and Bert Rhodes put on 241 without being separated at Portsmouth in 1948. More than fifty years went by after that before Mathew Dowman and Dominic Cork set the current best of 258 against Durham at Derby.

Alf also had Robin Buckston as his partner during 1938 in a stand of 91 for the ninth wicket against Kent at Tonbridge. As at Edgbaston, he got into the seventies, but this time was not out, and he turned in one of his best all-round performances in taking 5-68 in Kent's first innings. George Pope, who had first followed his elder brother into Derbyshire's first team five years before, then did most to round off an emphatic victory by taking 7-57 when the home side followed on.

Alf and George, lean and lanky (at 6ft 2in they were among the tallest first-class cricketers of the Thirties) could be confusing enough simply because of their similarity on the field when, with George's bald pate covered, both wore a cap. As a bowling partnership, they caused more confusion at Guildford in the last pre-war season when they took eleven wickets between them in the defeat of Surrey inside two days. And only a few days afterwards, on 24 June 1939, they bowled unchanged in routing Yorkshire for 83 in two and a half hours at Sheffield after rain had delayed the start until early afternoon, George taking 6-44 and Alf 4-37. Victory in that match, however, went to the home county, who, after Derbyshire's intervention of 1936, resumed their familiar role as champions in each of the last three seasons before the war. In reply, Derbyshire were demolished in 40 minutes for 20, their lowest total since their 17 against Lancashire at Old Trafford in 1888. Jim Smurthwaite, a 23-year-old from North Ormesby who had neither batted nor bowled in his only previous county match, took 5-7 in four overs, two of which were maidens, with his fast-medium inswingers.

A century by Wilf Barber then helped Yorkshire to total 310 in their second innings, after which Derbyshire tottered to defeat by 276 runs as the medium-paced Frank Smailes followed up his first-innings 4-11 by taking all ten wickets for 47 runs in their dismissal for 97. It all made for a dismaying debut for a young man whose first-class career, with war looming, then threatened to be about as brief as that of his father Joseph, a fast bowler whose wickets for Glapwell had taken him into the Derbyshire team during the two seasons either side of the previous world war. His name: Clifford Gladwin, of whom more later.

Alf and George Pope also combined to particular effect while playing for Sir P F Warner's XI against England Past and Present at the Folkestone Festival in September 1938. They shared all but five of their opponents' eighteen wickets before rain brought the game to a premature close after only twenty-five minutes' play on the third day. Alf's 6-70 in the first innings included Arthur Fagg, who that season uniquely scored two double-centuries in one match for Kent, his county colleague Frank Woolley, who was making his first-class farewell, and two England captains, Walter Hammond and Percy Chapman. It was the sixth time Alf had dismissed Hammond, and in that year he captured the wicket of another leading batsman, Herbert Sutcliffe, for the seventh time in getting rid of him in both innings of Yorkshire's two matches with Derbyshire.

In the previous match of the Folkestone Week, another rained-off draw, the Popes were also in the England XI that drew with the Australians, and, although they were less successful that time, Alf twice cheaply claimed the wicket of opener Bill Brown, who had earlier in the season scored an undefeated double-century in one of Derbyshire's heaviest defeats, by an innings and 234 runs, at Chesterfield.

Alf Pope gained one of his other successes against Hammond when he played for the North against the South at Lord's in 1937, in one of the matches commemorating the MCC's 150th anniversary. He had him caught by Bill Voce for 86 in the South's first innings, but was as powerless as the rest when Hammond condemned the North to a six-wicket defeat with a not-out century on the final day.

During the war Alf Pope, having for some while varied his medium-pace deliveries with off-breaks, reaped more wickets in the Bradford League with Saltaire, Windhill and Baildon Green. After it, by then into his late thirties, he did not return to the Derbyshire staff but continued in league cricket by spending four seasons with Mitchell's and Butler's, for whom he scored an undefeated century besides playing a prominent part with the ball. From there he went to Canada as coach at Trinity College in Ontario, and he played for Ontario in the Dominion cricket championship, heading the Canadian bowling averages, before the first of his two spells as professional with Forfarshire, the Scottish champions. His other engagements took him to Falcon College in Bulawayo, Berkhamsted School and Trent College, and he did not give up playing until he was in his seventieth year. The fact that I was on the opposing side in the first match he played, at Borrowash, on his return to the Derby area in the mid-1950s showed that he was in much diminished cricketing circumstances, so it was not surprising that he enjoyed himself with three sixes in a not-out half-century before taking a couple of wickets in a brief spell of bowling as his team gained a convincing win.

His son Tony and grandson Tim played for Alvaston and Boulton in the Derbyshire County League. Tony, who was also given the family name Vardy to have the same initials as his father, made one appearance in the Derbyshire second team at Worcester in 1971. He did not have the chance to bat, but took a couple of wickets – one of them, in the home first innings, that of Peter Stimpson, who in his second knock, after two Derbyshire declarations, steered his side to a seven-wicket victory with an unbeaten century. Two months later, Stimpson scored his maiden first-class hundred against Glamorgan.

George Pope more than made up for his disappointment of missing most of the county's title-winning year of 1936 through injury by being one of their most influential players in the remaining three seasons before the war. Indeed, he made such astonishing progress as an all-rounder in 1937 that he not only scored the first of his eight Derbyshire centuries but also hit two more in the same month, totalled 1,318 runs for the county at 35.62, and narrowly missed the double with 92 wickets in all at 20.84. That was enough to earn him selection, along with Stan Worthington, for the tour of India undertaken in 1937-38, but without the usual MCC sponsorship, under the captaincy of Lord Tennyson.

As already recalled, his lordship was often hard put to raise a full eleven because of injuries and illness, with George Pope among those afflicted. And thereby hangs a sorry story as related by one of the other tourists, Ian Peebles, the Middlesex and England spin bowler. It began when Alf Gover, the Surrey and England fast bowler, joined those stricken with dysentery in spectacular fashion. He tore in along his usual long run-up, but instead of delivering the ball he carried on straight down the pitch, much to the consternation of the batsman taking strike, and then kept going in his desperate dash off the field to avail himself of the facilities of the pavilion. Someone had to go after him to reclaim the ball from what Peebles called his 'convulsive grasp', and there was a further delay while a junior groundsman who was pressed into service as a substitute fielder had to be persuaded to wear boots. This is how Peebles described what happened next:

'During this pause another disaster befell us. I was idly bowling the ball to and fro with George Pope, our one remaining bowler of any consequence, when, unfortunately, something distracted his attention. The ball took him rather below his grievously upset tummy, and to my horror he went down with a terrible hissing sound. When I reached the other end he was in the arms of several helpers who had heard the thud, sweating in a fearful manner and showing the whites of his eyes. When at this moment the Lord turned to ask him to bowl he was astonished and infuriated to see his one remaining hope apparently writhing in his last agonies. As the victim couldn't speak, and no-one else had seen the incident, no answer was forthcoming to his testy demand as to what the hell had happened now. Personally, I thought that a tactful silence would be best in the circumstances, so without more ado poor George was carted off to be erroneously treated for sudden heat-stroke.

In other matches on that tour, however, Pope steered clear enough of the health risks to give several telling performances. In the third unofficial Test at Calcutta, which India won by 93 runs after losing the first two, he followed a spell of 5-15 with an undefeated 41. He next took 5-51, and held three catches, in Madras, despite which Tennyson's team became the first from England to be beaten by an innings in India. Then came the decider back at Bombay in which Pope completed match figures of 8-77, besides just missing a half-century in his partnership with Stan Worthington, as the tourists clinched a 3-2 series win.

Back home for the 1938 season, Pope continued to improve by achieving the double for the first time while playing in the Folkestone Festival after the completion of Derbyshire's programme. For the county he scored 903 runs and captured 91 wickets; his full figures were 1,040 at 29.71 and 103 at 24.13. He also took part in a Test trial and, though excluded from the final eleven, was among the players from whom the England team was chosen for the first match of that season's series with the Australians at Trent Bridge.

That unfortunate experience was repeated when the Aussies paid their next visit ten years later. He found himself summoned the short distance to Nottingham on the eve of the 1948 series because Doug Wright, the Kent leg-break and googly bowler, was doubtful with lumbago. In the event, neither of them played.

In 1939, George Pope headed Derbyshire's batting averages with his biggest aggregate of 1,457 (1,464 in all) at 32.37, but fell seventeen wickets short of the double. He added to his hundreds by scoring 121 against Nottinghamshire at Ilkeston's Rutland Ground, a homely, immaculate little enclosure which, sadly, was discarded as a County Championship venue almost forty years later after the Derbyshire and Surrey captains, and also the umpires, had complained to Lord's about its 'very poor pitch'. Regrettably, its eventual reprieve was short-lived.

Derbyshire had little cause to complain about Ilkeston's pitch on the first two days of that match in sweltering late summer weather only a few weeks before the Second World War put county cricket on hold for six years. A sixth-wicket century stand by the Pope brothers (Alf's share was 43) provided the main boost to their total of 319 on Saturday, 19 August, and when stumps were drawn at the close of Monday's play (no first-class cricket on Sundays then) they had increased the lead they gained on first innings to 256 with seven wickets in hand. But it was not only the war clouds that were looming.

The weather broke with a vengeance that evening, as I remember only too well. That second day's play was the first in a county game that I, not yet a teenager, attended, in the company of my step-father, and we were thoroughly drenched as we cycled home. Next day, the last seventeen wickets toppled for 171 runs in not much more than three hours, Derbyshire rounding off a comfortable win even though Bill Voce produced an inspired spell of fast left-arm bowling as those last seven home wickets fell for the addition of only 36 runs. The Popes shared six wickets when Notts found batting hardly less difficult in the changed conditions.

With the 1939-40 tour of India, for which he was among those selected, called off because of the war, George Pope had to wait until 1947 for his full Test debut, against South Africa at Lord's. Unfortunately, but not unexpectedly because he was then thirty-six, he did nothing to warrant a second chance. In a ten-wicket win for England he was still there, but with only eight runs to his name, at the declaration, then took just one wicket – and that of last man Ian Smith, the spin bowler who was the youngest and least experienced player in the visitors' side – at a cost of 85 runs in his 338 deliveries spread over the Springboks' two innings. That was the series dominated by the 'Middlesex Twins', Bill Edrich and Denis Compton, and at Lord's they excelled themselves by establishing a world Test record for the third wicket with a stand of 370, Compton scoring 208 and Edrich 189. It broke the previous best, set up by Alan Melville, the South African captain, and Dudley Nourse, in the first Test at Nottingham only a fortnight earlier, by 51 runs, and was only a dozen below the then biggest for any England wicket – by the second pair, Len Hutton and Maurice Leyland, against Australia at The Oval in 1938.

For wickets, England were best served against South Africa at Lord's in 1947 by the spin of Doug Wright, who took ten in the match, Eric Hollies and Compton, though Alec Bedser, who shared the opening attack with Edrich, had at least four catches dropped off his bowling.

George Pope did himself more justice when he played in three of the 1945 'Victory Tests' against the Australian Services side – and it would have been four if, in keeping with his blunt, no-nonsense character, he had not turned down one invitation. Having been overlooked for the opening match of that celebration series, won by the Australians at Lord's with only two deliveries to spare, he was one of the big successes of the second, won by England, in what *Wisden* termed 'the finest match of the season', on the ground where he was to excel so regularly in league cricket – Bramall Lane, Sheffield. It was the first time England and Australia had met there for forty-three years. In surroundings that had been knocked about a bit by Hermann Goering's bombers, skipper Walter Hammond took the batting honours with exactly 100 in England's first innings. Pope, his junior partner with 35 in a century stand, shared most of the Australian wickets with another newcomer to that level, Lancashire's Dick Pollard. Pope had match figures of 8-127, Pollard 6-118. Just over a month later Pope was back at Bramall Lane for his only Derbyshire appearance of that season, scoring 113 and taking 5-62 in a drawn game with Yorkshire.

Lord's was again the venue for the third 'Test', and it was because of the cost of spending a few days in London that Pope startled officialdom by pulling out for 'business reasons'. He wanted to play for his country, but not at a financial loss. He was then player-coach with the Colne club in the Lancashire League, and he had to find, and pay, a professional to take his place in their team – something he was not prepared to do without being guaranteed expenses on top of his match fee of £10.

Those expenses were not forthcoming, so Pope took his stand on behalf of his fellow professionals. He felt that men earning a living from the game ought to be compensated. After his death at Chesterfield in 1993, aged 82, *Wisden* was to comment that he 'somehow came to seem the embodiment of the county's professionals: hard, rough-hewn, under-appreciated', though the almanack conceded that 'he was mellower' during his years as a first-class umpire.

Eddie Phillipson, one of Pollard's colleagues at Old Trafford, would have filled the England vacancy Pope caused had he been fit. The cry was for another fast bowler. Instead, the choice fell on a future Derbyshire (and England) captain and top MCC official, D B Carr, who was a right-hand batsman of considerable promise, but a left-arm spin bowler. Carr, then very recently a Repton pupil and shortly to be three times an Oxford Blue following Army service, had developed into one of the best schoolboy cricketers of 1944 under the guidance of 'Bill' Blaxland and Garnet Lee after receiving his first serious cricket tuition from the Rev R M Chadwick, a former Rugby School and Dorset player, while at a boarding school at Swanage.

Two of Carr's contemporaries, John Dewes, later a batting force with Middlesex, and the Hon L R White, both of Cambridge University, were already in the twelve from whom the final selection was made. The mistake was made of fielding all three, each of them only eighteen and unequal to the task. England, having also lost Hammond with lumbago, and with opener Cyril Washbrook handicapped by a badly bruised thumb, went one down again, despite a hundred and half-century from Yorkshire's Len Hutton. The young inexperienced trio mustered fewer than fifty runs in their six innings, and Carr, the only bowler among them, went without a wicket through his nine overs. 'I managed to bowl a maiden each to Hassett and Miller,' he said afterwards, 'and I was feeling pretty elated until I realised they were playing out the last few balls before tea.'

George Pope, his point made and satisfactory arrangements concluded, was back for the remaining two 'Victory Tests' – and back among the wickets, if not the runs. England drew one (at Lord's) and won the other (their first victory against an Australian team at Old Trafford for forty years) to square the series. Pope emerged from it with fifteen wickets for just over twenty-one runs each, a tally second only to Pollard's twenty-five, at 23.64, among the bowlers on either side. Pope managed fewer than fifty runs in his four innings, but in his other first-class match that season he scored 84 for an Over-33 team in a rain-ruined draw with an Under-33 side at Lord's, driving fiercely in a stand of 155 in 110 minutes with Jack Davies, the former Cambridge Blue who eleven years earlier had caused a sensation by bowling Bradman for his first nought in England.

Although he failed to trouble the Australians unduly with the bat, Pope was by then so highly rated as an all-rounder that he must surely have won more than just his one full cap but for being deprived of the best years of his first-class career by the war – and of another one, the first post-war season of 1946, by his shock decision to continue in his playing and coaching engagement at Colne instead of resuming his career with the county. His absence caused much dismay and disappointment, mixed in with not a little disapproval, as a Derbyshire team that had also lost Harry Elliott, Tommy Mitchell and Leslie Townsend in addition to Alf Pope sagged to third from the foot of that year's final Championship table.

Instead of being for Derbyshire, George Pope was against them when they went to Dublin, where he was coaching, for a two-day warm-up match that Leinster just managed to draw with their last pair together and more than a hundred runs still needed to avoid the innings defeat. Pope made no bones about his refusal to resume his county career from where he had been forced to break it off in 1939, readily admitting that it was for financial reasons. During the war he had played his league cricket with Lidget Green, Saltaire and

Spen Victoria in the Bradford League. With Colne he was the Lancashire League's best all-rounder of 1946, scoring 613 runs and taking 81 wickets at respective averages of 36.05 and 9.88, yet after that one season he changed his mind completely and was welcomed back into the Derbyshire fold after reputedly turning down offers from half-a-dozen league clubs. 'I am not interested in those offers,' he said. 'I wish to play in only one kind of cricket, county cricket.'

That he was still capable of doing himself justice in that sphere was soon clearly evident. It was no mere coincidence that when he did again agree terms with Derbyshire they revived to figure strongly in the title race in each of the two seasons of his comeback. In 1947, when they finished fifth, he took a hundred wickets for Derbyshire for the first time (113 at 17.79 to be exact). In 1948, when they were sixth, he headed their batting averages with 1,152 runs at 38.40 and took 100 wickets at 17.24, becoming the first player in the country to do the double that year.

Nottinghamshire again suffered at his hands at Ilkeston in both those seasons. In 1947, in the first match of Harry Elliott's emergency comeback, Pope did the hat-trick against them and in one spell had five wickets for as many runs, altogether taking 12-101. In 1948, he had to be content with a couple of wickets but scored the last of his Derbyshire centuries, 129, in sharing a sixth-wicket partnership of 149 with George Dawkes, who was only five runs from his own hundred when he became one of wicketkeeper Eric Meads's six victims in the innings. Derbyshire won on both occasions – the first narrowly, by fifteen runs, the second convincingly, by an innings and thirty-three runs.

Somerset had even more reason than Notts to rue Pope's reappearance in the Championship. On 11 June 1947, they were skittled out for 68 and 38 at Chesterfield, Pope bowling unchanged in grabbing six wickets for 34 runs in their first innings and seven for 16 in their second – after conceding two dozen runs with his medium-paced inswingers before gaining the first of those thirteen successes (see p.341). What a hectic few hours those were for Len Aitken, one of my senior colleagues at the *Derby Evening Telegraph,* as the men from the West Country crashed to defeat by an innings and 125 runs after Derbyshire had built up a lead of 163. He turned up to report on a county cricket match for the first time soon after his return to journalism from traumatic wartime service in the RAF – and ran straight into the first Championship game to be all over in one day since 21 May 1925.

And Somerset it was who were also the vanquished on that former occasion, losing to Lancashire by nine wickets at Manchester after being dismissed for 74 and 73. Twice before, in 1892 and 1894, Somerset had been beaten by Lancashire in one day, also at Old Trafford, and it happened to them for a fourth time against that county, on a newly laid pitch at Bath, on 6 June 1953. That was the day Bertie Buse contributed to the financial undoing of his own benefit match by taking six wickets cheaply in Lancashire's dismissal for 158, only for England off-spinner Roy Tattersall to upstage him with 13-69 as the home county subsided to 55 and 79.

For reducing the length of his own benefit game, and therefore its receipts, even Buse was outdone. At Lord's on Whit Monday 1907, Albert Trott, the Australian who played for Middlesex, not only took four wickets in four balls but also brought play to its premature end with his second hat-trick in the same innings. Yes, Somerset were the sufferers that time too – as they had also been when Trott had taken all ten wickets in one innings seven years before. Another beneficiary in a hurry was Gloucestershire's Charlie Parker, who for many years was one of the best left-arm slow bowlers in county cricket. Against Yorkshire, who inflicted another of Somerset's one-day defeats at Huddersfield in 1894, he hit the stumps with five consecutive deliveries in taking 9-36 on a rain-damaged pitch at Bristol in 1922, though the second of them was a no-ball. A year earlier Somerset had also wilted at his hands, losing all ten of their first-innings wickets to him at the same ground.

The season after demolishing Somerset, George Pope gave one of his best all-round displays at Yorkshire's expense. Watched by a record crowd of 14,000 at Chesterfield, he snapped up 6-12 when they were bundled out for 44, skipper Brian Sellers top-scoring with eight. It was the Tykes' smallest total since their 31 against Essex at Huddersfield in their only defeat in their thirty matches on their way to the title of 1935, the year in which they also registered the season's highest score of 582 for seven against Surrey in Sheffield. In Yorkshire's second innings at Queen's Park in 1948, Pope took four more wickets for thirteen runs as they sagged again, to 37 for six, before rain, which had washed out the second day's play, denied Derbyshire the rare chance of an innings victory over those formidable neighbours. In between, he also enjoyed himself with the bat, leading the way with 73 in the home total of 277.

As a batsman, Pope revelled in his finest hours, just under five of them, down at Portsmouth the month before that game with Yorkshire. Derbyshire, put in, lost half their side cheaply, but George then plundered the biggest score of his career, smiting a six and twenty-two fours in 207 not out. That was the match in which he and 'Dusty' Rhodes, who carried his bat for 105, were associated in their unbroken record stand of 241 for Derbyshire's seventh wicket at the same United Services Recreation Ground where, in 1933, a slow left-arm bowler named Stuart Boyes had propelled the county to one of their most calamitous collapses by taking six wickets for only five runs. From 41 for one Derbyshire had capitulated to 47 all out, yet had emerged from a rain-shortened game with a draw. Not until the young South African Ian Smith wreaked his six for one havoc in 1947, recalled in an earlier chapter, did Derbyshire disintegrate even more dramatically.

In the 1948 encounter at Portsmouth, Hampshire, replying to a declared total of 445 for six, were saved from the follow-on largely by a stubborn century from Dawson, a Yorkshireman who was known as Gerry instead of his given name of Gilbert, but they only narrowly avoided defeat after Derbyshire, without needing Pope to bat again, had declared a second time. Dawson, who some twenty years later was found dead in his crashed car, aged only 55, after having been taken ill while umpiring in a club game, once more made his team's top score, 68, but Hampshire were still more than a hundred runs behind when their last man, George Heath, went in with only four minutes remaining for play. Heath survived two deliveries, after which Desmond Eagar played a true captain's part by keeping his wicket intact with fieldsmen crowded around his bat.

Although it was not realised at the time, George Pope was playing his last match for Derbyshire, against Surrey at Chesterfield on 5 August, when he became the first in the country to complete the double of 1,000 runs and 100 wickets in 1948. No Derbyshire player has done that double since then, though Cliff Gladwin went close with 914 runs and 117 wickets in 1949, and Derek Morgan, several times, and Geoff Miller, once, were also not far off before the slimmer first-class programme made it enough of an achievement to get to 500 runs and 50 wickets – as done for Derbyshire by Dominic Cork and Graeme Welch, and almost by Philip DeFreitas. In 2005 Welch scored 792 runs and took 58 wickets for the county in only sixteen games.

Only two players have accomplished the 1,000 and 100 double since Middlesex's Freddie Titmus in 1967, and both did so for Nottinghamshire – New Zealander Richard Hadlee in 1984 and Franklyn Stephenson, the Barbadian he recommended as his successor with the county, in 1988. And only Pakistani Mushtaq Ahmed, for Sussex in 2003 and 2006, has taken a hundred first-class wickets in a season since Courtney Walsh (Gloucestershire) and Andy Caddick (Somerset) both did so in 1998.

In 1948, injury kept George Pope out of Derbyshire's last four fixtures – and then came his unexpected decision to desert the county scene again as he and his wife decided to move to Jersey for the sake of Mrs Pope's health. He left with first-class totals of 7,518 runs at 28.05 (6,606 of them in his 169 matches for Derbyshire), 677 wickets at 19.92 (567 for the county) and 156 catches (125).

Attractive as life in the Channel Islands was, it did not take Pope long to catch attention once more as a cricketer away from there, both in the leagues (first in Lancashire, later Yorkshire) and also abroad. He paid his second visit to India in 1949-50, when he was one of the players then prominent in league cricket who formed most of a Commonwealth squad that took over the itinerary, also including games in Pakistan and Ceylon (as Sri Lanka was then known), after the MCC had declined to send a team. That was the tour in which George Dawkes also took part.

Pope scored no runs and took no wickets in the only one of the five unofficial Tests in which he played – it was drawn, at Kanpur, though India won the rubber 2-1 after starting with a defeat – but he finished on a strong note with six wickets in an innings defeat of Ceylon in Columbo, five more in a rain-hit draw there with a Combined XI who were bustled out for 75, and a top score of 85 in a 12-a-side winding-up match in Bombay. He also scored a half-century in a seventh-wicket stand of 123 against West Zone at Poona with Bill Alley, the colourful Australian left-hander who a decade later, while with Somerset, surprised himself as much as everybody else in cricket by amassing more than three thousand first-class runs in a season – the last player to do so – when into his forties. Against West Zone, Alley, a league cricketer with Colne and Blackpool, was unbeaten on 209, his second not-out double-century of the tour.

The two defeats in the unofficial Tests were the only ones the Commonwealth side suffered in their twenty-one matches, and there were only a few minutes left for play when India clinched the series with a three-wicket win in the final 'Test' at Madras. The tourists gained ten victories, with the nine other games drawn.

Following his return to England, George Pope gave a number of outstanding displays as Heywood's professional – most memorably all ten wickets, including a hat-trick, for only nine runs in a Crompton innings. There were to be more hat-tricks – three of them in one season – during his subsequent very eventful six years as a regular player with Sheffield United CC, a club with which his service was extended to fourteen seasons in all from 1952 with his appointment as their senior coach. In one Yorkshire Council game against Scarborough he scored an unbeaten half-century and twice took two wickets with successive deliveries during an in innings in which the only one to elude him was a run-out. Not bad going for a 44-year-old.

As a first-class umpire, he stood in 156 County Championship matches from 1966, the year in which Albert Alderman also first joined the list, to 1974. He was eighty-two when he died at Chesterfield on 29 October 1993. Alf Pope survived him until 11 May 1996.

18. Third in 1934

Third in 1934, second in 1935, champions in 1936. Such was Derbyshire's inexorable progress to what was to remain their only major honour, once the 1874 title had been taken away from them, until they became the first winners of the NatWest Bank Trophy in 1981.

After the appalling seasons of 1920 and 1924, the long-awaited improvement started despite the departure of Bill Bestwick, Sam Cadman. Garnet Lee and Arthur Morton as the benefits of the nursery began to bear fruit with the development of Leslie Townsend, Stan Worthington, Albert Alderman, Denis Smith, Tommy Mitchell, Bill Copson and two of the Pope brothers that formed such a strong foundation along with the Harrys Storer and Elliott under the astute captaincy of Arthur Richardson. The county's record number of wins per season was pushed up to eight in 1927, when they finished fifth, to ten in 1929, when they were seventh, and then to eleven in 1933 (sixth) before the climb to the top really got under way with twelve in 1934 and sixteen, a total yet to be exceeded, in 1935.

From 1933 to 1937 each county had to fulfil 24 fixtures to qualify for the Championship, and Derbyshire comfortably managed that with 28 each time. During that period 15 points were awarded for a win instead of eight. In drawn games a lead on first innings was worth five points, three were allowed for a deficit at that stage, and four went to each side if no decision was reached on first innings – or if the scores were then level, or if there had been no play at all.

On that method of reckoning, Derbyshire got off to an unpromising start in 1934 by taking only three points from their first two matches. The worst of a draw with Lancashire at Ilkeston's Rutland ground, where they had to follow on, was the prelude to defeat by Sussex at Hove. Lancashire lost only three wickets, one each to Copson, Mitchell and Armstrong, before declaring at 337, a total built on a third-wicket partnership between century-makers Frank Watson and Jack Iddon. It was only one run from being worth 200 when Watson was trapped lbw by Armstrong for 128. Iddon went on to carry his bat for 121.

These two batsmen were both in a Lancashire title-winning team for the fifth time that year, but their first-class careers, in which both also scored more than 20,000 runs, were to come to an end that, for one, was confidence-shattering, and the other tragic. Watson, one of the most obdurate batsmen of the inter-war years, lost form, and soon afterwards his place, after being struck in the eye by a ball from Bill Bowes, the Yorkshire and England pace bowler; Iddon was killed in a car accident at Crewe in April 1946 while returning home from a business trip to the Rolls-Royce works. Watson's sight was not ultimately impaired, but he was never again a stoic and assured player of fast bowling. Iddon, technical representative for a brake-lining firm in Manchester, had not re-signed as a Lancashire professional for the first post-war season, but had hoped to continue playing occasionally as an amateur. He was the second Lancashire player to meet his death in a road accident in less than ten years, Ted McDonald, the Australian Test fast bowler, having been struck by a car on the Manchester to Chorley road near Bolton early in a July morning in 1937.

Another of Lancashire's five-times champions, the crinkly haired Frank Sibbles, added to Derbyshire's discomfiture in that opening match of 1934 at Ilkeston by taking six wickets for 44 runs with his off-breaks in their dismissal for 115. At Buxton in 1932 he had got rid of three Derbyshire batsmen in four balls, and in Derbyshire's own title year of 1936 he was to send back six more for only nine runs. At least those victims had the perhaps dubious consolation of knowing that, according to Sir Neville Cardus, 'a nicer mannered cricketer never wore flannels.'

Derbyshire lost only one more wicket in the follow-on against Lancashire at the Rutland ground, that of Arthur Richardson. Leslie Townsend, who opened with the captain, just had time to complete a half-century out of 88 before the close.

Harry Storer was back from his football commitments as Coventry City's manager to open with Richardson at Hove, and although he was cheaply dismissed by Maurice Tate in Derbyshire's first innings of 167, he provided most of the resistance in their second with a typically forthright 80. That, however, was not quite enough to earn an away victory, Sussex passing their low target of 95 with their ninth-wicket pair together. Copson and Mitchell each took three wickets as Derbyshire went so close to snatching the 15 points instead of having to settle for three, Copson striking a crucial blow by quickly sending back Tommy Cook, top scorer with 82 in Sussex's first innings of 279. Cook, one of the finest all-rounders Sussex have produced, was, like Storer, an England soccer international. He both played for and managed Brighton and Hove Albion, and was also briefly with Bristol Rovers before suffering the broken collar-bone that ended his career as a professional footballer. He was the sole survivor of an aeroplane crash while in the South African Air Force before rejoining Brighton as manager, but was only a few days beyond his 49th birthday when he died early in 1950, apparently by his own hand.

James Langridge, an all-rounder who played for England and became what was then a cricketing rarity in captaining Sussex as a professional during the 1950s, shared most of Derbyshire's wickets with Tate in that 1934 game at Hove, but his younger brother John, an opening batsman most unlucky to miss Test selection, was to be the most troublesome member of the family as far as Derbyshire were concerned. In the counties' two meetings of 1949 the rosy-cheeked John plundered 526 runs in three innings for only once out – and that was a run out. After carrying his bat for 234 at Ilkeston he twice scored

146 in the return match at Worthing, hitting two hundreds in one game for the second time that season. With a Sussex record dozen centuries altogether and nearly three thousand runs at an average of sixty, no wonder *Wisden* made him one of the Cricketers of the Year. A year later he took 184 off Derbyshire at Burton and 78 not out at Hove. And the year after that he scored 200 not out at Derby. Yet none of those magnificent efforts brought his team victory. Each of the matches was drawn.

In 1934, Derbyshire had three days off after their literally pointless visit to Hove before gaining their first success of the season by the same two-wicket margin against Warwickshire at Derby. They trailed by four runs on first innings, despite half-centuries by Harry Elliott (72 not out), Leslie Townsend (64) and Harry Storer (52), but four wickets apiece for Stan Worthington and Tommy Mitchell kept the home side in check, and a target of 179 was achieved mainly through a stand of 98 between Storer, who again rose to the occasion with 79, and Denis Smith (45). Mitchell claimed eight wickets in the match, giving skipper Bob Wyatt reason to regard him highly by twice dismissing him cheaply.

Next came a one-sided victory at Northampton, where Worthington scored the same number of runs, 147, by which the home team failed to equal Derbyshire's 345 in their two innings, collapsing for 78 in the follow-on. Mitchell again twice took four wickets in making up for the absence of the unfit Copson.

A third win in a row looked likely when Yorkshire's reigning champions were bundled out for 99 at Chesterfield, Mitchell including Herbert Sutcliffe, Maurice Leyland and the captain, Brian Sellers, among his five victims at a cost of only 26 runs, but Bill Bowes countered with 5-60 as Derbyshire squeezed only three runs ahead. Yorkshire then showed more of their mettle when they batted again, Wilf Barber and Ken Davidson leading the way with half-centuries, though Mitchell once more emerged with the best bowling figures, taking 6-96 in a total of 271. This left Derbyshire needing 269, and they fell 102 short against the speed-spin attack of Bowes and Hedley Verity. Davidson, better known as a badminton player but a good enough cricketer to score a thousand runs that year, went to the United States in 1935. Nearly twenty years later, while returning to his New York home from a world tour with an American badminton team, he was killed in an aeroplane crash at Prestwick airport on Christmas Day 1954, the day after his 49th birthday.

Derbyshire bounced back from that Yorkshire defeat to gain their first-ever away win against Nottinghamshire, beating them by 28 runs at Trent Bridge. Charlie Harris, one of cricket's humorists whose habitual greeting when he went in to bat at the start of a day's play was 'Good morning, fellow workers', alone reached a half-century on either side, scoring exactly 50 in his first innings. With Mitchell out of the side as well as Copson, the Derbyshire bowling was mainly shouldered by Les Townsend and Tom Armstrong, and a right good job they made of it. Armstrong took 5-72 and 3-76, Townsend 4-59 and 7-47. Notts hopes were raised when Derbyshire's slump to 135 in their second innings (Voce 7-53) left them requiring 196, seven fewer than they had made earlier, but Pat Vaulkhard could find nobody to stay with him for long enough as he remained undefeated on 40 against the county he was to captain after the war.

That long overdue success might have been expected to have put Derbyshire's players in the right frame of mind to account for another county against which they had so often had to concede second best, but they got off to a disappointing start when they met Surrey at The Oval and finished well beaten by seven wickets. They were up against it from the moment Alan Skinner, who resumed at the fall of the ninth wicket, had to retire hurt with only twenty runs on the board – a setback quickly followed by the cheap dismissal of his opening partner, Albert Alderman, and Denis Smith. Both those wickets fell to Freddie Brown, the ebullient all-rounder under whose captaincy both England and Northamptonshire were revived after the 1939-45 war, but the main damage in Derbyshire's dismissal for 137 was done by Alf Gover, whose six wickets cost him only 37 runs.

Surrey then tightened their grip with a century from Bob Gregory and scores in the sixties by Laurie Fishlock and Stan Squires, guiding them to a lead of 185 that looked even more commanding when Derbyshire reduced it by only 38 runs for the loss of their first four second-innings wickets, especially as the incommoded Skinner was again down to go in last (he was the not-out batsman both times). A recovery was led, however, by Smith, whose 126 was resolutely backed up by Worthington (65) and Neville Ford (60), although a total of 321 set Surrey a modest target of 137 that Gregory enabled them to make light of by adding 50 to his first-innings 124. In the continued absence of Copson and Mitchell, Worthington completed one of his best all-round performances, totalling 96 runs and seven wickets. His 31 was the top score in Derbyshire's first innings, and he took 6-90 when Surrey first batted.

From London, Derbyshire travelled to Portsmouth – and to their biggest defeat of the season. Again they did better in their second innings after faltering in the first, but this time it was in the follow-on, and Hampshire thrashed them by an innings and 82 runs. The home side's formidable total of 481 was built on a third-wicket stand of 259 between John Arnold and the prolific Philip Mead, who, having been discarded as a left-arm bowler by his home county of Surrey, was to retire in 1936 as the fourth highest scorer in first-class cricket behind Jack Hobbs, Frank Woolley and 'Patsy' Hendren. Their respective scores of 144 and 138 were the biggest individual ones of the year against Derbyshire. South African-born Len Creese, like Mead a hard-hitting left-hander, weighed in with 74, and the captain, William Lowndes, made 54.

Creese was another of those cricketers caught up in tragedy. While groundsman at Hastings after the 1939-45 war he had the traumatic experience of seeing his small grandson killed by a heavy roller during the interval between innings at a festival match.

Derbyshire's most successful bowlers at the United Services ground in Portsmouth were the Pope brothers, with four wickets apiece. An uphill struggle was inevitable after a first-innings collapse for 108, but Albert Alderman (124) and Leslie Townsend (86) restored some lost pride with a century stand for the third wicket. Support, however, was sadly lacking. Of the other batsmen, only Harry Storer, with 30, reached double figures.

In Arthur Richardson's first absence of the season, the captaincy for this match was taken over by John Southern, a Derby-born naval officer, in his fifth and final first-class appearance for the club. On his debut he had made what was to remain his top score at that level – the 43 that had also been the top score for Derbyshire in their defeat of the Australian Imperial Forces side in 1919. This time, however, he managed only a single in his two innings. Southern, who had skippered the Malvern XI in 1917, was the son-in-law of Thomas Usborne, a batsman who played in India for the Europeans and Bombay.

With eight matches completed after the pounding at Portsmouth, Derbyshire had lost as many as they had won (three), with the two others drawn. But they now embarked on a sequence of sixteen games in which their only setback was suffered in July against the Australian tourists at Chesterfield, where Don Bradman (who else?) was top scorer in a total of 255 that left Derbyshire's two responses below 150 wide open to a beating by nine wickets. At least the Don was denied one of his frequent centuries, Townsend having him caught by Harry Elliott for 71. Mitchell hit the stumps five times in taking seven wickets for 105 runs. Elliott helped him to the two others, stumping Bill Brown and catching Stan McCabe, both going cheaply.

The unbeaten spell at county level, from mid-June to the second week of August, began with a draw at Derby in which the other master batsman of the day, Walter Hammond, did get to a century. His 134, ended by an Alderman catch off the returning Mitchell, who held a stinging return catch to dismiss him, for 42, in his first innings, did most to snuff out a Derbyshire sniff of victory after Gloucestershire had entered the final day's play with one wicket down and 16 runs still to be cut from their deficit of 37. For that slender advantage Derbyshire, captained by Harry Elliott, were largely indebted to solid innings of 89 by Storer and 82 by Alderman, whose opening partnership realised 172, and a typically brisk 68 by Townsend. In the time left after Gloucestershire had ended their second innings 270 ahead, Denis Smith just managed to complete a half-century in taking over as Alderman's partner in an unbroken stand of 93. On a pitch that most favoured spin bowlers, Mitchell upstaged the visitors' Charlie Parker and Tom Goddard with five wickets in one innings and four in the other, though on both occasions he again conceded more than a hundred runs.

Derbyshire next returned to the winning path against Leicestershire at Aylestone Road, Leicester. Copson was also back for this one, but, with five wickets in the match, he had to take a back seat to Mitchell, who took eleven. To the 7-55 that ensured a useful first-innings lead, the tormenting Tommy added 4-67 as the home side sagged to defeat by 124 runs. The batting honours for Derbyshire went to Alderman and Worthington. Alderman made 64 on the first day after soon losing another opening partner, Alan Skinner, who was the fourth captain in as many games in the continued absence of Richardson; Worthington's 68 in the second innings was the highest individual score of the match.

Three successive draws followed, with Kent at Chesterfield, Northamptonshire at Derby, Sussex at Buxton. Guy Jackson had failed to get into double figures in either innings (out for a duck in the first) of his only previous County Championship appearance of the season, against Warwickshire, but on his return against Kent he totalled 117 runs, missing a century by just seven when he batted a second time. Townsend (62) and Skinner (57), who again led the side, provided the backbone of Derbyshire's 278 on the first day, but Kent claimed five points to the home team's three as half-centuries by their own captain, Old Reptonian Bryan Valentine (77), and Bill Ashdown (run out for 64) helped to edge them ahead on first innings despite five more wickets for Mitchell.

Derbyshire's second innings of 299, one run fewer that Kent's first, put them 277 ahead, but there was time for only thirty more overs, in which the visitors scored 96 against six bowlers for the loss of two wickets.

Mitchell reaped ten more wickets against Northants, that season's bottom club, his 6-73 doing most to pick up the five points for a first-innings lead after Alderman had given Derbyshire the impetus of a century that monopolised their total of 238. Alderman's opening partner, Denis Smith, was the next highest scorer to his 115 with a mere 26, but fortune turned against Alderman when he opened with his former Derby County clubmate Harry Storer in the second innings. He retired hurt before he could get off the mark, and with only seven runs on the board, though he was fit to continue in the next game. Townsend took over the leading run-getting role with a fine knock of 85 that led to a declaration with a lead of 282 and nearly eighty overs available, but an unbeaten century by John Timms steered the visitors to the safety of 196 for seven.

Sussex had slightly the better of the draw at Buxton, where the weather washed out the second day's play after they had scored 385 for eight on the first against an attack again deprived of Copson. Jim Parks, who three years later was to perform the unique double of 3,000 runs and 100 wickets, shared century stands with opening partner John Langridge (61) and Tommy Cook (71) before being stumped for 138 – the first of four batsmen to fall victim to Harry Elliott in that manner off the bowling of Mitchell, who, however, once more conceded over a hundred runs. George Pope took three wickets at a cost of 64, the other going to Worthington.

Harry Parks, Jim's younger brother, was left eight runs from a half-century by the prompt declaration on the third morning. In Derbyshire's reply there were two more stumpings, by Walter ('Tich') Cornford, one of cricket's smallest wicketkeepers at not much over 5ft, at the expense of Storer and Alf Pope, both off the bowling of James Langridge, but some consistent batting through nearly 150 overs carried them to the respectability of 340 with three wickets still in hand at the close. Denis Smith's 120 was the smallest of his four centuries that season.

Harry Storer (113) was the century-maker in Derbyshire's next match, convincingly won against Somerset at Chesterfield. He and Alderman (67) started with a stand of 151, and, although the tail failed to wag after Skinner (53) and Worthington (24) had added 66, a total of 310 proved well beyond Somerset's ability to avoid the follow-on. The hard-hitting Arthur Wellard was stranded on 40 as the visitors' first innings closed at 115. Sterner resistance was provided second time round by 'Dickie' Burrough (79) and the brothers Jack and Frank Lee, whose opening partnership realised 81, but Derbyshire were still left with a target of only 62 that was reached without loss. Somerset's wickets were shared by Worthington (seven), Copson and Mitchell (six each), though the spinner again conceded more than a hundred runs in the second innings.

That season was Jack Lee's most successful, and during the August he and his younger brother shared three century stands for the first wicket in three successive innings against Surrey and Sussex in the course of four playing days. Jack was serving as a private in the Pioneers when he was killed in action early in the Normandy campaign in 1944. Like Frank, who became a highly respected umpire best remembered for his no-balling of the South African Geoff Griffin in the Lord's Test of 1960, he joined Somerset from Middlesex, with whom their elder brother Harry went in first for a number of years.

The defeat of Somerset was the first of four consecutive victories for Derbyshire in the County Championship, with the others gained against Kent at Tunbridge Wells, Worcestershire at Stourbridge, and Middlesex at Derby. Tommy Mitchell hit a hot streak after Copson's 5-36 had been the main undoing of Kent for 114 on the first day. In the home side's second innings of that match and in the opponents' four of the next two games Mitchell plundered thirty wickets for 215 runs: 4-14 when Kent went in again, 8-22 and 5-66 at Stourbridge, 6-56 and 7-57 against Middlesex.

Alf Pope also took four wickets as Kent were dismissed for 120 in their second innings after having bundled Derbyshire out for 92 (Freeman 5-29). That left 143 needed for victory, and Harry Storer batted through for an unbeaten 54 as they were obtained for the loss of six wickets.

For the away match with Worcestershire, the unavailable Skinner was replaced as captain by Harry Elliott and as batsman by Eli Carrington, who celebrated his recall with the top score of 70 not out in a victory by an innings and 115 runs. Only one batsman nudged into double figures as Mitchell wrought his havoc in the home side's first reply of a paltry 48 to Derbyshire's 306. Openers 'Doc' Gibbons (he acquired that nickname after turning up for his debut with his kit in a little black bag) and Charlie Bull checked that smooth progress at the beginning of the second day's play with a half-century stand, but after both had gone for 41 Mitchell was assisted in mopping up the rest by Townsend, who finished that second innings with 5-48.

At Whitsun that year Worcestershire suffered a grievous loss with the sudden death of Maurice Nichol at a Chelmsford hotel while there for a match with Essex, and by a most macabre coincidence Bull was killed in a road accident at Margaretting, near Chelmsford, at Whitsun five years later. Nichol, a North-Easterner who had scored a century on his first appearance for Worcestershire against the West Indians in 1928, and had been England's 12th man for the 1931 Test with New Zealand at Lord's, had been taken seriously ill with pneumonia during the winter of 1931-32, and, by what *Wisden* called 'another dramatic coincidence', he had been forced to drop out of the county's Whitsun game with Essex at Leyton in 1933 after being taken ill at a railway station.

Later in the 1930s, Worcestershire's team also included Syd Buller, and after one match in which both he and Charlie Bull had batted with extreme caution an exasperated onlooker is said to have said thankfully: 'Well, we've had Bull, and we've had Buller. Thank goodness we're not getting Bullest!' Buller was badly injured in the car crash that took Bull's life, but he was able to resume his playing career and subsequently became a respected umpire who, however, was caught up in the Griffin no-balling affair and then had to seek a police escort from the Chesterfield ground after slamming down the lid on the England career of Derbyshire's Harold Rhodes by also adjudging him guilty of throwing during the opening match of the South Africans' 1965 tour. Buller, too, met an untimely end. While at Edgbaston as one of the umpires for a game between Warwickshire and Nottinghamshire in 1970, he collapsed during a hold-up in play because of rain and never regained consciousness.

With Guy Jackson called upon to lead Derbyshire for the visit by the 1934 Australians that came straight after the game at Stourbridge, there was again a fourth captain in as many matches when Richardson returned for the encounter with Middlesex. Derbyshire twice totalled just under 250, declaring with only six wickets down in a second innings dominated by Skinner's 79, whereas Mitchell-muddled Middlesex collapsed for 91 and 117 to lose by 278 runs.

Next came three successive draws, all missed by Mitchell. Derbyshire gleaned just three points from the first one at Gloucester, but five from each of the two others, against Worcestershire at Chesterfield and Surrey at Ilkeston. Gloucestershire were guided to a lead of 113 by a century from Cecil

Dacre, a stocky, strongly built batsman who seven years earlier had struck eight sixes and 21 fours in a brilliant 176 at Derby for the first New Zealand tourists of England, but the spectre of defeat was banished by Denis Smith (131) and Alan Skinner (102), whose third-wicket stand was worth 215 in a total of 333 that was just four runs fewer than Gloucestershire's first-innings score. In the fifteen overs of the home team's second innings that were possible before the close Dacre and Basil Allen scored 54 without being separated.

Gloucestershire's captain in that match, succeeded by Allen, was Dallas Page, another county cricketer to be the victim of a fatal road accident. He died after his car crashed into a wall near Cirencester while he was on his way home after leading his county to an innings victory over Nottinghamshire at Gloucester on the last day of the 1936 season. Other first-class cricketers killed in motor accidents between the world wars included George Street, a Sussex and England wicketkeeper, Dudley Pope, an Essex batsman (near Chelmsford only a few days after Page's death) and, as already recalled, Reg Northway, of Northamptonshire.

Worcestershire, who ended that season next to the foot of the table, were routed for 76 after their captain, Bernard Quaife, son of the famous Willie, had decided to bat first on winning the toss at Queen's Park, Copson and Alf Pope both taking four wickets for little more than twenty runs apiece. The rot set in from the moment Gibbons, one of the best uncapped batsmen of his era, was snapped up by Harry Elliott off Worthington without getting off the mark, but when he went in again he made amends with one of the eight centuries he scored, four of them in five successive innings, in the most successful season of his career. His second-wicket stand with Syd Martin, a South African who batted right-handed but bowled with his left, took the score from 75 to 201 before he was bowled by Copson for 105. Martin, who also played for Natal and Rhodesia, carried on to be 80 not out as Worcestershire reached the close of the second day's play with all but one run of their first-innings arrears of 250 wiped out for the loss of just three wickets.

That morning, Derbyshire's top scorer, Carrington, had added only eight runs to his overnight 72 before being bowled by Reg Perks, and Martin was to share a similar, even speedier fate, when he resumed his innings twenty-four hours later. Three more runs were his ration, Copson then upsetting his stumps, only for the weather soon afterwards to snatch victory from Derbyshire's grasp by intervening when Worcestershire were only 38 runs ahead with seven wickets down.

Surrey also had the worst of their draw at Ilkeston, the premature end coming with Smith, on 40 after scoring 125 in the first innings, and Townsend going well and Derbyshire's target reduced from 159 to 83 for the loss of only Skinner's wicket. Surrey were only eighteen behind after both sides had batted once, but Stan Squires (60) alone stayed for long as Copson, Alf Pope and Townsend evenly shared the wickets in their second innings of 176.

A third consecutive home match, at Derby, brought comprehensive revenge for the mauling in Hampshire. The Derbyshire century-maker this time was Worthington, whose 154 received sound backing from Townsend (86) and Richardson (58). Replying to a declared total of 377 for seven, Hampshire fell foul of the fit-again Mitchell, who took 6-90 in their first innings of 192 and 4-74 in their second of 186, Copson chipping in with 4-67. This left Derbyshire needing only two runs for victory, and after a wide had brought the scores level Smith struck the winning boundary off Philip Mead's third delivery. Derbyshire's keen attack was held up mostly by Alec Kennedy, who was only one run from a half-century when Mitchell nailed him in Hampshire's first innings, and John Arnold, who was also a Mitchell victim after scoring 85 in their second.

So Derbyshire entered August with an outside chance of becoming champions, only for more bad weather to intervene after they had worked themselves into a strong position on the first day of their match with Yorkshire, winners of the title in each of the preceding three seasons, at Bramall Lane, Sheffield. Consistent batting at the top of the order, Alderman, Smith, Townsend and Skinner each getting to a half-century and Worthington not far from one, guided them to within eight runs of 350 with two wickets in hand by the close, but the whole of the second day's play was then washed out.

Although Hedley Verity wrapped up the innings for the addition of only three runs the next morning, Yorkshire also quickly lost a couple of wickets, including that of the redoubtable Herbert Sutcliffe to the Elliott-Copson combination without a run on the board. Apart from a resolute 62 by Maurice Leyland and an unbeaten 32 by wicketkeeper Arthur Wood, they continued to struggle as Mitchell got to work with the enthusiastic assistance of Townsend. All out for 187, they were forced into the indignity of having to follow on, Mitchell finishing with 5-81 and also holding the catch offered by skipper Sellers that gave Townsend one of his three wickets. Not enough time was left, however, to give any realistic prospect of fifteen points instead of five, and the game ended with Yorkshire's deficit reduced to 61 without loss and Sutcliffe, imperturbability restored, just past his half-century.

On next to Birmingham – and another drawn game influenced by the weather. After dismissing Warwickshire for 219 (four wickets for Copson, three for Mitchell), Derbyshire gained a slender lead largely through an opening century stand by Storer (69) and Alderman (64) and an undefeated 45 by Les Townsend, but no further play was possible on the third day after the home side had added 32 runs to their overnight 44, giving them an overall lead of 55 for the loss of only one wicket. The batsman out, Norman Kilner, was caught by Townsend off Copson for 47, making him his team's second highest scorer in the match behind his captain, Bob Wyatt, whose 63 in the first innings was interrupted by injury soon after he had completed his fifty. Again he was Mitchell's bunny.

Kilner began his career with his home county of Yorkshire, but, unlike his elder, and more famous, brother Roy, was unable to command a regular place in their side. This made him open to the offer from Warwickshire, and for the dozen seasons from 1926 they reaped from him an annual harvest of over a thousand runs. Both brothers were wounded in the 1914-18 war – Norman the more severely, though he outlived Roy by more than fifty years. Roy was only thirty-seven years old when he died of enteric fever in 1928.

From Edgbaston, Derbyshire ran straight into two defeats in three matches that ruined their remote title prospects. Unusually, fielding lapses contributed to their failure by 135 runs at Old Trafford, but the biggest reason was the best bowling performance given against them all season. In Derbyshire's first innings of 170, John Hopwood took 5-32 with his slow left-arm teasers; in their second innings of 137 he claimed 8-58. As he was also an opening batsman (right hand) who that year had a double-century against Gloucestershire among his 1,500 or so runs to go along with his 110 wickets, which also included a 7-13 haul against Glamorgan, it can be easily understood why *Wisden* expressed the view that Lancashire 'could never have won the [1934] Championship without him'. John Kay, who for many years was an authority on Lancashire cricket, described Hopwood as 'an all-rounder of moods', and he did disappoint in his two Tests that summer against Australia (he failed to get into double figures and, like Tommy Mitchell, took nought for plenty as Bradman piled up one of his triple centuries at Leeds), but he was a dependable, if generally unexciting, contributor for his county throughout most of the 1930s, and more than forty years later became the first professional to be their president.

Derbyshire's attack was most heavily punished in Manchester during that match five from the end of their 1934 programme by Peter Eckersley, who was bowled by Copson eleven runs short of a century in Lancashire's first innings of 240, and by Ernest Tyldesley, who was not out for two runs fewer when the second innings was declared closed just after the 200 had gone up with only half the side out. Eckersley, the captain, was known as the 'cricketer airman' for his habit of often flying to matches in his own plane. He was killed in a flying accident in 1940 at the age of 36.

For Derbyshire, a true captain's example in adversity was set by Alan Skinner, who had resumed the leadership against Warwickshire in another of Richardson's absences. He made 47 in a fourth-wicket stand of 96 with Worthington (56) when he first batted, then scored 55 before becoming fourth in Hopwood's sequence of second-innings successes that was interrupted only by the early running-out of Worthington. The last wicket, Mitchell's, went to Dick Pollard.

Derbyshire's other setback in August, their sixth and last of the season, was suffered rather unexpectedly at the hands of Middlesex, who in those pre-Compton and Edrich days, and with 'Patsy' Hendren and 'Young Jack' Hearne nearing the end of their illustrious careers, were trundling along just below halfway in the Championship table. The reclaiming of Storer by football was again felt as Derbyshire responded disappointingly to a home total of only just over 200 built on half-centuries by Hearne and William ('Tagge') Webster, a Cambridge Blue and future president of both Middlesex and the MCC.

Middlesex's lead of 69 on first innings was increased to 296, leaving Hendren unbeaten on 72 after exactly doubling the score at which he had had to retire hurt. 'Big Jim' Smith, whose excellent form on his entry into first-class cricket that season earned him immediate Test selection in the West Indies, followed up his 5-51 in Derbyshire's 136 with a typically slogging 53, but then had to take a back seat as Jim Sims bagged 6-85 in the sealing of a victory by 84 runs. The only Derbyshire players to take any real credit from the match were Bill Copson, whose eight wickets included 5-63 in Middlesex's second innings, and Denis Smith, who on the last day went close to batting right through a total of 212 in missing his fifth century of the season by only three runs.

Between those reverses at Old Trafford and Lord's, Derbyshire demolished lowly Somerset by an innings and 69 runs at Clarence Park, Weston-super-Mare. That was Leslie Townsend's match. He was not out for 106 when Derbyshire declared at 351 for eight, Smith (84) and Worthington (66) making the other major contributions, then took 6-66 and 5-64 as the home county wilted for 159 and 123.

From the failure against Middlesex, Derbyshire bounced back to win both their remaining matches. They completed a rare double over Nottinghamshire, beating them by 201 runs at Ilkeston, then accounted for Leicestershire at Chesterfield by 42. Alf Pope's best display of the season undermined Notts. After making the top score of 40 in Derbyshire's first innings of 220, he did most to gain a lead of 90 by taking six wickets for only 21 runs. Bill Voce hit back with 6-52, dismissing Smith and Townsend for ducks, and Alderman and Alf Pope for a single each, but determined batting by Worthington (93) and Harry Elliott (46 not out) helped to set a target of 302 that proved well out of the visitors' reach as Copson reaped another five-wicket haul at a cost of 40 runs.

Leicestershire edged eight runs ahead on first innings at Queen's Park, mainly through a half-century by Norman Armstrong and a single short of one by 19-year-old Charles Edgson, after seven of Derbyshire's players had failed to get into double figures in a total of 181 that did not make best use of winning the toss. Skinner, again captain, hit 48 of those runs, and he also top-scored with 60, ably supported by Harry Elliott (50), in a second-innings of 229. This left Leicestershire needing 222, and they looked quite capable of getting them before Leslie Berry (67), Armstrong and Edgson, who both made 43, were removed. The score then slumped from 168 for five to 179 all out, Copson finishing things off for the best return of 3-22 as the ten wickets in the innings were evenly shared among five bowlers.

Edgson, who had been a heavy scorer at Stamford School, played only occasionally for Leicestershire and missed a Blue at Oxford despite making a half-century in the Freshmen's match of 1936, but Armstrong and Berry were two of the heaviest scorers in the county's history – Armstrong after not starting his professional career until he was 33. Armstrong, who was the second oldest former English first-class cricketer at the time of his death at 97 in 1990, became the first to hit 2,000 runs in a season for Leicestershire in 1933; Berry, who also found time earlier in his career to keep goal for Bristol Rovers and Swindon Town, rose to the county's captaincy and retired in 1951 as their record maker of runs, just over 30,000 of them.

Four Derbyshire players scored more than a thousand runs in County Championship matches in 1934 – Smith (1,565), Alderman (1,290), Townsend (1,149) and Worthington (1,185) – and Storer, who headed the averages with 881 at 38.30, would almost certainly also have done so if he had not missed 13 of their 28 games. Skinner went close with 921, but just managed to top the thousand with the inclusion of his innings for Cambridge University against Yorkshire and the Australians. Mitchell and Copson, who both missed seven matches, headed the bowling with 138 (at 17.39) and 91 (17.61) Championship wickets respectively. Townsend took 75, Worthington 59, and Alf Pope 51. Harry Elliott, who, with Smith, Townsend, Smith and Worthington, had an ever-present record, was awarded a well-deserved testimonial. Alderman and Alf Pope were both absent from only two Championship games, but Richardson, like Storer, was available on only fifteen occasions. Skinner, so often the captain in his absence, played twenty times. Final table for 1934:

	P	W	L	1st inns W	L	NR	Points Poss	Act	%
Lancashire	30	13	3	10	4	0	450	257	57.11
Sussex	30	12	2	7	8	1	450	243	54.00
DERBYSHIRE	28	12	6	6	3	1	420	223	53.09
Warwickshire	24	10	4	4	4	2	360	190	52.77
Kent	30	12	7	6	5	0	450	225	50.00
Yorkshire	30	12	7	5	4	2	450	225	50.00
Gloucs	30	12	10	2	4	2	450	210	46.66
Essex	28	9	4	5	9	1	420	191	45.47
Notts	28	8	7	7	6	0	420	173	41.10
Middlesex	28	8	9	7	2	2	420	169	40.23
Surrey	26	6	8	9	3	0	390	144	36.92
Leics	24	6	9	3	6	0	360	123	34.16
Glamorgan	24	3	8	5	5	3	360	97	26.94
Hampshire	28	3	11	8	5	1	420	104	24.76
Somerset	24	3	10	0	11	0	360	78	21.66
Worcs	28	3	12	3	9	1	420	91	21.66
Northants	24	2	17	3	2	0	260	51	14.16

Sussex, one of the original members of the Championship, made the running until late July, but they won only one of their last ten matches and had to be content with second place for the third successive year. They had also finished runners-up in 1902 and 1903, and were to do so again in 1953 and 1981. In 2001, under the captaincy of former Derbyshire batsman Chris Adams, they won the Division Two title in the second season of split sections, and in 2003, while Derbyshire languished at the foot of Division Two, they were county champions for the first time after a wait of 164 years, also led by Adams. Three years later, Adams guided them to the top again.

19. Second in 1935

As if the lbw law was not already controversial enough, the debate about it was racked up another notch at a meeting at Lord's on 21 November 1934, when it was decided to give a trial the following season to a critical amendment. Law 24 was altered to read:

'The striker shall be out lbw if with any part of his person (except his hand) which is between wicket and wicket he intercept a ball which, in the opinion of the umpire at the bowler's wicket, shall have been pitched in a straight line from the bowler's wicket to the striker's wicket, or shall have been pitched on the off-side of the striker's wicket and would have hit it.'

The change to what is now Law 36 was the additional phrase that meant a batsman could be out to a ball that pitched outside the off stump, as well as one that landed in a straight line, if, in the opinion of the umpire, it would have hit the wicket but for intercepting 'any part of his person (except his hand)' that was between wicket and wicket at the moment of impact. Those who agreed to this spreading of the danger area wanted to even things up a bit for the bowlers after several seasons of high scoring, but what a division of views they aroused!

Those in favour saw it not only as a benefit for off-break bowlers and in-duckers but also as an antidote to fast leg-theory. Those against viewed it as a discouragement to play attractive strokes on the off-side, a move to the detriment of leg-spinners and the orthodox left-arm bowlers, and an added reason for cricket to become more defensive-minded. Some very respected and knowledgeable people in the game were among the strongest critics, and Frank Chester, one of the most respected umpires, was to say that if he could change one law in cricket it would be the new lbw one, but *Wisden* threw its considerable weight in the opposite direction after finding that in the 1935 first-class season there were 483 dismissals under the new rule out of 1,560 leg-before decisions. It declared: 'Those who watched cricket day after day in variable weather on all kinds of pitches could see how the game benefited from the alteration.'

The experiment was continued for another season, then officially incorporated into the law the year after that. Despite continued adverse comments, it was not until 1970 that the next change was introduced for the English season, following a try-out in Australia and the West Indies in their 1969-70 seasons. Designed mainly to curb what *Wisden* called the 'negative and unfair practice' of pad play – something the detractors of the 1935 experiment had predicted would be a consequence – the new wording read:

'A batsman will be out lbw if, with any part of his body except his hand, he intercepts a ball which has not first touched his bat or hand, and which, in the opinion of the umpire, would have hit the wicket provided that either: (a) the ball pitched, or would have pitched, in a straight line between wicket and wicket, or (b) the ball pitched outside a batsman's off stump and, in the opinion of the umpire, he made no genuine attempt to play the ball with his bat.'

Another experimental law came into force in 1972:

'Should the umpire be of the opinion that the striker has made no genuine attempt to play the ball with his bat, he shall, on appeal, give the striker out lbw if he is satisfied that the ball would have hit the stumps even though the ball pitched outside the off stump, and even though any interception was also outside the off stump.'

The current law stipulates that the striker is out lbw if:

'The bowler delivers a ball, not being a no-ball, and the ball, if it is not intercepted full pitch, pitches in line between wicket and wicket or on the offside of the striker's wicket and the ball not having previously touched the bat, the striker intercepts the ball either full pitch or after pitching, with any part of his person, and the point of impact, even if above the level of the bails, either is between wicket and wicket, or is either between wicket and wicket or outside the line of the off stump, if the striker has made no genuine attempt to play the ball with his bat, and but for the interception, the ball would have hit the wicket.'

There is more, detailing what is meant by 'interception of the ball', but that is quite enough! It all prompts a great deal of sympathy for the poor umpire.

No mention was made of an lbw law until 1744, when the striker was out if, *with design,* he prevented the ball hitting his wicket with a leg. In 1788 the design clause was omitted, and the ball had to pitch straight to get an lbw verdict. In the early 1820s the ball did not need to be pitched straight, but it had to be 'delivered straight'. In 1839 the law reverted to that of 1788, and this remained in force until 1935. There was a strong move in 1901 to omit the words 'pitch straight', but it did not get the necessary two-thirds majority at the MCC meeting.

Dismissals under the 1935 experiment were recorded as lbw (n), and umpires signalled them to the scorers by opening the palm of an upraised hand. Peter Sunnucks, of Kent, had the dubious distinction of being the first to fall for it, trapped without scoring by Leicestershire's Haydon Smith, uncle of Terry Spencer who later also opened the county's attack, at Gravesend on the first day of May in 1935. Derbyshire's first victim, at Chesterfield on 14 May, was Albert Alderman, but he had scored exactly 100 when dismissed in his second innings by Horace Fisher, the Yorkshire left-arm spinner who, against Somerset at Sheffield three years earlier, had been the first to achieve a hat-trick of lbw victims.

Derbyshire, full of confidence after finishing so close to Lancashire's champions the previous year, got off to a most impressive start in that opening match of 1935 against Yorkshire, who were to end the season back in their familiar first place. In his first innings Alderman endured a complete contrast to the century he was to score on the last day of the match in being bowled by Bill Bowes without getting off the mark, and with only six runs on the board, but his partner Denis Smith settled in to get within eleven runs of a double-century before Hedley Verity spun the ball through his defence. Leslie Townsend (37) gave good support in a stand of 105 for the third wicket after Worthington had also swiftly bowed to Bowes, and Eli Carrington (74) was an even stauncher ally in a partnership of 202 for the fourth.

With George Pope contributing a brisk and unbeaten 30 after Arthur Richardson and Arnold Townsend had also gone cheaply to the Bowes-Verity combination of speed and spin, Derbyshire amassed a total of 382 that was highly creditable for one day – especially as there was still time for Herbert Sutcliffe and Arthur Mitchell to take Yorkshire's reply to 67 without loss by the close.

Next morning, Mitchell had no sooner reached his fifty than he was bowled by his namesake, but Sutcliffe proceeded on his serene way until George Pope deceived him with the aid of the lbw amendment nine runs from a century. Wickets, meanwhile, had been tumbling at the other end, and a healthy home first-innings lead seemed certain when seven were down for 174, only just doubling the value of the first-wicket stand. Half-centuries by Arthur Wood (run out for 64) and Frank Smailes (52), ably abetted by 30 from Verity, then ensured a very lively wagging of the tail, however, and Derbyshire had their advantage cut to 54 before being able to begin their second innings.

Even so, victory might still have been theirs, instead of having to settle for five points to Yorkshire's three, if a mixture of rain and snow had not cost some playing time in the final day. Arthur Richardson, despite being without his Copson spearhead, attempted to force a definite result by declaring 265 ahead with four wickets still in hand, but the end came with Yorkshire 102 for four after another solid start by Sutcliffe and Mitchell, who both fell just short of a fifty. As in the visitors' first innings, the wickets were shared evenly around, with Alf Pope benefiting from the lbw (n) to claim each of his three in that manner. Verity outdid Tommy Mitchell with five wickets in both Derbyshire innings for match figures of 10-192. His spinner rival had to pay 143 runs for six wickets.

From that creditable display against the most consistently successful county of the 1930s, Derbyshire surged on a roll with four consecutive wins, each inside two days. Copson was back for the visit to The Oval, and he and Mitchell ripped through the batting with four wickets apiece as Surrey slumped to a total of 60. Only Laurie Fishlock and Percy Fender, widely regarded as the shrewdest county captain of his generation, reached double figures. Leslie Townsend (89), George Pope (53) and Worthington (44) showed how it should be done as Derbyshire replied with 253, after which victory would have been gained by an innings but for a Fender flourish that finished only sixteen runs from a century. As it was, Surrey were all out just seventeen ahead, Mitchell taking 8-78, and, with Alderman failing for the second time in the match, the winning margin was by nine wickets.

It was Copson's turn to do most of the damage when Leicestershire were then swept aside by ten wickets at Derby, his nine wickets costing only 80 runs. Alderman was back in form with a half-century, and Harry Storer celebrated his first appearance of the season by top-scoring with 79. On to Brentwood, where Copson and Mitchell combined with five wickets each in an Essex first innings that staggered to 116 with the late assistance of a defiant 54 by Claude Ashton. Derbyshire's lead was limited to 34 mainly by Laurie Eastman, who added to his 5-36 by taking all six wickets that the visitors lost in progressing to fifteen more points under the guidance of Denis Smith's 82. That the requirement was as high as 186 was due mainly to Essex's more consistent batting in their second innings, headed by Jack O'Connor (49) and Ashton (38), as the wickets were spread evenly among five bowlers.

Ashton, a Cambridge Blue at cricket and hockey, and an amateur soccer international who played in all forward and half-back positions for the Corinthians, at full-back and in goal for the Casuals, and at centre-forward for England, was the youngest of the three sons of Hubert S Ashton, who was president of the Essex club from 1936 until his death in his 82nd year in 1943. Claude died, aged 41, only a few months before his father, while on active service in the RAF. Roger Winlaw, a fellow Old Wykehamist and double light Blue, perished in the same plane. Laurie Eastman, who did not enjoy the best of health, also died during the war – following an operation, but as some consequence of the shock caused when a bomb exploded near him while he was carrying out his duties as an ARP warden.

Derbyshire's run of success in the Championship was interrupted after their return from Essex by defeat at Ilkeston at the hands of the South African tourists, but they promptly bounced back with a trouncing of Hampshire at Chesterfield before luck turned against them with reverses at Worcester and Edgbaston.

As on their previous visit in 1929, the Springboks found Derbyshire setting the pace in the Championship, but whereas they had had the worst of a rain-affected draw at Derby six years earlier (Derbyshire had led by 42 runs on first innings with three wickets still to fall), this time they recovered from losing their first four men for 75 to be put firmly on top by a stand of 262 for the fifth wicket by Ken Viljoen (152) and the noted hitter 'Jock' Cameron (132). With Arthur Langton, at 23 the youngest member of the side, weighing in with a lusty 43 not out at No 10, the total reached 443, the second biggest of the season against Derbyshire. In another Copson absence, Tommy Mitchell was again the county's most successful bowler, but he had the pay the high price of 167 runs for his five first-innings wickets. The high standard of fielding that had become a Derbyshire speciality was reflected in the fact that both South African opening batsmen, Jack Siedle and Eric Rowan, were run out.

All but Arthur Richardson of the top seven in Derbyshire's batting order got into double figures in their reply, the 22-year-old Gilbert Hodgkinson marking his debut in first-class cricket with the team's top score of 44 that included nine fours and was to remain his highest at that level, but they were all out 207 in arrears. Herbie Wade, soon to become captain of the first South African team to win a Test in England, decided against enforcing the follow-on, and declared his second innings closed immediately Siedle was fourth out at 200 – caught by Smith off Mitchell only two runs from his fourth century of the tour. Facing a deficit of just over 400, Derbyshire wilted after Smith (37) and Worthington (49) had been parted, and they would have lost even more heavily than by 209 runs but for the late defiance of Alf Pope, who was left unbeaten on 39.

Cameron and Langton were two others to die prematurely. Cameron, one of South Africa's finest wicketkeepers, succumbed to enteric fever shortly after his return home from that tour. He was only 30, the age at which Langton, a 6ft 3in-tall medium-pace bowler, was killed in action with the air force in November 1942.

Gilbert Hodgkinson, who had been in the team at Derby School, was a natural forcing batsman whose inability to resist the temptation of trying to hit every ball limited him to a first-class career average below fifteen. After playing in only a few more matches before the 1939-45 war he came back from the dead to take on the difficult task of captaining the county in the first post-war season of 1946, for in the 1943 *Wisden* he was reported to have been killed in action while serving as an officer with the Sherwood Foresters. The head wounds he suffered in the summer of 1940 were indeed serious, but it was eventually learned that he had been taken prisoner, and he made a remarkable recovery on being repatriated. He was a popular leader in his one season of Derbyshire captaincy, if not, perhaps, a strict enough one, and he set a good example in the field.

By far the dominant feature of Hampshire's eclipse at Queen's Park in the 1935 season was Denis Smith's personal-best 225 after an attack again without Copson had whisked the visitors out for 140, Worthington conceding only 19 runs for his three wickets. The one substantial stand of Derbyshire's innings, which Richardson declared closed at 378 for nine, was monopolised by Smith to such an extent that just 52 of the 235 runs added came from Les Townsend's bat. Worthington, Mitchell and Townsend then each took three wickets as John Arnold (52) alone delayed the inevitable end for long as Hampshire faded to defeat by an innings and 104 runs.

Bad weather played its part in the two away defeats that followed. Put in to bat by Cyril Walters, the stylish Welsh-born batsman who captained England as well as Worcestershire, Derbyshire got to within three runs of 200 mainly through a partnership of 70 between Carrington (52) and Richardson (43), and were then helped to a first-innings lead of 36 by five more wickets for Mitchell despite an undefeated half-century by Bernard Quaife. That, however, was where things began to go wrong. Early in Derbyshire's second innings rain stopped play until the final morning, and when the game got under way again Worcestershire's imported spinners found the conditions so much to their liking that a mere 54 runs were on the board when the last wicket fell. Dick Howorth, a Bacup-born left-arm slow bowler who came right to the fore that season but, because Hedley Verity was then an automatic England choice, had to wait until after the war for his Test chance, took six wickets for only 16 runs; with half his dozen overs maidens; 'Peter' Jackson (like 'Peter' Perrin he was christened Percy), an off-spinner from Scotland, snapped up the four others, Howorth holding the catch for one of them, at a cost two runs fewer. This left Worcestershire needing 91, and they got them for the loss of Walters, bowled by Mitchell after an opening stand of 62 with Gibbons.

The rib injury that delayed Denis Smith's Test debut, and some costly dropped catches, combined with the weather to aid Warwickshire's six-wicket defeat of Derbyshire in Birmingham. Although dismissed for only 119, of which Smith made 61, Derbyshire again claimed the five points for a first-innings lead as Wyatt declared when the home reply reached 100 with the last pair together. Another good score by Smith would at least have given Warwickshire a bigger target to aim at, but his handicap put him well down the batting order when Derbyshire went in again, and he was left stranded, 11 not out, at the fall of the last wicket for a paltry 75. So in successive matches Derbyshire had been routed for their smallest totals of the season, and their only comfort in another severe blow to their title aspirations was that Warwickshire lost four wickets after being set to get only 95. Three of them were taken by Mitchell, giving him seven in the match, and one was again Wyatt's – bowled without scoring. Though thus denied the last laugh, the Warwickshire captain could be content with the second last, having taken 5-30 in Derbyshire's second-innings collapse.

More rain had a bearing on Derbyshire's next game, drawn at Leicester in another low-scoring encounter that confined them to five points. Copson was back, but this was the match in which Tommy Mitchell became only the county's second player, after Bill Bestwick, to take all ten wickets in an innings. After Haydon Smith and George Geary had equally shared the ten wickets in Derbyshire's modest total of 140, Leicestershire were hurried out for 123 by the bespectacled spinner, only for time to run out with their second-innings score at 111 for three (two more for Mitchell). They then still required 134, with Alan Shipman, a bowler converted into an opening batsman, going well on 60 not out.

As much of a stir as Mitchell's achievement caused, there was something even more remarkable – 'sensational' was Major Eardley-Simpson's word for it in his booklet about that season – to come straight afterwards. Having fallen just two runs short of being able to enforce the follow-on against Somerset at Derby, Richardson sent Mitchell in with Harry Elliott to open the home side's second innings, declared after Elliott had taken a single off only one ball (skipper Reggie Ingle put himself on to deliver it), and then saw his bowlers sweep Somerset all out for 35 in an hour for a victory by 114 runs. Copson's five wickets cost only 15 runs; Les Townsend conceded just a single in taking three. Worthington and Mitchell had to be satisfied with one each. In Derbyshire's first innings, declared at 237 for eight, Alderman (77), Les Townsend (58) and Alf Pope (51 not out) showed that batting was not as difficult as Somerset also found it in their first total of 89 (Mitchell 4-40).

The freak declaration was just one of a series over several seasons spawned by the decision to increase the number of points for a win after the 1930 season, a move designed to encourage captains to go for an outright victory. When bad weather delayed the start of the match between Yorkshire and Gloucestershire at Sheffield in 1931, it was turned into a one-innings contest by the agreement between the captains, Frank Greenwood and Beverley Lyon, to declare their first innings closed after one ball had been bowled straight through to the boundary for four byes.

There were two outcomes to this. One was Yorkshire's only defeat of that season after being put in to bat, though they still ended comfortably ahead of the runners-up – Gloucestershire. The other, which took seven more years to arrive, was the further tinkering with the regulations whereby the number of points for a win was reduced from 15 to 12, and for a lead on first innings from five points to four – but with no points for a team behind on first innings in a drawn match. The peculiar anomaly was left, however, of a county retaining their four points for a first-innings lead if they lost, but not if they went on to gain the dozen for a win. Not until 1966 were the winners allowed to keep any first-innings points they had gained, but even at that time they still picked up just the dozen – ten for the win, two for the lead.

From their comfortable win against Somerset in 1935, Derbyshire went to the other extreme of beating Lancashire at Old Trafford by seven runs with only three minutes to go after claiming the extra half-hour. This was the match in which Harry Elliott caught eight batsmen and stumped two others, setting a Derbyshire record since equalled by only Bob Taylor. Replying to a total of 227 in which Smith scored 63 and Alderman 43, Lancashire were dismissed for 168 and then set to score 320 by a declaration at 260 for nine. Alderman duplicated Smith's first-innings score when he batted a second time, after Storer (77) and Smith (58) had opened with a stand of 138.

That man Iddon, who had taken Denis Smith's place in that year's first Test, was again the biggest obstacle in Derbyshire's path when Lancashire embarked upon their daunting task. He scored 131 and partnered Watson (43) in a second-wicket stand of 104 following the departure of Hopwood, to one of Elliott's catches off Copson, before a run had been obtained. None of the other batsmen got beyond 30, but the outcome remained in the balance right until Alf Pope snatched the extra ten points by bowling George Duckworth with the second ball of his 25th over. Mitchell was again Derbyshire's chief wicket-taker, with four in each innings, if at a total cost of 186 runs.

Ilkeston was Derbyshire's next stop, and their triumphant progress continued with an even more satisfying defeat of their neighbouring rivals Nottinghamshire, after once more gaining a first-innings lead. In the absence of Mitchell, only Copson went without a wicket as the Pope brothers and Leslie Townsend each dismissed three batsmen, and Worthington one, while Notts just managed to struggle past 200 on the opening day. Most of their runs, 78 of them, came from George Vernon Gunn, one of whose uncles, Ernest Stapleton, had played once for Derbyshire in 1902. Gunn, whose other cricketing uncle, John, was a nephew of William Gunn, was no mean batsman in his own right, but his main claim to fame was to have scored his maiden century, 100 not out, in the same Notts innings, at Edgbaston in 1931, in which his father George, then 53, had also hit a hundred (183).

The century-maker in that match of 1935 with Notts at Ilkeston was Stan Worthington, whose 126 in Derbyshire's reply of 253 (48 ahead) was his first of the season. Given most assistance by Harry Storer's 56, he eventually had his stumps upset by Bill Voce, who outshone his pace partner Harold Larwood by five wickets to one. Charlie Harris almost matched Worthington when Notts batted again, getting within eight runs of three figures before being run out. Joe Hardstaff, also run out, was the next highest scorer, eight from a half-century, in a total of 233 that left Derbyshire needing 186. Shrugging off the dismissal of Storer for a duck by Larwood, they knocked them off with seven wickets to spare. Alderman carried his bat for 76 after sharing a second-wicket stand of 70 with Smith, who was caught at the wicket, off Voce, three runs from fifty.

Having notched his first century of the season at the nineteenth attempt, Worthington promptly scored another one, 107, in the following game with Surrey at Chesterfield. There was not to be a third one, though he got into the nineties in the return match with Notts at Trent Bridge and against Sussex at Hove. Neither did his splendid effort lead to a fourth successive victory, although there was still some chance of it until rain intervened. Errol Holmes, Surrey's new captain – one of those, incidentally, who was strongly against the new lbw law – had twice been out without scoring, first to Copson and then Mitchell, in the May match between the clubs at The Oval, but this time, in the absence of Copson through injury and Mitchell, rested after being in the England team with Holmes in the Lord's Test that had finished only the day before, he indulged himself with a masterly innings of 206 in a total of 430. One of the most gifted amateur batsmen of his day, Holmes was a great believer in brighter cricket, and he certainly lived up to his reputation at Queen's Park in century stands with Laurie Fishlock (80) and Ted Whitfield (43).

Derbyshire conceded a first-innings lead of 186 despite Worthington's hundred, losing six of their wickets to the fast-medium bowling of Eddie Watts, brother-in-law of clubmate Alf Gover. Holmes then declared in Surrey's second innings at 164 for seven (Alf Pope 5-34) after Tom Barling (65 not out) and Fishlock (41) had rescued the visitors from the toils of 22 for four, and in the time remaining Derbyshire wiped out 150 of their 350 arrears for the loss of only one wicket. The opening partnership between Storer (57) and Smith (67 not out) was worth 133.

Copson and Mitchell also missed the ensuing draw with Lancashire at Buxton, where Alan Skinner, the third successive stand-in for Richardson as captain (after Harry Elliott and Wilfred Hill-Wood), provoked a divergence of opinion by deciding not to enforce the follow-on after Tom Armstrong, in his only appearance of the season, and Les Townsend had made the Red Rose men red-faced with five cheap wickets apiece in their rout for 86 in reply to a total of 237 to which Storer contributed another fifty. Townsend followed up his good work with the ball by just missing a half-century in support of Denis Smith's 62 before Skinner declared Derbyshire's second innings closed with the lead increased to 342 for the loss of nine wickets, but by the close Lancashire had chipped 176 off that deficit with their fifth pair together. Once more Iddon was the man mainly in the way, unbeaten on 76.

Having gained just eight points from those two unsatisfactory draws, Derbyshire proceeded to drop all thirty from their next two matches, away to Gloucestershire and Nottinghamshire, despite welcoming back their speed and spin spearheads. Under the renewed captaincy of Hill-Wood with both Richardson and Skinner absent, they gave one of their most disappointing displays of the season in losing by 68 runs in Bristol. Then, with Richardson back, they frittered away a most promising position at Trent Bridge after again controversially scorning the follow-on in not wishing to bat last, and were beaten by three wickets ten minutes from time.

There were three half-centuries, by Billy Neale (67), Eric ('Dick') Stephens (54 not out) and Walter Hammond (53), in Gloucestershire's 250 to just one for Derbyshire, by Denis Smith (76), on first innings, but the home team went in again only 17 runs to the good. When that slim advantage was increased by a mere 50 runs with half the side out Derbyshire looked to be on easy street, only for Stephens (65) and Monty Cranfield (50) to put a sting in the tail that helped to raise their requirement to 226. The famous spin combination of Goddard and Parker put that out of reach with reasonable comfort, Leslie Townsend, with 52, alone offering much of a fight. From a setback that should have been avoided Derbyshire at least had the consolation of a seven-wicket comeback by Mitchell and a fine second-innings return of 5-48 by the fast-improving Alf Pope.

The rarity of a double defeat of Nottinghamshire for the second consecutive season seemed certain when Derbyshire held a commanding lead on first innings after running up an imposing, if not exactly adventurous, total of 353. This was one of the occasions when Worthington narrowly missed a century in being bowled by Larwood eight runs short. Les Townsend (71) helped him to add 156, Carrington weighed in with a dour 63, and Harry Elliott made an unbeaten 40 after the Pope brothers had both departed without scoring. George Pope made up for his failure with the bat by equally sharing eight wickets with Mitchell in the Notts reply of 187, his victims including the two highest scorers, skipper George Heane (53) and Willis Walker (48) – both caught by Elliott.

The loss of an hour's play through rain on the last morning made the slowness of some of Derbyshire's batting even more regrettable, with the result that Richardson felt pressured into declaring in their second innings earlier than he would have liked in the hope of forcing a win. The closure at 124 for six left Notts needing 291, and they beat the odds to get them on the back of a century stand between Walker, one of four more victims for Mitchell after making 65, and Gunn, who saw the job through with a forceful 113 not out.

Undaunted by those two avoidable setbacks, Derbyshire immediately got back on track with seven wins in their next eight matches, beginning in emphatic fashion against Kent at Chesterfield and Gloucestershire at Burton-upon-Trent. Alf Pope started Kent's slide to a beating by an innings and 75 runs inside two days by taking 5-37 in their dismissal for 129, ably abetted by brother George's 3-13. Tommy Mitchell finished it off with 7-66 as the stylish Frank Woolley, bowled by Copson for 51, was one of the few to escape him in a second innings of 156. In between, Alf Pope underlined his all-rounder credentials with a knock of 62 in support of Alderman (74) and Worthington (63) in a Derbyshire total of 360.

Swift revenge for the defeat in Gloucestershire was gained by ten wickets, Bill Copson coming up with his best match figures of the season, 4-44 and 5-31. Derbyshire were in firm command after getting rid of Dacre (59) and Hammond (81), Gloucestershire fading to 234 all out after having 171 on the board with only two men out. Half-centuries by Alderman, Smith, Townsend and Worthington then guided Derbyshire to another total of more than 300, after which Mitchell (4-54) joined Copson in ensuring that Storer, who just had time to reach his half-century, and Smith needed no more than 81 runs to gather in fifteen more points.

Back then to Derby – and to the sobering experience of defeat after having to follow on against Sussex. Perhaps that reverse, by seven wickets, was not all that surprising, considering that these visitors had been runners-up to Yorkshire in each of the preceding three seasons, but they slipped to a final seventh place in 1935 and, like Gloucestershire, were speedily to be beaten by Derbyshire in the return game. The Parks brothers were at the hub of the victory in Derby. Jim Parks was out only seven runs short of a century after sharing a stand of 124 with his opening partner, John Langridge (55), and one of

66 for the second wicket with the elegant Alan Melville (54), captain of both the county and South Africa. Harry Parks forged nineteen runs past a century, and was still there when the last wicket fell at 415. Derbyshire were soon in the further toils of losing Smith, Alderman and Storer before their total reached fifty, and although Worthington (81) and Townsend (52) then staged a recovery, adding 101, they had to go in again 173 behind. Smith (70) this time gave Worthington (69) most support, but Sussex were left to get only 84, and Melville saw them home with another half-century, 51 not out.

Worthington was in a rich vein of form at this stage of the season, totalling almost 600 runs in nine innings dating back to his 92 against Nottinghamshire, and only twice failing, with 23 and 44, to get to a half-century. In the ten-wicket defeat of bottom-of-the-table Northamptonshire at Chesterfield that was the first of five victories in a row after the Sussex setback, he steadied the ship with 78 before the returning Skinner's 81 got it fully afloat with the able assistance of George Pope (57). Northants, already undermined by Mitchell's 8-67 despite an exceptional display by John Timms, who batted right through their first innings for 82 out of 156, left Derbyshire requiring only fourteen runs for victory after Townsend had claimed the best figures of 5-21 in their dismissal even more cheaply when they went in again. Mitchell, having finished with eleven wickets in the match, was promoted to be Alderman's opening batting partner for the completion of that simple task.

The success at Hove, by five wickets, that followed was gained in the face of some resolute batting by Melville, who made 74 in Sussex's first innings of 194, a hostile 7-76 by Jim Cornford in Derbyshire's reply of 213, and a dogged 106 by James Langridge in the home side's second venture before becoming one of the six batsmen Copson got rid of at a cost of 42 runs. Derbyshire's prospects of getting 226 to win looked decidedly shaky when half the side was out for 99 after Richardson (31) and Worthington, who added 46 to his first-innings 91, had put on 82 for the second wicket, but Skinner (64) and George Pope (60) then rose to the occasion in splendid style with an unbroken stand of 128.

Leslie Townsend, whose highest score of the season so far had been his 89 at The Oval back in May, took centre stage for the next two wins of August by scoring 103 not out and 55 in the Bank Holiday game against Warwickshire that attracted a record crowd at Derby on the Monday, and 102 at Northampton. With the back-up of another half-century by Skinner, Derbyshire led Warwickshire by 66 runs on first innings even though Fred Santall offset the loss of opener Arthur Croom, who was injured while fielding and unable to bat in either of the visitors' innings, by living up to his reputation as a fine driver of the ball in making 113 against their varied attack. That advantage was increased to 277 despite Eric Hollies making steady inroads with six wickets that cost 75 runs, and a 77-run victory was then rounded off by Mitchell (5-63) and Copson (4-48). Santall, whose father also played for Warwickshire, and his brother John for Worcestershire, had the contrasting experience in that second innings of being bowled by Copson without getting off the mark.

A big shock awaited Derbyshire on their visit to Northamptonshire before they were able to extend their winning run. Skinner, again deputising as captain, decided they would bat first on winning the toss, but 'Nobby' Clark and Reg Partridge had them all out before lunch for 85. This was one of those days when Clark, with his classic left-arm action, was a devastatingly fast bowler – not one of those when his fallible temperament let him down either because he had to do what he considered more than his fair share of bowling or became exasperated when catches off him were dropped.

There was no danger of those eventualities upsetting him in that Derbyshire innings. In hitting the stumps three times and trapping another batsman (Skinner) under the new lbw law, he needed the help of only one fielder in taking his five wickets for 33 runs. Four of the others fell for 26 runs to Partridge, who six years before had been subjected to the disconcerting experience of taking a day off from his work in a factory to attend a trial with Northants, only to find that nobody from the club had bothered to turn up to watch him. It said much for his perseverance and good humour that he still became one of the most dependable members of the county's attack through the bleakest years of their history.

It was, indeed, because Northamptonshire were then so regularly the whipping boys on the county circuit – last in seven seasons of the 1930s, and next to last in two of the three others – that the capitulation to them of Derbyshire's title-chasing team on that August morning caused such a sensation. Northants won only one game that season, and none at all in again finishing at the foot of the table in each of the following three. After beating Somerset at Taunton at the start of the 1935 season, they went through just one short of a hundred County Championship matches before winning another one, by an innings at home to Leicestershire, during the May of 1939. Hardly surprising, Leicestershire it was to whom they handed over the wooden spoon that season.

Hardly surprising, either, that it was Tommy Mitchell who got Derbyshire back into that 1935 game at Northampton by taking 7-73 as the home side's first-innings lead was confined to a manageable 101. Townsend's second century in as many matches then deducted that deficit on its own with a single to spare after Worthington had suffered the ignominy of a pair (out to Clark both times), and Carrington, who had alone survived the first-day carnage with an undefeated 35, kept up the good work by getting to 71 before hitting his wicket in attempting to deal with a rare delivery from opening batsman Bakewell. A total of 362 set Northants to get 261, and, with Timms and Partridge going close to half-centuries, they ended exactly 100 adrift. Mitchell polished them off with his tenth wicket of the match, but it was Copson's turn to cause the batsmen most trouble. His five wickets cost just under nine runs apiece.

On returning next to Chesterfield, Derbyshire landed another double in an exciting finish with Essex. They trailed on first innings by 21 runs, but that was exactly the amount by which they chalked up their fifth successive triumph. Mitchell collected seven more wickets, for 97 runs, as opener Jim Cutmore's 63 countered the four runs fewer scored by Skinner, who handed the captaincy back to Richardson, but the match-winner this time was George Pope. Just when things looked bleakest for Derbyshire, only 54 runs ahead with the fall of their sixth second-innings wicket at 75, he took the lead role in half-century stands with Carrington and his brother Alf, and by one run edged out Skinner as his side's top scorer of the match in a total of 216 that left Essex chasing 196. Then, with that target cut to 23, he snapped up the last two wickets for the addition of a single to end with 4-36. The four others that fell to Mitchell were nearly three times as expensive.

So, on the crest of a winning wave, Derbyshire travelled up to Scarborough for the return game with Yorkshire that had every prospect of being the title decider. And so it was, but, sadly, not to Derbyshire's benefit. It was bad enough that they were outplayed in losing by ten wickets. On top of that, Stan Worthington suffered the serious injury that put him out of the match early in his first innings – and also out of the county's remaining four matches of the season. He had scored only three runs after joining Richardson at the dismissal of Smith with the total 20 when his jaw was fractured in his misjudged attempt to pull a no-ball from 'Sandy' Jacques, a fiery customer with an action Len Hutton said was the finest by a fast bowler he had ever seen. Derbyshire were in real difficulties when Jacques, off whom Smith had been caught at the wicket, trapped Worthington's replacement, Alderman, for nought, and he went on also to send back Richardson and Alf Pope, the modestly highest scorers in a dismal total of 133.

This was in reply to a score that would have been much smaller than 304 but for dropped catches that enabled Brian Sellers and Arthur Wood to add 72 for Yorkshire's sixth wicket after half the side had gone for 131. Sellers played a true captain's part with the top score of the match, 73. Following on, Derbyshire wobbled again, this time against Frank Smailes, and, with spinner Cyril Turner lopping off the tail, Skinner was left seven from a half-century when the last wicket went down only three runs into a credit balance. This was the occasion when Harry Elliott opened the bowling, Hedley Verity striking the winning four off his third delivery.

Yorkshire were beaten only once that season – sensationally, a fortnight before demolishing Derbyshire, by an innings at home to Essex after being routed for 31 and finding themselves behind before lunch on the first day. The fact that Jacques did not play in that match, in which Stan Nichols excelled for the visitors with eleven wickets and a century, leads to the mention that Yorkshire never lost when he was in their team, though there were only twenty-eight such occasions. He played in a Test trial after just six appearances for the county, but after turning professional amid high expectations he soon found that his legs could not stand the strain of six-days-a-week first-class cricket. Not even the wearing of five pairs of socks could lessen the pain, but he continued to be a force in league cricket.

Derbyshire drew the first two of their last four matches in 1935, and won the last two. They were without Alf Pope as well as Worthington against Worcestershire at Derby, and suffered another big blow when Copson broke down again on the first evening. He, too, was out for the season. Les Townsend's third century in five games, 180, piloted them to their biggest total of the season, 406, aided by Skinner's 73 and Carrington's 58. Worcestershire responded with 364, Bernard Quaife (91) and 'Doc' Gibbons (53) prospering against them again, after which Derbyshire declared at 259 for six, Townsend taking his aggregate for the match to 238 and joining Smith (74) in a century stand. The game ended with Worcestershire having cut their deficit of 301 by 104 for the loss of only the wicket of Charlie Bull, who had made 71 in their first innings.

From soaring to their own top total, Derbyshire, still without Copson but welcoming back Alf Pope, went straight to conceding the largest made against them that year. Kent's 560 at Dover was monopolised by the second triple century of Bill Ashdown's career. The year before he had taken 332, still his county's record, off Essex at Brentwood. This time he carried his bat right through the innings for 305, receiving most assistance from the amateurs Bryan Valentine (62) and Percy Chapman (49). Richardson (59) and Smith (48) got Derbyshire's reply off to a good start with a century partnership, George Pope added 67 to his 5-126, and there were other sound contributions from Carrington and Harry Elliott, but a follow-on 180 behind could not be avoided. There was never any danger of defeat by that stage, however. Charlie Elliott celebrated his first appearance of the season with a half-century, for a match tally of 83, as the second-innings total was taken to 121 for two by the close.

The concluding victories, for the club record of sixteen in the season, were gained in low-scoring matches by 80 runs against Hampshire, and by 41 runs against Somerset, doubling Derbyshire's number of doubles. Alf Pope ended on a strong note with five wickets in each Hampshire innings at Bournemouth, and five more at Taunton; Smith, Les Townsend and Skinner scored half-centuries against Hampshire, Townsend following his with seven wickets; and Mitchell rounded off his record season with seven wickets at Taunton.

Yorkshire set a pace that was just too hot for Derbyshire to handle by gaining six consecutive victories in both July and August. This was the final table:

	P	W	L	1st inns W	L	NR	Points Poss	Act	%
Yorkshire	30	19	1	3	7	0	450	321	71.33
DERBYSHIRE	28	16	6	4	2	0	420	266	63.33
Middlesex	24	11	5	6	1	1	360	202	56.11
Lancashire	28	12	6	8	1	1	420	227	54.04
Notts	28	10	3	8	5	2	420	213	50.71
Leicestershire	24	11	9	2	2	0	360	181	50.27
Sussex	32	13	10	3	2	*4	480	232	48.33
Warwickshire	24	9	6	3	6	0	360	168	46.66
Essex	28	11	12	3	2	0	420	186	44.28
Kent	30	10	12	5	2	1	450	185	41.11
Surrey	26	7	5	5	7	2	390	159	40.76
Worcs	30	9	16	0	4	1	450	151	33.55
Glamorgan	26	6	11	5	2	2	390	129	33.07
Somerset	26	5	11	4	6	0	390	113	28.97
Gloucs	30	6	16	2	6	0	450	118	26.22
Hampshire	30	5	16	1	8	0	450	104	23.11
Northants	24	1	16	3	2	*2	360	44	12.22

* Including one tie on first innings

Of the twenty-two players called upon by Derbyshire during the season, including the game with the South Africans, only Alderman and Harry Elliott had an ever-present record, though Alf Pope and Les Townsend both missed just one Championship match. In only about a third of their fixtures were they at full strength.

Alderman, Smith, Townsend and Worthington each exceeded a thousand runs, and Copson, who headed the bowling averages, would surely have followed Mitchell (160 at 19.11) to a hundred wickets, instead of sticking on 71 (at 16.53 each), if he had not been absent ten times. Smith was the top batsman with 1,697 runs at 42.42, ahead of Skinner, who averaged 36.66 for his 550 runs in only ten matches, Townsend (1,560 at 35.45) and Worthington (1,276 at 33.57). Storer, limited to fifteen appearances by his soccer duties, came next with 635 at 27.60, just ahead of Alderman (1,134 at 24.65).

The Pope brothers made a significant advance, Alf taking 85 Championship wickets at 19.28 and George, in his first full season (he missed only five games) 62 at 19.62.

At the end of the season, Denis Smith and Les Townsend were in H D G Leveson-Gower's XI against the MCC West Indies touring team at Scarborough. Townsend did nothing of note, but Smith completed a half-century in his second innings shortly before being run out. The MCC tourists won by just two runs.

20. Champions in 1936

And so we come to the season of 1936 that has so obstinately remained unique in Derbyshire cricket history for being the only one in which they are now officially recognised as having been champions. It was quite a year for top sport in the county. Derby County were runners-up in the First Division of the Football League and Chesterfield won promotion from the Third (North).

With their number of victories three below their record sixteen, Derbyshire finished with 27 fewer points from their 28 matches than they had done the year before. They had 36 to spare over the runners-up, resurgent Middlesex, but were only nine ahead of Yorkshire, who, however, fulfilled 30 fixtures and therefore ended third on the percentage system. Some play was made of the fact that, in an unusually wet summer, Yorkshire were prevented from setting their customary pace because eighteen of their matches were left drawn, but Derbyshire themselves drew eleven times, and they forced the dethroned champions to follow on in the first of the two rain-hit drawn encounters with them that were both reduced to two days. They might well have led them again on first innings in the return match at Bramall Lane but for a dropped catch, and even then the advantage they yielded was only two runs.

Another slight criticism aimed at Derbyshire was that they did not meet Middlesex on their way to the title. It was boom time for that county, too, under the lively leadership of Walter Robins, with Denis Compton coming strongly onto the scene at the tender age of 18, Norfolk-born Bill Edrich soon eligible to join him, and 'Patsy' Hendren still a force at 47. Some were not slow to point out that Middlesex would have pipped Derbyshire at the post with the one extra victory they were twice denied when rain intervened at Northampton and Maidstone.

After their several years in the doldrums, Middlesex had been third behind Yorkshire and Derbyshire in 1935, and they were now to be second for five Championship seasons in succession before winning the title in two of the next three (with another third-place finish in between). Glamorgan, last but one in the final table, were the only other county who did not have a match with Derbyshire in 1936; each of the fourteen others were met twice.

To set against their unwanted avoidance of Middlesex, Derbyshire twice trounced fourth-placed Gloucestershire by ten wickets, besides giving a good account of themselves in their two drawn meetings with Yorkshire. And although they lost at Ilkeston to Nottinghamshire, who finished fifth, they led them on first innings in the drawn return game. Another big point in their favour was that all but one of their five Championship victories by an innings were gained on away grounds. Furthermore, they notched up three more wins than all three of their closest challengers, and only Yorkshire, with two, had fewer than their four defeats. It also has to be remembered that, although this was the most successful season of their careers for Bill Copson and Alf Pope, Tommy Mitchell had his leanest year (if 121 wickets can be called lean) since 1932 before becoming one of the casualties with which the club had to contend, George Pope missed most of the season through his injury, and Denis Smith lost form and confidence to such an extent that it was not until the end of July that runs once more flowed with some consistent freedom from his bat.

Yes, despite all their difficulties, Derbyshire were most worthy champions, though the manner in which they began certainly did not indicate that they were going to be, and their batting at times could still be as alarmingly fallible as ever. After only just managing to scrape a draw with Hampshire in their opening match at Southampton, they crashed to a ten-wicket defeat before lunch on the second day of their game with Kent at Gravesend, then wriggled through to a slender success against Surrey at Derby after being led on first innings for the third time.

Copson's combination with the at-times-expensive Mitchell was to have a key influence on the bringing of the genuine title to Derbyshire at long last now that, a stone heavier, he had built up his strength and was no longer so susceptible to breakdowns, but it failed to click straight into top gear as Hampshire built on a first-innings lead of 52 with a second-wicket stand of 183 between 21-year-old Dick Moore and Cecil Paris.

Moore, an enterprising batsman who was in his first match as captain after missing most of the previous season because of scarlet fever, had no sooner got into three figures than Alf Pope dismissed him lbw without recourse to the experimental amendment. Paris, a much more circumspect batsman, who 32 years later became the first chairman of the Test and County Cricket Board, and then president of the MCC, made just one run more than Moore before being bowled by Worthington. Two years later, Moore made Hampshire's biggest individual score of 316 against Warwickshire at Bournemouth, reaching three figures off the ball before lunch, but soon afterwards his cricket had to take second place to the family's bakery business.

Hampshire's next highest scorer against Derbyshire before Moore's second-innings declaration at 334 for seven was John Arnold, who became the first of Copson's only two victims in the match (at a total cost of 90 runs) on reaching 65. Mitchell's four wickets, all taken in the first innings of 256 (Mead 62), altogether cost him 145 runs on a pitch responsive to spin.

Facing daunting arrears of 386, Derbyshire got to within two runs of 150 for the loss of openers Alderman and Smith before 'Lofty' Herman broke a stand of 84 between Les Townsend (eight fours in his 67) and Worthington (44). After that, however, only Wilfred Hill-Wood, again captaining the side in the absence of Richardson on his last appearance for the county, offered much resistance before Harry Elliott and Mitchell played out the extra half-hour to finish at 255 for eight. Elliott batted 55 minutes for just a single. Those swept aside in the middle order included Eli Carrington, who, making the most of some good fortune, had got off to a good start to the season in the first innings by smiting two sixes and five fours in his 72, but he was shortly to lose his place and was released the following year.

Mention of Herman, a fast-medium inswing bowler who stood more than 6ft and was the mainstay of the Hampshire attack for several years, leads to the recollection of a remark attributed to him while he was batting one murky day. His partner, his captain Lord Tennyson, called to him down the pitch, saying that he was thinking of appealing against the light, and how did he feel about it? 'I can hear you, my lord,' replied Herman, 'but I can't see you.'

Between their hard-fought draw in Hampshire and the caning in Kent, Derbyshire had the luxury of victory by an innings and 130 runs over the university at Oxford, if with the considerable assistance of some poor bowling and even poorer fielding by the home side. The account by 'Isis' in *The Cricketer* said that 'the number of catches missed was appalling'. No doubt the fact that the conditions on the first day, a Saturday, were most un-May-like, cold and dismal, had something to do with that, Derbyshire taking full advantage to plunder 456 by 5.15pm before the deteriorating light delayed the start of Oxford's reply until the Monday. Stan Worthington hit out recklessly in an attempt to give away his wicket after reaching 100, but not until he had advanced to 174 in only 180 minutes was a catch off him held. Denis Smith (77) partnered him in a century stand, Les Townsend just missed a half-century, and George Pope hit out heartily to be left unbeaten on 62.

When play was resumed after the Sunday break, the plumb pitch was contrastingly bathed in brilliant sunshine, and, to quote 'Isis' again, 'the bowling was first-class, the fielding magnificent, and almost all the batting puerile.' John Gilbert, an amateur from Chellaston Manor who also took over the Derbyshire captaincy for his farewell appearance, readily rang the changes as Oxford lost eight wickets for 54 runs before the tail-enders helped their captain, Norman Mitchell-Innes, to raise the total to 153.

Mitchell-Innes, who the previous year had played his one Test against South Africa, took particular toll of Mitchell, whose two wickets cost 91 runs, in his 67 not out. Following on, Oxford sagged again, with six wickets down for 47, but were revived to 173 by opener Michael Barton, later captain of Surrey, who made 70, and William Murray-Wood (42), later of Kent, whom he also captained. Copson, with six wickets in the match, was the most successful of the bowlers on either side.

Mitchell-Innes made his debut for Somerset at sixteen, and captained them after the 1939-45 war, but his first-class cricket was restricted by asthma brought on by his being allergic to pollen, and also by his work in the Civil Service taking him to the Sudan.

After that frolic in the Parks, Derbyshire were brought down with a bump at the appropriately named Gravesend, where the swift defeat by ten wickets gave Niel Walker, their third captain in as many games, a most unhappy send-off as he too played his last game for the club. 'Tich' Freeman, with 7-29 in the first innings, and Doug Wright, with 5-31 in the second, were the men chiefly responsible for Derbyshire's collapses for 119 and 99 on a pitch affected by rain. Copson did best with 5-57 as the home side were restricted to a lead of 60, but openers Ashdown and Fagg made light work of the simple task their visitors' renewed and even severer slump set them.

Albert Alderman, whose 47 had made him Derbyshire's highest scorer against Kent, again led the way against Surrey, hitting eleven fours in his 77 and partnering Les Townsend in a stand of 105 after Smith had gone without scoring and Worthington for a single. Alderman was also top scorer, with 43, in a second-innings total of 136 that left Surrey needing only 94 to win. They were just over halfway there with only two men out, but then collapsed to startling defeat by sixteen runs against Copson, who plundered six wickets for eight runs in his final spell of seven overs, three of which were maidens, after tea on the second day. He altogether took 7-19 and had 12-52 in the match, hitting the stumps nine times. Two of his other victims were lbw, one of them under the new law, and not until he finished things off did he require a colleague's assistance in having Alf Gover caught by Harry Elliott for the fifth duck of Surrey's second innings – and the ninth in all.

From that thrilling triumph, gained under a fourth captain with the belated return of Arthur Richardson to take up his appointed post, Derbyshire really got down to business by thrashing Sussex by an innings at Chesterfield and Gloucestershire by ten wickets in Bristol. As at Oxford, they made hay on the first day against Sussex, scoring 351 for seven after losing Alderman and Worthington with only 23 runs on the board. Les Townsend, dropped at 33, led the recovery with first Smith (53), then Harry Elliott (63), and he was still there on 165 at the close. Next day, he went on to carry his bat for 182 in a total of 387, hitting a six and 22 fours in a stay of five and a half hours. Copson (5-42) and Mitchell (4-64) carried on the good work as Sussex were forced to follow on 258 behind, and the Pope brothers and Townsend joined Copson in ousting them a second time with 25 runs to spare after the breaking of a second-wicket stand of 109 by John Langridge and Harry Parks, who both got into the fifties before being caught by Worthington off George Pope. The rejuvenated Copson was again at his most accurate in skittling all but two of his eight victims in the match.

With four Championship matches played, Derbyshire were then sixth in the table with 33 points out of 60 for a 55 percentage. Kent, who had won four of their six games, were at the top with 63 points out of 90 and a percentage of 70, followed by Leicestershire, Surrey, Yorkshire and Nottinghamshire. Gloucestershire were down near the bottom with only one win in five matches – and that newly gained against Glamorgan in Bristol by just one wicket.

Indifferent light interfered with play during Derbyshire's away match with Gloucestershire, whose total on the first day would have been even lower than 164 but for a half-century by Charlie Barnett and a late show of defiance by Tom Goddard. Both were among the four batsmen dismissed by Copson, all of them bowled, though Goddard spoiled his figures somewhat by hitting five fours off him in one over. George Pope struck the first blow by bowling Barnett's opening partner, Reg Sinfield, but he had to retire from the attack soon afterwards with the knee injury that kept him out for the rest of the season, and for which he had to have a cartilage operation.

Derbyshire inched 29 runs ahead on first innings despite losing Smith, Worthington, Townsend and Carrington before any of them could get into double figures. Harry Elliott helped Alderman (42) to stop the rot with a sound 61 before being ably supported by Alf Pope (40), but Sinfield quickly lopped off the tail to return the impressive figures of 7-54. Alf Pope and Worthington then equally shared the four second-innings wickets Gloucestershire lost in getting just beyond 50, after which Tommy Mitchell took over to end with 5-40 in the collapse for 123. That left Derbyshire requiring 95, and Alderman and Smith knocked them off without being separated, the left-hander just having time to complete a half-century.

That was Derbyshire's most productive opening partnership in their first nine innings, and it was to be surpassed only once during the rest of the season – halfway through it when Alderman and Harry Storer put on 108 at Worcester on the first day of July. Indeed, the county's first wicket fell before the total got into double figures on no fewer than seventeen occasions that year – and on eight of them it went down without even one run on the board. It said much for the resilience of the side, and the potency of its bowling, that a convincing victory was extracted from all eight of those shock starts, four by an innings. Alderman had Smith as by far his most frequent opening partner, at both the early and late stages of the season, but he also went in first with Richardson and Worthington as well as Storer, who also opened with Smith and Worthington during his soccer-limited appearances.

There was a slight check to Derbyshire's progress after their success in Bristol, only three points being gained from a drawn game with Essex at Derby in which play was possible on only the second day because of rain, but they promptly bounced back by winning at Northampton and completing the double over Gloucestershire. A total of 179 never looked like being big enough to net the five points for a first-innings lead against an Essex team that had declared beyond 500 on the way to beating Sussex at Hove a fortnight earlier, and so it proved as a century stand by Stan Nichols and Jim Cutmore guided the visitors to a reply of 193 for six.

And still fewer would have been needed for that lead but for a partnership of 77 in 45 minutes between Worthington and Mitchell after Derbyshire had lost their eighth wicket at 101. Worthington, who hit 13 fours in a stay of 110 minutes, was left stranded fifteen runs from a century when Copson was last out.

After that one-day draw with Essex, Derbyshire were up to third place on 51 points out of 90 (average 56.66), having played one game fewer than Kent (68 points out of 105, average 64.76) and two fewer than second-placed Surrey (75 out of 120, 62.50). The next match at Northampton was one in which Derbyshire twice lost their first wicket before opening their scoring, Alderman collecting a couple of ducks. On a rain-affected pitch, the outcome was in the balance for the first two days, which ended with Northamptonshire 21 runs ahead with nine wickets in hand after first collapsing for 59 and then dismissing Derbyshire for 93. Les Townsend, off whom only three runs were scored in his ten overs, and Mitchell both took four wickets; five fell to Austin Matthews, who ended his ten years with Northants after that season and then enjoyed the most successful period of his career with Glamorgan. Matthews, who had captained the Northampton rugby club, made his Test debut against New Zealand at the age of thirty-three only a fortnight after first playing for the Welsh county.

Derbyshire took a firm grip on the third morning of the Northampton game as Copson, with the assistance of a strong wind, added five wickets to his previous evening's dismissal of Norman Grimshaw for nought. His six cost him only two dozen runs, but two of the batsmen who eluded him were the two who delayed Derbyshire the longest – John Timms, whose 69 was the biggest individual score of the match, and Ken James, the former New Zealand Test wicketkeeper. Undeterred by Alderman's repeated swift failure, Derbyshire knocked off the 125 runs they were left to get for the loss of three wickets, Townsend and Worthington completing the task after Denis Smith had scored 59 out of 78.

With Surrey going without a point from their drawn games at Worcester and Old Trafford, the win lifted Derbyshire above them behind Kent, who kept up the pace by beating Somerset at Frome. Middlesex, home winners against Nottinghamshire, also overtook Surrey, moving up to third.

Tommy Mitchell provided the highlight of the defeat of Gloucestershire at Derby by taking his thousandth wicket for Derbyshire in his 207th appearance. Combining with Copson, who took the three other wickets, he had a devastating spell of 7-15, after conceding eleven runs before his first success, as the visitors subsided from 64 for one to 95 all out. A forceful innings by Worthington, who batted 100 minutes for his 90, then helped Derbyshire to a lead of 105 after Richardson, promoting himself to open, and Alderman, out for a third successive duck, had gone for only six runs.

Gloucestershire – though without Hammond, who had made the mistake of returning to the game too quickly after undergoing an operation for tonsils and adenoids – offered some sterner opposition when they went in again, Sinfield defending with particular dourness in a stay of two hours for an unbeaten 41, but they still left Derbyshire needing only 91 for their victory inside two days after Mitchell had this time found his main ally in Alf Pope. Both took four wickets, Pope for just 29 runs but Mitchell for 98. Smith, renewing his opening partnership with Alderman, struck eight fours in his 63 not out as the target was reached without loss.

Derbyshire next had the better of a draw with Yorkshire at Chesterfield in what also became a two-day match after a rain-delayed start. Both sides were below strength, though the reigning champions were worst hit in providing three players, Arthur Mitchell, Leyland and Verity, to the home county's one, Copson, for the North team that drew with the South at Lord's (Copson's one wicket there cost him 103 runs). With Charlie Elliott also excluded, Derbyshire's two changes brought in Arnold Townsend, for the first of only two matches in which he joined his brother in the county side that season, and Harry Storer.

Again a Derbyshire innings got off on the wrong foot, with Alderman, Smith and Storer back in the pavilion and only 18 scored, but Les Townsend, missed at slip before opening his account, and Worthington then added 154. Both were eventually caught by skipper Sellers – Worthington off the bowling of Cyril Turner for 80; Townsend, who hit two sixes and a dozen fours, off Frank Smailes for 101. Bill Bowes made short work of the rest, finishing with 5-66, and the innings closed at 253 with the running-out of Tommy Mitchell, who then got down to bowling so enthusiastically that the first five of his six wickets cost only 20 runs. The other one cost him 40 more.

Alf Pope joined Mitchell in getting rid of Yorkshire's openers, the experienced Sutcliffe and up-and-coming Hutton, for a mere 14 runs, and he returned the economical figures of 3-14 in taking the last wicket shortly after the total had struggled to 109. Following on, Yorkshire again lost Sutcliffe cheaply – as in the first innings to a catch at the wicket, but this time off Townsend – but Hutton and Sellers played out time without further ado, the young England captain-to-be getting to a half-century and Sellers to a quarter of one in raising the score from 36 to 102.

From that creditable showing, Derbyshire tumbled to a shock ten-wicket defeat by lowly Somerset, who came to Ilkeston straight from being well beaten by Kent at Tonbridge. To say that the Rutland ground's pitch was helpful to bowlers would be something of an understatement, for twenty-two wickets toppled on the first day and Derbyshire lost the last eight in their second innings for 47 runs in just over an hour the next morning – five of them for seven runs at one stage. Put in to bat, Storer and Smith reached 44 without excessive alarm, but the procession then set in against the off-spin of Bert Hunt and pace of Arthur Wellard, the innings closing at 152. Hunt, whose elder brother George had been an all-rounder with Somerset for some ten seasons up to the early Thirties, turned in a career-best 7-49, but he was not needed when Derbyshire's second collapse was engineered by Wellard and Bill

Andrews with four wickets each – plus one for Bertie Buse and one run-out (of Richardson). All out for 62, with only Alf Pope and Denis Smith into double figures, Derbyshire left Harold Gimblett and Frank Lee with the simple task of obtaining 25 runs for the fifteen points. Gimblett, who had hit the previous season's fastest century on his debut, was top scorer of the match with 43 in his first innings.

The only redeeming feature from Derbyshire's viewpoint was the bowling of Mitchell and Worthington when Somerset first batted, though Mitchell had to pay 90 runs for his five wickets in the favourable conditions. Worthington's four cost 31. Sobering as the defeat was, there was to be another, and a most untimely one at that, when Derbyshire went to Wells for the return game towards the end of August, but more about that in its turn.

As before, Derbyshire wasted no time after adversity in getting back onto the winning path, beating both Warwickshire and Worcestershire by an innings. At Edgbaston, however, they once more made a faltering start, losing Smith and Storer for only nine runs on a pitch perfect for batting, before recovering to end the first day's play on 280 for six and then progressing to a total of 318. But even then they required some good luck. Worthington made 81 out of 107, hitting thirteen fours, after being dropped at 17, and Charlie Elliott, in only his third appearance of the season, was missed before scoring, and again at 65, in compiling his then highest score of 97. Alderman, temporarily dropped down the order because of his recent lean spell as an opener, helped Harry's nephew to add 92 for the fifth wicket.

With the pitch drying out after overnight rain, Warwickshire were then caught in conditions that Mitchell and Les Townsend gratefully exploited in each taking five wickets for a fraction more than eight runs apiece. Following on 209 behind, the home side lost their first two wickets – both to Copson, who had not got on to bowl in the first innings – with the deficit reduced by only eight, but the inevitable was delayed by Norman Kilner (48) and Bob Wyatt (72), who added 80, and George Paine, a slow left-arm bowler who defended doggedly for his 41 before being last out with ten runs still needed to make Derbyshire go in to bat again. In hitting his wicket, Paine provided Mitchell with his only success of the innings at the high expense of 99 runs. The match-winner was Townsend, whose 7-46 gave him a match return of 12-90. He twice dismissed Wyatt, who thus escaped Mitchell's customary clutches.

Meanwhile, Kent were also offsetting a home defeat with a prompt away victory. Having lost at Tonbridge to Nottinghamshire on the same two days that Derbyshire succumbed to Somerset, they won convincingly at Worcester despite being held up by a thunderstorm. This enabled them to stay at the top of the table with seven wins and 113 points to Derbyshire's six wins and 101 points, both from eleven matches, with Notts closing up in third place above Middlesex and Yorkshire.

In the following round of matches, Derbyshire took over at the top for the first time that season with the fifteen points they gained from their three-wicket defeat of Worcestershire at Chesterfield while Kent were left pointless in losing to Lancashire by two wickets on their first visit to Liverpool since 1891. But Derbyshire's own failure to beat Lancashire, taking only three points from a rain-hit drawn game at Buxton after the win against Worcestershire, dropped them straight back to second place, Kent ending the month of June nine points clear with an eight-wicket victory over Essex at Tunbridge Wells.

Les Townsend, Copson and Storer were Derbyshire's key players in the home match with Worcestershire. It was largely due to Townsend, who was especially severe on Dick Howorth in smiting four sixes and eight fours in his 76, that a precarious lead of fourteen runs was achieved on first innings after Copson had taken 5-34 in a total of 233 which 'Doc' Gibbons dominated in having the misfortune to miss a century by just one run after a stay of nearly three hours.

Townsend then took over the main strike role with 4-34 as the winning target was confined to 149, and Storer's 62, his highest score of the season, provided the steadying answer to a wobble the lively Reg Perks caused. It was not a match for the other opening batsmen. Worcestershire's Charlie Bull, twice dispatched by Copson, bagged a pair, his partner Grant Righton, whose father had also played for the county, was run out for a single in the visitors' second innings after doing little better in the first, and Denis Smith, twice bowled by Perks, made two and nought.

Against Lancashire at Buxton, Derbyshire's batting was even more brittle, if by only one run, than it had been against Somerset at Ilkeston. Both sides completed an innings on the first day, Derbyshire losing half their side for two dozen runs, and the other half for only 37 more, in reply to a total of 194 in which Jack Iddon, like Gibbons before him, yet again presented the biggest obstacle. Norman Oldfield gave Iddon the best backing before they became two of the four victims Copson claimed for nine runs after having to go off for attention to a split finger – Iddon trapped under the experimental lbw law when just past his half-century, Oldfield caught and bowled a few runs short of his.

Derbyshire's 61, in the thirteenth of their twenty-eight matches, was their lowest score for a completed innings all season, but very little play was possible on the second day and they had no undue difficulty in salvaging the draw, though still 135 behind with four men out, after Copson had exactly repeated his full first-innings figures of 4-35, and Alf Pope had taken 5-53, in Lancashire's second-innings slump for 94.

The rain again played a part as Derbyshire reached the halfway point of their programme by again beating Worcestershire, and again by an innings, in the return game at Worcester despite the hold-ups, while Kent, more adversely affected by the downpours, had time to extract only first-innings points from their home match with Sussex. This enabled Derbyshire to inch back into the lead by a single point, 134 to 133 – and this time it was a lead they were not to lose.

Bill Copson, off whom Harry Elliott smartly held four catches at the wicket, was the man who made all the difference as Derbyshire rushed to beat the weather as well as Worcestershire. He had match figures of 12-54, following 5-38 in the home side's rout for 64 in their first innings with 7-16 as they folded up even more feebly for 47 in their second. This was after Derbyshire, given the impetus of their only century opening stand of the season, had scored 135 for the loss of four wickets on the rain-restricted first day and then added 99 for another four before declaring.

Albert Alderman, ending his short stint down the batting order, shared his partnership of 108 as Harry Storer's third successive opening partner (Smith and Worthington were the others) and he was the highest scorer in the match with 61. Storer made 52, after which a stutter of three wickets falling for as many runs was offset as Charlie Elliott joined Alf Pope in a stand of 54 before the declaration came with his dismissal one run from following the openers to a half-century.

With Alf Pope adding to his good batting form by ably abetting Copson with a couple of wickets, and Mitchell joining in with the aid of a slick stumping by Harry Elliott, Worcestershire were as good as beaten, weather permitting, as soon as they lost half their side in their first innings for a mere six runs. When rain again stopped play they were 39 for six, and on the third morning Alf Pope helped Copson to polish them off by taking two more wickets for a total cost of only a dozen runs. Ten of his sixteen overs were maidens. In the follow-on Worcestershire showed the minimal improvement of losing their first five wickets for seven runs, and seven were down for 16 before Joe Horton (whose brother Henry played for Worcestershire and Hampshire) and Reg Perks offered some belated sound defence in putting on 19 for the ninth wicket. Mitchell, who had been given only two overs in the first innings, was Copson's co-operator this time, swiftly dismissing the last man after ending that late resistance to finish with 3-26.

Down at Tunbridge Wells, Kent could not get under way until after lunch on the first day, could not play at all on the second, and gained their first-innings lead only by playing on in rainy conditions on the third. Their opening pair put them well on the way to overhauling Sussex's 187 with a stand of 125, Bill Ashdown going on to carry his bat for 120 in a total of 261 for three as the bowlers were handicapped by a wet ball on a lifeless pitch. At that point, Kent, like Derbyshire, had eight wins from fourteen games, but they were to gain only one more from their last fourteen – and that, paradoxically, against a full-strength Yorkshire team Derbyshire were to dethrone – as they dramatically faded away to a final eighth place, 65 points adrift of Arthur Richardson's title winners. At one stage they sank as low as tenth.

Even when they were setting the pace Kent attracted some criticism that their form did not justify such good results. In reviewing their season, *The Cricketer Annual* stated:

'Both without and within the confines of the county the view was that much could be ascribed to the unusual situation of three captains being provided. One local newspaper asked: 'How can three captains carefully watch the performances of the eleven and make the best selection?'

That question arose from the fact that Kent did not have a selection committee but left the choice of the team to those captains, the senior of whom was the former England captain Percy Chapman. His deputy was Bryan Valentine, and when both were unavailable the leadership was taken over by Ian Akers-Douglas, an Old Etonian who was another of those first-class cricketers who met an unfortunate and untimely end. He died as the result of a shot-gun accident at his home in 1952, aged 43.

The Cricketer also criticised Kent for bowling that 'often seemed terribly inadequate', adding that 'the very patchy fielding did not suggest team spirit, for it appeared to be demonstrative of individualism rather than the co-operative work so ably and admirably exhibited by Derbyshire, Middlesex, Yorkshire and Gloucestershire'. Those were the counties in the top four positions in the final table, in that order.

In the next chapter it is recalled how Derbyshire resisted the challenge presented by their main rivals after Kent's decline, with neighbouring Nottinghamshire for several weeks the closest of them before slipping to the fringe of the title race.

21. Final Steps to the Title

As one of the four counties playing twenty-eight matches (the others were Kent, Notts and Worcestershire), Derbyshire embarked upon the second half of their 1936 season with an innovation – the Chesterfield Week. It began auspiciously with a second successive innings victory, gained against Warwickshire (who joined Leicestershire and Northants in fulfilling the minimum of twenty-four fixtures) with the generous margin of 159 runs to spare.

It was their biggest win of their title year, and it lifted them sixteen points clear of Kent, who were without a game and therefore now had one in hand. Under the complicated percentage system, Derbyshire also led by 66.22 to Kent's 63.33, with Nottinghamshire third with 111 points and a percentage of 61.66 from twelve games. Yorkshire had the same number of points as Notts, but were fourth on percentage – 52.85 after fourteen of the thirty matches they were playing in company with Gloucestershire, Hampshire, Lancashire, Surrey and Sussex. The remaining four counties, Essex, Glamorgan, Middlesex and Somerset, had a programme of twenty-six games.

All rather complicated, especially in comparison with that venerable method of fewest defeats. The county obtaining the greatest proportionate number of points on the percentage basis was to be adjudged winner of the Championship, and 'for the purpose of calculating the result the unit of 100 per cent in all matches was the equivalent of fifteen points'. Quite so! I have tried fathoming it all out to no avail, but, then, I am no mathematician.

This first match of the first cricket week to be staged by Derbyshire was an immediate success story for Copson and Mitchell as Warwickshire lost their first five wickets for 27 runs and were all out for 117. Copson, at his fastest and swerving the ball disconcertingly, took 4-38, Mitchell, tweaking eagerly and luring two of his victims to stumpings by Harry Elliott, had 5-52. Derbyshire again lost a wicket (Storer's) before scoring, and his opening partner Alderman was also out cheaply, but Worthington then settled in to form a productive partnership with Charlie Elliott that earned a lead of 118 by the close of the first day's play with six wickets in hand.

Next day, their fourth-wicket stand altogether lasted for 90 minutes and was worth 127 before Elliott, trapped lbw (n), missed a half-century by one run for the second successive match. His uncle Harry just managed to follow him into the forties before departing in the same manner as Worthington – caught by Tom Collin off spinner Eric Hollies, who had to pay a hundred runs for those two wickets. Worthington hit seventeen fours in his stay of 255 minutes for 163 in a total of 381.

Needing 265 to make Derbyshire bat again, Warwickshire lost their first two wickets to Alf Pope for one run and only Bob Wyatt delayed the inevitable end for long as the visitors inched into three figures. Wyatt once more escaped

Mitchell's clutches in getting to 40 before falling lbw to Townsend, who equally shared nine of the wickets with Copson and Pope.

Derbyshire also outplayed their second opponents of the Chesterfield Week, but the weather prevented play on the third day after they had bundled Hampshire out for 88, declared at 336 for eight, and then snapped up two more wickets for eight runs. Copson began the first-innings collapse; Alf Pope and Mitchell completed it with four wickets each, Pope taking the last three for three runs. With Harry Storer having returned to his football, Alderman had Worthington as his opening partner, but both were back in the pavilion before Townsend got into his most aggressive stride with a superb unbeaten 153 that included four sixes, all off Len Creese, and nineteen fours. The extent to which he dominated the proceedings was shown by the fact that the next highest score in his half-century stands with Smith, Alf Pope and Mitchell was Pope's 37.

So Derbyshire had to be content with ten fewer points than they had seemed certain to gain, but only Kent of their three main rivals made any advance in the corresponding series of matches – and that was only because the rules allowed four points to each side when no result was reached on first innings in their game with Glamorgan at Folkestone. Rain washed out play on the second day and limited it to just over half-an-hour on the third. Nottinghamshire were led on first innings by Northants at Trent Bridge, where there was no play on the last day, and Gloucestershire, having shot out Yorkshire for 56 in 90 minutes at Bristol, just had time to go one run ahead, with half their side out, before the rain prevented any addition to the three hours' play of the first day.

It was Derbyshire's turn, with Lancashire, to be given four points for a 'no result' when play was possible on only the last day of their next match at Old Trafford. This was the game in which Sibbles took six wickets for nine runs as they struggled to 116 before declaring with eight men out after Alderman and Les Townsend had taken them to 84 for one. In the short time remaining Lancashire scored 37 without loss. After seventeen matches, Derbyshire then had 158 points and an average of 61.96. Kent, beaten by Surrey at Blackheath with five minutes to spare, stayed second with 137 points from sixteen games and an average of 57.08, and Notts (117 from fourteen and an average of 55.71) remained third after being saved by rain from likely defeat by Yorkshire at Bradford. The first-innings points took fourth-placed Yorkshire to 119 from sixteen games for an average of 49.58.

Despite a continuance of the bad weather, cutting play to 50 minutes on the first day of their crucial clash with Kent at Burton-upon-Trent, Derbyshire made up for lost time by establishing a lead of 134 with all their second-innings wickets intact by the close of the second. Les Townsend hit two sixes and fifteen fours in another forceful innings, reaching 115 in a total of 268 before giving a return catch, and, in the absence of Copson on duty for the

Players against the Gentlemen at Lord's, Alf Pope kept up the good work with 5-48 in Kent's reply of 184. Frank Woolley was seen at his stylish best in scoring 61, and Alan Watt, the noted hitter of the time along with Middlesex's Jim Smith and Arthur Wellard, of Somerset, supplied the fireworks by smiting 6, 4, 4, 6 off consecutive deliveries from Mitchell, whose one wicket cost 84 runs.

Derbyshire declared at 204 for three in their second innings, Worthington making 53 after sharing an opening stand of 80 with Alderman and Townsend again excelling with an undefeated 78 that included two more sixes. This set Kent to get 289 and they were comfortably beaten by 141 runs as all but one of their wickets, which went to Mitchell, were evenly shared by Pope, Townsend and Worthington. With 193 runs for once out and six wickets in the match, it was one of Townsend's finest all-round performances.

A boisterous wind provided a change from the rain as the weather remained unkind for the break Derbyshire then took from the Championship by meeting All-India at Derby. So boisterous at the start that the bails had to be dispensed with at the pavilion end. Copson, back from dismissing four of the Gentlemen in the drawn game at Lord's, went without a wicket as the tourists laboured to 62 for three in the two hours before lunch, but afterwards snapped up five of the remaining seven for 44 runs in an innings that ended at 228 from an overnight 219 for eight. Cottari Nayudu, who had captained India in their first Test against England in 1933, hit two sixes and five fours in his 60 and added 79 with Laxmidas Jai (43) for the fifth wicket in 70 minutes.

Derbyshire appeared to be heading for a comprehensive defeat when Carrington, back in the side for the first time since the upset against Somerset at Ilkeston in mid-June, was sixth out at 51, but the two Elliotts then put on 88, Charlie including ten fours in his impressive 77 and Harry getting within eight runs of a half-century.

Even so, Derbyshire trailed by 68 on first innings, and those arrears were increased to exactly 300 before the Indians declared at the fall of their seventh second-innings wicket, their leading batsman, opener Vijay Merchant, completing his thousand runs for the tour in batting 135 minutes for 75. Derbyshire responded with a second-wicket stand of 135 in 90 minutes by Alderman and Les Townsend, and they salvaged a commendable draw with a score of 169 for two. Townsend was out for 77 after getting to 50 in 40 minutes. Alderman stayed unbeaten for 61.

Meanwhile, Kent failed to exploit Derbyshire's three days away from the Championship by going near defeat through a rain-reduced draw with Middlesex at Maidstone, and Notts conceded a first-innings lead to Yorkshire in Larwood's benefit match at Trent Bridge, where time lost through the weather also prevented a definite outcome. Derbyshire's chief rivals had already lost ground in matches that had coincided with their victory over Kent, rain having curtailed drawn games in which Notts, at Northampton, and Yorkshire, at Leicester, had been led on first innings – Yorkshire by only five runs.

These were the leading positions at close of play on 21 July:

	P	W	L	1st inns W	1st inns L	NR	Points Poss	Points Act	%
DERBYSHIRE	18	10	2	2	3	1	270	173	64.07
Kent	18	8	5	2	2	1	270	140	51.85
Notts	16	6	1	3	6	0	240	123	51.25
Yorkshire	18	5	1	7	3	2	270	127	47.03
Middlesex	14	4	2	5	2	1	210	95	45.23
Hampshire	19	5	1	7	6	0	285	128	44.91

The stage was now set for one of the most keenly-awaited matches of the season – Derbyshire's visit to play Yorkshire at Bramall Lane, Sheffield. Yet again, however, the wretched weather was to have the over-riding influence, making a draw inevitable after washing out the second day's play, but there was then a tense battle for first-innings lead which Yorkshire won by just a couple of runs. Put in to bat by Sellers, Derbyshire were indebted to another magnificent innings by Worthington in totalling 216. Again opening with Alderman, he made 82 out of 123 for two by lunch, and altogether hit 24 fours in his 135. The next highest scorer was Skinner, with 17.

Yorkshire ended that first day 114 behind with six wickets in hand, having lost Sutcliffe to the rampant Copson before opening their account, Hutton for 31 at 68, and Norman Yardley and Hedley Verity in rapid succession just after getting into three figures. As in Derbyshire's case, their innings was held together by one man, Arthur Mitchell, whose 103 was the brightest batting spot of his disappointing year. He eventually fell to a catch by Charlie Elliott off Alf Pope, who took 4-58 in sharing the main burden of Derbyshire's attack with Copson, whose 6-60 included his hundredth wicket of the season. Yorkshire lost their ninth wicket at 211, but a skied catch was then missed, enabling Jacques and Bowes to scramble the runs required for five points instead of three. In the time left, Derbyshire made 148 for five, Les Townsend scoring a half-century.

After that match Derbyshire had gone through ten without defeat since the Somerset shock at Ilkeston, a run that promptly ended back at the Rutland ground with the visit of Nottinghamshire. Both teams were without one of their best batsmen, on Test duty at Old Trafford. Joe Hardstaff kept his England place despite having failed in the nine-wicket victory over India at Lord's; Worthington was called up for his home Test debut when Yorkshire's Maurice Leyland withdrew through injury.

And a big success both made of it, though England were denied another win when India's opening pair, century-makers Merchant and Mushtaq Ali, ensured a draw with a stand of 203 after following on 368 behind. As already recalled, Worthington helped Hammond to add 127, and Hardstaff 86, before his faultless 87 was ended by the brilliant right-handed catch Nayudu brought off from a powerful drive at extra cover. Hardstaff went on to miss following Hammond to a hundred by only six runs.

In Worthington's absence against Notts, Denis Smith was restored to open with Alderman. He had been having a surprisingly lean time after his fine form of the previous season, but he responded in a manner that was to keep him in his old place at the top of the order for the rest of the season by resisting for nearly three hours in top-scoring with 59. Support for him was sadly lacking, however. Although four catches were dropped at slip, Derbyshire still lost six wickets in getting to 154 before rain stopped play at four o'clock, George Gunn Junior having a spell of 3-12.

Next day, only 33 runs were added for the last four wickets, but Notts speedily lost openers Keeton and Harris to Pope and Copson before Tommy Mitchell suddenly came good again with six wickets as the score slumped to 126 for nine after a stand of 64 by Willis Walker and Gunn. A decent first-innings lead for Derbyshire then seemed assured, only for Larwood, who was given two lives, and Frank Woodhead to reduce it to five runs with a partnership of 56.

By the end of the second day's play, Derbyshire were 99 ahead with only two men out, a stand of 83 by Alderman and Smith having given them a sound start, but on the final morning they suffered a startling collapse and were all out for 125. Apart from the opening pair, only Harry Elliott got into double figures – and only just, though he was unbeaten – against the renowned attack of Larwood and Voce. Like Mitchell, Voce took six wickets, but for 43 runs as against the Derbyshire spinner's 87. So Notts were left an easy target of 131 and, most untypically, more dropped catches made it even easier for them, if still for the loss of four wickets. Two of those took Alf Pope to 64 for the season at 15.65, and to seventh in the national bowling averages headed by Verity (146 at 11.28) from Copson (106 at 11.80).

Notts moved up to second place in the Championship table with the addition of those 15 points to the five they had gained from the preceding home draw with Glamorgan in which, after the loss of the second day's play through rain, Charlie Harris and Joe Knowles had overhauled the Welsh county's total with an unbroken double-century stand for the second wicket.

With the weather continuing to disrupt play throughout the country, Kent had to be content with eight points from drawn games with Warwickshire and Surrey, and Yorkshire slipped below both Surrey and Hampshire after squeezing to a first-innings lead at home to Sussex, who were left just under a hundred runs from victory with six wickets in hand on the rain-hit last day. Surrey had strengthened their position with an innings defeat of Worcestershire at The Oval, Hampshire with a home win against Glamorgan at Bournemouth after taking only three points from a draw with Middlesex at the same ground. Middlesex, led on first innings by Somerset at Taunton, where no play was possible on the opening day for the first time this season, dropped out of the top six. These were now those leading positions:

	P	W	L	1st inns W	L	NR	Points Poss	Act	%
DERBYSHIRE	20	10	3	2	4	1	300	176	58.66
Notts	18	7	1	4	6	0	270	143	52.96
Kent	20	8	5	3	3	1	300	148	49.33
Hampshire	21	6	1	7	7	0	315	146	46.34
Surrey	21	7	4	4	4	2	315	145	46.03
Yorkshire	20	5	1	9	3	2	300	137	45.66

With Derbyshire without a fixture in the next round of matches, Nottinghamshire failed to take full advantage of one of the two matches they had in hand over them by going close to the follow-on at home to Kent, and then only just managing to hold out for a draw with their last pair together after Doug Wright had taken four wickets without conceding a run in his last spell of half-an-hour. Hampshire, meanwhile, accounted for Lancashire by eight wickets at Southampton, dismissing them for 98 (Boyes 6-16) and 99 (Creese 8-37), and Yorkshire, for whom Sutcliffe scored 202 and Leyland 107, thrashed Middlesex by an innings and 170 runs at Scarborough.

Surrey, like Derbyshire, were without a match during those last three days of July, and on their return to action they lost ground as Larwood, who took six wickets in each of their innings, and Voce hurried them to a 45-run defeat by Notts at The Oval. Hampshire, in a game against Kent reduced to two days by rain at Canterbury, and Yorkshire, whose visit to Lancashire was affected by the weather on the third day, both picked up only five more points, whereas Derbyshire staged a remarkable recovery to glean all fifteen from their visit to Chelmsford.

Essex, and Kenneth Farnes in particular, exploited a damp pitch after rain had held up play for 90 minutes. The tall England fast bowler took five wickets for only 20 runs, eight of which came from two boundaries by Copson during his last over, in Derbyshire's collapse for 80 after losing half their side for 29. Nichols and Stephenson shared the other five, and, with Farnes, they then added to Derbyshire's discomfort as batsmen. Not that any of them scored a lot of runs, but Nichols helped Jack O'Connor to add 61 in an hour and Stephenson joined this son of a former Derbyshire player in a stand of 53. As for Farnes, well, he was missed four times in making just eleven runs. And, as if that was not amazing enough considering that fielding was usually one of Derbyshire's strongest points, he enjoyed three of those lives off consecutive deliveries from the hapless Alf Pope.

From 102 for four at the first day's close, Essex built up a lead of 139 before Albert Alderman ended their innings by holding another catch given by Farnes off Pope. O'Connor also left, 13 runs from a century, to a catch (off Townsend) by Alderman, who proceeded to lead the Derbyshire fight-back by making his top score of the season, 79, in a second-innings total of 240 that still left Essex looking the likeliest winners with a quest for 102. That, though, was where Tommy Mitchell stepped in to bring about a startling transformation. In just five overs he took six wickets for 25 runs, and Essex, all out for 81, were beaten by 20. O'Connor was again their top scorer, but this time with only 21. These were now the leading positions in the table:

	P	W	L	1st inns W	L	NR	Points Poss	Act	%
DERBYSHIRE	21	11	3	2	4	1	315	191	60.63
Notts	20	8	1	4	7	0	300	161	53.66
Hampshire	23	7	1	8	7	0	345	166	48.11
Yorkshire	22	6	1	10	3	2	330	157	47.57
Kent	22	8	5	4	4	1	330	156	47.27
Surrey	22	7	5	4	4	2	330	145	43.93

Derbyshire's next match, at The Oval, was the one in which Tom Barling was so spectacularly caught for 57 by Alderman on the leg boundary after adding 91 with Stan Squires for Surrey's second wicket. Copson was the bowler to benefit, but Mitchell went one wicket better than his 4-41 with 5-88, his victims including Watts, maker of the other half-century of the innings. Derbyshire ended the first day 53 runs behind Surrey's 204 with eight wickets still standing, and, although time was subsequently lost through rain, Denis Smith and Alan Skinner made their third-wicket stand worth 152 before Skinner was caught for 58. Smith, whose previous highest score this season had been his 77 at Oxford on 9 May, and who had got to a half-century only six times in 35 innings, at last regained his touch with an admirable 106.

Alderman, having had to retire hurt after only five runs had been scored, did not stay long on resuming when Skinner was out at 171, but a first-innings lead was gained shortly before Harry Elliott and Alf Pope tightened the grip with a partnership of 88. The advantage was extended to 117 before the last wicket fell with Elliott unbeaten on 79, his highest score of the season, and Surrey might then have been in deeper difficulties if there had not been another untypical outbreak of dropped catches. As it was, Barling scored 102 and Fishlock 71, the pair adding 160 for the third wicket, and stumps were drawn with Surrey 198 ahead at 315 for seven.

From London, the Derbyshire team travelled back to Derby, where their chief speed-spin strike force was at its peak. Copson took nine wickets (5-40 and 4-39) and Mitchell ten (5-57 and 5-52) in a two-day victory over lowly Leicestershire by nine wickets. Copson blew away the middle of these neighbours' first innings with three of his wickets in four balls, but a total of 117 was made to look less inadequate when George Geary conceded only six runs in his first 15 overs and Derbyshire's top six were back in the pavilion before at least five points were assured.

The lead eventually amounted to only 42, Geary lopping off the tail with three wickets for three runs to finish with five for 39, only for Leicestershire to fold up again even more unaccountably on a pitch that by then was less favourable for the bowlers. Their total of 94 left only 53 required, and Alderman and Worthington saw Derbyshire home after Geary, who earlier in the season had taken 12 Warwickshire wickets in a day for only 12 runs, had deceived Smith for his sixth wicket of the match.

Yorkshire had by now climbed above Notts (fractionally) and Hampshire into the runners-up position by defying the weather with victories over Worcestershire, by an innings and 215 runs at Leeds, and Warwickshire, by 42 runs at Bradford. Maurice Leyland's century at Headingley was his fiftieth for the county. Notts, without the injured Larwood, picked up ten points for first-innings leads in drawn matches at Leicester and at home to Lancashire – both with more time lost to rain. Hampshire, beaten by an innings and 86 runs by Sussex at Hastings, and by nine wickets by Somerset at Weston-super-Mare, dropped to fifth below Middlesex, who followed a nine-wicket defeat of Gloucestershire in Bristol with five points from a draw (yes, more rain) at The Oval, where Hendren made the 162nd century of his career. Kent lost to Lancashire by five wickets in the cold and wintry weather at Canterbury and were easily led on first innings at Hastings in facing the total of 554 that Sussex made on the first day of a match in which heavy rain prevented play on the third. Top placings:

	P	W	L	*1st inns* W	L	NR	*Points* Poss	Act	%
DERBYSHIRE	23	12	3	3	4	1	345	211	61.15
Yorkshire	24	8	1	10	3	2	360	187	51.94
Notts	22	8	1	6	7	0	330	171	51.81
Middlesex	20	6	3	7	3	1	300	138	46.00
Hampshire	25	7	3	8	7	0	375	166	44.26
Kent	24	8	6	4	5	1	360	159	44.16

Having given themselves an extra day off by so swiftly seeing off Leicestershire, Derbyshire now had three further days without a fixture during which Yorkshire and Notts took five points apiece from drawn games with, respectively, Leicestershire at Scarborough and Warwickshire in Birmingham. At the same time, Middlesex beat Hampshire by 192 runs at Lord's, where Denis Compton and Hendren had a partnership of 95 in only 55 minutes, and Kent lost to Essex by an innings and 216 runs in the benefit match at Southend for Nichols, who fittingly scored a century (as also did O'Connor, his partner in a double-century stand).

Derbyshire returned to the Championship trail with the return game against Nottinghamshire at Worksop – but again without Worthington, who was at The Oval enjoying his greatest Test success in the defeat of India by nine wickets that gave England a 2-0 win in the series. Although purists observed that Worthington's bat was not as straight as they would have liked, he created an excellent impression as he unleashed his wide range of powerful strokes and emphasised the calmness of his temperament in sharing his record fourth-wicket stand of 266 with Walter Hammond, who was back to full health, before being bowled for 128 in having a go at Mahomed Nissar. He edged the ball through the slips a few times, but his only real blemish was in being missed at the wicket off Amar Singh with his score on 104.

Hammond, profiting from escapes at three and 96, had reached 217 when he too was bowled in attacking Nissar shortly before Worthington's departure. Nissar, who topped the tourists' bowling averages for the three Tests, took five wickets for 46 runs in nine overs with the third new ball but altogether conceded 120. Worthington did not get the chance to bat again in the match as only 64 runs were required. Hammond, who headed England's batting averages for the series with 194.50 to the Derbyshire man's 107.50, made the winning hit.

With Alderman labouring for 140 minutes over 31 and Harry Elliott two hours for 17, Derbyshire's progress against Notts, who lacked Voce (on England duty) as well as Larwood, was contrastingly tedious in the extreme – until, that is, Mitchell livened things up in a last-wicket stand of 44 with Copson in as many minutes. Copson contributed only seven. Mitchell, who had started in a brief partnership with Alf Pope, reached 45, his highest score for the county, but was then stumped in going for another big hit. That closed the Derbyshire innings at 218, and before stumps were drawn for the day Notts lost their first three wickets for only 11 runs. Two more fell next morning before the 50 went up, but Derbyshire went in again only 66 to the good after the collapse had been checked by 57 from skipper Heane and ten fewer from Arthur Staples, whose brother Sam also played for the county. Their sixth-wicket stand was worth 62.

The excessive caution with which Derbyshire had started was cast aside as they went for the runs in their second innings, Smith hitting a five and nine fours in his 85 and Skinner making 60. A declaration at 270 for eight left Notts with a possible four hours and ten minutes in which to get 337, but, although the pitch was by now perfect for batting, the match ended uneventfully in a draw as Copson and Mitchell, who had shared seven wickets in the first innings, were thwarted along with Alf Pope, Les Townsend and George Langdale while Keeton and Harris both got to a century in taking the total to 215 without being separated. Langdale, the Nottingham University left-hand batsman and right-arm bowler from Clay Cross, was making his debut.

Yorkshire, though without Leyland and Verity at the Test, strengthened their hold on second place by beating Somerset by an innings and 155 runs at Sheffield, their England pace bowler Bill Bowes taking five of his eleven wickets in the cider county's second-innings dismissal for 75. Middlesex, who gave

'Gubby' Allen and Jim Sims to the England cause, drew with Warwickshire at Edgbaston – foiled by a century partnership between Bob Wyatt (100 not out) and Tom Dollery after gaining a first-innings lead based on a magnificent 156 by Hendren, and then declaring 365 ahead after a second innings dominated by an undefeated century from Joe Hulme, the Arsenal and England footballer.

An England call-up also deprived Surrey of a key player, Laurie Fishlock, but big centuries by Andy Sandham and Tom Barling carried them to victory over Glamorgan in Cardiff by an innings and 331 runs – and up to fifth place in the table. Hampshire slipped below them after a draw with Essex at Southend, where a first-day total of just over 500 was well beyond them, despite a century by Philip Mead and a near one by Neil McCorkell, while Kent dropped out of the top six in crashing to defeat by an innings and 52 runs against Worcestershire at Dover. Essex's trump card was played by Denys Wilcox (133) and Stan Nichols (205), whose second-wicket partnership realised 221. Wilcox, a Cambridge Blue, was headmaster of a preparatory school at which the pupils included Trevor Bailey, the all-rounder who went on to play with such distinction for Essex and England. There were three centuries in Worcestershire's 482 for nine declared against Kent – by Dick Howorth (his first in county cricket), Charlie Bull and 'Doc' Gibbons. This was how they now stood at the head of affairs:

	P	W	L	*1st inns* W	L	NR	*Points* Poss	Act	%
DERBYSHIRE	24	12	3	4	4	1	360	216	60.00
Yorkshire	26	9	1	11	3	2	390	207	53.07
Notts	24	8	1	7	8	0	360	179	49.72
Middlesex	22	7	3	8	3	1	330	158	47.87
Surrey	26	8	6	4	6	2	390	166	42.56
Hampshire	27	7	4	8	8	0	405	169	41.72

Now that they had only four games left to play, Derbyshire showed some further signs of nerves in taking only eight points from the first three of them. They got off to a reasonably good start against Sussex at Eastbourne, Worthington and Skinner scoring half-centuries, but then lost their last five wickets for only 30 runs. Sussex, facing a total of 228, lost both openers, Jim Parks and John Langridge, with their score stuck at nine, and, although they reached 30 without further loss before rain set in, they appeared likely to go further into trouble when strong sunshine after more rain overnight made the pitch tricky for batsmen. Another wicket did go down with just three runs added, but only one more was lost – that of Tommy Cook, who was in bright form for his 53 – before James Langridge and Harry Parks earned a first-innings lead with a stand of 185. Langridge hit fourteen fours in his excellent 126; Parks made 75. The rest were soon swept away, Copson finishing off the innings with four wickets for three runs to give himself full figures of six for 87.

Going in again 88 behind, Derbyshire ended the second day at 41 for two after quickly losing Alderman and Smith, and it therefore demanded a determined rearguard action to force the draw. Worthington (45), Les Townsend (46) and Charlie Elliott (39 not out) fought it so dourly that at one stage the score crawled along at a rate of 38 in two hours. At the close, with runs of no importance, skipper Richardson, who missed only three Championship matches all season, was helping to hold the fort at 191 for six. It was a commendable backs-to-the-wall effort, but one that could have been avoided if more of their batsmen had shown greater application on a good pitch on the opening day.

Down at Dover, Kent checked their recent run of disappointing results with one of the big upsets of the season, beating Yorkshire by nine wickets after reducing them to 37 for six in their first innings. Verity and Smailes revived the defending champions by adding 99 for the ninth wicket, but Kent forged into a lead of nearly 200, largely through a brilliant 120 from Leslie Ames, the wicketkeeper who had temporarily lost his England place to Lancashire's George Duckworth for the series with India. Yorkshire's improved start to their second innings took them to 170 for three, Len Hutton scoring 71, and although there was then another slump Verity again showed he was no mean batsman besides having exceptional ability as a spin bowler before Kent were able to tackle the simple task they were left for full points.

The only other defeat Yorkshire suffered all season had been their first by Worcestershire since 1909 – by just eleven runs when caught on a drying pitch at Stourbridge back in mid-May. Having begun the last day 55 runs from victory with only two men out, they had lost three wickets to 'Peter' Jackson in four balls, and four to Dick Howorth for one run.

In the other corresponding matches, while Yorkshire were so narrowly failing to take advantage of Derbyshire's restriction to three points at The Saffrons, Middlesex lost at Lord's by ten wickets after following on against Lancashire, Notts and Hampshire (who were completing their programme) gleaned five points each from respective drawn home games with Leicestershire and Gloucestershire, and Surrey compelled Warwickshire to end their season without a win at Edgbaston by defeating them there by five wickets.

Derbyshire's next match, at Chesterfield, was the one from which Northamptonshire's opening batsmen were returning home when one of them, Reg Northway, was killed in the car crash that left the other, 'Fred' Bakewell, seriously injured. Northants went into the game, their twenty-fourth and last of the season, still seeking their first victory – and they went so close to it, after being led on first innings, that they claimed the extra half-hour and had Derbyshire clinging on for the draw with only two wickets left. Mitchell was unable to bat because of an injured thumb.

The fact that Derbyshire finished the first day 23 runs ahead with three wickets in hand was due mainly to Copson and Alf Pope, who both took four wickets in Northants' 144, and Les Townsend, who hit eight fours in his 67. The lead was extended by only 42 runs before Bakewell dominated the rest of the second day's play by scoring 221 not out in a total of 374 for four against an attack deprived of the injured Mitchell. After putting on 93 for the third wicket with Timms, who added 41 to his top first-innings score of 47, Bakewell was joined by Brookes in a stand of 211 in 190 minutes for the fourth, Brookes reaching what was then his highest score for the county of 81. When William Brown, the Northants captain, declared on the last morning at 411 for six Bakewell had batted flawlessly for ten minutes over six hours and hit 19 fours in his unbeaten 241. A special mention is also merited here for Alf Pope, who, manfully shouldering his increased burden for 42 overs, took all six of those second-innings wickets for 129 runs.

With their slim lead of 65 having been transformed into a daunting deficit of 346, Derbyshire understandably made no effort to attempt a victory chase at 70 runs an hour. Indeed, they were just thankful to avoid defeat after losing Worthington and Harry Elliott for ducks, and Townsend for a single, in struggling to 121 for six. Skinner stayed two hours for 41, and Alf Pope rounded off his excellent display with the ball by holding out with his captain for the tense final overs.

Meanwhile, two of Derbyshire's main rivals faltered but another revived. Yorkshire had the worst of a draw with Surrey at The Oval, where centuries by Errol Holmes and Freddie Brown outweighed one by Maurice Leyland; Notts, despite scores of 103 and 70 by Joe Hardstaff, lost at Clacton by 34 runs to Essex, who, bolstered by another O'Connor hundred, followed up an innings win at Taunton to climb into the top six; Middlesex whisked Kent out for 85 at Lord's, Allen including a spell of four wickets for no runs in his 6-39, and beat them by eight wickets. With the finishing post now in sight, this was how they then stood:

				1st inns			Points		
	P	W	L	W	L	NR	Poss	Act	%
Derbyshire	26	12	3	5	5	1	390	224	57.43
Yorkshire	28	9	2	11	4	2	420	210	50.00
Middlesex	24	8	4	8	3	1	360	173	48.05
Notts	26	8	2	8	8	0	390	184	47.17
Essex	24	8	6	5	5	0	360	160	44.44
Surrey	28	9	6	5	6	2	420	186	44.28

Somerset bounced back from their trouncing by Essex to beat Worcestershire by 97 runs at Kidderminster – and then tarnished for Derbyshire the match in which, paradoxically, Richardson and his men became assured of the Championship by also defeating them, by just one wicket, at Wells to complete a memorable double over the new champions. Smith and Worthington offset the early loss of Alderman with a second-wicket stand of 90, Smith unfortunate to miss a century by seven runs, but Bill Andrews then got among the wickets to take five for 42 in a total of 216. The last four fell for the addition of nine runs.

Somerset also found runs hard to come by, with Alf Pope (5-35) again in fine form as they lost their last five wickets for 30 runs after resuming at 116 overnight. That gave Derbyshire a lead of 70, yet they promptly slumped again in conditions that so obviously favoured the bowlers. Seven of their second-innings wickets were down for 98 before Richardson, who hit eight fours in his 50, and Pope added 66. A total of 200 set Somerset to get 271, and they were 93 for two at the end of the second day's play.

To say there was some thrilling cricket on the last day was something of an under-statement. Copson claimed three of the six wickets with which he was to finish at a cost of 81 runs as Somerset lost half their side for 140. That left 131 still needed, and dearly Derbyshire were to pay for dropping Reggie Ingle before he had scored and Arthur Wellard when he had obtained only a single. The sixth-wicket pair added 77 runs in 45 minutes, the majority of them plundered by Wellard. This was the occasion when this Kentish man (his home county failed to recognise his potential) struck seven sixes – five of them from successive deliveries in one over – off Tom Armstrong, who had been brought back into the Derbyshire team because of Mitchell's injury. Wellard, who smote as many as 3,000 of his career total of 11,000 runs in sixes, scored 86 out of 102 in 62 minutes before giving a catch to Townsend off Copson. Ingle was caught off the same bowler, by Smith, for just 16.

When Wellard was seventh out, the target was 29 runs away. 'Peter' McRae (his given first names were Foster Moverley) then defended stubbornly for his 14 not out, and last-man Horace Hazell made the winning hit after going in with six required. McRae, who was born at Buenos Aires, last played for Somerset in 1939. He was killed when the destroyer, *HMS Mahratta*, on which he was serving as a Surgeon Lieutenant in the RNVR, was sunk in the Barents Sea in the Arctic Ocean early in 1944.

Wellard's spectacular punishment of Armstrong, who conceded 64 runs for one wicket in his eight overs, was unparalleled in first-class cricket at that time, but he repeated it at the same small ground two years later in an over from Kent's Frank Woolley – and was dropped in front of the sightscreen off the sixth ball. Five consecutive sixes have since been hit by two South Africans. Denis Lindsay finished off Essex in that grand manner at the expense of Bill Greensmith while playing for the SA Fezela side at Chelmsford in 1961, and Mike Procter equalled the feat for Western Province, off Ashley Mallett of the Australian touring team, at Cape Town in 1970.

The world record of six off every ball of an over, set by the West Indian all-rounder Gary Sobers for Notts off Glamorgan's Malcolm Nash at Swansea in 1968, has been equalled by Ravi Shastri, for Bombay against Baroda in 1985. In 1979, Procter hit six of his eight sixes for Gloucestershire against Somerset at Taunton off six successive deliveries from Dennis Breakwell – the last two of one over, the first four of his next.

With Yorkshire taking just the five points for a first-innings lead in being held to a draw by Sussex at Hove, and overtaken for second place by Middlesex, winners by 255 runs at Worcester, Derbyshire could no longer be caught, despite their desperately close failure at Wells. So it was that on the last day of their visit to Somerset, Friday 28 August 1936, they were finally crowned champions – this time undisputedly. When this glad news reached the Derbyshire club's president, the Duke of Devonshire, he hurriedly left his shooting party at Bolton Abbey and travelled to Derby to attend the public reception the players were given on their return. The Duke was an active president, attending home games regularly and always ready to help to resolve financial problems, from 1909 until his death in 1938. He was succeeded from 1939 to 1950 in the club's presidency by his son, who in turn was followed in that post by his son, the 11th Duke, from 1951 to 1990. As already recalled, Guy Willatt and Charlie Elliott are among those who have been president since then, and another former player, Les Jackson, has also had the honour.

In September 1936, the *Derbyshire Advertiser* published a cricket supplement to celebrate the title triumph. It included a complete review of the season by Major Eardley Simpson, statistics by Frank Peach, who after the war was to be a leading figure in the formation of a Supporters' Club, and an article on Derbyshire cricket of the old days by L G Wright.

To quote *The Cricketer Annual,* Derbyshire's success was 'immensely popular'. That popularity stemmed from their scorning of safety-first tactics – not only during the season but also throughout the years leading up to it. *Wisden* remarked:

'Derbyshire, acknowledged as exponents of attractive cricket, continued to hold victory as the highest prize, and if at times this urge caused their downfall, the county gained tremendously in popularity and respect among both supporters and rivals.'

The season ended on a fitting note of triumph for Derbyshire, winners at Oakham of their final match by an innings and 66 runs against Leicestershire, the county third from the foot of the table. Brilliant fielding backed up accurate bowling as the home side lost their first five wickets for 47 runs, then struggled to 151 after Alan Shipman had spent three hours over his 37 not out and shared a stand of 51 with Ewart Astill that lasted two hours. Astill, one of county cricket's first professional captains, did nothing outstanding in that match, but he was one of the more remarkable cricketers of his time – scorer of a thousand runs and taker of a hundred wickets in each of nine seasons during a career with Leicestershire that lasted from 1905, when he joined the staff at the age of 15, until 1939, when, at 49, he rejoined the Army with the commission he had earned in the First World War. The only break he took from competitive cricket in one period of seven years was when he did not go on a tour in 1928-29.

After losing Albert Alderman to the first ball of their first innings, bowled by Shipman, Derbyshire were put in a match-winning position by Denis Smith and Stan Worthington, whose second-wicket partnership took the total to 103 by the end of the opening day and was worth 209 by the time Worthington was dismissed for 102. Smith, back to his best, was seventh out at 328 after hitting a six and 13 fours in a masterly innings of 169. The extent to which Derbyshire relied on that pair for a lead of 187 was shown by the fact that Harry Elliott's 24 was the next highest score.

By the close of the second day Leicestershire were almost as badly off as they had been in their first innings, with five wickets down and their arrears reduced by only 59. Copson and Alf Pope, who between them took 13 wickets in the match, soon saw off the rest on the season's final day, the first one of September. Leicestershire's innings of 121 was one of the completed 25 in that year's Championship in which Harry Elliott conceded no byes – while 3,661 runs were scored. And he also allowed none in Oxford University's second innings at Oxford.

For Copson and Worthington the season was crowned by their selection for the MCC's tour of Australia – Copson as the only member of the party of 17 who had not yet played in a Test. As we have seen, he was to return still to make his England debut, but Pelham Warner observed that 'the voyage should do him the world of good'. Copson's 153 wickets at 12.54 put him well clear at the head of Derbyshire's bowling averages, and, with 160 in all at 13.34, third to Larwood (119 at 12.97) and Verity (216 at 13.18) in the national list. Worthington, scorer of 1,519 runs at 37.97, was the county's top batsman for both runs and average; his overall total of 1,734 at 41.28 put him 13th nationally. Pride of place went to Hammond, whose 2,107 runs in three fewer innings than Worthington gave him an average of 56.94.

In addition to Copson, who was seventeenth in 1933 and sixth in both 1934 and 1935, Derbyshire had previously had ten bowlers in the top twenty of a season's final overall bowling averages – Leslie Townsend as many as six times, Bill Bestwick five, Tommy Mitchell four, and George Davidson three. But not since 1923 had they had a batsman in the top twenty. Wilfred Hill-Wood had then only just squeezed in with 1,082 runs in 30 innings at 36.06, and for Derbyshire alone that year his average for 961 runs had been down to 34.32. Before him, five Derbyshire batsmen had been in the top twenty – William Chatterton (twelfth in 1894, ninth in 1896), William Storer (sixth in 1896, ninth in 1898), Harry Bagshaw (nineteenth in 1896), L G Wright (twelfth in 1905) and A E Lawton (fourth in 1907).

While Derbyshire were winding up their 1936 programme by beating Leicestershire for the second time, their two main rivals also won – Middlesex by 256 runs against Surrey at Lord's, where Hendren scored a century in both innings; Yorkshire by ten wickets against Hampshire at Bournemouth – but Notts lost by an innings and 70 runs at Gloucester and Essex, who dropped out of the top six, by 185 runs at Worcester. Gloucestershire's victory, which hoisted them above Notts to fourth in the final table – a remarkable rise after their poor start to the season – had the firm foundation of a dazzling innings of 317 by Hammond. In the course of it he beat W G Grace's record of 1,278 runs in August by three runs and completed his 2,000 for the season. His team-mates could afford to be without him for the final day, which he missed because of a badly bruised instep.

THE FINAL COUNTY CHAMPIONSHIP TABLE FOR 1936

	P	W	L	1st inns W	L	NR	Points Poss	Act	%
DERBYSHIRE	28	13	4	5	5	1	420	239	56.90
Middlesex	26	10	4	8	3	1	390	203	52.05
Yorkshire	30	10	2	12	4	2	450	230	51.11
Gloucs	30	10	7	*4	8	1	450	203	45.11
Notts	28	8	3	9	8	0	420	189	45.00
Surrey	30	9	7	6	6	2	450	191	42.44
Somerset	26	9	10	2	3	2	390	162	41.53
Kent	28	9	9	4	5	1	420	174	41.42
Essex	26	8	8	5	5	0	390	160	41.02
Hampshire	30	7	5	9	9	0	450	177	39.33
Lancashire	30	7	6	7	6	5	450	175	38.88
Worcs	28	7	9	4	7	1	420	150	35.71
Warwicks	24	4	8	2	7	3	360	103	28.61
Sussex	30	4	10	7	6	3	450	125	27.77
Leics	24	2	5	8	8	1	360	98	27.22
Glamorgan	26	1	12	6	5	2	390	68	17.43
Northants	24	0	9	5*	9	1	360	61	16.94

Including ten points for a win on first innings in a match played under the laws for one-day games.

22. Undermined by Unrest

Derbyshire cricket has been anything but champion-like in recent years – and in quite a few other years too since the county title was won in 1936. Even when they rose to their highest final position after that long overdue success, second to Leicestershire in 1996, they immediately sank back to the bottom three in the turbulent wake of a gigantic upheaval behind the scenes in which, within four months, they lost their chairmen (yes, there were two of them), commercial manager, captain and coach.

And, as if all that was not quite enough to be going on with, they soon afterwards suffered other unwelcome additions to the exodus of key players that had resulted from unrest and bad feeling in the dressing room. It was the attitude of some senior members of the team that came in for strong criticism by Dean Jones after the former Australian Test player had resigned from the captaincy so soon after leading the team to the runners-up position, and departed with Les Stillman, the fellow countryman who had been frozen out as coach. Jones complained of a lack of support.

More fuel was piled on the fire of discontent when former skipper Kim Barnett was fined £500 for 'a blatant and deliberate disregard of club policy' after ignoring a warning to the players not to comment to the media that was issued by the chairman, Mike Horton, and the chairman of the cricket committee, former player and captain Ian Buxton. Barnett, who said on Radio Derby that the players' case should be heard, also incurred a suspended fine of £1,000 that was applied after he had missed a session of a home match with Sussex to frame a reply and give notice of appeal. Horton blamed a lack of committee support when he resigned after returning from a business trip to the United States to find that Barnett had been successful with that appeal, vindicated because of England and Wales Cricket Board regulations that permitted players to comment with certain provisos.

It said much for Barnett's dedication and powers of concentration that he maintained his batting form despite being involved in so much trouble off the field. In 1997 he passed a thousand runs for the fourteenth season and shared in two stands that broke Derbyshire records – 316, unbroken, for the third wicket with Adrian Rollins at Leicester, and the 417 for the second wicket with Tim Tweates, in the final game against Yorkshire at Derby, that is the biggest in the club's history. He totalled 235 runs in that latter match without being dismissed as Derbyshire lost only four wickets in winning by nine. The assurance Tweats displayed in making 189, his maiden first-class century, made his sudden and irreversible decline the following season all the more inexplicable.

The turmoil into which the county had been thrown further unsettled batsman Chris Adams, a firm supporter of Jones and Stillman. He had been hankering after a change of club for some time, and he got his wish with a year still to run on his Derbyshire contract, leaving to join a Sussex side he was to captain to their first county title – and to another one, this time coupled with the Cheltenham and Gloucester Trophy, as they enjoyed the most successful seasons in their history. His departure was a blow Derbyshire could ill afford so soon after the exit of two other reliable batsmen, Peter Bowler and John Morris, and another one was quickly to be felt in the bowling department as paceman Devon Malcolm, whose analysis of 16.3-2-57-9 in England's defeat of South Africa at The Oval in 1994 was the sixth-best in Tests, threw in his lot with Northamptonshire (and later Leicestershire).

It did not take long for the self-destruct button to be pressed again. The new captain, Test all-rounder Dominic Cork, complained about the committee acting against his wishes and said he would not continue if Harold Rhodes, the club's former England bowler who was on the committee, and Andy Hayhurst, the director of coaching and development, retained influence over decisions about senior staff. This precipitated the resignation of another chairman, Vic Brownett, a few days before another heated annual meeting.

It also led to the departure of Barnett, the most prolific scorer of runs the club have ever possessed. Cork wanted him to be appointed player-coach, but he was released at his own request after again topping the thousand and Derbyshire's averages in 1998. Barnett moved on for several more successful seasons with Gloucestershire in the wake of a dispute over the extent of Cork's powers that split the membership and led to the resignation of the committee after a vote of no confidence in it had been carried by 501 votes to 348 – though four of those committee members, including Brownett's successor, Trevor Bowring, were voted back only three months later.

Derbyshire's inability to hang on to some of their best players – five more, including Rollins and the former England all-rounder Phillip DeFreitas, left after the 1999 season – gave them reason to rue the fact that, whereas a dozen or more of them were so readily taken on by other first-class counties, their own resources became so shorn of sufficient talent that the dramatic dip in their fortunes was inevitable during the seasons following their challenge for the title under Jones's resourceful leadership.

In those unhappy circumstances, they did amazingly well, while the inspiring but often impulsive Cork was still at the helm before his own move to Lancashire, to finish just inside the top half of the table in 1999 and thus qualify to be in the new First Division with the splitting of the Championship into two sections.

They did so, however, only by gaining one more victory than Warwickshire, who were level with them on points – and that after a controversial final match with Hampshire at Derby in which the captains, Cork and Robin Smith, were unsuccessfully accused of collusion by Warwickshire.

Hampshire began that game needing a win, and Derbyshire two batting points, to make sure of being among the elite at the expense of Warwickshire and Sussex. Warwickshire themselves dashed Sussex's hopes by defeating them inside two days on what *Wisden* called 'a blatantly unsatisfactory pitch' at Edgbaston. Then they too were squeezed out as Derbyshire, who had collected three bonus points (but would have been fourth instead of ninth if they had scored just three more runs) were beaten by only two runs. The third declaration of the match, setting Derbyshire a target of 285 in four sessions with rain threatening, was hurried along by some generous bowling that provoked protests from the watching members but also conjured up the enthralling finish.

If Derbyshire's presence in the inaugural top flight was unexpected in view of all the discord, their swift relegation was not. There was a suggestion that they might have survived had they not been weakened by Cork's recall to the England team he helped to a 3-1 win in the five-match series against the West Indies after he had missed the opening game they lost. Derbyshire were beaten by an innings in three of their corresponding games and were helped to a draw in the other by dropped catches after being led on first innings. Gratifying as it was for Cork and his county to have him back in the national team, the more galling aspect of his call-up from Derbyshire's viewpoint was that, because he was not a contracted England player, they received no financial compensation when they complied with the request of officialdom by resting him from their match with relegation rivals Kent at Canterbury before the third Test at Old Trafford.

So, their slender resources over-stretched, down Derbyshire went with Hampshire and Durham. Although they finished only one point behind those demoted companions, they were more than thirty away from safety. They would therefore still have descended even if they had not been given something else to complain about in having eight points deducted, but if that penalty had not been controversially imposed they would at least have been spared the ninth and last place. Contrary to the opinions of the two umpires, the pitch was deemed below the acceptable standard by official liaison officers after Derbyshire had gained one of their two victories in defeating Surrey at rain-swept Derby. If Hampshire had not also been similarly punished, Durham would have been alone at the foot of the table.

Last place was again to be Derbyshire's fate in three of the next five seasons, taking the club to a record authorised total of fourteen wooden spoons. And it would have been seventeen with the inclusion of three of the seasons before 1890 that are no longer officially recognised. And eighteen if that last place in Division One in 2000 were to be taken into account. *Wisden* has decreed that Sussex, as the county at the bottom of Division Two, should have the only wooden spoon allowed that year.

That is something I would argue more strongly about if it were not to Derbyshire's detriment, though their number of wooden spoons could arguably be raised beyond twenty by including their seasons at the foot of the league, no longer confined to Sundays, that has undergone so many changes of name since it was introduced with John Player sponsorship in 1969 (no fewer than 14 to date). *Wisden* once felt moved to say that this one-day competition had 'gone through more incarnations than a Buddist lama'.

The depressing monotony of Derbyshire's monopoly of the booby prizes – two of them when misguidedly known as the Sunday League's Scorpions – was interrupted, despite another pitch penalty of eight points, with a rise to sixth out of the Division Two Championship's nine in 2002 under the impetus of wins in five of their first six matches, and a basement swap with Durham that edged them up to penultimate position in 2005. Little wonder that chief executive John Smedley, who at the age of twenty-six in 1997 had become Derbyshire's youngest secretary since Will Taylor began his 51-year reign at twenty-three in 1908, left after a lengthy absence with work-related stress, claiming a lack of committee support.

Nor perhaps, in seasons of such a dearth of quality, was it all that surprising that spectators at Derby went through three whole seasons and more than thirty matches before seeing another Derbyshire victory in the Championship, against Somerset in 2006. It was a bleak sequence that included the county's worst run of seven defeats in the competition for more than seventy years and their heaviest, by an innings and 231 runs at home to Northamptonshire, in twenty-eight. In 1975, their beating by Lancashire by an innings and 348 at Buxton had been the biggest of the lot – after the loss of a day's play because of a snowstorm in June.

Before their prolonged delve into the depths during the early years of the twenty-first century, Derbyshire fetched up at the bottom of the final Championship table in four of the seasons after the Second World War. In 1963, they were last for the first time since 1924 – a most unfortunate start to Yorkshire-man Charlie Lee's captaincy in succession to Donald Carr, and a most inappropriate end for the career of record-breaking bowler Les Jackson. Even so, Jackson bowed out of his seventeenth and final season with the county in his customary place at the head of their bowling averages.

Five years earlier, when his opening partner Cliff Gladwin himself retired from first-class cricket as the county's reigning record wicket-taker (he overtook Bestwick's record during a hat-trick, at the age of forty-two, against the New Zealand tourists), Jackson had topped the national averages with figures that *Wisden* said were 'impressive enough in any circumstances', but 'represented a feat of the first magnitude' considering that he achieved them, aged thirty-seven, in one of the wettest of summers despite being dogged by a persistent groin strain that at times reduced his approach to the wicket to little more than an abbreviated trot. He kept himself going by having regular treatment and the occasional match off. Curiously, he was at his most effective while experiencing his severest discomfort, collecting sixty-two of his wickets for fewer than eight runs apiece in his last eight Championship games.

Jackson, the first Derbyshire player to be among *Wisden's* Five Cricketers of the Year since Copson and Worthington after the 1936 title season (Donald Carr, Bob Taylor, Mike Hendrick, Kim Barnett, Devon Malcolm and Dominic Cork have since been added to the list), altogether took 143 wickets for 1,572 runs in 829 overs, 292 of them maidens, for an average of 10.99. All but eight of those wickets were captured for Derbyshire, at the still lower average of 10.09, and they included a unique hat-trick with three catches by wicketkeeper George Dawkes in the very next match, at Kidderminster, after Gladwin's feat against the Kiwis. It was the lowest final season's bowling average for the county, with a comparable number of wickets, since William Mycroft's 98 at 8.66 (116 in all at 10.31) in 1878. It was also the lowest by any first-class bowler taking at least a hundred wickets in a season since 1894, when Surrey's Tom Richardson had bagged 196 at 10.32 apiece.

Since the turn into the twentieth century, the previous meanest figures among regular bowlers in top-class cricket had been recorded by two left-arm spinners from Yorkshire. Wilfred Rhodes took 134 at 11.54 in 1923, Arthur Booth 111 at 11.61 in 1946. Leicestershire's Dick Pougher had averaged 9.35 for 56 wickets in 1894, but he had delivered fewer overs than any other bowler in the top twenty.

Les Jackson had also been as good as the leading bowler in the country in 1953. Though third in the list with 103 wickets at 15.28, the two men above him had been only occasional bowlers – Jack Bailey, of Essex, with 25 wickets at 13.04, and Charlie Knott, of Hampshire, with 38 at 13.71. As already recalled, two years after Jackson's retirement Derbyshire had the distinction of seeing their opening bowlers, Harold Rhodes and Brian Jackson (no relation to Les), first and second in the national averages. Rhodes showed great strength of character to attain that exalted position under the shadow of being no-balled for throwing.

In 1960, two years after topping the national averages, Les Jackson was runner-up to Lancashire's Brian Statham in achieving his highest total of wickets in a season – 150 for Derbyshire, 160 in all – at a cost of fewer than fourteen runs each. He was unlucky indeed to play in only two Tests – and those a dozen years apart, the second one at the age of forty when he was not even an original choice.

It was his misfortune to have his career coincide with those of such speed merchants as Fred Trueman, Brian Statham, 'Typhoon' Frank Tyson and Peter Loader, and to be at the mercy of selectors who looked unfavourably on his unorthodox slinging type of action because they felt he did not make full use of his height. Even Bill Edrich, primarily a batsman, was among those preferred to the collier from the village of Whitwell that also produced the billiards and snooker champion Joe Davis. If it had been left to umpires and the batsmen he tested so rigorously on the county circuit, Jackson would have been an automatic choice.

His other appearances in teams labelled 'England' were in festivals at Kingston-upon-Thames, Hastings and Torquay, and he was selected for the Players against the Gentlemen. He also did get to go on an overseas tour, with a Commonwealth team to India and Ceylon (as it then was) in 1950-51, but had to return home after playing in only one game, in Bombay, because of a swollen 'tennis' elbow for which he underwent an operation. It was a fate that a year later befell another Derbyshire player, Bert Rhodes, who accompanied Donald Carr on the MCC's trip to India and Pakistan, but had to cut it short after taking part in only four matches. A hernia was at first diagnosed, but it was for deep-seated muscle trouble that he had to have an operation. Originally a leg-spinner, the Cheshire-born Rhodes changed to bowling fast-medium outswingers off a long run unsuited to his slight build, but reverted to spin to fill the gap left by Tommy Mitchell's retirement. His son was also a spinner before switching to speed.

After 1963, two of Derbyshire's other post-war finishes in last place in the Championship came in succession, directly after they had been seventh in their centenary year of 1970 – and they then escaped being at the bottom for four seasons in a row only by the narrowest of margins.

In 1971, when there was a record loss of £15,000 and attendances were considerably down partly due to bad weather, their only Championship victory was gained against a Kent side weakened by Test calls, and they also provided Oxford University with their first win over a first-class county for two years.

In 1972, they again won only once in the Championship (by three wickets with six overs to spare against Sussex, the county immediately above them in the table), but had a chance of honours in the fifth year of the John Player League until losing all but one of their last six games. The season ended with another change of captain – Yorkshireman Brian Bolus for Ian Buxton – and one of the severest clear-outs among the playing staff in the club's history.

A notable exception to the general air of decline was the continued immaculate form of wicketkeeper Bob Taylor, who had the misfortune to be kept at home by an ear infection after so deservedly earning his selection for the MCC's tour of India and Pakistan. Another gleam in the gloom was the emergence of Mike Hendrick as a fast-medium bowler in the true Derbyshire tradition.

In 1973, not until the final day of the season did Derbyshire avoid ending at the foot of the table for the third time in succession – and then it was by only one bonus point that they pushed Nottinghamshire into that unenviable position in drawing with them at Trent Bridge. This was the season in which Alan Ward was dismissed from the field by Bolus for refusing to bowl during the match with Yorkshire at Chesterfield.

In 1974, it was back to the bottom once more, despite outplaying Sussex in their opening match on a Derby pitch of questionable quality. That win remained the county's only one in the Championship even though they had six players of Test experience on the books (there have since been even more than that, still without the desired results). Furthermore, the financial situation stayed so desperate that the position of coach was dispensed with, more cuts were made in the full-time playing staff, and a second team was dispensed with for a short time. Derbyshire have rarely been free from cash problems throughout their history, yet it was at another time when their playing fortunes were at their lowest ebb – last in 1994 for the first time since 1974 – that they cleared an overdraft of some £480,000. That was partly due to a legacy of £235,000 from the estate of Frank Stretton, a Derbyshire farmer, but much credit could also be attributed to the guidance of another in the long line of chairmen, Mike Horton, for the record profit of more than £60,000 declared that autumn. A year later the profit was up to just over £123,500, and £175,000 in loans had been cleared.

Some long overdue improvement in playing standards after the dreadful slump in the early years of the 1970s was brought about under the dynamic leadership of the South African Test all-rounder Eddie Barlow, the county's fourth captain in five seasons, but there were to be three more captains after him before Derbyshire claimed their first honour since the title of 1936. The first real signs of a recovery were beefed up by Barlow with a rise to seventh place in 1977, when the batting was strengthened by the arrival of New Zealander John Wright, and four of the seven wins in the Championship (the first to be sponsored, by Schweppes) were gained in consecutive matches. Middlesex, joint champions with Kent that year, were beaten by an innings inside two days, but some ground was lost because no points were acquired from three matches ruined by rain in one of the worst summers for weather since the war. At the end of the season Derbyshire had three locally-produced players, Hendrick, Taylor and Geoff Miller, in an overseas tour, to Pakistan and New Zealand, for the first time.

In the following season of 1978 – the last for Barlow with the county, but the first for another gifted South African, Peter Kirsten, who was to compile the club's record of six double-centuries before leaving in 1982 – there was another first for Derbyshire. They finally got beyond the group stages of the Benson and Hedges Cup competition, in its seventh year. Better still, they won through to the final – only to fade to demoralising defeat at Lord's, where Kent, runners-up the year before, lifted the trophy for the third time. Kent went on land a notable double by becoming champions, whereas Derbyshire won only one more match in all competitions and fell back to fourth from the foot of the Championship table.

Derbyshire had also given a disappointing display in losing to Yorkshire on their first appearance in a knock-out final – the eighth one of the Gillette Cup competition, at Lord's in 1969. That was a particularly big let-down after the emotional scenes of their defeat of Sussex in front of a Chesterfield crowd of

11,000 who brought in record receipts of more than £3,500 for a match in the county. Peter Eyre, a right-arm fast bowler and left-hand batsmen from the Hathersage club whose first-class career was to be so cruelly cut short as a consequence of the glandular fever he contracted within a year, was the man of that match. He took six wickets for 18 runs in 10.2 overs, four of which were maidens, in the rout of Sussex for 49, then the lowest total in the competition.

The defeat by Yorkshire in the final denied Derek Morgan a most fitting farewell. At the age of forty, the Middlesex-born all-rounder was in the last of his twenty seasons of splendid service to Derbyshire, and of his five years as captain. Although he had not done the double of a thousand runs and one hundred wickets in any of those seasons, he retired as one of only ten players in the game's history to have scored more than 15,000 runs, taken over 100 wickets and held more than 500 catches.

Morgan was an automatic selection throughout the captaincies of Guy Willatt (1951-54) and Donald Carr (1955-62) during which Derbyshire enjoyed some of their most successful seasons of those earlier post-war years. There had been a gradual slide down the table in the three remaining pre-war seasons after the 1936 title year – to third in 1937, fifth in 1938 and ninth in 1939 – and the fifteenth final position of the first post-war season of 1946 had been their lowest since the mid-1920s.

One major explanation for that slump to third from the foot of the table was that the team had lost Harry Elliott, Tommy Mitchell, Les Townsend and Alf and George Pope. Another was that three other key members of the pre-war side who were still available, Albert Alderman, Bill Copson and Denis Smith, were not far off forty, and a fourth, Stan Worthington, had already got there. It may be said that life begins at forty, but not for first-class cricketers. Two others from the 1930s, Arnold Townsend and Charlie Elliott, both celebrated their thirty-fourth birthday before taking the field for the resumption of the County Championship in May 1946 after the loss of six first-class seasons; another, Harold Rhodes's father Bert, turned thirty that year.

In those circumstances, Derbyshire were fortunate to possess a proficient player as eager to do well as Cliff Gladwin. He was thirsting to make up for lost time after having gone without either a run or a wicket through his debut as a 23-year-old in Derbyshire's thunderous crash to defeat by Yorkshire at Sheffield in the last pre-war season, and he had remained wicketless despite room having been made for him in the county's last three matches of that year by resting Harry Elliott and calling upon Alderman to keep wicket. Now, though aged thirty, Gladwin was a far more formidable proposition. Not only had he gained valuable experience playing in league cricket with Saltaire and Lidget Green. He had also avenged himself against Yorkshire by taking eight of their wickets for only 27 runs during a two-day game at Chesterfield in 1945.

In 1946, Gladwin set out as he was to go on, taking more than a hundred wickets for the first of twelve seasons – a Derbyshire record most closely approached by Tommy Mitchell and Les Jackson, with ten each. In 1950, the only year in which big Cliff failed to get into three figures during his post-war first-class career (he was only six short), he missed a dozen Championship games through unfitness.

On that consistent form Gladwin deserved to play more than eight times for England, keen though the competition was, but he still had a major Test memory to cherish as a central figure in one of the most feverish finishes in cricket history. In the first match of the 1948-49 series in South Africa England were set to score only 128 to win in a little over two hours, but tottered towards defeat when Cuan McCarthy, making his Test debut at nineteen, took six wickets for 33 runs in ten overs of splendidly hostile fast bowling. With just three deliveries remaining any one of four results was possible that late December day in Durban – a draw, a tie, or victory for either side. Eight wickets were down, and Gladwin, having survived an easy chance off the first ball he received, was batting with Surrey's Alec Bedser, who then brought the scores level with a single off the sixth ball of the final eight-ball over, bowled by Lindsay Tuckett.

In failing light, and with rain about, the seventh delivery eluded Gladwin's bat, but also the stumps. So, after a mid-pitch conference, with few of their team-mates in the pavilion able to bear the strain of watching, the ninth-wicket pair decided to run off the last ball regardless of what happened unless the wicket was hit. As Tuckett started his run-up the fieldsmen closed in quickly to try to prevent the winning run. Gladwin once more swung heartily, but again missed. The ball struck him on the thigh, and, although it bounced only a yard or two in front of him, 'Tufty' Mann's desperate pounce from short-leg was to no avail. The vital single was scampered in a veritable Cliff-hanger.

It went down as the most celebrated of all leg-byes. 'Coometh the hower, coometh the man,' exulted the jubilant Gladwin. He and Bedser danced a jig of delight, then were chaired off as hundreds of spectators flocked onto the field. *Wisden* commented:

'No greater support could have been given to the contention of cricket lovers that an exciting cricket match can provide as intense a thrill as anything else in sport than by the drama of the final stages.'

Gladwin only wished he could have carried the bruise on his thigh around him for the rest of his life, but he did the next best thing by having a photograph taken of it. He also obtained another souvenir to treasure – a recording of commentator John Arlott's description of those nerve-jangling closing minutes. England went on to draw each of the next three Tests before winning the final one in Port Elizabeth to clinch the series, in which Gladwin was an ever-present. He had then not been on the losing side in seven appearances for England, all against the Springboks, but was discarded after being chosen for just one of the four drawn three-day home Tests with New Zealand later in 1949.

That 1949 season was the one in which Gladwin went closest to doing the double, combining his 117 wickets with 903 runs that included his one first-class century – an unbeaten 124 at Trent Bridge. But it was a disappointing year for Derbyshire as they slipped back to fifteenth place after being involved in the Championship race in each of the previous two seasons under the captaincy of the greying and bespectacled Eddie Gothard, the former Staffordshire player who was then into his forties and who later also served Derbyshire as honorary secretary and treasurer.

In 1947, when Gothard did the hat-trick against Middlesex, Derbyshire headed the table for a short time, but, handicapped by injuries and Test calls, finished fifth. In 1948, when Gothard bowled Bradman, they were at the top in early June and late July, still had a chance of the title until the closing stages, but ended sixth – two dozen points behind the new champions Glamorgan, who were well beaten at Derby in their only meeting that year.

It was by no mere coincidence that Derbyshire prospered during those two seasons while George Pope was back in their ranks. Nor was it just a coincidence that they floundered the following year when they were again without him. Since Gladwin's near-miss, only Derek Morgan and Geoff Miller have been anywhere near emulating Pope's double for Derbyshire, though that achievement has petered out among all the counties now that fewer fixtures are fulfilled in the Championship in these days of so much one-day cricket. Miller might have got there during the 1984 season in which he at last scored his maiden century, in his 380th innings, if England had not needed him for the one-day internationals and two Tests.

After a climb back to fifth place in 1950 with Pat Vaulkhard captain of a team that contained the new imports Arnold Hamer, John Kelly and Derek Morgan, Derbyshire enjoyed some further seasons of comparative prosperity in the early post-war years under the leadership of Guy Willatt and Donald Carr. Team spirit flourished, batting was more consistently reliable, and one of the best attacks in the country had the magnificent support of the superb close catching of Carr, Morgan, Alan Revill and Charlie Elliott besides George Dawkes' exemplary wicketkeeping.

There was also a slightly built, ruddy-faced off-spinner from Grassmoor named Edwin Smith who went near a hat-trick in dismissing eight Worcestershire batsmen for 21 runs at the age of seventeen in only his second first-class game in 1951. When he took five Australian wickets for 36 runs two years later he was hailed by the Aussies' former Test bowler Bill O'Reilly as 'undoubtedly England team material', and 'one of the most promising lads I have seen in this country, or my own, in years'. Although that Test prophecy did not come true, Smith met with enough success over the next twenty years to join Jackson, Gladwin, Bestwick, Mitchell, Morgan and Copson as one of the seven bowlers to have taken more than a thousand wickets for Derbyshire. And after that he rendered further service by following another Smith (Denis) in the post of county coach that had previously been filled by Harry Elliott, the man who discovered him.

Willatt, a left-hand batsman with a crouching stance and determined defence, had played some first-class cricket either side of the war with Cambridge University (where he also gained a soccer Blue), Nottinghamshire and Scotland. His release from teaching at Repton for the summer term was therefore seen as a real coup for Derbyshire, though his settling into the captaincy had to be delayed when he had the misfortune to suffer a fracture of the left hand when struck by a rising ball in only the second over of his debut against Warwickshire at Edgbaston. When he took over for the first of his four seasons in charge in 1951 he immediately gained the respect of his men by abolishing separate dressing rooms for amateurs and professionals. He also won approval for his willingness to press for victory with what he called 'method cricket' that was 'gritty, purposeful, combative and intensely competitive' without compromising his belief in fair play.

In 1952, when Willatt won the toss in all but two of fifteen home games, and eighteen times in all, Derbyshire finished fourth. That was then their highest position since the war, but two years later they improved on that by rising to third for the first time since 1937 despite being held up by the weather in crucial matches during the last few weeks. In the intervening season of 1953 they were joint sixth, but had bad luck with injuries and were also handicapped by the weather. No decision could be reached in three matches. Even so, they defeated Surrey's habitual champions by an innings inside two days, beat Leicestershire, one of the title contenders, by ten wickets, and twice dismissed the Australian tourists for less than 200 in a drawn game at Chesterfield.

Willatt's appointment as headmaster at Heversham Grammar School in Westmorland (he was later head at Pocklingtion School in Yorkshire) caused the vacancy in the Derbyshire captaincy that Donald Carr filled from 1955 to 1962 – though he, too, had an unpleasant setback soon after being confirmed in the post. Shortly before Christmas in 1954 he was suddenly taken ill with appendicitis and had to be rushed to Derbyshire Royal Infirmary for an operation. Only once during his eight seasons as skipper did Derbyshire end outside the top half of the table, and in that year, 1956, they were third before dropping to twelfth in failing to add to their seven wins in their last eight Championship games. A faltering finish also prevented their being higher than fourth in 1957. They led the way early in June, but gained only three victories in sixteen Championship matches in the wetter second half of the season.

In taking over from Willatt, after being his vice-captain for two years, Carr paid this tribute:

'His keenness for the game, his determination and his will to win, together with a completely straight and open approach to those under him, meant that it was a privilege and a pleasure to play with him. I believe there is no happier side than Derbyshire in the County Championship, and this can be attributed to a very large extent to Guy Willatt's ability to blend eleven individuals into a well-disciplined and loyal team.'

Carr himself earned high praise as a captain, quite apart from his ability as a batsman whose 2,165 runs in 1959 have yet to be bettered for one season by a Derbyshire player. Tony Lock, the Surrey, Leicestershire and England spinner who had Carr as his captain on the MCC's first 'A' team tour abroad, to Pakistan in 1955-56, chose Derbyshire's Old Reptonian as captain of the team he would 'most like to field with' in his book *For Surrey and England*. Lock, no mean fielder himself, wrote:

'Carr is a great skipper in the field. He has a wonderful personality and he starts with the admiration, as well as the respect, of all his fellow players. Furthermore, he understands people. He is not a worrier. He offers advice when he thinks something should be done, but he does not bicker and bully his bowlers. He will always pay the bowler the courtesy of speaking to him before moving a fielder – as, indeed, does Peter May [Lock's captain with Surrey]. The main reason, however, why I prefer Donald Carr to Peter May is that he is such a superb fieldsman. May is good, but Carr can be brilliant. Carr seldom misses even half-chances. Either at slip or short-leg, he is an expert.'

As with George Pope, so with Donald Carr. Not just by coincidence did Derbyshire decline straight after Carr had left to join J G Dunbar at Lord's as secretarial assistant to S C ('Billy') Griffith, the former Cambridge University, Surrey and Sussex wicketkeeper-batsman who, as a makeshift opener in the West Indies in 1948, had become the only man to score his maiden first-class century on his England debut. Carr, who filled the vacancy created by Griffith's promotion to succeed Ronald Aird as MCC secretary, was later secretary of both the newly-formed Test and County Cricket Broad and the reconstituted Cricket Council, the governing body for England and Wales, until his retirement in 1986 – and after that he retained some influence as chairman of the TCCB Pitches Committee.

23. The Other Honours

With the best of the rest deliberately left to the last in this final chapter, so that some bright notes can at least be struck after Derbyshire's fortunes have again been at such a low ebb in recent years, we now come to the trophies the club have claimed since topping the Championship in 1936.

The first one after that success took thirty-nine years to arrive (excluding the six of the war), but it was well worth waiting for. In 1981 they became the first winners of the NatWest Bank Trophy, beating Northamptonshire at Lord's in the tightest of finishes – by losing fewer wickets with the scores tied. Geoff Cook set a captain's example for Northants, who made 235 for nine in their sixty overs, by scoring a century and partnering Wayne Larkins (52) in an opening stand of 99. Derbyshire, with their imports from overseas, John Wright (76) and Peter Kirsten (63) setting the pace, replied with 235 for six, Geoff Miller beating Allan Lamb's throw at the stumps as he tore through for the decisive single off the last ball.

Miller had started the season as Derbyshire's captain, but it was Barry Wood who lifted the trophy. The former Lancashire and England all-rounder took over only six weeks before the final after having been among those who failed to persuade Miller not to resign. And that was not the only resignation during another year of disruption behind the Derbyshire scenes. The chairman and chief executive also quit. Miller, too, was also on his way out with his fellow Test player Mike Hendrick, who moved to Nottinghamshire, and, although he changed his mind (and regained his England place), he did eventually leave for a short stint with Essex before having one last season with Derbyshire in 1990.

Neither was it long before Wood also left. For the fifth time in nine years Derbyshire were forced into a change of captain during a season when, during the first week of May in 1983, he stepped down because he found it 'too demanding to captain the team and maintain the standards I have set myself'. Bob Taylor and David Steele, the grey-haired former England batsman recruited from Northamptonshire, were others who had given up the post because they thought it was affecting their play. Miller's contract as a player was also terminated by mutual consent a couple of months after Wood's departure, by which time Kim Barnett's appointment, after Miller had temporarily taken over again, had brought what proved to be record stability to the captaincy.

The next prize to be landed by Derbyshire was a comparatively minor one – the Asda Challenge Trophy at Scarborough in September 1985. After beating Yorkshire by three wickets in the last over they won more comfortably, by eight wickets, in the final against Lancashire, who had knocked out Nottinghamshire in their semi-final. Five of Lancashire's wickets were taken for 32 runs by Roger Finney, the right-hand batsman and left-arm bowler from

Darley Dale who had been awarded his county cap during a break because of snow after taking five of Northamptonshire's first six wickets on a bleak opening day of that season at Derby.

Also deserving of mention is a success for Derbyshire's second team, although they achieved it at the end of the 1987 season in which they were a poor last in the Second XI Championship without a win in their thirteen games. Under the captaincy of former first-team opener Alan Hill, they retrieved some credibility by beating Hampshire's second team by seven wickets in the Bain Dawes Trophy final at Southampton, thanks chiefly to an opening partnership of 140 between Iain Anderson and Andrew Brown. Last place has since been the Seconds' lot on three more occasions in four years, but when, in 2002, they avoided it during that period they soared to runners-up – as fractionally close on average to becoming champions as they had been in 1999.

Derbyshire went near another trophy in 1987. Their first team were in contention for the Sunday League title under its new sponsorship of Refuge Assurance, after eighteen seasons as the John Player League, right until their last match, having been in the top three since the end of May. Ironically, Somerset edged Derbyshire into fifth place, and out of £2,625 in prize money, by gaining one more away win than Barnett's men with a victory by fourteen runs at Derby on that final day. Both had forty points – six behind Worcestershire's champions.

That season, in which Derbyshire's sixth place was their highest in the Championship for twenty years, was also notable for the first tied match in their history (with Gloucestershire in Bristol), and for the dismissal by Bernie Maher, successor to Bob Taylor behind the stumps, of more batsmen (76) than any first-class wicketkeeper in the country. On the downside, however, there was more friction off the field. Roger Pearman spoke of a breakdown in his relations with the committee when he resigned after five and a half years as chief executive.

Derbyshire's next major honour, their first for nine years and only their third in the 120 since their formation, came in 1990, when they did hold on to win the Refuge Assurance League title – and with it £24,000 that was especially welcome for a county with the smallest membership among the first class. Again the last day was decisive, and it pitted them at Derby against Essex, a county they had not defeated in any competition since 1982, and who had outplayed them in winning by an innings and 94 runs inside two days in a Championship match at the same ground the previous Thursday and Friday. This time they upset the form book by overhauling Essex's 40-over total of 203 for four off the third ball of their final over for the loss of five wickets. Adrian Kuiper, the Western Province all-rounder who was in his only season with the county after having scored 2,000 runs and taken 100 wickets in South Africa's Currie Cup, reached a half-century off thirty-one balls.

Derbyshire had shared the early Sunday League lead with Kent and Middlesex after winning four of their first five matches, and, with games in hand, returned to the top of the table, alongside Middlesex, in mid-July. The finish was so close that Lancashire – last-day winners by 49 runs against Warwickshire at Old Trafford, where they had lost to Derbyshire by just five runs a few weeks earlier – would have been champions on away wins if Derbyshire had not taken all four points from that vital home game with Essex on 26 August. And if Derbyshire and Lancashire had both lost that day Middlesex would have taken the title on run rate with a victory against Yorkshire at Scarborough. As it was, Middlesex, winners of nine of their first ten games, suffered their fourth defeat in the last six – the penultimate one of which, at Derby of all places, had been washed out before a result could be reached. Yorkshire beat them by 44 runs after making their biggest Sunday League total of 271 for seven.

Derbyshire gave themselves the chance to land the first League and Cup double in the third year of the Refuge Assurance Cup by reaching the final with a 22-run win over Nottinghamshire at Derby, but their total of 197 for seven in their 40 overs on a sluggish pitch at Birmingham was overhauled by Middlesex, who had beaten Lancashire in the other semi-final at Old Trafford, with five wickets and two deliveries to spare. After losing three wickets in a dozen balls, Middlesex required 62 from the last ten overs, 30 from five, and seven from the last. The boundary that took the £6,000 first prize south, and left Derbyshire with the consolation of half as much, was struck after there had almost been a run-out in levelling the scores off the third ball.

Only a few weeks before that match, in which Barnett was Derbyshire's lone survivor from the team that had won the NatWest Bank Trophy nine years before, Middlesex had been beaten by 171 runs at Derby – their only defeat in the twenty-two games they played on the way to winning the Championship that was then sponsored by Britannic Assurance. That, however, had become a hollow victory with the deduction of twenty-five points that dropped Derbyshire four places to twelfth in the final table. Having had a pitch there reported unsatisfactory for being too green earlier in the season, they had shaven to order and, as a consequence, had produced one deemed 'clearly unsuitable for first-class cricket' by the umpires and inspectors who included Donald Carr. But it certainly did not appear to trouble Mike Gatting, the Middlesex captain. His unbeaten century prompted Chris Middleton, another of Derbyshire's chairmen, to thank him in writing for his enterprising attitude in circumstances the home county found embarrassing.

No Derbyshire batsman emulated Gatting in that game, but there were a record number of first-class hundreds for the county during the season in other matches – twenty-one of them. The five scored by Barnett took him past Denis Smith's Derbyshire record of thirty that had stood for forty years. Final placings of third (for the first time since 1954) and fifth in the

Championship in the next two seasons were followed by another plunge to the depths in 1993, but that was the year in which Derbyshire had another trophy to display. This was the Benson and Hedges Cup, which they won for the first time in its twenty-two years by beating Lancashire, the hot favourites they had incensed less than a fortnight earlier by hinting at alleged malpractice during their Championship match at Derby. Lancashire won that one by 111 of the record aggregate of 1,497 runs for a game involving Derbyshire (beating the 1,391 when Essex were at Chesterfield in 1904). The unpleasantness arose on the final afternoon when Wasim Akram, the Pakistan all-rounder, took six wickets for eleven runs after Derbyshire had reached nearly 250 for two. Derbyshire were sufficiently concerned about the ball he used to send it to the TCCB at Lord's for examination, but officialdom decided there was no case to answer.

The omens were far from bright for Derbyshire when they themselves went to Lord's. They entered the final burdened by the financial crisis that threatened their existence, making three senior officials redundant, and without their West Indian fast bowler Ian Bishop through injury. That was the first year in which the competition was played on a straight knock-out basis, the group matches having been abolished, and Derbyshire got through to the last stage by beating Gloucestershire in Bristol (though only by losing fewer wickets with the scores level), Middlesex at Derby (by 14 runs), Somerset at Taunton (by 6-3 in a bowling contest after the match had been declared void with Derbyshire at 69 for no wicket before the downpour), and Northants at Derby (by eight wickets).

Derbyshire had been badly awry when the 'bowl out', cricket's version of soccer's penalty shoot-out, had first been used in the NatWest Bank Trophy competition in 1991 because no play had been possible, even with the extension to a second day, in their first-round match with Hertfordshire at Bishop's Stortford. The bowlers had let them down that time, only Steve Goldsmith registering a strike, with their ninth delivery, after five players from each team had been required to bowl two deliveries each at the three unguarded stumps, and the home side had won 2-1 with four deliveries to spare. Against Somerset, Derbyshire relied more on their batsmen after the TCCB had refused permission to postpone the game for a week. All their choices managed one hit, and Chris Adams two, whereas only four of Somerset's had the chance to try their aim after Andy Hayhurst, a few years later briefly a Derbyshire Director of Cricket, had missed twice.

It looked like being third time unlucky for Derbyshire after their defeats by Kent and Hampshire in the finals of 1978 and 1988 when their top four batsmen, Barnett, Bowler, Morris and Adams, were all back in the pavilion with only 66 scored against Lancashire in sixteen overs. There had been an even worse start in the final flop against Hampshire, the first four wickets having gone down for 32 runs – all of them to Steve Jefferies, a South African left-arm pace bowler who had been with Derbyshire six years before. They cost him only one run in eight balls, and he later struck again for a full return of five for 13, the best for a B & H final. With wides and no-balls counting against bowlers, only nine of those runs came from the bat – and one of those resulted from the missing of a catch that would have given him a hat-trick.

Derbyshire's total of 117 was the lowest in a final of either of the two major knock-out competitions at Lord's, and Hampshire, who had been the only first-class county not to have appeared in a final at cricket's headquarters, lost only three wickets in overtaking it. Even Michael Holding, who that season set a world record for the limited-overs game with 8-21 (figures that included nine no-balls debited against him) in Derbyshire's defeat of Sussex at Hove in the first round of the NatWest Bank Trophy, was powerless to prevent Hampshire picking up the £21,000 first prize. Derbyshire had to be content with half that, to add to their £2,500 as NatWest losing quarter-finalists.

In the 1993 final, with Wasim coming in for particularly heavy punishment, Cork led an astonishing recovery, pluckily aided by Tim O'Gorman and Karl Krikken in stands of 109 and 77, and he was still there eight runs from a century when the allotted 55 overs were completed at 252 for six. It was the first major highlight of Cork's already burgeoning career, to be followed two years later by his explosive entry into Test cricket with 7-43 in West Indies' second innings at Lord's (the best bowling figures by an Englishman on his debut) and a hat-trick two matches later at Manchester – the first for England in a Test since Surrey's Peter Loader performed the feat in 1957. Sydney-born John Ferris had taken 7-37 in South Africa's second innings at Cape Town on his debut for England in 1891, but he had previously played in eight Tests for Australia.

I have good reason to remember Lancashire's reply in that Benson and Hedges final of 1993, for I was among those who were thoroughly soaked in the crush to get off the top of the uncovered stand at the nursery end when heavy rain stopped play just as 112 runs were needed to beat Derbyshire with seventeen overs and eight wickets in hand. Nothing seemed more certain than that the match would have to go into a second day, so my son and son-in-law had no hesitation in agreeing with me that it would be best to get back home as soon as possible and change into dry clothes. Imagine our surprise, therefore, when we arrived home in time to see play again in progress on the television screen, sterling work by the ground staff having limited the hold-up to just over an hour.

And what a dramatic finish there was to be seen. When the slight figure of Frank Griffith stepped up to shoulder the intimidating burden of bowling the last over in deteriorating light the result was still tantalisingly in the balance with eleven runs required and four wickets left. Neil Fairbrother, Lancashire's captain, took a single off the second ball, Phillip DeFreitas, who was to switch to Derbyshire for the following season, hit the next one to a height that kept wicketkeeper Krikken waiting for the catch, and the television replay's verdict narrowly saved Fairbrother from being run out off the fourth.

With the game as good as over by the time the last ball came to be bowled, the unbeaten Fairbrother was left thirteen runs from a century as Derbyshire ended winners by six and a very welcome £30,000 better off in addition to the winning bonuses they picked up in the previous rounds. Cork's Gold Award earned him £600. Kim Barnett declared it to be his greatest day as captain, but the lifting of the club's alarming overdraft was still a year away as the annual loss soared to the new heights of more than £120,000 and yet another chairman, Chris Middleton, decided that, after eight years in office, it was time to go.

Lancashire extracted ample revenge when Derbyshire next reached a Lord's final, overwhelming them by nine wickets to carry off the NatWest Trophy in 1998.

So there you have it – one Championship lost and another gained, two major knock-out trophies, and a Sunday League title. Those have been Derbyshire's chief visits to cricket's honours board – plus, regrettably, plenty of wooden spoons for the humble pie. Though the signs have been far from good of late, those with Derbyshire's best interests at heart can only hope for another revival in the not-too-distant future.

Appendix 1

DERBYSHIRE'S FINAL AVERAGES IN 1874, YEAR OF THE LOST TITLE
(Eleven-a-side matches only: Played 6, won 3, drew 3)

BATTING

	Inns	NO	Runs	HS	Avg
Dr W G Curgenven	4	0	113	74	28.25
T Foster	3	1	54	20	27.00
A Shuker	2	0	46	41	23.00
J Platts	9	2	121	29	17.28
G Frost	10	1	151	37	16.77
J Smith	6	2	63	27	15.75
R P Smith	10	0	156	50	15.60
S Richardson	6	0	88	28	14.66
W Hickton	3	0	37	21	12.33
J Flint	7	1	70	24	11.66
Rev W J Humble	7	1	51	19*	8.50
R Allsop	6	0	45	33	7.50

Also batted: T Attenborough 0, 0; W Boden 2*, 0; J Cooke 0, 6; J Davidson 0*, 3; E Estridge 4; W Mycroft 2, 0*, 0, 0*, 0; W Rigley 25; U Sowter 19; J Tye 0, 11, 3, 7, 11, 0.
Not out

BOWLING

	Overs	Maidens	Runs	Wickets	Avg
W Hickton	103.2	42	144	17	8.47
W Mycroft	210	104	262	25	10.48
J Flint	255	91	402	28	14.35
J Davidson	48	13	89	5	17.80
J Platts	147	48	258	12	21.50

Also bowled: T Attenborough 12-2-24-2; T Foster 7-0-22-1; J Smith 8-2-27-1; R P Smith 2-1-6-0; J Tye 17.1-4-33-1.
Four balls per over)

Catches: 6 – Platts; 5 – Flint; 4 – Smith (J), Smith (R P); 3 – Allsop, Humble, Tye; 2 – Frost (G), Frost (J), Richardson, sub; 1 – Curgenven, Davidson (J), Hickton, Rigley, Shuker.

County Championship appearances (4 matches): 4 – Flint, Frost (G), Smith (R P); 3 – Humble, Mycroft, Platts, Smith (J), Tye; 2 – Allsop, Attenborough, Hickton, Richardson, Shuker; 1 – Boden, Cooke, Curgenven, Davidson (J), Estridge, Foster, Frost (J). 20 players.

Other appearances (2 matches): 2 – Allsop, Flint, Frost (G), Platts, Richardson, Tye.
1 – Curgenven, Davidson (J), Foster, Humble, Mycroft, Rigley, Smith (J), Smith (R P), Sowter.

DERBYSHIRE'S FINAL AVERAGES IN THEIR TITLE YEAR OF 1936
(For all first-class matches: Played 30, won 14, drew 12, lost 4)

BATTING

	Inns	NO	Runs	HS	Avg
T S Worthington	43	3	1,519	174	37.97
L F Townsend	46	4	1,454	*182	34.61
D Smith	47	5	1,333	169	31.73
A E Alderman	49	5	1,145	79	26.02
A F Skinner	21	0	443	62	21.09
C S Elliott	27	3	503	97	20.95
H Elliott	43	9	666	*79	20.17
G H Pope	7	1	112	*62	18.66
H Storer	13	0	205	62	15.76
E Carrington	14	1	199	72	15.30
A V Pope	40	6	460	40	13.52
G R Langdale	5	0	64	29	12.80
A W Richardson	34	4	378	50	12.60
T B Mitchell	34	7	272	45	10.07
S M Hunt	5	0	48	17	9.60
W H Copson	31	14	95	17	5.58

Also batted: T R Armstrong 8*, 7, 1; J D Gilbert 16; G R Jackson 4;
Capt N A McD Walker 13, 7; A Townsend 21, 1, 1; W W Hill-Wood 10, 38.
Not out

BOWLING

	Overs	Maidens	Runs	Wickets	Avg
W H Copson	863.3	226	1,919	153	12.54
G H Pope	76.1	16	161	9	17.88
A V Pope	918	279	1,795	99	18.13
L F Townsend	559	165	1,198	59	20.30
T B Mitchell	700.2	73	2,593	121	21.42
T S Worthington	258.5	57	675	22	30.68

Also bowled: T R Armstrong 33-9-95-4; C S Elliott 5.5-1-22-1; S M Hunt 1-0-3-0;
G R Langdale 26-3-95-0; A F Skinner 3-0-15-0; D Smith 3-1-13-1;
A Townsend 6-1-23-0; Capt N A McD Walker 2-0-10-0.

Catches: 54 – Elliott (H), plus 13 stumped; 22 – Smith; 19 – Worthington; 17 – Mitchell;
15 – Alderman, Skinner, Townsend (L F); 11 – Copson; 8 – Pope (A V), Elliott (C S);
7 – Richardson, Storer; 2 – Hill-Wood, Pope (G H), sub; 1 – Carrington.

County Championship appearances (28 matches): 28 – Alderman, Elliott (H), Pope (A V), Smith, Townsend (L F); 26 – Copson, Mitchell, Richardson, Worthington; 18 – Elliott (C S); 12 – Skinner; 9 – Storer; 7 – Carrington; 5 – Hunt; 4 – Pope (G H); 3 – Langdale; 2 – Armstrong, Townsend (A); 1 – Hill-Wood, Walker. 20 players.

Other appearances (2 matches): 2 – Alderman, Carrington, Copson, Elliott (H), Mitchell, Pope (A V), Townsend, Worthington; 1 – Elliott (C S), Gilbert, Jackson (G R), Pope (G H), Skinner, Smith.

Appendix 2. DERBYSHIRE'S CHAMPIONSHIP MATCHES IN 1874

(Match 1)   LANCASHIRE v DERBYSHIRE
At Old Trafford, Manchester, on June 5 and 6, 1874
Derbyshire won by nine wickets

DERBYSHIRE	*First innings*		*Second innings*	
R P Smith	c McIntyre b Watson	13	b Watson	6
A Shuker	c Hillkirk b Watson	41		
G Frost	st Roberts b Watson	32	not out	18
S Richardson	run out	10		
R Allsop	st Roberts b Watson	33		
J T B D Platts	c & b Watson	11	not out	3
T Attenborough	b Watson	0		
J Tye	st Roberts b Watson	0		
J Smith	not out	15		
J Flint	c McIntyre b Watson	23		
W Mycroft	b Watson	2		
	Extras (b 10)	10	Extras (b 3)	3
	Total	190	Total (1 wkt)	30

Fall: 1-14, 2-78, 3-91, 4-101, 5-135, 6-145, 7-145, 8-148, 9-188.

1-21.

Bowling: Watson 53.3-5-118-9; McIntyre 35-17-44-0; Jervis 9-6-4-0; Harrop 7-2-14-0.

Watson 10.3-3-13-1; McIntyre 11-4-14-0.

LANCASHIRE	*First innings*		*Second innings*	
W R Craig	c Flint b Mycroft	7	c Platts b Mycroft	1
G Walsh	b Flint	0	(5) b Platts	15
J R Hillkirk	b Mycroft	1	(6) b Tye	26
A Watson	c Allsop b Mycroft	0	(7) lbw b Flint	8
H Mellor	c Smith (J) b Flint	17	(2) b Flint	3
W S Jervis	b Mycroft	0	(8) c sub b Platt	6
A Ollivant	b Mycroft	6	(9) not out	24
R Roberts	c Shuker b Mycroft	0	(10) c Richardson b Flint	20
R Walker	c Smith (R P) b Flint	1	(4) b Flint	19
W McIntyre	not out	5	(3) c Flint b Mycroft	48
J Harrop	c Tye b Flint	0	b Attenborough	5
	Extras (lb 1)	1	Extras (b 3, lb 3)	6
	Total	38	Total	181

Fall: 1-0, 2-1, 3-3, 4-12, 5-12, 6-20, 7-20, 8-24, 9-34.

1-15, 2-18, 3-51, 4-73, 5-99, 6-117, 7-137, 8-161, 9-178.

Bowling: Mycroft 15-7-23-6; Flint 15-6-14-4

Mycroft 21-5-43-2; Flint 29-4-83-4; Platts 14-5-39-2; Attenborough 7-1-9-1; Tye 1.1-0-1-1.

(Match 2)   DERBYSHIRE v KENT

At Derby Road ground, Wirksworth on July 13 and 14, 1874

Derbyshire won by 33 runs

DERBYSHIRE	*First innings*		*Second innings*	
R P Smith	lbw b Remnant	5	(6) b Willsher	3
G Frost	c & b Draper	37	c Henty b Willsher	17
J H Frost	c McCanlis G, b Willsher	18	b Willsher	1
W G Curgenven	b Willsher	5	(1) b Draper	0
J T B D Platts	c Remnant b Draper	16	(4) b Willsher	0
Rev W J Humble	b Draper	7	(7) b Willsher	0
J Tye	b Willsher	3	(8) b Draper	7
W Boden	not out	2	(5) c Byass b Willsher	0
J Flint	b Willsher	4	(9) c Draper b Willsher	2
W Mycroft	c Hodgson b Willsher	0	(11) not out	0
J Cooke	b Willsher	0	(10) b Draper	6
	Extras	0	Extras	0
	Total	97	Total	36

Fall: 1-15, 2-56, 3-65, 4-65, 5-88, 6-91, 7-95, 8-95, 9-97.

1-16, 2-17, 3-17, 4-17, 5-21, 6-21, 7-22, 8-28, 9-36.

Bowling: Willsher 35-18-36-6; Draper 18-9-22-3; Remnant 16-2-39-1.

Willsher 16-7-22-7; Draper 17-11-14-3.

KENT	*First innings*		*Second innings*	
W McCanlis	c Platts b Flint	6	c Smith b Platts	28
T F Swinford	b Mycroft	6	(3) b Mycroft	1
G H Remnant	run out	1	(4) c Humble b Flint	11
R G Hodgson	c Frost (JH) b Mycroft	0	(6) b Mycroft	4
G McCanlis	b Mycroft	2	(2) b Flint	2
W Draper	b Mycroft	0	(10) b Mycroft	3
H Croxford	lbw b Flint	3	(5) b Platts	0
J E Byass	b Mycroft	0	(7) run out	2
E Willsher	c Frost (G) b Flint	7	(8) c Platts b Flint	9
E Henty	c Frost (JH) b Flint	0	(9) not out	7
R Palmer	not out	0	b Flint	5
	Extras	0	Extras (b 2, lb 1)	3
	Total	25	Total	75

Fall: 1-12, 2-12, 3-13, 4-13, 5-13, 6-18, 7-18, 9-19.

1-6, 2-9, 3-39, 4-39, 5-44, 6-47, 7-58, 8-61, 9-66.

Bowling: Flint 12-6-17-4; Mycroft 11-8-8-5.

Flint 27-9-35-4; Mycroft 39-30-15-3; Platts 12-5-22-2.

(Match 3)   KENT v DERBYSHIRE

At Higher Common ground, Tunbridge Wells on July 23, 24 and 25, 1874

Derbyshire won by three wickets

KENT

	First innings		*Second innings*	
W McCanlis	b Flint	6	b Mycroft	19
G McCanlis	c Smith (J) b Hickton	30	c Smith (J) b Hickton	27
W Foord-Kelcey	c & b Flint	8	(4) b Mycroft	4
E Henty	run out	5	(7) b Platts	0
T F Swinford	b Hickton	6	b Mycroft	9
R G Hodgson	b Hickton	5	(8) c Humble b Foster	47
E A White	b Hickton	12	(9) c Humble b Hickton	5
E A Parke	b Mycroft	9	(6) b Hickton	47
W Draper	c & b Hickton	0	(10) b Hickton	5
G H Remnant	c Flint b Hickton	0	(11) not out	12
E Willsher	not out	3	(3) c Smith (J) b Hickton	11
	Extras (b 2, lb 1, nb 1)	4	Extras (b 5, lb 6, nb 1)	12
	Total	88	Total	198

Fall: 1-16, 2-32, 3-51, 4-51,
5-61, 6-66, 7-75, 8-75, 9-75.

1-42, 2-56, 3-67, 4-71,
5-80, 6-91, 7-159, 8-180, 9-180.

Bowling: Flint 31-11-45-2; Hickton 24-15-15-6; Mycroft 11-2-24-1.

Flint 7-1-13-0; Hickton 45-19-68-5; Mycroft 52-24-73-3; Foster 7-0-22-1; Platts 5-0-10-1.

DERBYSHIRE

	First innings		*Second innings*	
R P Smith	b Foord-Kelcey	0	b Draper	47
G Frost	b Foord-Kelcey	22	(3) c Remnant b Willsher	4
R Allsop	c & b Willsher	0	(5) b Draper	4
S Richardson	c Henty b Draper	10	lbw b Draper	24
T Foster	c Henty b Foord-Kelcey	15	(8) not out	19
J Smith	b Foord-Kelcey	0	(2) c McCanlis (W) b Willsher	27
W Hickton	b Draper	21	b Draper	13
Rev W J Humble	run out	1	(9) not out	19
W Mycroft	st Henty b Draper	0		
J T B D Platts	b Draper	11	(6) c Foord-Kelcey b Draper	26
J Flint	not out	0		
	Extras (b 7, nb 1, w 4)	12	Extras (b 2, lb 1, w 10)	13
	Total	92	Total (7 wkts)	196

Fall: 1-5, 2-11, 3-30, 4-54,
5-54, 6-61, 7-65, 8-65, 9-91.

1-49, 2-57, 3-105,
4-108, 5-138, 6-151, 7-155.

Bowling: Foord-Kelcey 28-14-40-4; Willsher 19-9-20-1; Draper 17-11-20-4.

Foord-Kelcey 23-8-43-0; Wilsher 32-15-80-2; Draper 48.2-32-51-5; Remnant 5-3-6-0; Parke 2-0-3-0.

(March 4)   DERBYSHIRE v LANCASHIRE
At Saltergate ground, Chesterfield on August 3 and 4 (no play on August 5)
Match drawn

LANCASHIRE	*First innings*	
V P F A Royle	b Hickton	1
A Watson	b Hickton	8
R Roberts	b Hickton	4
J R Hillkirk	c Smith (RP) b Attenb'gh	15
F W Wright	b Davidson	43
E J Bousfield	c Tye b Davidson	13
C W Landon	b Davidson	11
W M Hardcastle	c Davidson b Hickton	9
R Dewhurst	not out	26
W McIntyre	b Hickton	13
F R Reynolds	b Hickton	0
	Extras (b 9, lb 9)	18
	Total	161

Fall: 1-5, 2-18, 3-19, 4-71, 5-92, 6-99, 7-117, 8-119, 9-161.

Bowling: Hickton 34.2-8-61-6; Flint 16-4-31-0; Attenborough 5-1-15-1; Davidson 19-5-33-3; Tye 3-2-3-0.

DERBYSHIRE	*First innings*	
R P Smith	b Watson	17
G Frost	b Watson	17
A Shuker	st Roberts b Watson	5
E Estridge	run out	4
J Smith	b Watson	7
W Hickton	b McIntyre	3
Rev W J Humble	b McIntyre	10
J Flint	c Bousfield b Watson	24
J Tye	b Watson	11
T Attenborough	c Bousfield b McIntyre	0
J Davidson	not out	0
	Extras (b 4, lb 2)	6
	Total	104

Fall: 1-23, 2-29, 3-33, 4-46, 5-51, 6-55, 7-85, 8-103, 9-103.

Bowling: McIntyre 34.2-17-41-3; Watson 29-10-43-6; Landon 5-1-14-0.

OTHER MATCHES PLAYED BY DERBYSHIRE IN 1874

Nottingham (May 25 & 26): Sixteen of Derbyshire 163 (R P Smith 42) and 28 for one; Eleven of Nottinghamshire 65 (R Daft 19) and 125 (T Wright 34). J Flint and W Mycroft each took eight wickets. Sixteen of Derbyshire won by 14 wickets.

Derby (July 2 & 3): Derbyshire 105 (W G Curgenven 34) and 223 for seven (Curgenven 74, R P Smith 50); Yorkshire United 232 (C Ullathorne 59, W Smith 50,
J Hicks 49, W Mycroft 5-77). Match drawn.

Leeds (August 7 & 8): Yorkshire United 183 (R Iddison 52, J Flint 4-59, J T B D Platts 3-75) and 152 for nine (J Hicks 34 not out, Flint 4-38, Platts 4-62); Derbyshire 129 (W Rigley 25). Mycroft and Hickton absent. Match drawn.

Derby (August 17, 18 & 19): Sixteen of Derbyshire 202 (W Hickton 52, J Tye 43) and 52 for two (Platts 26, Rigley 18 not out); United Eleven 167 (W G Grace 51, F Silcock 49, J Flint 6-51) and 86 (Flint 5-36, W Mycroft 3-32). Sixteen of Derbyshire won by 13 wickets.

Appendix 3. DERBYSHIRE'S CHAMPIONSHIP MATCHES IN 1936

(Match 1)   HAMPSHIRE v DERBYSHIRE
At Southampton on May 6, 7 and 8, 1936
Match drawn; Hampshire won on first innings

HAMPSHIRE	*First innings*		*Second innings*	
R H Moore	c Smith b Townsend	11	lbw b Pope (A V)	100
N McCorkell	c Hill-Wood b Townsend	41	b Pope (A V)	1
C G A Paris	st Elliott b Mitchell	1	b Worthington	101
C P Mead	c Pope (G H) b Mitchell	62		
J Arnold	c Worth'ton b Townsend	8	b Copson	65
W L Creese	b Pope (G H)	36	c Hill-Wood b Copson	25
G S Boyes	b Mitchell	25	b Pope (A V)	13
A E Pothecary	c Townsend b Mitchell	7	not out	20
G Hill	run out	10		
H M Lawson	not out	36	c Pope (G H) b Pope (A V)	0
O W Herman	b Pope (G H)	5		
	Extras (b 6, lb 6, w 1, nb 1)	14	Extras (b 1, lb 8)	9
	Total	256	Total (7 wkts dec)	334

Fall: 1-21, 2-30, 3-82, 4-92, 5-167, 6-167, 7-175, 8-206, 9-241.

1-8, 2-191, 3-221, 4-293, 5-304, 6-307, 7-334.

Bowling: Copson 17-6-26-0; Pope (A V) 16-3-45-0; Mitchell 28-5-93-4; Townsend 33-15-43-3; Pope (G H) 18.1-4-35-2.

Copson 22-6-74-2; Pope (A V) 29.5-3-122-4; Mitchell 9-0-52-0; Townsend 2-0-14-0; Pope (G H) 8-1-26-0; Worthington 11-1-37-1.

DERBYSHIRE	*First innings*		*Second innings*	
A E Alderman	b Lawson	25	c Herman b Hill	23
D Smith	c Pothecary b Lawson	8	c McCorkell b Creese	34
L F Townsend	b Herman	5	b Herman	67
T S Worthington	b Herman	9	b Herman	44
E Carrington	c Pothecary b Herman	72	b Creese	1
G H Pope	b Creese	12	c Paris b Creese	4
A V Pope	c Paris b Boyes	10	c McCorkell b Boyes	1
W W Hill-Wood	c Moore b Boyes	10	c McCorkell b Herman	38
H Elliott	not out	35	not out	1
T B Mitchell	c Lawson b Herman	8	not out	27
W H Copson	b Lawson	3		
	Extras (lb 5, nb 2)	7	Extras (b 4, lb 8, w 1, nb 2)	15
	Total	204	Total (8 wkts)	255

Fall: 1-20, 2-33, 3-49, 4-49, 5-82, 6-113, 7-136, 8-179, 9-195.

1-64, 2-64, 3-148, 4-155, 5-173, 6-174, 7-220, 8-235.

Bowling: Lawson 19.4-4-41-3; Herman 16-1-57-4; Creese 12-3-24-1; Boyes 15-2-65-2; Hill 4-1-10-0.

Lawson 29-8-31-0; Herman 29-7-88-3; Creese 28-10-40-3; Hill 13-5-28-1; Boyes 18-8-27-1; Arnold 4-0-26-0.

(Match 2)   KENT v DERBYSHIRE
At Gravesend on May 13 and 14, 1936
Kent won by 10 wickets

DERBYSHIRE	*First innings*		*Second innings*	
A E Alderman	b Freeman	47	lbw b Wright	20
D Smith	st Levett b Freeman	17	c Ashdown b Watt	12
T S Worthington	c Levett b Wright	7	c Todd b Watt	0
L F Townsend	st Levett b Freeman	9	b Watt	4
E Carrington	b Freeman	1	c Valentine b Wright	25
C S Elliott	st Levett b Wright	3	b Freeman	0
A V Pope	c Wright b Freeman	10	b Freeman	18
N A McD Walker	c Lewis b Freeman	13	c & b Wright	7
H Elliott	not out	4	not out	5
T B Mitchell	c Lewis b Freeman	2	b Wright	1
W H Copson	c Fagg b Wright	1	b Wright	0
	Extras (b 5)	5	Extras (b 7)	7
	Total	119	Total	99

Fall: 1-42, 2-53, 3-68, 4-72,
5-89, 6-99, 7-103, 8-112, 9-115.

1-19, 2-19, 3-27,
4-62, 5-63, 6-81, 7-87, 8-93, 9-99.

Bowling: Todd 6-1-16-0; Watt 7-0-20-0;
Freeman 16-7-29-7; Wright 14.1-1-49-3.

Todd 9-1-16-0;
Freeman 11-2-23-2;
Watt 9-3-22-3; Wright 7-1-31-5.

KENT	*First innings*		*Second innings*	
W H Ashdown	c Elliott (H) b Pope (A V)	2	not out	17
A Fagg	b Copson	14	not out	25
F E Woolley	c Copson b Mitchell	34		
B H Valentine	lbw b Mitchell	28		
L J Todd	c Elliott (H) b Copson	55		
I Akers-Douglas	c Smith b Mitchell	12		
D V P Wright	b Copson	21		
W H V Levett	c Worthington b Copson	2		
A E Watt	c Alderman b Worthington	8		
A P Freeman	b Copson	0		
C Lewis	not out	1		
	Extras (lb 2)	2	Extras	0
	Total	179	Total (no wkt)	42

Fall: 1-9, 2-33, 3-73, 4-86, 5-122,
6-157, 7-170, 8-171, 9-171.

Bowling: Copson 16-2-57-5; Pope (A V)
9-1-36-1; Mitchell 11-1-52-3; Townsend
7-0-14-0; Walker 2-0-10-0; Worthington 2-1-8-1.

Copson 5-1-26-0;
Pope (A V) 4-0-11-0;
Mitchell 1-0-5-0.

Scorecards from 1874 and 1936

(Match 3)   DERBYSHIRE V SURREY
At Derby on May 16 and 18, 1936
Derbyshire won by 16 runs

DERBYSHIRE	*First innings*		*Second innings*	
D Smith	c Brown b Gover	0	c Watts b Parker	15
A E Alderman	b Gover	77	c Brooks b Brown	43
T S Worthington	bw b Watts	1	c Gover b Parker	11
L F Townsend	c Parker b Brown	38	c Brooks b Parker	3
E Carrington	c Parker b Gover	12	b Brown	10
G H Pope	c Fishlock b Brown	14	c & b Brown	9
A W Richardson	c Barling b Brown	0	c Barling b Brown	4
A V Pope	c Fishlock b Brown	9	lbw b Gover	1
H Elliott	b Gover	6	b Watts	24
T B Mitchell	b Gover	3	st Brooks b Brown	3
W H Copson	not out	5	not out	0
	Extras (b 3, lb 5, nb 2)	10	Extras (b 9, lb 2, nb 2)	13
	Total	175	Total	136

Fall: 1-1, 2-4, 3-109, 4-126, 5-146, 6-146, 7-150, 8-166, 9-166.

1-37, 2-59, 3-67, 4-87, 5-97, 6-102, 7-103, 8-122, 9-136.

Bowling: Gover 18.5-4-63-5; Watts 8-3-22-1; Parker 8-1-21-0; Brown 15-2-52-4; Gregory 1-0-7-0.

Gover 16-6-25-1; Parker 15-4-26-3; Watts 8.1-4-19-1; Brown 20-7-53-5.

SURREY	*First innings*		*Second innings*	
A Sandham	b Copson	53	b Copson	5
R J Gregory	lbw b Mitchell	22	lbw b Pope (A V)	0
H S Squires	lbw b Mitchell	0	st Elliott b Mitchell	20
T H Barling	b Copson	95	b Copson	23
L B Fishlock	c & b Mitchell	0	not out	17
E W Whitfield	b Copson	1	lbw b Copson	0
E A Watts	b Mitchell	3	b Copson	8
F R Brown	b Copson	0	b Copson	2
J F Parker	not out	18	b Copson	0
E W J Brooks	lbw b Copson	0	c Smith b Pope (A V)	0
A R Gover	c Worthington b Pope (A)	9	c Elliott b Copson	0
	Extras (b 9, lb 7, nb 1)	17	Extras (lb 1, w 1)	2
	Total	218	Total	77

Fall: 1-46, 2-46, 3-102, 4-103, 5-104, 6-115, 7-116, 8-207, 9-209.

1-2, 2-10, 3-49, 4-53, 5-53, 6-63, 7-73, 8-75, 9-76.

Bowling: Copson 16-6-33-5; Pope (A V) 20.5-5-50-1; Worthington 9-2-19-0; Mitchell 23-5-89-4; Townsend 6-1-10-0.

Copson 14-5-19-7; Pope (A V) 9-3-8-2; Worthington 4-1-20-0; Mitchell 6-0-28-1.

(Match 4)   DERBYSHIRE v SUSSEX
At Queen's Park, Chesterfield on May 23, 25 and 26, 1936
Derbyshire won by an innings and 25 runs

DERBYSHIRE	*First innings*	
A E Alderman	b Nye	0
D Smith	c Langridge (John) b Tate	53
T S Worthington	b Nye	9
L F Townsend	not out	182
E Carrington	b Parks (J H)	35
H Elliott	b Wensley	63
G H Pope	c Parks (J H) b Tate	4
A W Richardson	c Holmes b Parks (J H)	5
A V Pope	c Cornford b Nye	2
T B Mitchell	c Langridge Jm b Parks J	0
W H Copson	c Holmes b Parks (J H)	17
	Extras (b 9, lb 5, nb 3)	17
	Total	387

Fall: 1-0, 2-23, 3-112, 4-177, 5-314, 6-321, 7-351, 8-366, 9-367.

Bowling: Nye 24-2-100-3; Tate 27-7-42-2; Wensley 31-8-78-1;
Parks (J H) 25.1-7-56-4; Oakes 11-3-36-0; Langridge (James) 19-2-58-0.

SUSSEX	*First innings*		*Second innings*	
J H Parks	c Elliott b Copson	3	c Smith b Pope (A V)	3
John Langridge	b Copson	3	c Worthington b Pope (G H)	58
H W Parks	lbw b Mitchell	15	c Worthington b Pope (G H)	52
G Cox	not out	42	c Worthington b Copson	39
James Langridge	lbw b Mitchell	0	b Copson	27
A J Holmes	run out	1	lbw b Townsend	5
M W Tate	b Copson	34	c Pope (A V) b Townsend	6
C Oakes	b Copson	0	b Copson	31
A F Wensley	b Copson	1	not out	5
W Cornford	c Copson b Mitchell	7	b Pope (A V)	0
J K Nye	c Copson b Mitchell	14	c Elliott b Pope (A V)	0
	Extras (b 2, lb 7)	9	Extras (lb 7)	7
	Total	129	Total	233

Fall: 1-6, 2-7, 3-35, 4-35,
5-37, 6-86, 7-86, 8-88, 9-105.

1-4, 2-113, 3-126, 4-163, 5-172,
6-184, 7-227, 8-228, 9-229.

Bowling: Copson 17-5-42-5; Pope (A V)
8-4-7-0; Pope (G H) 6-3-7-0; Mitchell
14.4-2-64-4.

Pope (A V) 16.2-7-14-3; Copson
18-7-36-3; Worthington 5-2-11-0;
Pope (G H) 18-3-42-2; Mitchell
19-0-97-0; Townsend 21-12-26-2.

(Match 5)   GLOUCESTERSHIRE v DERBYSHIRE
At Bristol on May 27 and 28, 1936
Derbyshire won by 10 wickets

GLOUC'SHIRE	*First innings*		*Second innings*	
R A Sinfield	b Pope (G H)	9	lbw b Pope (A V)	9
C J Barnett	b Copson	59	b Pope (A V)	11
B O Allen	st Elliott b Mitchell	1	c Copson b Worthington	18
W R Hammond	b Pope (A V)	20	c Elliott b Worthington	8
W L Neale	run out	16	st Elliott b Mitchell	28
E J Stephens	b Copson	5	b Mitchell	22
D A C Page	c Elliott b Pope (A V)	7	b Mitchell	0
C Monks	b Copson	12	b Mitchell	17
V Hopkins	c Elliott b Mitchell	2	c & b Mitchell	0
T W Goddard	b Copson	23	c sub b Pope (A V)	4
G P Surman	not out	2	not out	0
	Extras (lb 8)	8	Extras (b 3, lb 2, w 1)	6
	Total	164	Total	123

Fall: 1-37, 2-40, 3-94, 4-94,
5-99, 6-110, 7-132, 8-135, 9-139.

1-11, 2-40, 3-40, 4-53, 5-84, 6-84,
7-110, 8-110, 9-119.

Bowling: Copson 20.3-2-72-4; Pope (A V)
18-6-26-2; Pope (G H) 6-0-18-1; Mitchell
12-1-33-2; Worthington 4-0-7-0.

Copson 6-1-26-0; Pope (A V)
13-3-30-3; Worthington 8-0-21-2;
Mitchell 10.1-2-40-5.

DERBYSHIRE	*First innings*		*Second innings*	
A E Alderman	lbw b Sinfield	42	not out	40
D Smith	b Surman	1	not out	51
T S Worthington	b Surman	8		
L F Townsend	c Hammond b Sinfield	6		
E Carrington	c Hammond b Sinfield	0		
H Elliott	c Hopkins b Sinfield	61		
A W Richardson	b Sinfield	7		
A V Pope	c Monks b Goddard	40		
G H Pope	b Sinfield	7		
T B Mitchell	not out	5		
W H Copson	b Sinfield	2		
	Extras (b 5, lb 8, nb 1)	14	Extras (lb 2, w 1, nb 1)	4
	Total	193	Total (no wkt)	95

Fall: 1-7, 2-19, 3-33, 4-33,
5-71, 6-85, 7-162, 8-172, 9-183.

Bowling: Surman 15-1-60-2; Monks 5-2-3-0;
Goddard 33-12-62-1; Sinfield 23.3-8-54-7.

Surman 8-2-23-0; Monks 5-2-4-0;
Goddard 10-3-29-0; Sinfield
10-1-23-0; Neale 4.3-0-12-0.

(Match 6)   DERBYSHIRE v ESSEX
At Derby on May 30, June 1 and 2, 1936
Match drawn; Essex won on first innings. No play on first and third days (rain)

DERBYSHIRE	*First innings*	
A E Alderman	b Nichols	26
D Smith	lbw b Nichols	5
H Storer	b Nichols	0
L F Townsend	b Stephenson	5
T S Worthington	not out	85
E Carrington	c Ashton b Stephenson	1
H Elliott	lbw b Smith (T P B)	9
A W Richardson	lbw b Smith (T P B)	10
A V Pope	lbw b Smith (T P B)	0
T B Mitchell	b Evans	25
W H Copson	b Smith (T P B)	1
	Extras (b 9, lb 2, nb 1)	12
	Total	179

Fall: 1-19, 2-21, 3-43, 4-43, 5-53, 6-79, 7-99, 8-101, 9-178.

Bowling: Nichols 17-2-66-3; Stephenson 15-6-41-2; Smith (T P B) 10.2-1-32-4; Evans 0-1-29-1.

ESSEX	*First innings*	
J R Sheffield	b Pope (A V) b Copson	24
R M Taylor	lbw b Worthington	14
M S Nichols	c Smith b Mitchell	76
J O'Connor	b Worthington	1
J A Cutmore	c & b Mitchell	45
C T Ashton	not out	13
T N Pearce	st Elliott b Mitchell	6
	Extras (b 4, lb 9, w 1)	14
	Total (6 wkts)	193

Did not bat: J W A Stephenson, W J Evans, T H Wade, T P B Smith.

Fall: 1-41, 2-41, 3-47, 4-162, 5-175, 6-193.

Bowling: Copson 16-5-32-1; Pope (A V) 15-2-40-0; Worthington 12-1-31-2; Mitchell 9.5-0-52-3; Townsend 13-5-24-0.

(Match 7)   NORTHAMPTONSHIRE v DERBYSHIRE
At Northampton on June 3, 4 and 5, 1936
Derbyshire won by seven wickets

NORTHANTS	First innings		Second innings	
A H Bakewell	b Copson	6	(4) b Copson	0
N Grimshaw	st Elliott b Mitchell	11	(1) b Copson	0
D Brookes	c Richardson b Pope (A V)	5	(2) b Copson	26
J E Timms	lbw b Mitchell	0	(3) lbw b Townsend	69
A L Cox	c Copson b Townsend	2	st Elliott b Mitchell	2
K C James	lbw b Mitchell	0	c Mitchell b Pope (A V)	29
H J H Lamb	c Townsend b Mitchell	17	b Copson	8
A D G Matthews	c Smith b Townsend	0	b Townsend	4
R J Partridge	c Elliott b Townsend	2	not out	3
C Perkins	not out	4	c Elliott b Copson	14
E W Clark	c & b Townsend	0	b Copson	0
	Extras (lb 2)	2	Extras (lb 3)	3
	Total	59	Total	158

Fall: 1-6, 2-23, 3-23, 4-23, 5-23, 6-47, 7-51, 8-53, 9-59.

1-0, 2-63, 3-71, 4-78, 5-120, 6-132, 7-147, 8-154, 9-158.

Bowling: Copson 11-3-15-1; Pope (A V) 8-3-7-1; Townsend 10-7-3-4; Mitchell 16-4-32-4.

Copson 22-13-24-6; Pope (A V) 14-3-33-1; Townsend 16-5-30-2; Mitchell 22-1-68-1.

DERBYSHIRE	First innings		Second innings	
A E Alderman	c Matthews b Clark	0	lbw b Matthews	0
D Smith	c & b Matthews	4	c Bakewell b Clark	59
H Storer	c Bakewell b Clark	12	c Partridge b Clark	18
L F Townsend	c & b Matthews	31	not out	17
T S Worthington	c Bakewell b Clark	9	not out	30
H Elliott	b Matthews	4		
S M Hunt	c Cox b Perkins	17		
A W Richardson	b Matthews	2		
A V Pope	c Clark b Matthews	8		
T B Mitchell	b Perkins	0		
W H Copson	not out	0		
	Extras (b 1, lb 2, w 2, nb 1)	6	Extra (b 1)	1
	Total	93	Total (3 wkts)	125

Fall: 1-0, 2-4, 3-25, 4-36, 5-47, 6-75, 7-77, 8-93, 9-93.

1-0, 2-78, 3-79.

Bowling: Clark 24-12-24-3; Matthews 31.1-9-42-5; Perkins 8-2-16-2; Bakewell 1-0-2-0; Partridge 1-0-3-0.

Clark 12-1-39-2; Matthews 13-5-23-1; Partridge 13-2-37-0; Perkins 12-2-25-0.

(Match 8)   DERBYSHIRE v GLOUCESTERSHIRE
At Derby on June 10 and 11, 1936
Derbyshire won by 10 wickets

GLOUC'SHIRE	*First innings*		*Second innings*	
C J Barnett	c Elliott (H) b Mitchell	39	lbw b Pope (A V)	27
R W Haynes	b Copson	8	b Copson	16
W L Neale	b Mitchell	21	c Smith b Pope (A V)	6
E J Stephens	c Elliott (H) b Copson	8	b Mitchell	16
R A Sinfield	c Worthington b Mitchell	1	not out	41
C C Dacre	c Elliott (H) b Mitchell	4	c Elliott (H) b Copson	0
D A C Page	b Mitchell	2	b Mitchell	10
J F Crapp	not out	4	c Smith b Pope (A V)	22
C Monks	b Mitchell	6	b Mitchell	2
V Hopkins	c & b Mitchell	0	b Mitchell	16
T W Goddard	b Copson	0	c Elliott (H) v Pope (A V)	29
	Extras (w 2)	2	Extras (b 6, lb 2, w 1)	9
	Total	95	Total	194

Fall: 1-18, 2-64, 3-77, 4-79, 5-80,
6-83, 7-88, 8-94, 9-94.

1-26, 2-52, 3-64, 4-69, 5-90,
6-96, 7-115, 8-154, 9-157.

Bowling: Copson 12.5-2-34-3; Pope (A V)
7-3-19-0; Worthington 5-1-14-0; Mitchell
10-2-26-7.

Copson 19-2-48-2; Pope (A V)
16.3-6-29-4; Worthington
4-0-10-0; Mitchell 30-4-98-4.

DERBYSHIRE	*First innings*		*Second innings*	
A W Richardson	c Crapp b Monks	3		
A E Alderman	c Dacre b Stephens	0	not out	23
D Smith	run out	14	not out	63
L F Townsend	c Page b Sinfield	20		
T S Worthington	c & b Haynes	90		
H Elliott	c Crapp b Goddard	22		
S M Hunt	b Goddard	16		
C S Elliott	b Neale	18		
A V Pope	c Page b Neale	11		
T B Mitchell	b Haynes	3		
W H Copson	not out	2		
	Extra (lb 1)	1	Extras (lb 4, w 1)	5
	Total	200	Total (no wkt)	91

Fall: 1-0, 2-6, 3-31, 4-70, 5-143,
6-153, 7-172, 8-195, 9-198.

Bowling: Stephens 8-1-24-1; Monks 8-1-35-1;
Goddard 27-5-65-2; Sinfield 25-10-39-1;
Neale 5.1-0-18-2; Haynes 7-1-18-2.

Stephens 6-0-30-0;
Monks 6-0-12-0; Haynes 9.5-1-22-0;
Neale 4-2-6-0; Page 5-3-16-0.

(Match 9)   DERBYSHIRE v YORKSHIRE
At Queen's Park, Chesterfield on June 13, 15 and 16, 1936
Match drawn; Derbyshire won on first innings. Rain prevented play on the first day

DERBYSHIRE	*First innings*	
A E Alderman	Smailes b Bowes	4
D Smith	lbw b Bowes	9
H Storer	lbw b Smailes	1
T S Worthington	c Sellers b Turner	80
L F Townsend	c Sellers b Smailes	101
H Elliott	b Bowes	17
A F Townsend	c Sellers b Bowes	1
S M Hunt	lbw b Fisher	10
A W Richardson	lbw b Bowes	5
A V Pope	not out	7
T B Mitchell	run out	12
	Extras (b 3, lb 3)	6
	Total	253

Fall: 1-11, 2-14, 3-18, 4-172, 5-201, 6-208, 7-227, 8-229, 9-234.

Bowling: Bowes 32.3-12-66-5; Smailes 24-5-60-2; Fisher 24-10-60-1; Turner 13-3-40-1; Hutton 2-0-9-0; Wilson 7-2-12-0.

YORKSHIRE	*First innings*		*Second innings*	
H Sutcliffe	c Elliott b Pope (A V)	6	c Elliott b Townsend (L F)	11
L Hutton	lbw b Mitchell	8	not out	56
A B Sellers	c & b Mitchell	2	not out	25
C Turner	b Mitchell	8		
J R S Raper	lbw b Mitchell	15		
J H Pearson	b Townsend (L F)	10		
G A Wilson	b Mitchell	1		
A Wood	b Pope (A V)	26		
T F Smailes	b Pope (A V)	13		
H Fisher	c Worthington b Mitchell	1		
W E Bowes	not out	10		
	Extras (b 3, lb 6)	9	Extras (b 4, lb 6)	10
	Total	109	Total (1 wkt)	102

Fall: 1-13, 2-14, 3-21, 4-24, 5-44, 6-48, 7-62, 8-99, 9-100.

1-36.

Bowling: Worthington 12-1-19-0; Pope (A V) 14.2-6-14-3; Mitchell 18-0-60-6; Townsend (L F) 5-1-7-1; Hunt 1-0-3-0.

Worthington 6-0-13-0; Pope (A V) 18-9-15-0; Mitchell 10-1-26-0; Townsend (L F) 7-4-15-1; Townsend (A) 6-1-23-0.

(Match 10)   DERBYSHIRE v SOMERSET
At Rutland ground, Ilkeston on June 17 and 18, 1936
Somerset won by 10 wickets

DERBYSHIRE	*First innings*		*Second innings*	
H Storer	lbw b Hunt	18	lbw b Wellard	2
D Smith	c Hazell b Hunt	22	c Luckes b Andrew	11
T S Worthington	c Andrews b Hunt	21	c Bennett b Andrews	2
L F Townsend	c Hazell b Hunt	0	c Wellard b Andrews	0
A E Alderman	lbw b Wellard	18	c Barnwell b Buse	3
E Carrington	c Lee b Wellard	0	c Gimblett b Wellard	0
H Elliott	lbw b Hunt	14	c Gimblett b Wellard	4
A W Richardson	c Andrews b Hunt	19	run out	7
A V Pope	Lee b Wellard	23	b Andrews	18
T B Mitchell	c Wellard b Hunt	6	c Gimblett b Wellard	4
W H Copson	not out	0	not out	3
	Extras (b 6, lb 5)	11	Extras (b 2, lb 5, nb 1)	8
	Total	152	Total	62

Fall: 1-44, 2-49, 3-49, 4-76,
5-77, 6-87, 7-114, 8-124, 9-146.

1-12, 2-15, 3-17, 4-17,
5-20, 6-21, 7-22, 8-38, 9-53.

Bowling: Wellard 14-3-43-3; Andrews
3-0-12-0; Hazell 12-2-37-0; Hunt 19.2-7-49-7.

Wellard 11.2-1-29-4;
Andrews 10-0-21-4, Buse 2-1-4-1.

SOMERSET	*First innings*		*Second innings*	
H Gimblett	c Mitchell b Townsend	43	not out	15
F S Lee	c Carrington b Worthington	32	not out	10
R A Ingle	c Alderman b Mitchell	10		
G M Bennett	b Mitchell	18		
H F T Buse	c Elliott b Worthington	37		
A W Wellard	c Worthington b Mitchell	3		
W H R Andrews	lbw b Mitchell	14		
W T Luckes	b Worthington	8		
C J P Barnwell	c Alderman b Mitchell	3		
H Hunt	not out	11		
H L Hazell	b Worthington	7		
	Extras (b 2, lb 2)	4	Extras	0
	Total	190	Total (no wkt)	25

Fall: 1-48, 2-60, 3-89, 4-127,
5-138, 6-160, 7-160, 8-167, 9-176.

Bowling: Copson 2-0-3-0; Pope (A V) 4-0-12-0;
Mitchell 22-2-90-5; Townsend 15-6-50-1;
Worthington 17.2-4-31-4.

Worthington 3-0-7-0;
Copson 2.2-0-18-0.

(Match 11)   WARWICKSHIRE v DERBYSHIRE
At Edgbaston, Birmingham on June 20, 22 and 23, 1936
Derbyshire won by an innings and 10 runs

DERBYSHIRE	*First innings*	
H Storer	lbw b Mayer	3
D Smith	c Smart by Mayer	0
T S Worthington	c Kilner b Mayer	81
L F Townsend	b Hollies	23
A E Alderman	lbw b Wyatt	34
C S Elliott	c Mayer b Hollies	97
H Elliott	c Paine b Hollies	33
A W Richardson	c Croom b Paine	32
A V Pope	not out	6
T B Mitchell	b Hollies	3
W H Copson	run out	3
	Extras (lb 3)	3
	Total	318

Fall: 1-0, 2-9, 3-79, 4-116, 5-208, 6-246, 7-298, 8-308, 9-315.

Bowling: Mayer 26-9-48-3; Wyatt 21-8-44-1; Santall 8-3-17-0; Hollies 35-10-114-4; Paine 30-8-83-1; Croom 2-0-9-0.

WARWICKSHIRE	*First innings*		*Second innings*	
N Kilner	c Townsend b Mitchell	13	b Townsend	48
A J Croom	c Elliott (C S) b Townsend	11	c Smith b Copson	0
W A Hill	c Storer b Townsend	0	b Copson	4
R E S Wyatt	c Storer b Townsend	14	b Townsend	72
F R Santall	b Mitchell	18	c Elliott (H) b Townsend	0
H E Dollery	c Alderman b Mitchell	22	lbw b Townsend	4
E G Barber	c Worthington b Townsend	13	b Townsend	9
G A E Paine	hit wkt b Mitchell	0	hit wkt b Mitchell	41
J H Mayer	not out	7	b Townsend	3
J Smart	c Smith b Mitchell	7	c & b Townsend	2
E Hollies	b Townsend	1	not out	8
	Extras (lb 3)	3	Extras (lb 8)	8
	Total	109	Total	199

Fall: 1-25, 2-25, 3-25, 4-59, 5-61, 6-92, 7-94, 8-96, 9-105.

1-0, 2-8, 3-88, 4-88, 5-94, 6-108, 7-149, 8-169, 9-179.

Bowling: Pope (A V) 7-3-10-0; Worthington 4-1-10-0; Townsend 18-4-44-5; Mitchell 15-2-42-5.

Copson 22-7-30-2; Pope (A V) 7-3-8-0; Townsend 32-11-46-7; Mitchell 23.4-2-99-1; Worthington 8-5-8-0.

(Match 12) DERBYSHIRE v WORCESTERSHIRE
At Queen's Park, Chesterfield on June 24, 25 and 26, 1936
Derbyshire won by three wickets

WORCS	*First innings*		*Second innings*	
C H Bull	b Copson	0	lbw b Copson	0
E G Righton	lbw b Mitchell	19	run out	1
S H Martin	b Copson	41	c Storer b Townsend	48
H H I H Gibbons	b Copson	99	lbw b Mitchell	12
B W Quaife	lbw b Mitchell	15	b Townsend	16
J Horton	b Copson	34	c Storer b Townsend	16
Hon C J Lyttelton	b Pope (A V)	4	not out	44
R Howorth	b Pope (A V)	3	c Pope (A V) b Mitchell	5
V Grimshaw	b Copson	0	b Townsend	1
R T D Perks	not out	4	c Copson b Pope (A V)	9
P F Jackson	c Storer b Pope (A V)	0	run out	1
	Extras (lb 14)	14	Extras (b 5, lb 3, w 1)	9
	Total	233	Total	162

Fall: 1-0, 2-30, 3-83, 4-106,
5-216, 6-225, 7-227, 8-229, 9-231.

1-1, 2-1, 3-23, 4-67,
5-91, 6-96, 7-121, 8-134, 9-160.

Bowling: Copson 27-8-34-5; Pope (A V)
25-9-41-3; Mitchell 23-0-83-2;
Worthington 7-1-32-0; Townsend 12-3-29-0.

Copson 18-4-38-1;
Pope (A V) 14-6-22-1; Mitchell
13-1-59-2; Townsend 13-3-34-4.

DERBYSHIRE	*First innings*		*Second innings*	
H Storer	c Quaife b Jackson	26	lbw b Perks	62
D Smith	b Perks	2	b Perks	0
T S Worthington	b Jackson	33	b Perks	35
L F Townsend	st Quaife b Howorth	76	b Howorth	7
A E Alderman	lbw b Howorth	25	not out	29
C S Elliott	b Jackson	0	c Quaife b Perks	0
H Elliott	b Perks	30	c Grimshaw b Howorth	4
A W Richardson	not out	23	b Perks	2
A V Pope	c Jackson b Perks	0	not out	1
T B Mitchell	c Perks b Howorth	10		
W H Copson	b Perks	0		
	Extras (b 11, lb 10, nb 1)	22	Extras (b 2, lb 3, w 1, nb 3)	9
	Total	247	Total (7 wkts)	149

Fall: 1-7, 2-51, 3-92, 4-175,
5-176, 6-176, 7-224, 8-224, 9-247.

1-0, 2-86, 3-99, 4-120,
5-122, 6-143, 7-145.

Bowling: Perks 20.2-2-56-4; Jackson
34-10-64-3; Howorth 25-8-79-3;
Martin 15-6-26-0.

Perks 20-4-63-5; Jackson 4-1-8-0;
Howorth 19.1-4-56-2; Martin
5-0-13-0.

SCORECARDS FROM 1874 AND 1936

(Match 13)   DERBYSHIRE v LANCASHIRE
At Buxton on June 27, 29 and 30, 1936
Match drawn; Lancashire won on first innings. Little play on second day.

LANCASHIRE	*First innings*		*Second innings*	
F Watson	lbw b Mitchell	29	lbw b Copson	11
J L Hopwood	lbw b Mitchell	13	c Elliott (H) b Copson	17
J Iddon	lbw b Copson	51	c Elliott (H) b Pope (A V)	15
E Paynter	b Worthington	15	lbw b Copson	7
C Washbrook	lbw b Worthington	0	c Townsend b Pope (A V)	8
N Oldfield	c & b Copson	44	c Worthington b Copson	6
W Farrimond	lbw b Copson	0	b Pope (A V)	0
W H L Lister	c Worthington b Townsend	0	b Pope (A V)	0
R Pollard	c Elliott (H) b Copson	5	not out	16
F S Booth	b Worthington	20	run out	5
F M Sibbles	not out	5	b Pope (A V)	3
	Extras (lb 12)	12	Extras (b 4, lb 2)	6
	Total	194	Total	94

Fall: 1-30, 2-65, 3-89, 4-89, 5-154,
6-154, 7-155, 8-161, 9-166.

1-16, 2-45, 3-53, 4-61, 5-70, 6-70,
7-71, 8-78, 9-78.

Bowling: Copson 17-6-35-4; Pope (A V)
8-3-10-0; Worthington 18.3-8-28-3; Mitchell
19-2-68-2; Townsend 16-3-41-1.

Copson 16-3-35-4;
Pope (A V) 15.4-0-53-5.

DERBYSHIRE	*First innings*		*Second innings*	
H Storer	b Sibbles	1	lbw b Iddon	10
T S Worthington	c Farrimond b Booth	3	lbw b Sibbles	25
L F Townsend	c & b Sibbles	1	b Oldfield	23
D Smith	c Pollard b Booth	0	not out	11
A E Alderman	lbw b Booth	18	lbw b Hopwood	15
H Elliott	c Watson b Booth	11	not out	1
C S Elliott	lbw b Booth	5		
A W Richardson	b Booth	7		
A V Pope	c Farrimond b Pollard	0		
T B Mitchell	not out	4		
W H Copson	b Pollard	0		
	Extras (b 2, lb 5, nb 4)	11	Extras (b 2, lb 3, w 1, nb 1)	7
	Total	61	Total (4 wkts)	92

Fall: 1-3, 2-5, 3-5, 4-7, 5-24,
6-29, 7-54, 8-55, 9-61.

1-30, 2-30, 3-76. 4-89.

Bowling: Booth 18-6-18-6; Sibbles 16-5-17-2;
Pollard 10.5-2-15-2.

Booth 10-2-18-0; Sibbles 14-5-19-1;
Hopwood 18-3-27-1;
Pollard 4-2-5-0; Iddon 9-4-9-1;
Watson 3-0-7-0; Oldfield 1-1-0-1.

(Match 14)   WORCESTERSHIRE v DERBYSHIRE
At Worcester on July 1, 2 and 3, 1936
Derbyshire won by innings and 123 runs. Rain held up play on first and second days.

DERBYSHIRE	*First innings*	
H Storer	c King b Grimshaw	52
A E Alderman	b Perks	61
D Smith	c Lyttelton b Jackson	25
T S Worthington	b Perks	1
L F Townsend	c Martin b Howorth	1
C S Elliott	b Jackson	49
H Elliott	c Horton b Martin	1
A W Richardson	c Howorth b Martin	10
A V Pope	not out	28
	Extras (b 3, lb 3)	6
	Total (8 wkts dec)	234

Did not bat: T B Mitchell, W H Copson.

Fall: 1-108, 2-119, 3-121, 4-122, 5-156, 6-162, 7-180, 8-234.

Bowling: Perks 21-4-50-2; Jackson 17.4-2-64-2; Howorth 37-17-61-1; Martin 16-4-44-2; Grimshaw 4-2-9-1.

WORCS	*First innings*		*Second innings*	
C H Bull	c Elliott (H) b Copson	2	b Copson	1
V Grimshaw	b Pope (A V)	0	c Elliott (H) b Copson	6
S H Martin	c Worthington b Pope (A V)	1	c Townsend b Mitchell	3
H H I H Gibbons	lbw b Copson	1	c Elliott (C S) b Copson	3
B W Quaife	b Copson	0	lbw b Copson	4
Hon C J Lyttelton	st Elliott (H) b Mitchell	11	b Copson	0
J Horton	c Elliott (H) b Copson	22	not out	15
R Howorth	c Elliott (H) b Copson	7	b Copson	3
B P King	c Elliott (H) b Pope (A V)	10	c Smith b Copson	0
R T D Perks	b Pope (A V)	4	c Elliott (H) b Mitchell	10
P F Jackson	not out	6	c & b Mitchell	0
	Extras	0	Extras (lb 4)	4
	Total	64	Total	47

Fall: 1-2, 2-2, 3-4, 4-4, 5-6, 6-27, 7-43, 8-48, 9-57.

1-0, 2-1, 3-5, 4-7, 5-7, 6-12, 7-16, 8-28, 9-47.

Bowling: Copson 18-2-38-5; Pope (A V) 16.3-10-12-4; Mitchell 2-0-14-1.

Copson 13-6-16-7; Pope (A V) 5-4-1-0; Mitchell 9.4-1-26-3.

(Match 15)   DERBYSHIRE v WARWICKSHIRE
At Queen's Park, Chesterfield on July 4, 6 and 7, 1936
Derbyshire won by an innings an 159 runs

WARWICKSHIRE	*First innings*		*Second innings*	
N Kilner	c Pope (A V) b Copson	12	c Elliott (H) b Pope (A V)	14
A J Croom	b Mitchell	7	c Storer b Pope (A V)	1
W A Hill	b Mitchell	5	c Elliott (H) v Pope (A V)	0
R E S Wyatt	c Elliott (H) b Copson	1	lbw b Townsend	40
F R Santall	b Copson	2	b Mitchell	3
H E Dollery	st Elliott (H) b Mitchell	22	b Copson	29
T Collin	b Pope (A V)	23	c Richardson b Townsend	14
J H Mayer	c Richardson b Copson	24	c Pope (A V) b Townsend	2
J Smart	b Mitchell	7	c Mitchell b Copson	0
K Wilmot	st Elliott H b Mitchell	1	c Storer b Copson	0
E Hollies	not out	13	not out	1
	Extras	0	Extras (lb 1)	1
	Total	117	Total	105

Fall: 1-15, 2-24, 3-25, 4-27, 5-27,
6-67, 7-81, 8-101, 9-102.

1-1, 2-1, 3-35, 4-47, 5-70, 6-94,
7-104, 8-104, 9-104.

Bowling: Copson 15-3-38-4; Pope (A V)
12-5-18-1; Mitchell 12.5-0-52-5; Townsend
4-1-9-0.

Copson 10.4-2-31-3;
Pope (A V) 10-5-12-3; Mitchell
10-0-26-1; Townsend 11-6-19-3;
Worthington 3-0-16-0.

DERBYSHIRE	*First innings*	
H Storer	c Wyatt b Mayer	0
A E Alderman	c Hollies b Wilmot	7
T S Worthington	c Collin b Hollies	163
L F Townsend	b Collin	32
D Smith	lbw b Mayer	24
C S Elliott	lbw b Mayer	49
H Elliott	c Collin b Hollies	40
A W Richardson	b Collin	1
A V Pope	b Wilmot	28
T B Mitchell	not out	16
W H Copson	c Smart b Wilmot	11
	Extras (b 4, lb 2)	6
	Total	381

Falls: 1-0, 2-26, 3-82, 4-131, 5-258, 6-321, 7-326, 8-332, 9-365.

Bowling: Mayer 21-4-61-3; Wyatt 11-4-37-0; Wilmot 18-2-75-3;
Hollies 30-3-100-2; Collin 20-2-80-2; Santall 5-2-11-0; Croom 4-1-11-0.

(Match 16)   DERBYSHIRE v HAMPSHIRE
At Queen's Park, Chesterfield on July 8, 9 and 10, 1936
Match drawn; Derbyshire won on first innings. No play on last day (bad weather)

HAMPSHIRE	*First innings*		*Second innings*	
J Arnold	c Skinner b Pope (A V)	24	not out	6
N McCorkell	lbw b Copson	3	lbw b Copson	2
A E Pothecary	c Elliott (H) b Pope (A V)	2	c Worthington b Pope (A V)	1
C P Mead	lbw b Copson	1	not out	1
R H Moore	lbw b Mitchell	7		
W L Creese	b Pope (A V)	14		
W Lancashire	b Mitchell	13		
G S Boyes	c Elliott (H) b Pope (A V)	1		
W L Budd	lbw b Mitchell	4		
H M Lawson	not out	11		
O W Herman	b Mitchell	5		
	Extras (lb 2, w 1)	3	Extras	0
	Total	88	Total (2 wkts)	10

Fall: 1-20, 2-23, 3-24, 4-38, 5-50,   1-7, 2-8.
6-54, 7-66, 8-68, 9-80.

Bowling: Copson 6-1-24-2; Pope (A V)   Copson 5-3-3-1;
11-5-15-4; Mitchell 6-1-46-4.   Pope (A V) 5-1-7-1.

DERBYSHIRE	*First innings*	
A E Alderman	b Boyes	9
T S Worthington	c McCorkell b Creese	17
L F Townsend	not out	153
A F Skinner	st McCorkell b Boyes	19
D Smith	c Pothecary b Lancashire	28
C S Elliott	run out	17
H Elliott	b Herman	6
A W Richardson	b Herman	4
A V Pope	c Arnold b Moore	37
T B Mitchell	not out	27
	Extras (b 6, lb 9, nb 4)	19
	Total (8 wkts dec)	336

Did not bat: W H Copson.

Fall: 1-35, 2-51, 3-74, 4-125, 5-175, 6-212, 7-218, 8-284.

Bowling: Herman 26-5-92-2; Lawson 8-1-27-0; Creese 21-7-72-1;
Boyes 19-3-56-2; Budd 7-1-19-0; Lancashire 6-0-23-1; Moore 5-0-28-1.

(Match 17)   LANCASHIRE v DERBYSHIRE
At Old Trafford, Manchester on July 11, 13 and 14, 1936
No result; No play on first and second days (rain)

DERBYSHIRE	*First innings*	
A E Alderman	b Sibbles	32
T S Worthington	c Nutter b Sibbles	1
L F Townsend	b Sibbles	46
D Smith	b Sibbles	5
A V Pope	c Washbrook b Sibbles	3
C S Elliott	not out	10
S M Hunt	c Duckworth b Sibbles	0
H Elliott	c Hudson b Sibbles	3
T B Mitchell	c Iddon b Booth	6
	Extras (b 6, lb 2, nb 2)	10
	Total (8 wkts dec)	116

Did not bat: A W Richardson, W H Copson.

Fall: 1-3, 2-84, 3-89, 4-93, 5-94, 6-94, 7-107, 8-116.

Bowling: Booth 18.1-4-24-1; Sibbles 19-4-36-7; Hudson 10-3-25-0; Nutter 7-4-7-0; Hopwood 4-0-14-0.

LANCASHIRE	*First innings*	
J L Hopwood	not out	21
C Washbrook	not out	15
	Extra (lb 1)	1
	Total (no wkt)	37

Did not bat: J Iddon, E Paynter, N Oldfield, A Nutter, W H Lister, G Duckworth, F M Sibbles, F S Booth, G N Hudson.

Bowling: Worthington 5-0-19-0; Pope (A V) 8-4-10-0; Townsend 4-2-7-0.

(Match 18)   DERBYSHIRE v KENT
At Burton-upon-Trent on July 15, 16 and 17, 1936
Derbyshire won by 141 runs. Only 50 minutes' play on the first day because of rain.

DERBYSHIRE	*First innings*		*Second innings*	
A E Alderman	run out	25	c Ashdown b Lewis	39
T S Worthington	c Valentine b Watt	15	c Watt b Lewis	53
L F Townsend	c & b Lewis	115	not out	78
A F Skinner	c Ashdown b Wright	49	c Watt b Lewis	12
D Smith	b Wright	4	not out	20
C S Elliott	b Freeman	12		
S M Hunt	b Wright	5		
A V Pope	c Watt b Freeman	9		
A W Richardson	b Freeman	19		
T B Mitchell	c Todd b Freeman	5		
H Elliott	not out	0		
	Extras (b 4, lb 6)	10	Extras (b 2)	2
	Total	268	Total (3 wkts dec)	204

Fall: 1-26, 2-84, 3-190, 4-195, 5-216, 6-225, 7-242, 8-243, 9-264.

1-80, 2-133, 3-178.

Bowling: Watt 16-3-47-1; Todd 9-0-24-0; Freeman 22.2-1-89-4; Wright 18-3-53-3; Lewis 9-1-45-1.

Todd 6-1-16-0; Watt 15-3-42-0; Freeman 11-2-27-0; Wright 7-1-34-0; Lewis 17-1-83-3.

KENT	*First innings*		*Second innings*	
W H Ashdown	lbw b Worthington	4	c Alderman b Pope (A V)	5
A Fagg	b Pope (A V)	1	c Alderman b Pope (A V)	46
F E Woolley	c Elliott (C S) b Townsend	61	b Worthington	21
P R Sunnucks	lbw b Townsend	5	c Richardson b Worthington	0
L J Todd	b Mitchell	23	b Worthington	0
B H Valentine	b Pope (A V)	43	c Elliott (H) b Pope (A V)	26
T W Spencer	c Worthington b Pope (A V)	4	not out	23
D V P Wright	c Townsend b Pope (A V)	12	lbw b Townsend	0
A E Watt	c Skinner b Townsend	30	c Smith b Townsend	4
C Lewis	b Pope (A V)	0	c Richardson b Mitchell	9
A P Freeman	not out	0	c Smith b Townsend	12
	Extra (lb 1)	1	Extra (lb 1)	1
	Total	184	Total	147

Fall: 1-4, 2-6, 3-32, 4-83, 5-100, 6-130, 7-151, 8-174, 9-184.

1-15, 2-45, 3-45, 4-51, 5-96, 6-106, 7-111, 8-115, 9-133.

Bowling: Pope (A V) 25.2-9-48-5; Worthington 7-2-19-1; Townsend 12-3-32-3; Mitchell 14-0-84-1.

Pope (A V) 16-7-30-3; Worthington 11-3-29-3; Townsend 17-1-59-3; Mitchell 6-1-28-1.

(Match 19)   YORKSHIRE v DERBYSHIRE
At Bramall Lane, Sheffield on July 22, 23 and 24, 1936
Match drawn; Yorkshire won on first innings. No play on second day (rain)

DERBYSHIRE	*First innings*		*Second innings*	
A E Alderman	c Barber b Smailes	13	c Mitchell b Smailes	23
T S Worthington	c Wood b Bowes	135	c Mitchell b Bowes	13
L F Townsend	c Hutton b Verity	9	c Barber b Smailes	50
A F Skinner	b Verity	17	c Barber b Jacques	16
D Smith	lbw b Bowes	1	not out	37
C S Elliott	run out	2	st Wood b Yardley	1
H Elliott	lbw b Verity	4	not out	3
A W Richardson	b Jacques	4		
A V Pope	c Yardley b Bowes	13		
T B Mitchell	b Smailes	5		
W H Copson	not out	0		
	Extras (b 7, lb 6)	13	Extras (lb 3, nb 2)	5
	Total	216	Total (5 wkts)	148

Fall: 1-59, 2-85, 3-154, 4-155,   1-18, 2-89, 3-90, 4-128, 5-129.
5-164, 6-177, 7-182, 8-211, 9-216.

Bowling: Bowes 21.4-3-47-3; Jacques 18-1-64-1;   Bowes 8-2-10-1;
Smailes 13-4-45-2; Verity 18-4-47-3.   Smailes 11-1-44-2; Verity
14-2-50-0; Jacques 8-1-19-1;
Yardley 7-1-10-1; Hutton 5-2-10-0.

YORKSHIRE	*First innings*	
H Sutcliffe	c Skinner b Copson	0
L Hutton	c Elliott (H) b Copson	31
A Mitchell	c Elliott (CS) b Pope (AV)	103
N W D Yardley	lbw b Pope (A V)	12
H Verity	c Skinner b Copson	0
W Barber	b Copson	8
A B Sellers	c Elliott (H) b Copson	0
A Wood b Copson		24
T F Smailes	c Richardson b Pope (AV)	22
T A Jacques	c Worthington b Pope (AV)	8
W E Bowes	not out	3
	Extras (b 1, lb 6)	7
	Total	218

Fall: 1-0, 2-68, 3-101, 4-102, 5-114, 6-120, 7-182, 8-186, 9-211.

Bowling: Copson 30-7-60-6; Pope (A V) 31.5-10-58-4;
Mitchell 10-0-41-0; Worthington 6-1-30-0; Townsend 9-3-22-0.

(Match 20) DERBYSHIRE v NOTTINGHAMSHIRE
At Rutland ground, Ilkeston on July 25, 27 and 28, 1936
Nottinghamshire won by six wickets

DERBYSHIRE

	First innings		*Second innings*	
A E Alderman	c Voce b Gunn	23	c Lilley b Voce	53
D Smith	c Lilley b Voce	59	b Voce	36
L F Townsend	c Woodhead b Larwood	8	b Woodhead	2
A F Skinner	b Gunn	2	lbw b Voce	5
C S Elliott	st Lilley b Gunn	16	c Lilley b Larwood	2
A F Townsend	b Larwood	21	b Voce	1
H Elliott	lbw b Woodhead	14	not out	10
A W Richardson	run out	6	c Lilley b Larwood	1
A V Pope	c Knowles b Voce	2	b Voce	0
T B Mitchell	c Lilley b Larwood	14	b Voce	7
W H Copson	not out	1	c Voce b Larwood	0
	Extras (b 12, lb 9)	21	Extras (b 4, lb 4)	8
	Total	187	Total	125

Fall: 1-55, 2-62, 3-69, 4-107, 5-121,
6-150, 7-169, 8-171, 9-174.

1-83, 2-94, 3-98, 4-105, 5-110,
6-110, 7-111, 8-112, 9-120.

Bowling: Larwood 29-10-54-3; Voce 27-7-45-2; Woodhead 12-2-34-1; Staples 5-1-11-0; Gunn 18-11-22-3.

Larwood 18.2-7-29-3; Voce 23-6-43-6; Woodhead 9-3-16-1; Gunn 7-1-18-0; Staples 4-1-11-0.

NOTTS

	First innings		*Second innings*	
W W Keeton	lbw b Pope (A V)	4	c Elliott (C S) b Pope (A V)	14
C B Harris	c Skinner b Copson	1	c & b Townsend (L F)	43
W Walker	b Mitchell	58	lbw b Townsenf (L F)	28
G V Gunn	c & b Mitchell	34	c Smith b Pope (A V)	12
J Knowles	c Pope (A V) b Mitchell	0	not out	23
A Staples	c Elliott (H) b Mitchell	0	not out	11
W Voce	lbw b Mitchell	9	B Lilley c & b Mitchell	7
G F H Heane	c Elliott (H) b Pope (A V)	2		
H Larwood	not out	38		
F G Woodhead	c Mitchell b Townsend (LF)	24		
	Extras (b 2, lb 3)	5	Extras (lb 2)	2
	Total	182	Total (4 wkts)	133

Fall: 1-3, 2-7, 3-71, 4-77, 5-97,
6-107, 7-117, 8-118, 9-126.

Fall of wickets: 1-27, 2-83,
3-96, 4-106.

Bowling: Copson 10-4-41-1; Pope (A V) 21-4-41-2; Mitchell 25-6-87-6; Townsend (L F) 6.1-0-8-1.

Copson 14-4-29-0; Pope (A V) 17-9-25-2; Mitchell 12-3-49-0; Townsend (L F) 11-2-28-2.

(Match 21)   ESSEX v DERBYSHIRE

At Chelmsford on August 1, 3 and 4, 1936
Derbyshire won by 20 runs. Rain held up play for 90 minutes on the first day.

DERBYSHIRE	*First innings*		*Second innings*	
A E Alderman	c sub b Farnes	0	c Wade b Farnes	79
D Smith	b Stephenson	7	b Stephenson	15
T S Worthington	c Wade b Stephenson	13	c Wilcox b Smith (T P B)	42
L F Townsend	c Wilcox b Farnes	0	lbw b Smith (T P B)	8
A F Skinner	lbw b Nichols	19	lbw b Smith (T P B)	7
C S Elliott	b Farnes	4	b Smith (T P B)	4
H Elliott	lbw b Stephenson	11	b Smith (T P B)	14
A W Richardson	b Nichols	2	c Wade b Stephenson	14
A V Pope	lbw b Farnes	9	b Stephenson	33
T B Mitchell	b Farnes	0	c Wade b Nichols	6
W H Copson	not out	9	not out	3
	Extras (b 1, lb 4)	5	Extras (b 7, lb 4, nb 4)	15
	Total	80	Total	240

Fall: 1-8, 2-22, 3-23, 4-23, 5-29, 6-52, 7-56, 8-68, 9-70.

1-35, 2-103, 3-118, 4-148, 5-156, 6-172, 7-186, 8-223, 9-236.

Bowling: Nichols 9-2-27-2; Farnes 13-6-20-5; Stephenson 11.3-4-27-3; Eastman 3-2-1-0.

Farnes 27-5-56-1; Nichols 18-3-51-1; Stephenson 18.5-4-56-3; Smith (T P B) 24-3-62-5.

ESSEX	*First innings*		*Second innings*	
L G Crawley	b Copson	6	b Copson	1
D R Wilcox	lbw b Pope (A V)	9	lbw b Townsend	15
M S Nichols	lbw b Copson	21	c Townsend b Pope (A V)	10
J O'Connor	c Alderman b Townsend	87	b Mitchell	21
B H Belle	b Mitchell	0	lbw b Mitchell	10
C T Ashton	lbw b Copson	10	lbw b Mitchell	0
T P B Smith	b Pope (A V)	6	b Townsend	8
J W A Stephenson	b Townsend	20	lbw b Mitchell	0
G Eastman	c Mitchell b Copson	31	lbw b Mitchell	6
T H Wade	not out	6	c Skinner b Mitchell	8
K Farnes	c Alderman b Pope (A V)	11	not out	1
	Extras (b 10, lb 1, nb 1)	12	Extra (lb 1)	1
	Total	219	Total	81

Fall: 1-16, 2-16, 3-77, 4-80, 5-103, 6-112, 7-165, 8-176, 9-202.

1-12, 2-26, 3-28, 4-57, 5-57, 6-66, 7-66, 8-71, 9-77.

Bowling: Copson 31-8-64-4; Pope (A V) 27.1-11-40-3; Townsend 19-7-38-2; Worthington 5-2-5-0; Mitchell 11-1-60-1.

Copson 13-6-20-1; Pope (A V) 7-1-16-1; Townsend 15-8-19-2; Mitchell 5-0-25-6.

(Match 22)   SURREY v DERBYSHIRE
At Kennington Oval on August 5, 6 and 7, 1936
Match drawn; Derbyshire won on first innings. Rain restricted play on second day.

SURREY	*First innings*		*Second innings*	
R J Gregory	c Townsend b Copson	2	c Elliott (C S) b Copson	15
H S Squires	lbw b Mitchell	36	b Copson	16
T H Barling	c Alderman b Copson	57	c Smith b Townsend	102
L B Fishlock	lbw b Copson	10	c Skinner b Copson	71
E R T Holmes	lbw b Mitchell	11	not out	38
T Mc Murray	c Townsend b Copson	0	c Alderman b Smith	35
E A Watts	b Mitchell	51	b Pope (A V)	18
E W J Brooks	b Townsend	18	run out	1
A R Gover	lbw b Mitchell	0	not out	9
K C W King	c Elliott (C S) b Mitchell	11		
J V Daley	not out	4		
	Extras (lb 4)	4	Extras (b 5, lb 5)	10
	Total	204	Total (7 wkts)	315

Fall: 1-2, 2-93, 3-103, 4-115,
5-117, 6-119, 7-173, 8-188, 9-189.

1-26, 2-45, 3-205,
4-208, 5-247, 6-289, 7-292.

Bowling: Copson 17-5-41-4; Pope (A V) 16-4-47-0; Mitchell 24-1-88-5; Townsend 10-3-20-1; Worthington 4-2-4-0.

Copson 23-8-60-3; Pope (AV) 36-8-86-1; Worthington 3-0-8-0; Mitchell 16-1-73-0; Townsend 22-6-56-1; Smith 3-1-13-1; Elliott (C S) 2-0-9-0.

DERBYSHIRE	*First innings*	
A E Alderman	lbw b Daley	14
D Smith	b Gover	106
T S Worthington	c & b Gover	2
L F Townsend	b Watts	0
A F Skinner	c Brooks b Daley	58
C S Elliott	lbw b Gover	3
H Elliott	not out	79
A W Richardson	lbw b Holmes	8
A V Pope	c Fishlock b King	39
T B Mitchell	b Daley	0
W H Copson	c Squires b King	6
	Extras (nb 6)	6
	Total	321

Fall: 1-18, 2-19, 3-171, 4-176, 5-185, 6-187, 7-208, 8-296, 9-298.

Bowling: Gover 30-5-92-3; Watts 17-2-41-1; King 13.1-0-61-2; Holmes 6-2-21-1; Daley 24-2-88-3; Gregory 3-0-12-0.

Alderman retired hurt with the score at five for no wicket. Resumed at 171-3.

(Match 23)   DERBYSHIRE v LEICESTERSHIRE
At Derby on August 8 and 10, 1936
Derbyshire won by nine wickets

LEICESTERSHIRE	*First innings*		*Second innings*	
L G Berry	c Elliott (H) b Mitchell	19	b Copson	4
F T Prentice	b Mitchell	5	lbw b Mitchell	6
N F Armstrong	st Elliott (H) b Mitchell	37	lbw b Copson	16
C S Dempster	c Smith b Copson	4	c Skinner b Copson	16
G S Watson	b Copson	21	b Pope (A V)	0
H C Graham	lbw b Copson	0	b Mitchell	1
G Geary	b Copson	2	b Mitchell	0
W E Astill	c Skinner b Mitchell	22	c Smith b Mitchell	14
H A Smith	c Mitchell b Copson	3	c Copson b Mitchell	17
P Corrall	c Elliott (H) b Mitchell	0	c Smith b Copson	2
W H Marlow	not out	0	not out	17
	Extras (b 4)	4	Extra (lb 1)	1
	Total	117	Total	94

Fall: 1-18, 2-27, 3-34, 4-74, 5-74,
6-76, 7-94, 8-115, 9-117.

1-4, 2-24, 3-36,
4-39, 5-40, 6-40, 7-58, 8-60, 9-72.

Bowling: Copson 18-5-40-5; Pope (A V)11-4-13-0; Mitchell 19.3-3-57-5; Townsend 7-4-3-0.

Copson 13-1-39-4; Pope (A V) 11-3-12-1; Mitchell 13.3-1-42-5.

DERBYSHIRE	*First innings*		*Second innings*	
A E Alderman	b Marlow	35	not out	27
D Smith	c Dempster b Smith	16	lbw b Geary	13
T S Worthington	lbw b Geary	9	not out	13
L F Townsend	c Prentice b Astill	4		
A F Skinner	b Smith	8		
H Elliott	b Smith	1		
C S Elliott	lbw b Geary	17		
A W Richardson	c Corrall b Geary	31		
A V Pope	c Astill b Geary	10		
T B Mitchell	not out	5		
W H Copson	b Geary	6		
	Extras (b 13, lb 3, w 1)	17	Extras	0
	Total	159	Total (1 wkt)	53

Fall: 1-38, 2-49, 3-54, 4-73, 5-77,
6-100, 7-121, 8-146, 9-147.

1-28.

Bowling: Geary 33.4-16-39-5; Smith 26-5-60-3; Astill 12-3-27-1; Marlow 5-0-16-1.

Smith 8-1-33-0; Geary 7-0-16-1; Marlow 0.2-0-4-0.

(Match 24) NOTTINGHAMSHIRE v DERBYSHIRE
At Town Ground, Worksop on August 15, 17 and 18, 1936
Match drawn; Derbyshire won on first innings

DERBYSHIRE	*First innings*		*Second innings*	
A E Alderman	b Woodhead	31	c Wheat b Robinson	29
D Smith	c Wheat b Robinson	22	c Harris b Gunn	85
A F Skinner	b Staples	8	c Wheat b Butler	60
L F Townsend	lbw b Butler	28	c Keeton b Woodhead	6
C S Elliott	lbw b Robinson	6	b Butler	26
H Elliott	c Keeton b Robinson	17	b Robinson	6
G R Langdale	c Butler b Woodhead	14	b Robinson	29
A W Richardson	c Knowles b Robinson	11	not out	12
A V Pope	b Butler	5	c Harris b Robinson	2
T B Mitchell	st Wheat b Harris	45	not out	1
W H Copson	not out	7		
	Extras (b 16, lb 6, w 1, nb 1)	24	Extras (b 6, lb 8)	14
	Total	218	Total (8 wkts dec)	270

Fall: 1-31, 2-50, 3-100, 4-102, 5-112, 6-139, 7-151, 8-160, 9-174.

1-78, 2-97, 3-155, 4-214, 5-215, 6-245, 7-254, 8-268.

Bowling: Butler 33-6-57-2; Woodhead 31-11-47-2; Robinson 35-17-54-4; Staples 17-8-36-1; Harris 0.4-0-0-1.

Butler 22-2-64-2; Woodhead 16-1-48-1; Robinson 26-4-87-4; Staples 17-5-42-0; Gunn 7-0-15-1.

NOTTS	*First innings*		*Second innings*	
W W Keeton	b Pope (A V)	0	not out	100
C B Harris	c Skinner b Pope (A V)	5	not out	107
W Walker	run out	2		
J Knowles	b Copson	4		
G F H Heane	c Smith b Mitchell	57		
G V Gunn	lbw b Copson	17		
A Staples	lbw b Copson	47		
F G Woodhead	c Copson b Mitchell	5		
A B Wheat	c Aklerman b Mitchell	11		
H J Butler	not out	0		
G W Robinson	b Copson	0		
	Extras (lb 4)	4	Extras (lb 7, nb 1)	8
	Total	152	Total (no wkt)	215

Fall: 1-1, 2-3, 3-11, 4-23, 5-49, 6-111, 7-127, 8-151, 9-152.

Bowling: Copson 23.4-6-47-4; Pope (A V) 17-4-25-2; Mitchell 21-5-51-3; Townsend 7-2-14-0; Langdale 4-1-11-0.

Copson 13-2-27-0; Pope (A V) 23-5-54-0; Mitchell 17-2-49-0; Townsend 19-3-49-0; Langdale 7-2-28-0.

(Match 25)   SUSSEX v DERBYSHIRE
At The Saffrons, Eastbourne on August 19, 20 and 21, 1936
Match drawn; Sussex won on first innings. Rain interrupted play late on the first day.

DERBYSHIRE	*First innings*		*Second innings*	
A E Alderman	b Tate	6	c Langridge (Jas) b Nye	7
D Smith	c Cornf'd (W) b Langr' (Ja)	34	c Holmes b Nye	7
T S Worthington	c Cornford (J) b Parks (JH)	56	c Holmes b Langridge (Ja)	45
L F Townsend	lbw b Langridge (Ja)	32	c Langridge (Jn) b Langridge (Ja)	46
A F Skinner	c Cornford (W) b Nye	62	lbw b Cornford (J)	8
C S Elliott	lbw b Cornford (J)	11	not out	39
H Elliott	b Nye	8	lbw b Langridge (Jn)	11
A W Richardson	lbw b Cornford (J)	11	not out	8
A V Pope	b Cornford (J)	1		
T B Mitchell	b Cornford (J)	0		
W H Copson	not out	5		
	Extras (lb 1, lb 1)	2	Extras (b 10, lb 8, w 1, nb 1)	20
	Total	228	Total (6 wkts)	191

Fall: 1-8, 2-89, 3-99, 4-153, 5-198,
6-209, 7-216, 8-217, 9-217.

1-14, 2-33, 3-110, 4-117, 5-125,
6-163.

Bowling: Tate 12-2-30-1; Nye 13-1-40-2;
Cornford (J) 17.1-2-59-4; Parks (JH)
24-4-59-1; Langridge (James) 21-3-38-2.

Nye 31-7-67-2; Cornford (J)
33-16-31-1; Parks (JH)
20-7-28-0; Langridge (James)
27-17-16-2; Cook 8-1-17-0;
Langridge (John) 8-4-6-1;
Cumming 1-0-5-0; Holmes 1-0-1-0.

SUSSEX	*First innings*	
Parks (J H)	lbw b Pope (A V)	9
Langridge (John)	lbw b Copson	0
B L Cumming	c Skinner b Pope (A V)	14
T E Cook	c Mitchell b Copson	53
Langridge (James)	c Elliott (H) b Mitchell	126
H W Parks	b Copson	75
A J Holmes	c Worthington b Copson	5
M W Tate	c Mitchell b Copson	0
W Cornford	c Copson b Mitchell	8
J K Nye	c & b Copson	5
J Cornford	not out	6
	Extras (b 7, lb 6, w 1, nb 1)	15
	Total	316

Fall: 1-9, 2-9, 3-33, 4-106, 5-291, 6-295, 7-295, 8-302, 9-308.

Bowling: Copson 35-8-87-6; Pope (A V) 30-9-55-2;
Townsend 25-8-52-0; Mitchell 21.3-4-81-2; Worthington 10-4-26-0.

(Match 26)   DERBYSHIRE v NORTHAMPTONSHIRE
At Queen's Park, Chesterfield on August 22, 24 and 25, 1936
Match drawn; Derbyshire won on first innings.

NORTHANTS

	First innings		*Second innings*	
A H Bakewell	b Pope (A V)	3	not out	241
R P Northway	b Pope (A V)	1	c Elliott (H) b Pope (A V)	1
N Grimshaw	lbw b Mitchell	15	c Skinner b Pope (A V)	16
J H Timms	lbw b Pope (A V)	47	lbw b Pope (A V)	41
D Brookes	c Pope (A V) b Copson	14	b Pope (A V)	81
K C James	lbw b Copson	9	b Pope (A V)	12
A L Cox	b Pope (A V)	12	c Elliott (H) b Pope (A V)	2
W C Brown	not out	30	not out	13
R J Partridge	b Mitchell	2		
C Perkins	lbw b Copson	3		
E W Clark	b Copson	2		
	Extras (b 4, lb 2, w 1)	7	Extras (lb 4)	4
	Total	144	Total (6 wkts dec)	411

Fall: 1-3, 2-8, 3-61, 4-86,
5-86, 6-95, 7-113, 8-124, 9-132.

1-2, 2-53, 3-146,
4-357, 5-376, 6-386.

Bowling: Copson 16.5-7-24-4; Pope
(A V) 21-3-58-4; Mitchell 16-1-38-2;
Townsend 5-0-17-0.

Copson 26-2-80-0; Pope (A V)
42-6-129-6; Townsend 38-7-90-0;
Langdale 11-0-45-0; Worthington
17-1-48-0; Skinner 3-0-15-0.

DERBYSHIRE

	First innings		*Second innings*	
A E Alderman	b Partridge	9	b Partridge	14
D Smith	lbw b Partridge	31	b Clark	25
T S Worthington	c James b Partridge	15	b Clark	0
L F Townsend	lbw b Timms	67	lbw b Cox	1
A F Skinner	lbw b Timms	1	lbw b Partridge	41
H Elliott	b Clark	8	lbw b Clark	0
G R Langdale	b Clark	8	c Brown b Bakewell	9
A W Richardson	c Bakewell b Clark	18	not out	27
A V Pope	c Perkins b Partridge	11	not out	13
T B Mitchell	c Brookes b Partridge	14		
W H Copson	not out	2		
	Extras (b 11, lb 3, w 1)	15	Extras (b 21, lb 13, w 4, nb 50	43
	Total	209	Total (7 wkts)	173

Fall: 1-45, 2-49, 3-73, 4-74,
5-111, 6-121, 7-167, 8-179, 9-201.

1-43, 2-43, 3-46, 4-56,
5-64, 6-94, 7-121.

Bowling: Clark 18-3-63-3; Partridge
26.3-5-69-5; Cox 7-1-17-0; Perkins
4-1-5-0; Timms 15-4-40-2.

Clark 27-10-41-3; Partridge
29-16-22-2; Cox 17-13-12-1; Timms
12-6-13-0; Bakewell 6-1-17-1;
Perkins 5-3-5-0; Grimshaw 11-6-20-0.

(Match 27)   SOMERSET v DERBYSHIRE
At Wells on August 26, 27 and 28, 1936
Somerset won by one wicket

DERBYSHIRE	*First innings*		*Second innings*	
A E Alderman	b Wellard	9	c & b Meyer	17
D Smith	b Andrews	93	b Wellard	2
T S Worthington	lbw b Wellard	35	lbw b Wellard	9
L F Townsend	b Andrews	7	b Wellard	5
A F Skinner	c Meyer b Andrews	9	st Luckes b Meyer	39
C S Elliott	not out	29	b Andrews	6
H Elliott	b Meyer	11	b Andrews	10
A W Richardson	b Wellard	8	c Meyer b Wellard	50
A V Pope	b Andrews	0	c Meyer b Gimblett	30
T R Armstrong	b Andrews	1	not out	8
W H Copson	b Wellard	1	c Luckes b Wellard	1
	Extras (b 4, lb 7, nb 2)	13	Extras (b 6, lb 14, nb 3)	23
	Total	216	Total	200

Fall: 1-27, 2-117, 3-147,
4-153, 5-162, 6-186, 7-212, 8-213, 9-215.

1-6, 2-17, 3-26,
4-60, 5-85, 6-87, 7-98, 8-164, 9-196.

Bowling: Wellard 15.1-2-52-4; Meyer 24-6-53-1;
Andrews 16-4-42-5; Gimblett
3-0-15-0; Hazell 9-4-41-0.

Wellard 22.1-4-47-5;
Andrews 16-2-56-2;
Meyer 17-3-46-2;   Hazell 7-4-14-0;
Gimblett 8-4-14-1.

SOMERSET	*First innings*		*Second innings*	
F S Lee	b Pope (A V)	35	c Elliott (H) b Copson	27
H Gimblett	b Worthington	4	b Copson	41
F M McRae	c Elliott (H) b Pope (A V)	2	not out	14
R J O Meyer	b Copson	2	b Copson	14
E F Longrigg	b Pope (A V)	44	c Smith b Armstrong	38
J H Cameron	lbw b Worthington	23	run out	8
R A Ingle	lbw b Copson	8	c Smith b Copson	16
A W Wellard	c Elliott (C S) b Pope (A V)	17	c Townsend b Copson	86
W H R Andrews	c Elliott (H) b Pope (A V)	4	c Alderman b Townsend	12
W T Luckes	b Copson	1	b Copson	0
H L Hazell	not out	0	not out	8
	Extras (lb 6)	6	Extras (lb 9, nb 1)	10
	Total	146	Total (9 wkts)	274

Fall: 1-23, 2-38, 3-41, 4-53,
5-99, 6-118, 7-122, 8-145, 9-146.

1-67, 2-76, 3-98, 4-115, 5-140,
6-217, 7-242, 8-263, 9-265.

Bowling: Copson 21-3-55-3; Pope (A V)
20.1-3-35-5; Worthington 7-1-34-2;
Townsend 4-0-16-0.

Copson 30-6-81-6; Pope (A V)
34-13-64-0; Worthington
5-0-20-0; Townsend 17.5-5-35-1;
Armstrong 8-1-64-1.

(Match 28)   LEICESTERSHIRE v DERBYSHIRE
At Oakham on August 29, 31 and September 1, 1936
Derbyshire won by an innings and 66 runs

LEICESTERSHIRE	*First innings*		*Second innings*	
L G Berry	c Elliott (H) b Copson	9	c Elliott (H) b Copson	4
F T Prentice	c Richardson b Copson	7	c Worthington b Townsend	13
N F Armstrong	lbw b Copson	2	b Pope (A V)	42
H C Graham	c & b Townsend	8	c Elliott (H) b Pope (A V)	1
G S Watson	b Pope (A V)	24	st Elliott (H) b Armstrong	13
M St J Packe	c Alderman b Townsend	3	b Armstrong	3
A Shipman	not out	37	not out	21
G Geary	b Pope (A V)	9	b Copson	0
W E Astill	c Elliott (H) b Armstrong	29	b Copson	4
H A Smith	b Townsend	10	b Pope (A V)	8
P Corrall	lbw b Copson	5	b Pope (A V)	12
	Extras (b 4, lb 4)	8	Extras	0
	Total	151	Total	121

Fall: 1-13, 2-18, 3-23, 4-43, 5-47,
6-57, 7-78, 8-120, 9-137.

1-6, 2-25, 3-28, 4-52, 5-56,
6-85, 7-86, 8-90, 9-101.

Bowling: Copson 23.4-7-34-4; Pope (A V)
28-9-49-2; Armstrong 19-4-29-1; Townsend
18-2-31-3.

Copson 17-3-56-3;
Pope (A V) 25.4-9-44-4;
Townsend 11-5-8-1; Armstsrong
6-4-2-2; Langdale 4-0-11-0.

DERBYSHIRE	*First innings*	
D Smith	b Astill	169
A E Alderman	b Shipman	0
T S Worthington	b Smith	102
A F Skinner	lbw b Shipmen	1
L F Townsend	c Corrall b Smith	2
G R Langdale	b Geary	4
H Elliott c Corrall	b Smith	24
A W Richardson	b Geary	7
A V Pope	not out	3
T R Armstrong	st Corrall b Astill	7
W H Copson	c Graham b Astill	0
	Extras (b 7, lb 10, nb 2)	19
	Total	338

Fall: 1-0, 2-209, 3-212, 4-225, 5-240, 6-307, 7-328, 8-328, 9-338.

Bowling: Shipman 16-2-49-2; Smith 34-3-119-3;
Geary 31-3-85-2; Astill 21-1-52-3; Prentice 6-0-14-0.

OTHER MATCHES PLAYED BY DERBYSHIRE IN 1936

OXFORD UNIVERSITY v DERBYSHIRE
At Oxford on May 9, 11 and 12, 1936
Derbyshire won by an innings and 130 runs

DERBYSHIRE	*First innings*	
D Smith	c Kimpton b Darwall-Smith	77
A E Alderman	b Darwall-Smith	9
T S Worthington	c Scott b Ballance	174
L F Townsend	c Grieve b Murray-Wood	48
E Carrington	b Ballance	34
G H Pope	not out	62
J D H Gilbert	b Dyson	16
A V Pope	c M'-Innes b Darwall-Smith	14
H Elliott	b Mitchell-Innes	5
T B Mitchell	c sub b Darwall-Smith	4
W H Copson	b Darwall-Smith	0
	Extras (b 10, lb 3)	13
	Total	456

Fall: 1-31, 2-170, 3-306, 4-329, 5-370, 6-404, 7-429, 8-447, 9-456.

Bowling: Darwall-Smith 24.5-0-134-5; Scott 16-1-57-0; Mitchell-Innes 14-1-81-1; Grieve 5-0-24-0; Murray-Wood 12-1-90-1; Ballance 12-2-37-2; Dyson 7-3-20-1.

OXFORD UNIV	*First innings*		*Second innings*	
M R Barton	b Copson	0	b Copson	70
M M Walford	b Pope (G H)	8	c Elliott (H) b Copson	4
C F Grieve	c Smith b Pope (G H)	6	c & b Mitchell	2
N S Mitchell-Innes	not out	67	lbw b Pope (G H)	9
R C M Kimpton	lbw b Mitchell	12	run out	15
B H Belle	lbw b Mitchell	0	b Pope (G H)	2
W Murray-Wood	b Copson	0	st Elliott (H) b Townsend	42
R F H Darwall-Smith	b Copson	0	b Mitchell	23
J B Scott	b Copson	3	c Elliott (H) v Pope (A V)	0
T G L Ballance	b Pope (A V)	16	not out	1
J H Dyson	c Alderman b Townsend	35	c Elliott (H) v Pope (A V)	1
	Extras (b 2, lb 4)	6	Extras (lb 2, nb 2)	4
	Total	153	Total	173

Fall: 1-4, 2-15, 3-20, 4-37, 5-39, 6-42, 7-42, 8-54, 9-82.

1-6, 2-16, 3-25, 4-31, 5-43, 6-47, 7-142, 8-168, 9-172.

Bowling: Copson 12-5-14-4; Pope (A V) 12-6-13-1; Pope (G H) 12-4-17-2; Mitchell 23-1-91-2; Townsend 2.3-0-9-1; Worthington 2-0-3-0.

Copson 14-3-27-2; Pope (A V) 12.5-2-29-2; Pope (G H) 8-1-16-2; Mitchell 13-0-57-2; Worthington 5-1-12-0; Townsend 5-0-28-1.

DERBYSHIRE v ALL INDIA
At Derby on July 18, 20 and 21, 1936
Match drawn

ALL INDIA	First innings		Second innings	
V M Merchant	lbw b Worthington	23	c Elliott (H) b Copson	75
S Wazir Ali	b Pope (A V)	2	(3) c Townsend b Worthington	10
Mushtaq Ali	lbw b Worthington	9	(2) c sub b Townsend	27
C K Nayudu	lbw b Pope (A V)	60	c Alderman b Townsend	30
L P Jai	b Copson	43	c Skinner b Copson	11
C Ramaswami	c Skinner b Copson	0	not out	40
M Jahangir Khan	b Copson	9	c Worthington b Elliott (C S)	21
M Baqa Jilani	not out	33	c Skinner b Townsend	9
C S Nayudu	c Pope (A V) b Mitchell	3		
S Bannerjee	b Copson	28		
K R Meherhomji	b Copson	0		
	Extras (b 6, lb 11, nb 1)	18	Extras (b 5, lb 4)	9
	Total	228	Total (7 wkts dec)	232

Fall: 1-3, 2-22, 3-55, 4-134,
5-134, 6-140, 7-158, 8-169, 9-228.

1-76, 2-109, 3-114,
4-135, 5-163, 6-195, 7-232.

Bowling: Copson 25-9-44-5; Pope (A V) 21-8-26-2; Worthington 18-7-42-2; Mitchell 25-4-72-1; Townsend 11-3-26-0.

Copson 24-6-42-2; Pope (A V) 27-7-61-0; Townsend 22-4-73-3; Worthington 11-4-34-1; Elliott (C S) 3.5-1-13-1.

DERBYSHIRE	First innings		Second innings	
A E Alderman	lbw b Nayudu (C K)	1	not out	61
T S Worthington	b Bannerjee	9	b Nayudu (C S)	14
L F Townsend	b Bannerjee	7	b Bannerjee	77
A F Skinner	b Bannerjee	2		
C S Elliott	lbw b Jahangir Khan	77		
G R Jackson	lbw b Nayudu (C S)	4		
E Carrington	b Bannerjee	2	not out	6
H Elliott	lbw b Jahangir Khan	42		
A V Pope	st Meherhomji b Nayudu(CS)	5		
T B Mitchell	c Jai b Jahangir Khan	1		
W H Copson	not out	6		
	Extras (b 1, lb 2, nb 1)	4	Extras (b 9, lb 1, w 1)	11
	Total	160	Total (2 wkts)	169

Fall of wickets: 1-8, 2-12, 3-14, 4-27, 5-48, 6-51, 7-139, 8-152, 9-154.

Fall of wickets: 1-27, 2-162.

Bowling: Bannerjee 13-0-51-4; Nayudu (C K) 5-2-14-1; Jahangir Khan 10-3-28-3; Jilani 7-4-5-0; Nayudu (C S) 8-0-45-2; Mushtaq Ali 5-2-13-0.

Bannerjee 7-1-22-1; Nayudu (C K) 5-0-30-0; Jahangir Khan 17-4-28-0; Jilani 1-0-5-0; Nayudu (C S) 7-1-37-1; Mushtaq Ali 8-1-16-0; Ramaswami 4-0-11-0; Wazir Ali 2-0-3-0; Jai 3-2-6-0.

Appendix 4. MISCELLANEOUS SCORECARDS 1871-1947

LANCASHIRE v DERBYSHIRE
At Old Trafford, Manchester, on May 25, 26 and 27, 1871
Derbyshire won by an innings and 11 runs

LANCASHIRE	*First innings*		*Second innings*	
A N Hornby	c Gregory b Hickton	1	run out	0
J Ricketts	b Hickton	2	b Gregory	7
C Coward	c Burnham b Hickton	1	c & b Hickton	36
J R Hillkirk	c Sowter b Hickton	1	b Gregory	17
W Burrows	b Gregory	0	c Sowter b Hickton	3
A B Rowley	b Gregory	0	b Platts	1
T Whatmough	b Gregory	5	not out	28
A Smith	not out	11	b Gregory	7
E Wadsworth	b Gregory	2	b Hickton	8
W Mills	b Gregory	2	b Platts	1
F Reynolds	c Davidson b Gregory	0	c Attenborough b Platts	0
	Extras	0	Extras	3
	Total	25	Total	111

Fall: 1-2, 2-4, 3-4, 4-5, 5-5, 6-5, 7-15, 8-19, 9-25.

1-1, 2-16, 3-36, 4-39, 5-54, 6-67, 7-104, 8-105, 9-111.

Bowling: Hickton 12-5-16-4; Gregory 12.3-7-9-6.

Bowling: Hickton 37-15-58-3; Gregory 32-11-46-3; Platts 6-5-4-3.

DERBYSHIRE	*First innings*	
R P Smith	b Mills	17
J Smith	c Reynolds b Whatmough	1
T Attenborough	c Smith b Whatmough	8
J W Burnham	b Reynolds	31
U Sowter	not out	47
J Tilson	run out	8
J Davidson	b Reynolds	8
J T B D Platts	c Whatmough b Reynolds	2
W Hickton	st Smith b Mills	7
S Richardson	st Smith b Reynolds	5
D Gregory	st Smith b Reynolds	5
	Extras	8
	Total	147

Fall: 1-4, 2-20, 3-40, 4-74, 5-95, 6-112, 7-116, 8-130, 9-139.

Bowling: Reynolds 35-10-54-5; Whatmough 25-5-52-2; Mills 23-12-22-2; Rowley 13-8-11-0.

Note: There were then four balls in an over in English cricket.

SIXTEEN OF DERBYSHIRE v ELEVEN OF NOTTINGHAMSHIRE

At Wirksworth on September 4 and 5, 1873
Derbyshire won by an innings and 8 runs

DERBYSHIRE	*First innings*	
J Smith	c Selby b Shaw	5
W Rigley	c Oscroft b Daft	15
S Richardson	run out	21
G Frost	b Oscroft	15
Rev R C Moncrieff	b Oscroft	0
R P Smith	b Oscroft	2
T Howarth	b Morley	7
T Foster	c McIntyre b Shaw	0
J Frost	b Morley	2
J Flint	b Shaw	12
R Allsop	c McIntyre b Daft	22
J T B D Platts	c McIntyre b Shaw	1
W Hickton	run out	3
W Allen	c & b Shaw	2
E Tatlow	not out	0
W Mycroft	b Shaw	2
	Extras	5
	Total	114

Bowling: J C Shaw 6-40.

NOTTS	*First innings*		*Second innings*	
T Bignall	b Flint	0	b Mycroft	3
F Wild	b Mycroft	1	hit wkt b Flint	11
W Oscroft	c Flint b Mycroft	4	c Flint b Mycroft	12
C Clifton	c & b Flint	0	st Richardson b Flint	0
R Daft	c Platts b Mycroft	5	st Richardson b Flint	0
R Tolley	c & b Flint	0	c & b Flint	0
J Selby	lbw b Mycroft	0	not out	14
M McIntyre	c J Smith b Flint	1	b Hickton	23
G Martin	c & b Flint	0	run out	23
F Morley	not out	0	b Hickton	0
J C Shaw	b Flint	2	b Platts	3
	Extras	1	Extras	3
	Total	14	Total	92

Bowling: Mycroft 16-12-6-4;
Flint 16-10-7-6.

Mycroft 28-9-34-2;
Flint 26-9-44-4; Platts 6-4-5-1;
Hickton 5-3-6-2.

LANCASHIRE v DERBYSHIRE

At Old Trafford, Manchester, on August 10, 11 & 12, 1896
Match drawn

DERBYSHIRE	*First innings*	
L G Wright	c Sugg b Hallam	3
H Bagshaw	b Briggs	13
W Chatterton	b Hallam	104
G A Davidson	c Sugg b Briggs	274
W Storer	c Paul b Briggs	116
W Sugg	c Paul b Briggs	11
J J Hulme	c Tyldesley b Hallam	5
G A Marsden	st Smith v Briggs	4
H G Curgenven	c Sugg b Hallam	13
W B Delacombe	not out	2
G Porter	b Briggs	0
	Extras (22b, 6lb, 4w)	32
	Total (271 five-ball overs)	577

Fall: 1-0, 2-26, 3-234, 4-542, 5-553, 6-558, 7-558, 8-573, 9-577.

Bowling: Briggs 90-32-185-6; Hallam 73-31-127-4; Baker 20-8-45-0; Lancaster 46-18-97-0; Ward (F) 20-9-39-0; Paul 11-2-28-0; Ward (A) 4-1-11-0; Tyldesley 3-1-6-0; Sugg 4-2-7-0.

LANCASHIRE	*First innings*		*Second innings*	
E B Rowley	b Davidson	50	c Curgenven b Chatterton	14
A Ward	b Davidson	8		
A G Paul	b Porter	50	c Curgenven b Chatterton	0
J T Tyldesley	c & b Hulme	1	not out	20
F H Sugg	st Wright by Storer	96	not out	26
F Ward	b Davidson	10		
G R Baker	c & b Hulme	30		
J Briggs	lbw b Hulme	18		
T Lancaster	c Curgenven b Hulme	7		
C Smith	not out	1	c Wright b Curgenven	3
A W Hallam	b Hulme	4		
	Extras (1b, 1lb, 1w)	3	Extras	0
	Total (156.3 overs)	278	Total (3 wkts, 31 overs)	63

Fall: 1-24, 2-8, 3-82, 4-173, 5-203; 1-13, 2-21, 3-25.
6-233, 7-259, 8-273, 9-274.

Bowling: Davidson 57-34-75-3; Hulme 48.3-19-94-5; Porter 29-10-75-1; Curgenven 7-1-16-0; Storer 15-3-33-1.

Curgenven 15-4-31-1; Chatterton 12-4-16-2; Bagshaw 4-0-16-0.

DERBYSHIRE V HAMPSHIRE
At County Ground, Derby, on August 1, 2 & 3, 1898
Match drawn

DERBYSHIRE	*First innings*	
L G Wright	c Barrett b Webb	134
S H Evershed	b Steele	67
H Bagshaw	c Barton b Steele	19
W Storer	c Bennett b Martin	100
W Chatterton	c & b Quinton	142
G A Davidson	c Steele b Quinton	108
W Sugg	c Martin b Quinton	33
E M Ashcroft	c Webb b Quinton	10
A Charlesworth	c Poore b Lee	4
F Davidson	not out	0
J Hancock	c Bennett b Quinton	0
	Extras (7b, 15 lb, 5 nb, 1 w)	28
	Total (190.1 overs)	645

Fall: 1-134, 2-174, 3-297, 4-376, 5-552, 6-621, 7-634, 8-645, 9-645.

Bowling: Tate 39-7-118-0; Martin 33-6-109-1; Steele 37-8-109-2; Lee 21-4-56-1; Quinton 20.1-0-93-5; Webb 30-4-91-1; English 4-1-16-0; Barton 6-0-23-0.

HAMPSHIRE	*First innings*		*Second innings*	
V A Barton	b Davidson (G)	5	c Storer b Davidson (F)	2
E I M Barrett	c Storer b Davidson (G)	18		
A S Webb	c Chatterton b Davidson (G)	5	lbw b Davidson (F)	51
F W D Quinton	c Evershed b Davidson (G)	0	not out	101
R M Poore	not out	121	b Davidson (F)	15
E A English	c Chatterton b Davidson (G)	0	not out	14
E C Lee	b Davidson (F)	44		
D A Steele	b Chatterton	17		
R A Bennett	b Chatterton	4	b Davidson (G)	16
E Tate	c Evershed b Storer	15		
G Martin	c David'n (F) b David'n (G)	3		
	Extras (6 b, 2 lb)	8	Extras (26b, 3lb, 3nb, 1w)	33
	Total (94.4 overs)	240	Total (4 wkts, 111 overs)	232

Falls: 1-22, 2-23, 3-28, 4-29, 5-31, 6-141, 7-172, 8-184, 9-222.

1-35, 2-37, 3-172, 4-201.

Bowling: Davidson (G) 31.4-14-42-6; Davidson (F) 31-12-68-1; Storer 19-0-77-1; Hancock 6-0-23-0; Chatterton 7-2-22-2.

Davidson (G) 42-19-73-1; Davidson (F) 36-20-42-3; Storer 5-0-16-0; Hancock 14-1-36-0; Sugg 10-1-26-0; Bagshaw 4-1-6-0.

DERBYSHIRE v WARWICKSHIRE
At Miners' Welfare Ground, Blackwell, June 18, 20 & 21, 1910
Match drawn

WARWICKSHIRE	*First innings*		*Second innings*	
A F A Lilley	c Humphries b Warren	19		
S P Kinneir	st Humphries b Cadman	87		
C Charlesworth	c Warren b Root	216	not out	16
W G Quaife	c Warren b Morton	88		
C S Baker	lbw b Cadman	3		
F E Tayler	c Jelf b Morton	6	c Morton b Higson	34
S Santall	b Warren	37		
E J Smith	not out	18	st Humphries b Morton	7
F R Foster	not out	12		
	Extras (1 b, 14 lb, 2nb, 1 w)	18	Extras (1 b, 5 lb)	6
	Total (7 wkts dec)	504	Total (2 wkts)	63

Did not bat: J H Phillips, E F Field.

Fall: 1-40, 2-206, 3-378, 4-400, 5-413, 6-442, 7-484.

1-13, 2-63.

Bowling: Warren 41-8-199-2; Cadman 30-6-104-2; Morton 43-6-137-2; Higson 5-0-33-0; Root 5-1-13-1.

Cadman 10-0-24-0; Morton 6-1-24-1; Higson 0.2-0-0-1; Needham 4-0-9-0.

DERBYSHIRE	*First innings*		*Second innings*	
F A Newton	c Foster b Santall	87	lbw b Quaife	21
E Needham	c Foster b Field	8	c Charlesworth b Foster	34
J Handford	c Smith b Phillips	18	c Foster b Field	16
S W A Cadman	lbw b Foster	18	b Foster	0
A Morton	c Smith v Field	22	b Santall	13
T A Higson	b Foster	36	(7) c Charlesworth b Field	2
H F D Jelf	c Charlesworth b Foster	33	(9) c Charlesworth b Field	0
A Warren	b Foster	15	c Phillips b Field	123
C F Root	not out	0	(6) run out	34
J Chapman	c Foster b Santall	0	b Foster	165
J Humphries	b Foster	3	not out	8
	Extras (14 b, 8 lb)	22	Extras (7 b, 5 lb, 1 nb, 1 w)	14
	Total	262	Total	430

Fall: 1-34, 2-123, 3-123, 4-146, 5-194, 6-218, 7-253, 8-254, 9-259.

1-41, 2-69, 3-69 4-85, 5-115, 6-126, 7-131, 8-131, 9-414.

Bowling: Foster 28.1-10-62-5; Field 23-6-81-2; Santall 20-5-46-2; Quaife 6-1-21-0; Phillips 7-0-30-1.

Foster 26.4-4-119-3; Field 29-5-124-4; Santall 22-4-66-1; Quaife 12-2-47-1; Phillips 9-0-37-0; Charlesworth 4-0-16-0; Baker 2-0-7-0.

GLAMORGAN v DERBYSHIRE
At Arms Park, Cardiff, on June 18, 19 & 20, 1921
Derbyshire won by two wickets

GLAMORGAN	*First innings*		*Second innings*	
T A L Whittington	b Tomlinson	19	b Bestwick	0
W N Gemmill	b Bestwick	11	b Bestwick	2
W E Bates	c & b Tomlinson	67	b Bestwick	48
H Tomlinson	b Bestwick	8	c Storer b Bestwick	20
G E Cording	c Storer b Bestwick	25	b Bestwick	4
H G Symonds	c Elliott b Bestwick	6	b Bestwick	1
W L T Jenkins	c Curgenven b Tomlinson	5	c Elliott b Bestwick	6
A O'Bree	c Curgenven b R-Blackton	22	c Storer b Bestwick	16
J C Clay	b Storer	3	b Bestwick	5
H Creber	run out	1	b Bestwick	1
A Nash	not out	0	not out	0
	Extras (6 b, 3 lb)	9	Extra (1b, 2 lb)	3
	Total	168	Total	106

Fall: 1-31, 2-35, 3-37, 4-93, 5-109,
6-122, 7-151, 8-163, 9-163.

1-0, 2-9, 3-48, 4-60, 5-71,
6-80, 7-89, 8-105, 9-106.

Bowling: Bestwick 30-9-71-4; Storer 15.2-2-35-1;
Tomlinson 16-3-41-3; Reader-Blackton 8-2-12-1.

Bestwick 19-2-40-10;
Storer 6-1-24-0; Tomlinson
6-0-17-0; Reader-Blackton 6-1-22-0.

DERBYSHIRE	*First innings*		*Second innings*	
G M Buckston	c Symonds b Nash	0	(8) c Jenkins b Nash	0
W Carter	c Cording b Clay	0	(9) not out	50
G R Jackson	lbw b Bates	15	b Nash	4
G Curgenven	b Clay	0	(1) c Jenkins b Bates	46
S W A Cadman	b Nash	25	c Gemmill b Creber	31
H Storer	run out	13	(4) b Clay	12
J M Hutchinson	c & b Bates	19	(6) lbw Nash	0
W Reader-Blackton	b Clay	4	(7) b Nash	0
W J V Tomlinson	not out	3	(2) lbw Nash	5
H Elliott	b Bates	0	not out	20
W Bestwick	lbw Bates	0		
	Extras (3 lb, 1 w)	4	Extras (18 b, 7 lb)	25
	Total	83	Total (8 wkts)	193

Fall: 1-0, 2-0, 3-0, 4-29, 5-53, 6-63,
7-72, 8-80, 9-80.

1-35, 2-63, 3-67, 4-96, 5-107,
6-115, 7-115, 8-116.

Bowling: Clay 18-6-26-3; Nash 15-6-19-2;
Bates 6.5-1-17-4; Creber 8-2-17-0.

Clay 16-2-62-1; Nash 25-9-56-5;
Bates 10.2-1-31-1; Creber 3-0-19-1.

DERBYSHIRE v ESSEX
At Queen's Park, Chesterfield, on July 18, 19 & 20, 1904
Derbyshire won by nine wickets

ESSEX	*First innings*		*Second innings*	
F L Fane	lbw b Curgenven	3	b Warren	2
H A Carpenter	b Bestwick	5	c Warren b Bestwick	2
P A Perrin	not out	343	c & b Warren	8
C P McGahey	b Bestwick	32	c Cadman b Bestwick	5
F H Gillingham	c & b Warren	43	absent hurt	0
E H D Sewell	b Warren	10	c Cadman b Curgenven	41
W Reeves	b Warren	0	b Bestwick	0
R P Keigwin	lbw b Ashcroft	14	c Needham b Warren	0
J W H T Douglas	b Ollivierre	47	not out	27
A E Russell	c Humphries b Cadman	23	b Curgenven	0
C P Buckenham	lbw b Bestwick	3	b Warren	8
	Extras (2b, 5lb, 4nb, 3w)	14	Extras (1lb, 1nb, 2w)	4
	Total (138.1 six-ball overs)	587	Total (39.1 overs)	97

Fall: 1-12, 2-132, 3-179, 4-300,
5-314, 6-314, 7-383, 8-513, 9-586.

1-4, 2-4, 3-17, 4-21, 5-21, 6-25,
7-33, 8-83, 9-97.

Bowling: Warren 29-3-143-3; Bestwick
42.1-8-160-3; Cadman 22-3-65-1; Storer
7-0-41-0; Curgenven 16-1-67-1; Ashcroft
7-1-38-1; Morton 8-1-39-0; Wright 4-0-15-0;
Ollivierre 3-0-15-1.

Bestwick 16-4-34-3;
Warren 16.1-5-42-4; Cadman
2-0-10-0; Curgenven 5-2-7-2.

DERBYSHIRE	*First innings*		*Second innings*	
L G Wright	c Fane b Reeves	68	c Carpenter b Buckenham	1
C A Ollivierre	b Reeves	229	not out	92
W Storer	b Buckenham	44	not out	48
E M Ashcroft	b Sewell	34		
E Needham	b Reeves	47		
G Curgenven	b Buckenham	31		
A Morton	b Reeves	16		
A Warren	b Douglas	18		
S W A Cadman	c Douglas b Reeves	34		
J Humphries	not out	2		
W Bestwick	lbw b Douglas	0		
	Extras (6b, 18lb, 1w)	25	Extras (4b, 2lb, 1nb, 1w)	8
	Total (134.3 overs)	548	Total (1 wkt, 30 overs)	149

Fall: 1-191, 2-319, 3-378, 4-401;
5-462, 6-478, 7-499, 8-530, 9-544.

1-11.

Bowling: Buckenham 43-5-176-2; Keigwin
7-1-36-0; Reeves 51-7-192-5; Douglas
15.3-1-54-2; McGahey 11-2-34-0; Sewell 7-0-31-1.

Buckenham 13-0-78-1;
Reeves 13-1-43-0; Douglas
2-0-14-0; McGahey 2-1-6-0.

YORKSHIRE v DERBYSHIRE
At Queen's Park, Chesterfield, on August 18, 19 & 20, 1898
Yorkshire won by an innings and 397 runs

YORKSHIRE	*First innings*	
J T Brown	hit wkt b Storer	300
J Tunnicliffe	c Davidson (F) b Storer	243
Lord Hawke	c Walker b Storer	14
D Denton	b Davidson (F)	45
G H Hirst	c Davidson (G) b Walker	0
F S Jackson	c Storer b Walker	14
W Rhodes	c Storer b Walker	6
F W Milligan	c Chattertonn b Davidson F	4
E Smith	c Storer b Walker	4
S Haigh	c Ashcroft b Davidson (F)	13
D Hunter	not out	0
	Extras (14 b, 4 lb, 1 nb)	19
	Total (156.3 overs)	662

Fall of wickets: 1-554, 2-569, 3-578, 4-582, 5-600, 7-611, 7-625, 8-630, 9-662.

Bowling: Davidson (G) 1-0-3-0; Walker 55-11-199-4; Davidson (F) 39.3-9-133-3; Sugg 5-0-27-0; Bagshaw 11-1-50-0; Storer 26-1-142-3; Ashcroft 6-1-21-0; Evershed 3-0-13-0; Wright 3-0-24-0; Charlesworth 7-1-31-0.

DERBYSHIRE	*First innings*		*Second innings*	
S H Evershed	c Hunter b Jackson	18	b Smith	12
L G Wright	c Lord Hawke b Hirst	0	st Hunter b Rhodes	5
H Bagshaw	c Haigh b Jackson	20	b Jackson	2
W Storer	c Denton b Milligan	13	c Rhodes b Jackson	25
W Chatterton	b Milligan	6	c & b Rhodes	54
G A Davidson	b Jackson	36	lbw b Jackson	2
E M Ashcroft	c Hunter b Jackson	1	not out	21
W Sugg	c Brown b Smith	8	b Rhodes	3
F Davidson	c Haigh b Smith	3	retired hurt	5
A Charlesworth	c Haigh b Rhodes	7	absent hurt	0
G G Walker	not out	0	b Haigh	7
	Extras (5 b, 1lb)	6	Extras (15 b, 6 lb)	21
	Total (58.1 overs)	118	Total (102.1 overs)	157

Fall: 1-4, 2-39, 3-48, 4-59, 5-76,
6-77, 7-102, 8-105, 9-118.

1-20, 2-50, 3-74 4-80, 5-95,
6-112, 7-118, 8-137, 9-157.

Bowling: Hirst 10-3-19-1; Jackson 28-12-52-4;
Milligan 12-3-36-2; Smith 7.1-6-5-2;
Rhodes 1-1-0-1.

Jackson 37-22-26-3;
Milligan 4-2-6-0; Smith
21-10-35-1; Rhodes 29-13-47-3;
Brown 4-1-9-0; Haigh 7.1-4-13-1.

DERBYSHIRE v AUSTRALIAN IMPERIAL FORCES
At County Ground, Derby, on July 14 and 15, 1919
Derbyshire won by 36 runs

DERBYSHIRE	*First innings*		*Second innings*	
L Oliver	c Oldfield b Lampard	19	c Oldfield b Gregory	8
S W A Cadman	b Gregory	8	b Gregory	8
G Beet	b Gregory	0	c Stirling b Collins	18
W N Malthouse	c Winning b Collins	30	b Gregory	9
A Morton	b Lampard	36	b Gregory	1
J D Southern	c Oldfield b Gregory	7	c Lampard b Gregory	43
T F Revill	b Winning	16	c Winning b Collins	0
H Wild	st Oldfield b Trenerry	31	c Gregory b Collins	2
A Severn	not out	21	c Gregory v Collins	10
J Horsley	st Oldfield b Stirling	0	lbw b Gregory	0
G Ratcliffe	st Oldfield b Trenerry	3	not out	5
	Extras (1 b, 5 lb, 4 nb)	10	Extras (2 b, 3 lb, 3 nb)	8
	Total (84.4 overs)	181	Total (32.5 overs)	112

Fall: 1-26, 2-26, 3-36, 4-84, 5-93, 6-121, 7-125, 8-175, 9-176.

1-15, 2-18, 3-42, 4-47, 5-48, 6-50, 7-68, 8-100, 9-106.

Bowling: Gregory 29-5-75-3; Collins 16-5-23-1; Lampard 17-2-47-2; Winning 13-6-15-1; Stirling 7-3-6-1; Trenerry 2.4-1-5-2.

Gregory 16.5-2-65-6; Collins 16-3-39-4.

IMPERIAL FORCES	*First innings*		*Second innings*	
H L Collins	c Ratcliffe b Horsley	0	c Ratcliffe b Horsley	16
W L Trenerry	b Horsley	69	c Beet b Horsley	9
E A Bull	c Malthouse b Morton	2	lbw b Morton	5
C E Pellew	b Morton	15	b Horsley	0
C B Willis	c Horsley b Morton	0	b Horsley	1
J T Murray	b Horsley	0	b Morton	54
A W Lampard	lbw b Horsley	0	b Horsley	0
W S Stirling	b Horsley	0	b Morton	0
J M Gregory	b Horsley	28	c Wild b Horsley	5
W A Oldfield	not out	2	not out	26
C S Winning	lbw b Morton	5	st Beet b Ratcliffe	10
	Extras (2 b, 2 nb)	4	Extras (2 b, 2 lb, 2 nb)	6
	Total (38 overs)	125	Total (44.5 overs)	132

Fall: 1-0, 2-6, 3-42, 4-42, 5-55, 6-55, 7-55, 8-101, 9-118.

1-19, 2-26, 3-26, 4-28, 5-36, 6-41, 7-42, 8-60, 9-105.

Bowling: Horsley 19-6-55-6; Morton 19-6-66-4.

Horsley 21-6-62-6; Morton 22-2-54-3; Ratcliffe 1.5-0-10-1.

MCC AUSTRALIAN TOURING TEAM v REST OF ENGLAND
At Lord's on May 26, 27 & 28, 1937
MCC Australian Touring Team won by 69 runs

MCC AUSTRALIA	*First innings*		*Second innings*	
C J Barnett	c Langridge b Gover	12	b Gover	7
T S Worthington	not out	156	c Todd b Gover	12
W R Hammond	c Jones b Stephenson	47	c Hutton b Todd	45
M Leyland	c & b Stephenson	25	c Holmes b Todd	28
R E S Wyatt	c Maxwell b Stephenson	0	b Gover	42
J Hardstaff	lbw b Gover	2	c sub b Gover	24
L E G Ames	c Jones b Gover	45	c Holmes b Gover	4
H Verity	c Dollery b Jones	17	b Gover	0
R W V Robins	c Paynter b Langridge	58	not out	3
G O Allen	b Langridge	0	lbw b Gover	0
K Farnes	b Stephenson	5	b Stephenson	1
	Extras (3 b, 4 lb, 2 nb)	9	Extras (5 b, 2 lb)	7
	Total	376	Total	173

Fall: 1-24, 2-98, 3-145, 4-145,
5-154, 6-223, 7-258, 8-345, 9-348.

1-19, 2-28, 3-95, 4-100, 5-161,
6-167, 7-172, 8-172, 9-172.

Bowling: Gover 27-3-76-3; Todd 9-2-50-0;
Stephenson 25.4-3-90-4; Langridge
20-4-68-2; Jones 9-0-46-1; Hutton 5-0-24-0;
Parks 7-1-13-0.

Bowling: Gover 14-1-44-7;
Todd 11-2-46-2; Stephenson
12.2-1-63-1; Langridge 3-0-13-0.

REST ENGLAND	*First innings*		*Second innings*	
L Hutton	c Hammond b Robins	18	c Allen b Verity	50
J H Parks	lbw b Allen	2	b Farnes	64
E Paynter	c Worthington b Farnes	1	c Farnes b Verity	21
H E Dollery	b Robins	15	c Worthington b Wyatt	41
L J Todd	c Ames b Allen	24	c Ames b Verity	3
E R T Holmes	b Verity	11	c Hammond b Wyatt	8
J Langridge	c Hammond b Farnes	80	not out	22
C R N Maxwell	b Allen	4	c Hammond b Allen	17
J W A Stephenson	not out	68	b Allen	1
A R Gover	b Hammond	1	b Allen	7
E C Jones	absent hurt	0	absent hurt	0
	Extras (1 b, 4 lb, 5 nb, 1 w)	11	Extras (1 b, 7 lb, 3 nb)	11
	Total	235	Total	245

Fall: 1-4, 2-13, 3-34, 4-41, 5-67,
6-77, 7-86, 8-234, 9-235.

1-107, 2-125, 3-180, 4-182, 5-195,
6-195, 7-219, 8-230, 9-245.

Bowling: Farnes 20-3-54-2; Allen 16-2-50-3;
Hammond 7.3-2-18-1; Robins 16-0-58-2;
Verity 9-4-13-1; Leyland 3-0-15-0; Wyatt
6-1-12-0; Worthington 2-0-4-0.

Farnes 16-4-30-1;
Allen 15-2-65-3; Hammond
9-0-31-0; Robins 8-1-40-0;
Verity 18-5-55-3; Wyatt 8-1-13-2.

MISCELLANEOUS SCORECARDS

LEICESTERSHIRE v DERBYSHIRE
At Leicester, June 15, 17 & 18, 1935
Match drawn

DERBYSHIRE	*First innings*		*Second innings*	
A E Alderman	b Geary	0	b Marlow	29
H Storer	lbw b Geary	5	lbw b Geary	33
T S Worthington	b Geary	44	c Berry b Marlow	37
L F Townsend	b Geary	5	c Marlow b Smith	35
E Carrington	c Astill b Smith	40	c Geary b Smith	24
G F Hodgkinson	b Geary	0	c Corrall b Smith	0
A Townsend	not out	24	c Smith b Marlow	9
A V Pope	c Corrall b Smith	0	c Prentice b Marlow	21
H Elliott	b Smith	2	not out	9
T B Mitchell	c Prentice b Smith	6	b Smith	1
W H Copson	c Prentice b Smith	9	c Corrall b Marlow	9
	Extras (b 1, lb 3, nb 1)	5	Extras (b 16, lb 1, w 1, nb 2)	20
	Total	140	Total	227

Fall: 1-4, 2-14, 3-22, 4-78,
5-80, 6-112, 7-112, 8-120, 9-130.

1-67, 2-67, 3-115, 4-169, 5-169,
6-174, 7-204, 8-207, 9-210.

Bowling: Smith 20.5-7-51-5; Geary
29-13-46-5; Marlow 18-5-23-0; Astill 8-2-15-0.

Smith 23-5-57-4; Geary 26-8-57-1;
Astill 8-0-24-0; Marlow 16.2-3-69-5.

LEICESTERSHIRE	*First innings*		*Second innings*	
A W Shipman	c Worthington b Mitchell	10	not out	60
L G Berry	b Mitchell	11	c Storer b Townsend (L)	18
N F Armstrong	c Worthington b Mitchell	13	c Copson b Mitchell	5
F T Prentice	lbw (n) Mitchell	10	hit wkt b Mitchell	4
G S Watson	b Mitchell	0	not out	16
C A Coleman	b Mitchell	8		
W E Astill	b Mitchell	18		
G Geary	b Mitchell	16		
H A Smith	c Worthington b Mitchell	6		
W H Marlow	st Elliott b Mitchell	14		
P Corrall	not out	8		
	Extras (b 5, lb 4)	9	Extras (lb 7, w 1)	8
	Total	123	Total (3 wkts)	111

Fall: 1-21, 2-30, 3-39, 4-39, 5-56,
6-57, 7-85, 8-92, 9-110.

1-29, 2-52. 3-72.

Bowling: Copson 16-3-30-0; Worthington
2-0-6-0; Mitchell 19.1-4-64-10;
Townsend (L)6-2-14-0.

Copson 4-0-20-0;
Worthington 3-1-7-0; Mitchell
17-4-39-2; Townsend (L)
15-5-35-1; Pope 4-3-2-0.

DERBYSHIRE v WARWICKSHIRE
At Derby, July 17 & 19, 1937
Derbyshire won by five wickets

WARWICKSHIRE	*First innings*		*Second innings*	
W A Hill	c Smith b Copson	0	b Mitchell	105
N Kilner	c Skinner b Copson	7	b Copson	0
F R Santall	b Copson	0	b Copson	1
J Buckingham	b Pope (A V)	9	(7) b Pope (G H)	7
R E S Wyatt	b Pope (A V)	1	(4) c Smith b Mitchell	30
H E Dollery	b Copson	7	(5) c Skinner b Copson	98
J S Ord	b Copson	1	(6) c Worthington b Mitchell	9
P Cranmer	not out	2	lbw b Pope (GH)	6
J H Mayer	b Copson	0	not out	14
W E Fantham	b Copson	0	c Pope (G H) b Mitchell	4
W E Hollies	b Copson	0	lbw b Mitchell	0
	Extras (lb 1)	1	Extras (b 9, lb 7, w 1)	17
	Total	28	Total	291

Fall: 1-0, 2-2, 3-17, 4-17,
5-18, 6-21, 7-26, 8-26, 9-28.

1-1, 2-3. 3-234, 4-238,
5-249, 6-264, 7-273, 8-273, 9-291.

Bowling: Copson 8.2-2-11-8; Rhodes
4-0-11-0; Pope (A V) 4-1-5-2.

Copson 32-4-82-3; Rhodes
5-2-12-0; Pope (A V) 21-1-56-0;
Pope (G H) 14-5-26-2; Mitchell
31.5-5-80-5; Townsend 2-1-2-0;
Worthington 5-0-16-0.

DERBYSHIRE	*First innings*		*Second innings*	
D Smith	b Mayer	6	c Cranmer b Mayer	32
A E Alderman	run out	8	lbw b Mayer	15
T S Worthington	b Hollies	5	c Buckingham b Mayer	18
A F Skinner	lbw b Mayer	13	(5) not out	12
L F Townsend	c Santall b Wyatt	52	(4) b Mayer	2
G H Pope	b Mayer	8	c Dollery b Mayer	6
A E G Rhodes	run out	58	not out	7
A V Pope	b Mayer	4		
H Elliott	b Wyatt	9		
T B Mitchell	st Buckingham b Mayer	21		
W H Copson	not out	30		
	Extras (b 12, lb 1)	13	Extras (lb 1)	1
	Total	227	Total (5 wkts)	93

Fall: 1-16, 2-20, 3-42, 4-52,
5-63, 6-148, 7-164, 8-165, 9-191.

1-39, 2-52, 3-59, 4-70, 5-82.

Bowling: Mayer 23-7-83-5; Wyatt
18.4-6-48-2; Hollies 11-1-42-1; Fantham
2-0-22-0; Santall 5-0-19-0.

Mayer 12.4-0-39-5; Wyatt
9-0-44-0; Hollies 3-0-9-0.

DERBYSHIRE v SOMERSET

At Chesterfield, June 11, 1947
Derbyshire won by an innings and 125 runs

SOMERSET	*First innings*		*Second innings*	
F S Lee	lbw b Pope	16	c Elliott b Gladwin	1
H Gimblett	c Vaulkhard b Gladwin	3	c Smith b Pope	2
M Coope	b Pope	13	b Pope	3
H F T Buse	c Alderman b Rhodes	23	c Smith b Gladwin	4
R J O Meyer	b Pope	0	c Revill b Pope	0
A W Wellard	b Pope	4	(10) c Elliott b Pope	0
G W L Courtenay	b Pope	1	(6) c Smith b Pope	3
W T Luckes	lbw b Rhodes	1	(7) b Rhodes	11
J Lawrence	lbw b Rhodes	0	(8) c Townsend b Pope	5
M F Tremlett	b Pope	1	(9) b Pope	1
H Hazell	not out	2	not out	8
	Extras (b 1, lb 2, nb 1)	4	Extras	0
	Total	68	Total	38

Fall: 1-3, 2-30, 3-37, 4-39,
5-43, 6-51, 7-60, 8-60, 9-63.

1-2, 2-6, 3-6, 4-6, 5-12,
6-14, 7-23, 8-30, 9-30.

Bowling: Pope 21-11-34-6; Gladwin
10-6-10-1; Rhodes 10.2-2-20-3.

Pope 9.1-2-16-7; Gladwin
8-3-14-2; Rhodes 1-0-8-1.

DERBYSHIRE	*First innings*	
A E Alderman	c Buse b Meyer	12
A F Townsend	st Luckes b Hazell	37
C S Elliott	c & b Hazell	46
P Vaulkhard	b Wellard	84
D Smith	c Wellard b Hazell	5
G H Pope	c Wellard b Hazell	2
A C Revill	lbw b Hazell	2
F E Marsh	b Lawrence	0
C Gladwin	b Buse	35
A E G Rhodes	c Wellard b Buse	0
E J Gothard	not out	2
	Extras (lb 5, nb 1)	6
	Total	231

Fall: 1-17, 2-92, 3-117, 4-125, 5-131, 6-137, 7-138, 8-221, 9-227.

Bowling: Wellard 11.2-2-35-1; Buse 3-2-3-2; Meyer 14-4-45-1;
Lawrence 11-0-71-1; Hazell 18-1-64-5; Tremlett 2-0-7-0.

Index

Abel R 59, 113, 118
Aberdeenshire 126
Adams C J 94, 125, 170, 231, 274, 289
Aird R 87, 285
Aitken L 214
Akers-Douglas I S 257
Alderman A E 133, 140, 155-56, 170-71, **176**, 186, 217-18, 221-24, 227, 229-30, 233-35, 238-39, 241-42, 244, 246, 248, 250-54, 256, 258-66, 268, 270, 272, 281
Aldred P 125
Allan F E 65
Allen B O 226
Allen G O 56, 107, 167-68, 196, 201, 267, 269
Alletson E 132
Alley W E 217
Allom M J C 166
Amarnath L 206
Amar Singh 266
Ames L E G 138, 162, 197, 268
Anderson I S 287
Andrews W H R 253-54, 270
Appleby A 23-24
Arlidge J 40
Arlott J 282
Armstrong H H 54
Armstrong N F 229-30
Armstrong T R 190, 218, 220-21, 240, 270
Armstrong W W 102, 124
Arnold J 221, 227, 236, 248
Arsenal 48, 97, 150, 158
Ashcroft Dr E M 55-56, 117, 187, 207
Ashdown W H 223, 245, 250, 256
Ashton C T 235
Ashton H S 235
Astill W E 271-72
Aston Villa 156-57
Attenborough T 24
Attewell W 80
Auckland 163, 166, 183, 202
Australians 64, 67-69, 71-72, 75, 80, 89-90, 96, 102-03, 107, 109, 113, 115, 121, 123-25, 135, 137, 139-40, 152, 163, 167, 183, 185, 188, 190, 194-96, 199, 208, 211-13, 222, 225, 270, 283-84
Azharuddin, Mohammad 118, 164

Bacchus F 200
Baggallay R R C 121-22, **179**
Bagshaw H 61-62, 76, 79, 82-83, 91-93, 96, 112, **179**, 272
Baildon Green CC 209
Bailey J 21, 278
Bailey P 57
Bailey T E 21, 267
Baker G 116
Bakewell A H ('Fred') 182, 243, 268-69
Baldwin H (Senior & Junior) 91-92
Bannerman A 80
Bannerman C 80
Bannister A 19
Barber W 181-83, 208, 220
Bari, Wasim 139

Barling T H 155, 240, 264, 267
Barlow E J 280
Barlow R G 24-25, 37, 86, 134
Barnes S F 103
Barnes W 38
Barnett C J 251
Barnett K J 94, 110, 118, 129-30, 134, 183-84, 186-87, 274-75, 278, 286, 288-89, 291
Barratt E 58
Barrington K F 142
Barrow I 202
Barton M R 249
Bassano C W G 95
Bassetlaw League 189, 194
Base S J 126
Bates W 57-58
Beaumont J 77
Bedser A V 188, 212, 282
Beet G 104-06, 125-26, **179**
Beet G A 104
Beet G H C 104
Bell G F 47
Belper Meadows CC 153
Bennett J **176**
Bentley J 21
Berkshire 190
Berry L G 171, 229-30
Berry R 199
Berwick J A 115
Bestwick R S 106
Bestwick W 100-01, 104-08, 124, 126, 129, 131-32, 136, 138, 162, **174, 179**, 185, 194, 198-99, 218, 272, 277, 283
Bicknell D 109
Billyeald J 22
Binks J G 141
Bird R E 151
Birmingham City 148, 150
Bishop I R 289
Blackburn Rovers 10, 115, 153, 187
Blackham J Mc 31, 67
Blacklidge H 135
Blackpool CC 217
Blackwell I D 95
Blaxland L B 133-34, 185, 212
Bligh, The Hon Ivo 38
Bloomer S 160
Blunt R C 109
Boden H 18
Boden W 18, **179**
Boje N 102
Boland 95
Bolton Wanderers 60
Bolus J B 71, 279
Booth A 189, 278
Border 95
Botha A G 95
Boulton C D 152-53
Bowden J 47, 50, 144-45, 185
Bowen R 7-10, 14-15, 29-30, 36
Bowes W E 189, 195, 218, 220, 234, 253, 261, 266
Bowler P D 94, 118, 164, 275, 289

Index

Bowley F L 143
Bowley T 77
Bowring T 275
Boycott G 71, 79
Boyes S 215, 263
Boyle H F 67
Bracey F C 119
Bradford City 159
Bradman D G 66, 167, 196, 213, 222, 228, 283
Brailsford F C ('Jim') 200
Brand D 51
Brand H 51
Brann G 96
Braund L C 135
Bray C 53, 116, 203
Breakwell D 271
Brelsford J 58
Brennan D V 141
Brentford 154
Bridges J J 145
Briggs J 25, 60, 92, 116-17
Brighton & Hove Albion 219
Bristol City 149
Bristol Rovers 157, 219, 230
Brockwell W 113, 118
Brookes D 182, 269
Brown A M 287
Brown F R 193, 221, 269
Brown J T 85, 112-15
Brown W A 208, 222
Brown W C 269
Brownett V 275
Buckenham C 108
Buckinghamshire 126
Buckston G M 128-29
Buckston R H R 129, **173**, 207
Bull C H 225, 245, 255, 267
Buller J S 225
Burnham G J **173**
Burnley CC 126, 131
Burnley FC 60, 97, 150, 153, 156
Burnup C J 48-49
Burns W 103
Burrough H D 224
Burton Albion 160
Bury 149-50, 153, 187
Buse H F T 214, 254
Butler H J 203
Butt H R 138
Buxton FC 157
Buxton I R 46, 156, 158-60, 274, 279

Caddick A R 216
Cadman J 64
Cadman S W A 127, 131, 135-37, 155, 162, 166, **174**, 183, 185, 207, 218
Calthorpe, the Hon F S 162
Cambridgeshire 162
Cambridge University 48, 50-51, 88, 94, 103, 120, 122, 129, 160, 162, 169, 184, 190, 202, 213, 229, 235, 285
Cameron H ('Jock') 182, 235-36

Canterbury 109
Cardiff City 148, 150
Cardus, Sir N 116, 219
Carpenter H 162
Carpenter R 162
Carr A W 132
Carr D B 43, 87, 118, 133, 160, 164, 186, 199, 212-13, 277-79, 281, 283-85, 288
Carr, Major D 71
Carrington E 186, 189, 224-26, 234, 236, 241, 243-45, 248, 251, 260
Carter H S 151-52, 158
Carter W 106, 144, 160
Cartland G H 21
Carver J 187-88
Castens H 83
Ceylon (see Sri Lanka)
Chadwick Rev RM 213
Chaplin H P 104
Chapman J 101-02, 120-21, 127, **179**
Chapman A P F 131, 168, 208, 245
Charlesworth A 114
Charlesworth C 101
Chatterton J 12
Chatterton W 12, 27-28, 37, 53-55, 60, 62, 65, 72-74, 76-77, 79-81, 84, 88-93, 96, 103, 112-13, 153, **179**, 181, 272
Chelsea 149, 159
Cheshire 49, 54-55, 80
Chester F 188
Chester FC 149
Chesterfield, Earl of 18
Chesterfield FC 160, 247
Cholerton N 87
Clark E W ('Nobby') 243
Clarke C C 130-31
Clough B H 149, 159
Cochrane R S T 86, **174**
Coles P 113
Collard A H 87
Collin T 258
Collins A E J 88-89
Collins H L 123-24
Colman S 113
Colne 212-14, 217
Commins J 102
Commonwealth XI 141, 171, 216-17, 279
Compton D C S 107, 150, 203, 211-12, 247, 265
Compton L H 139
Constantine, Learie 110
Constantine, Lebrun 110
Cook G 286
Cook T E 219, 223, 267
Cooper E 151
Cooper T 149
Copson W H 155, **173, 176**, 186, 193-94, 199-204, 206-07, 218-21, 223-24, 226-30, 234-35, 237-38, 241-43, 245-46, 248-56, 258-64, 266-70, 272, 278, 281, 283
Corinthians 131, 235
Cork D G 46, 94, 140, 144, 207, 216, 275-76, 278, 290-91

Cork City 152
Cornford J 242
Cornford W 224
Corrall P 142
Cotter A 137
Coventry City 148, 150, 187-88, 219
Cowdrey M C 188
Cranfield L M 240
Crawford J N 43, 119
Creese W L 221-22, 259, 263
Cromford Meadows CC 157-58
Crommelin-Brown J 131
Crompton CC 217
Crooks S D 138
Croom A J 242
Cropper W 11, 53-54, 58, 62-63, 76, 82, 89-90, 154
Crossland J 26
Cullinan D J 94-95
Cupitt J 80
Curgenven G 42-43, 170
Curgenven H G 42, 200
Curgenven Dr W G 42
Cuttell W 116-17
Cutmore J A 203, 244, 251

Dacre C C 225-26, 241
Daniell J 121
Darling J 71, 102, 107, 135, 137
Darley Dale CC 111, 159, 287
Darnley, Lord 38
Davenport G 80
Davidson F 23, 37, 112
Davidson G A 10, 25, 27-28, 37, 53-55, 59, 61-63, 72-73, 76-77, 79-85, 88-94, 96-97 113-14, 169, **179**, 207, 272
Davidson J 23, 94
Davidson K R 220
Davies J G W 213
Davis J 278
Davis J W 154
Dawkes G O 87, 141-43, 156, 158, 160, 171, 181, 200, 214, 216, 278, 283
Dawson G 215-16
Day J 119
Dean K J 125
DeFreitas P A J 216, 275, 290
Delacombe W B 81, 86, **179**
Derby County 10-12, 22, 28, 60, 97, 101, 138, 148-51, 153-56, 158, 160-61, 247
Derby Junction 153
Derby Midland 97, 153
Derbyshire Friars 81
De Smidt R 146
de Trafford C 74, 84
Devonshire Park 113
Dewes J D 213
Dexter E R 200
Disney J J 31, 139
Dixon J 115
Draper W 42
Docker F D 44
Docker L C 44-45, 58, 60

Docker R 44
Dollery H E ('Tom') 204, 267
Donnan H 89
Donnelly M P 156
Dorset 190, 213
Douglas J W H T 19-20, 102, 108, 121, 137
Dowman M P 207
Doyle D 11
Doyle, Sir Arthur Conan 35
Duckworth G 139, 141, 171, 239, 268
Dudleston B 118
Duke of Devonshire 271
Duleepsinhji K 166
Dunbar J G 285
Durham 46, 105, 107-08, 183, 207, 276
Dwyer E B 19
Dyson A H 161

Eadie W S 76
Eagar E D R 33, 216
Eardley-Simpson, Major 121, 128-29, 131, 136, 144, 237
Earle G F 145
East D 139
Eastman L 115, 235
Eckersley P T 228
Edgson C 229-30
Edrich J H 188
Edrich W J 168-69, 203, 211-12, 247, 278
Eggar J D **173**, 187
Elliott C S 138, 160, **173, 176**, 186-88, 200, 245, 253-54, 256, 258, 261, 268, 271, 281, 283
Elliott, Harold 139
Elliott, Harry 106, 129, 136-43, 145, 163, **173, 176**, 181, 185-86, 191, 197, 213-14, 218, 220, 222-24, 226-27, 229-30, 238, 240-41, 244-46, 248, 250-51, 256, 258, 262, 264, 266, 269, 272, 281, 284
Ellison Rev H 136
Emmett G M 143
Emmett T 57
Engel M 15-16
Essex 21, 27, 32, 34, 42-43, 53-54, 56, 73-74, 76-77, 81-82, 88, 90-91, 96, 99-100, 102, 108-12, 115-16, 127, 133, 137, 139, 143-45, 153-54, 158-59, 162, 164, 166, 187, 203, 215, 225-26, 230, 234, 244-46, 251-52, 255, 258, 263-64, 267, 269, 273, 286-89
Estridge E 41
Evans T G 138, 141
Evershed E 48
Evershed F 47, 73
Evershed S H 47, 76, 81-82, 93, 96, 117, **179**
Evershed W 47-48, 55
Everton 150, 153, 171
Exham P G 28, 153
Eyre T J P 281

Fagg A E 153, 208, 250
Fairbrother J 187
Fairbrother N H 290-91
Fairfax A G 195

Index

Fane F L 42, 108, 200
Farnes K 193, 201, 263
Farnsworth K 58, 112
Farrimond W 139
Fender P G H 200, 234
Ferris J J 64-65, 72, 290
Field F 102
Finney R J 161, 286
Fisher H 233
Fishlock L B 221, 234, 239-40, 264, 267
Fleetwood-Smith L O'B 152
Fletcher T 154
Flint J 24, 29-30, 40-41
Flint L E **179**
Flowers W 38, 74, 88
Foley E 22, 43
Ford A 43
Ford F 43
Ford N 43-44, 221
Ford W 43
Forester T 120, 126, **179**
Forfarshire 209
Foster H K 84, 143
Foster R E 84, 143, 163
Foster T 37, 139, **178**
Foster W L 84
Foulke W 159-60
Fowler A 104
Fraser G 148
Free Foresters 50
Freeman A P 32-33, 108, 224, 250
Frindall W 15, 34
Frost G **178**
Fry C B 43, 56
Fullwood W 142, 151

Gallian J 109
Garrett T W 65
Gatting M W 288
Geary G 237, 264-65
Gentlemen of England 47, 124
Gentlemen of Kent 18
Gentlemen of the North 30
Gentlemen v Players 20
Gibb P A 104, 168
Gibbons H H I H 225-26, 237, 245, 255, 267
Gibson A 8
Giffen G 64, 88
Gilchrist A C 140
Gilbert E 26
Gilbert J D H 249
Gilligan A E R 162
Gilligan A H H 162, 166
Gillingham 154
Gillingham F H 108
Gilman J 40
Gimblett H 254
Gladwin C 33, 105, 107, 151, **175**, 194-95, 199, 208, 216, 277-78, 281-83
Gladwin J 208
Glamorgan 96, 105-06, 132, 138-39, 146, 161, 182, 189, 191-92, 209, 228, 230, 246-47, 250, 252, 258-59. 262, 267, 270, 273, 283
Glossop North End 48, 97, 151, 154
Gloucestershire 7-10, 13-16, 27, 46, 49, 52, 56, 60, 84, 90-91, 104, 130-31, 140, 143, 165, 201, 222, 225-26, 228, 230, 238, 240-41, 246-47, 250-52, 258-59, 265, 268, 271, 273, 275, 287, 289
Glover A 36
Goddard T W 56, 168, 204, 222, 240, 251
Goldsmith S C 289
Golesworthy M 33
Gooch G A 168
Goodall J 151, 153
Goodman P 110
Gothard E J **173**, 196, 283
Gover A R 168, 193, 201, 210, 221, 240, 250
Grace E M 100, 120
Grace W G 10, 13, 23, 25, 35, 40, 61, 65-66, 68, 76, 88, 90, 96, 105, 118, 120, 273
Graham H 80
Grainger J 86
Grant G ('Jackie') 202
Grant R 202
Graveney T W 104
Greensmith W T 270
Greenwood F E 238
Gregory D 12, 19, 22, 30
Gregory J M 123-24
Gregory R J 221
Gregory S E 107, 135
Griffin G 26, 224-25
Griffith F A 290
Griffith S C ('Billy') 285
Grimsby Town 11, 97, 148-49
Grimshaw I 58
Grimshaw N 252
Grout A T W 139
Gunn G 37, 162, 239
Gunn G V 239, 241, 262
Gunn J 115, 119, 239
Gunn W 37, 90, 114-15, 239

Hassan, Adnan 95
Hadow E 82
Hadlee R J 216
Haig N E 163
Haigh S 102
Hall I W 156-58
Hall W 25, 76
Hallam A 92, 119
Hamer A 78, 160, 283
Hammond W R 162-63, 167-68, 195-96, 202, 208-09, 212-13, 222, 240-41, 252, 262, 266, 272-73
Hampshire 11, 19, 28, 32-34, 36, 46, 51, 54, 77, 85, 91, 93-94, 96, 100, 112-13, 118, 120, 124-25, 129, 142-43, 156-57, 170, 184-85, 204, 215-16, 221, 227, 230, 236, 245-46, 248-49, 256, 258-59, 261-65, 267-68, 273, 275-76, 287, 289-90
Hampshire J H 71
Hancock J W 94, **179**
Handford J 43
Hardinge H T W 153
Hardstaff J (Junior) 168, 181, 239, 261-62, 269

Hardstaff J (Senior) 181
Hare S N 102
Harris C B 220, 239, 262, 266
Harris, Lord 13, 18-19, 23, 26, 65
Harwich and Parkeston 160
Hassett A L 213
Hawke, Lord 19, 21, 44-45, 57, 70-71, 73, 90, 109, 113-14
Hay G 24
Hay J 24, 31-32
Hayhurst A 275, 289
Hayward T W 90, 113, 118
Hazare, Vijay 109
Hazare, Vivek 109
Hazell H 270
Headley G A 163, 202
Heane G F H 155, 241, 266
Heanor CC 105
Heanor Town 154
Hearne J T 90
Hearne J W 228
Heath G E M 216
Heckmondwike 199
Hemingway G E 49
Henderson R 59
Hendren E ('Patsy') 162, 197, 221, 228, 247, 265, 267, 273
Hendrick M 56, 72, 200, 278-80, 286
Hertfordshire 151, 289
Herman O W 248-49
Hewitt B 112
Heywood CC 217
Hickleton Main CC 199
Hicks J 42
Hickton W 19, 22, 25, 31, 40-42, **178**
Higson P 50
Higson T A (Senior) 49-50, 114, 196
Higson T A (Junior) 50
Hill, Alan 126, 287
Hill, Arthur 100
Hill, Aubrey 204
Hill C 89, 97, 102, 107
Hill-Wood B S H (also see S H Wood) 48, 117-18
Hill-Wood C K H 50
Hill-Wood D J C 50
Hill-Wood P 50
Hill-Wood W W H 50-51, 131, 144, 190, 240, 248, 272
Hind A **178**
Hirst G H 70-71, 114-15, 119, 135
Hives, Lord 87
Hobbs J B 20, 104, 118, 131, 162, 221
Hodgkinson G F 152, 236
Holder V 125
Holding M 66, 290
Hollies E 199, 212, 242, 258
Holmes E R T 183, 239-40, 269
Holmes P 115-16
Holmes Rev R S 8, 112
Hooper E A 87
Hopwood J L 228, 238
Hornby A H 49, 59, 90

Horsley J 124-26, 131-32, 162, **173, 179**
Horton H 256
Horton J 256
Horton M 274, 280
Howard N D 160
Howell R 159
Howorth R 237, 255, 267-68
Huddersfield Town 157
Huish F H 138
Hull City 152
Hulme J J 44, 60, 62, 73-74, 76, 82-85, 89-91, 94-95, 105, 113
Hulme J (Middx) 267
Humphries J 102-04, 117, 123, 125-26, 139-41, 143, 146, **174**
Hunt G 253
Hunt H 253
Hunt S W 186
Hunter D 138
Hunter J 138
Hutchinson J M 145-47, **173, 177**, 199
Hutton L 78, 152, 163, 189, 202, 211, 213, 244, 253, 261, 268
Hyslop H 32

Iddon J 218-19, 238, 240, 255
Idle CC 205
Ilkeston Town 154
India 109, 118, 130, 141, 143, 160, 168, 186, 189, 191, 199, 209, 216-17, 260, 265-66, 268
Ingle R A 238, 270
Iremonger J 56
Israr Ali 134

Jackman R D 204
Jacksdale 105
Jackson A 195
Jackson A B 30, 278
Jackson A H M 144
Jackson F S 21, 102, 114
Jackson G L 130
Jackson G R 86, 105, 129-32, 140, **173**, 186, 194, 223, 225
Jackson H L 30, 78, 105, 107, **175**, 187, 194, 199, 204, 277-79, 282-83
Jackson L **178**
Jackson P F 237, 268
Jackson V E 171
Jacobs R 139
Jai L P 260
James K C 252
James W 139
Jacques T A ('Sandy') 244-45, 261
Jardine D R 103, 195, 200
Jean-Jacques M 126
Jeeves P 35
Jefferies S T 289-90
Jephson D L A 118-19
Jervis Hon W M 18, 185
Jessop G L 84, 152
Jobey G 149, 155
Johnson G W 153

Johnson H L 142, 185
Johnson I W 125
Jones A 103
Jones D M 110, 125, 274
Jones S P 68
Joshi U C 204
Juniper J 55
Jupp V W C 133

Karachi Whites 116
Kay J 228
Keeton W W 262, 266
Kelleway C 123
Kelly J M 104, 157, 283
Kennedy A S 124, 227
Kent 8, 10, 13, 15-16, 18-19, 26, 32, 41-44, 48, 54-55, 76-77, 86, 116-17, 130, 132, 136, 138-39, 141, 153, 157, 162, 165-66, 185, 190, 192, 204, 207-08, 223-24, 233, 241, 245-46, 248-50, 252-65, 267-69, 273, 276, 279-80, 288-89
Key K J 59
Killick E H 132
Kilner N 227-28, 254
Kilner R 228
Kirsten P N 200, 280, 286
Knott C J 278
Knott A P E 138, 141
Knowles J 262
Kortright C J 96
Krikken K M 73, 144, 290-91
Kuiper A P 287

Lacey F 54
Laker J C 21, 125, 199
Lamb A J 155, 168, 286
Lancashire 8-10, 12-13, 15, 18-19, 21-28, 30-32, 40-41, 49-50, 52, 55, 59-60, 69, 76, 83, 88, 91-93, 109, 113, 116-18, 120, 124-25, 130, 138, 140, 142, 158, 160, 165, 194, 199, 203-04, 208, 214, 218-19, 228, 230, 238, 240, 246, 255, 258-59, 263, 265, 268, 273, 275, 277, 286, 288-89, 291
Lancaster A J 86
Langdale G R 189-90, 266
Langridge, James 168, 224, 242
Langridge, John 219-20, 223, 241, 250, 267
Langton A B C 197, 235-36
Lara B C 108
Larkins W 286
Larwood H 36, 103, 162, 194-96, 207, 239, 241, 260, 262-63, 265-66, 272
Lawton A E 100-01, 117-20, 170, **174**, 272
Laycock, Sir Joseph 137
Lee C 190. 277
Lee E 93
Lee F M 224, 254
Lee G M 132-33, 145, 164, **173**, 185, 207, 212, 218
Lee J 161
Lee J W 224
Leeds United 149
Leicester City 149, 152, 161
Leicestershire 34, 54-55, 62, 68-69, 72-74, 81-82, 84-85, 88, 97, 99, 101, 103, 105-07, 111-12, 117-19, 121, 127, 132-33, 138, 141-44, 146, 152, 156, 159, 161, 170-71, 185, 198-99, 206-07, 223, 229-30, 237, 243, 246, 250, 258, 260, 264-65, 268, 271-75
Leinster CC 213
Lester G 199
Leveson-Gower's XI 182, 193, 246
Levett W H 138
Leyland M 168, 181, 211, 220, 227, 253, 261, 263, 265-66, 269
Lidget Green CC 199, 205, 213, 281
Lilley A A 36, 96-97
Lillywhite J 65
Lincoln City 148-49
Lincolnshire 18
Lindsay D 270
Liverpool 97
Livingston L ('Jock') 141
Llanelly 105
Loader P J 278, 290
Lock G A R 142, 285
Locker W 115
Lockheed Leamington 157
Lockwood W 80
Lohmann G A 65, 77, 86, 91
London County 40, 105, 120
Long E 124
Loughborough Town 97, 154
Lowndes W G L F 221
Lowson F A 78
Lucas A 100
Luckhurst B W 153
Luton Town 159
Lyon B H 238
Lyttelton S 75

Macartney C G 124
Macaulay G G 129, 134
MacLaren A C 50, 90, 108, 113, 135
Magnall R 87
Maher B J M 287
Mailey A A 195-96
Makepeace H 171
Malcolm D E 134, 140, 204, 275, 278
Mallett A A 270
Malthouse S 73, 76, 83
Malthouse W N 73
Marples C 160
Manchester United 149, 154
Mann N B F ('Tufty') 282
Manning T B 121
Mansfield Town 110, 158
Mansoor Akhtar 116
Marlow J 54-55
Marsh F 200
Marsh F E 171-72
Marsh S 139
Marshall H 168
Marshall J 46
Martin F 68
Martin S H 226
Mason G W 187

Massie R A L 68
Matlock CC 157
Matthews A D G 252
Maxwell C R 92
May P B H 142, 188, 285
Maynard E A J 28, 53, 91
MCC 16-18, 20-21, 27, 30-31, 33, 35-39, 42, 44, 47-48, 50-52, 54, 62, 66, 76-77, 80, 87-88, 90-91, 96, 103, 110-11, 118, 130, 141, 158, 162, 164, 166-67, 183, 190-91, 195, 201-02, 209, 216, 229, 233, 246, 272, 279, 285
McCabe S J 222
McCarthy C N 282
McCorkell N 169, 267
McCormick E L 92
McDonald E A 219
McGahey C P 110, 116, 127
McIntyre W 18, 24, 41
McKibbin T 62
McLeod C E 97
McMillan S T 154-55
McRae F M ('Peter') 270
Mead C P 221, 227, 248, 267
Mead W 32, 74
Meads E A 214
Melville A 211, 242
Merchant V M 260-61
Merrick T A 204
Middlesbrough 160
Middlesex 8-11, 13, 15-16, 39, 41, 43-44, 49, 52, 56, 65-66, 70, 77, 82, 88-89, 103-04, 107, 111, 114, 136, 138-39, 157, 162-63, 184, 198, 203, 224-25, 228-30, 246-47, 252, 254, 258, 261-63, 265, 268-69, 272-73, 288-89
Middleton C 288, 291
Midland Counties 89
Miller G 72, 126, 216, 280, 283, 286
Miller K R 213
Milligan F 21
Milne A A 128
Mir, Parvez 190
Mirza, Waheed 116
Mitchell A 181-82, 234, 253, 261
Mitchell B 197, 203
Mitchell T B 133, **176**, 186, 190, 193-99, 206-07, 213, 218-25, 227-28, 230, 234-46, 248, 250-54, 256, 258-60, 262, 264, 266, 268-70, 272, 279, 281-83
Mitchell-Innes N S 249
Mitchell's & Butler's 206, 209
Mitchell St George's CC 154
Moir D G 81
Mold A 25-26, 39, 89, 111
Moore R H 248
Morgan D C 28, 137-38, 186, 216, 281, 283
Morley F 37-38
Morley H A 153-54
Morley W 153
Morren T 159
Morris J E 46, 118, 130, 155, 183, 275, 289
Morrison G W 113
Mortensen O 161

Mortimer G 171
Morton, Arthur (Bakewell) 127-28
Morton, Arthur (Glossop) 46, 121, 124, 126-27, 131, 137, **174, 179**, 218
Morton Colliery 200
Moss J 95
Moyes A G 66, 68
Murdoch W L 67
Murray J T 138
Murray-Wood W 249
Mushtaq Ahmed 216
Mushtaq, Ali 261
Mushtaq Mohammad 56
Mycroft T 30
Mycroft W 25, 29-36, 40-42, 44, 78, **178**, 278

Nash G 26
Nash M A 270
Nayudu C 260-61
Neale W L 240
Neath CC 105-06
Needham E 159-60, 170, **174**
Nelson CC 163
Nelson FC 149
New Brighton 151
Newcastle United 149, 187
Newman J A 71
New South Wales 102, 167, 183, 196
New Zealand 93, 109, 134, 139-40, 156, 162, 166-67, 169, 183, 188, 190, 196, 199-200, 203, 226, 252, 280, 283
Nichol M 225
Nichols M S 203, 244, 251, 263, 265, 267
Nissar, Mahomed 266
Noble M A 102
Norfolk 47, 73, 78, 189-90
Nornable C E 128
Northamptonshire 56, 99, 115, 118-19, 121, 132-33, 137-38, 141, 143-44, 156-58, 164-65, 169, 182, 187, 207, 220-21, 223, 230, 242-43, 246, 251-52, 258-60, 268, 273, 275, 277, 286-87
Northumberland 163, 171
Northway R P 182, 226
Nottinghamshire 8-9, 13, 15, 25-26, 29-30, 35-40, 43, 45-46, 53-57, 73, 80, 84, 91-92, 94, 99, 101, 112, 114-15, 117, 119, 121, 123-25, 127, 132, 138, 141, 146, 153, 159, 169-70, 181-84, 187, 191, 207, 211, 214, 220-21, 225, 229-30, 239-42, 246-47, 250, 252, 254, 257-69, 273, 279, 284, 286, 288
Nottingham Forest 56, 160
Notts County 115, 148, 159
Nourse A D 211

O'Connor J (Junior) 162, 203, 235, 263-65, 269
O'Connor J (Senior) 162
Oldfield N 255
Oldfield W A S 124, 167
Oliver L 122, 124, 126-27, 137, **174, 179**
Ollivierre C A 108-11, 119, 154
Ollivierre H 110
Ollivierre R 110

INDEX 349

O'Reilly W J 283
Otago 109, 183
Owen H 82
Owen-Smith H G O ('Tuppy') 184
Oxford University 44, 47, 49, 93, 118, 120, 127, 134, 142, 157-58, 160, 184, 188-90 204, 212, 249, 264, 272, 279

Packer K 141
Page D A C 226
Paine G A E 254
Pakistan 134, 139, 188, 190, 280, 285
Palairet L C H 43, 112, 135
Palairet R C N 43
Palmer C H 199
Palmer G E 65
Pardon C F 52
Paris C G A 248
Parker C W L 204, 215, 222, 240
Parker H **176**
Parkhouse W G A 138-39
Parkin C H 124
Parks H W 224, 241, 250, 267
Parks J H 168-69, 183, 223, 241-42, 267
Parr G 66
Partridge R J 243
Paynter E 195
Payton Rev W E G 184
Payton W R D 184
Peach F G 87, 271
Pearce T N 203
Pearman R 287
Peate E 57-58, 70
Peebles I A R 49, 168, 210
Peel R 70-73, 78, 89, 113
Pegasus 160
Pellew C E 123
Perks R T D 56, 226, 255-56
Perrin P A 108, 110, 196
Pervez Akhtar 92
Phillips J 26
Phillipson W E 212
Pickett H 74
Pilling R 31
Pinder G 31
Piper W J (Junior) 8, 18, 29, 32, 52, 70, 76, 78-79, 90, **179**
Platts J T B D 19, 22, 32, 36, 54, 56, **178**
Players of the North 30
Pocock P I 204
Pollard R 212-13, 228
Poole C J 110
Pooley E 139
Poole Town 158
Poore R M 93-94
Pope A V (Junior) 209
Pope A V (Senior) 133, **174, 176**, 186, 206-09, 211, 218, 222, 224, 226, 229-30, 234, 236, 238-41, 244-46, 248, 251, 253-56, 258-64, 266, 269-70, 272, 281
Pope D 226
Pope E 206

Pope F 207
Pope G H 138, 141, 168-69, 171, **173-74**, 186, 206-18, 222, 224, 234, 239, 241-42, 244-46. 248-51, 281, 283
Pope H **174**, 206
Pope J 206
Pope T 209
Porter G 25, 59, 73, 76, 78-79, 82, 85, 91
Portland, Duke of 11
Portsmouth 150
Port Vale 159-60
Pougher A D 62, 74, 278
Preston N 7
Preston North End 153
Procter M J 270-71

Quaife B W 106-07, 226, 237, 245
Quaife W 106-07
Queensland 167, 183, 195
Quetta 116
Quinton F W D 93

Ragg J 12
Ramage A 160
Ranjitsinhji 80, 111
Rashid, Tahir 139
Rasmussen F 186
Ratcliffe G 124
Read F 58
Read M 58
Read W W 25, 27, 45, 58-59, 65, 77, 79
Reeves W 109
Relf A 56
Repton School 28, 41-43, 103, 108, 119, 130-31, 133, 144, 156, 160, 162, 172, 187, 207, 212, 223, 284
Rest of England XI 88
Revill A C 186, 283
Revill T F **179**, 186
Rhodes A E G 78, 187, 204, 206, 215, 279, 281
Rhodes H J 26, 30, 142, 191, 204, 225, 275, 278
Rhodes W 33, 70-71, 102, 113, 115, 119, 135, 162, 278
Richards G H 159
Richardson, Arthur W **173, 176**, 186, 190-91, 206, 219, 222-23, 225, 227-28, 230, 234, 236, 240-42, 244-45, 250, 252, 268, 270
Richardson, Alistair W 192
Richardson G W 191-92
Richardson S 22, 41, 81
Richardson T 80, 86, 91, 278
Rickman R B 100, 119, **174**
Riddings CC 105
Righton G 255
Rigley W 24, **178**
Ripley Athletic 154
Ripley Town 148, 154
Robertson-Glasgow R C 127, 198
Robins R W V 167-68, 196-97, 247
Robinson E 129
Rochdale 157
Rollins A S 274-75
Root C F 103-04

Ross G 77
Roupell J H T 49
Rowan E A B 197, 235
Ruggles-Brise H 54
Russell E 108
Russell R C 140
Rylott A 54

SA Fezela XI 270
Sale R (Junior) 160, **173**
Sale R (Senior) **174**
Sales D 115
Saltaire 205, 209, 213, 281
Sandham A 118, 162-63, 200, 267
Santall F R 46, 242
Santall J F E 243
Santall S 46
Scarborough CC 217
Scotland 94, 144, 158, 284
Sellers A B 21, 215, 220, 227, 244, 253, 261
Sewell C O H 84
Shacklock F 35-36, 57, 60, 74, 80
Shastri R J 271
Shaw A 36-38, 44, 57, 65-67
Shaw J 29
Shearwood K A 160
Sheffield, Lord 38, 51
Sheffield United CC 128, 217
Sheffield United FC 159
Sheffield Wednesday (see The Wednesday)
Sheikh M A 126
Shepherd D R 95
Shepherd T 200
Shipman A 237, 271-72
Shirebrook 105
Shrewsbury A 37-38, 44, 114-15
Shrewsbury Town 157
Shuker A 41
Shuter J 11, 25, 59-60, 77
Sibbles F M 219, 259
Siedle I J 197, 235-36
Silcock F 40
Simpson R B 109
Simpson-Hayward G H 193
Sims J M 168, 229, 267
Sinfield R A 251-52
Skinner A F 169-70, **173**, 186, 191, 221, 223-30, 240, 242-46, 261, 264, 266-67, 269
Skinner D A 169-70
Slater A 45-46
Slater A G 45
Slater G H 45, 194
Slater Henry (Junior) 45
Slater Henry (Senior) 45, 55
Slater Herbert 45, 194
Slater Sam 45
Slater Stuart 45
Smailes T F 208, 234, 244, 253, 268
Smedley J 277
Smith A 31, **178**
Smith C A 44
Smith C I J 229, 260

Smith D 78, 92, 142, 151-52, 156, 164, 170, **173**, **176**, 181-87, 189, 191, 203, 218, 220-21, 223-24, 226-27, 229-30, 234-38, 240-42, 244-46, 248-56, 262, 264, 266, 268, 270-71, 281, 284, 288
Smith, Edwin 283-84
Smith, Ernest 112
Smith E J ('Tiger') 139
Smith F B 200
Smith H (Gloucs) 140
Smith H A (Leics) 233, 237
Smith, I 139
Smith J 21-22, 69, **178**
Smith M J K 142
Smith T P D 56
Smith, Ray 143
Smith, Robert 18, 21-22, 24, 40-42, 44, 54, **178**
Smith, Robin 275
Smith, Rick 65
Smith V I 134, 215
Smith W 42
Smith W C ('Razor') 119
Smurthwaite J 208
Soar T 91
Sobers G S 270
Somerset 26, 33, 36, 39, 46, 50, 53, 55, 82, 84, 89, 94-95, 112-13, 121, 126-27, 132, 137, 145-46, 157-58, 165, 182, 189, 214-15, 224, 229-30, 233, 237-38, 243, 245-46, 249, 252-54, 258, 260, 262, 265-66, 269-71, 273, 277, 287
South Africans 50, 83-84, 93, 129, 134, 140, 159, 181-82, 184, 196-97, 203, 211-12, 225, 235, 270, 275, 282
South Australia 102, 109
Southern J D 222
South of England 124
Southerton J 7, 66
Sowter U 21
Spencer C T 233
Spen Victoria CC 214
Spofforth F R 45, 64-70, 72-75, 81, 90, 110, 153, **180**
Squires H S 221, 226, 264
Sri Lanka 141, 216-17
Staffordshire 41, 130
Stanyforth R 140
Staples A 266
Staples S J 266
Stapleton E 239
Statham J B 278
Staveley 11, 159, 200
Steele D S 286
Steele J 118
Stephens E J ('Dick') 240
Stephenson F D 216
Stephenson G R 143, 156-57
Stephenson G T 156
Stephenson H 58
Stephenson J W A 201, 263
Stillman L 274
Stimpson P J 209
Stockport County 148
Stockton, Sir E 50
Stoddart A E 88-89, 96

Storer H (Junior) 97-98, 136-37, 143-46, 148-51, 155, 158, 165, 170, **173, 176**, 186-87, 218-20, 222-24, 227, 229-30, 235, 240-42, 246, 251, 253-56, 258-59
Storer H (Senior) 97-98, 148
Storer W 12, 27, 48. 61, 63, 76-77, 79-80, 83-85, 88-89, 91-93, 95-99, 103, 108, 114-16, 141-44, 154, 170, **179**, 186, 272
Stovold, A 143
Straw T 35-36, 84
Street G 226
Street J 49
Stretton F 280
Strudwick H 138
Strutt G H 18
Stubbings J 45
Stubbings S D 95
Stubbings W 45
Studd C T 65, 88
Sugg F H 12, 28, 54-55, 59-60, 92-93, 116, 153
Sugg W 28, 54, 72, 76, 84-85, 89, 91, 113, **179**
Summers G 36
Sunderland 151-52
Sunnucks P R 153, 233
Surrey 8-9, 11, 13, 15, 25-26, 28, 36, 43, 48-49, 52-53, 58-59, 63, 69, 76-80, 83, 85-86, 90-92, 107, 109, 112-13, 118-19, 125, 135, 138-39, 141-42, 151, 155, 159, 162, 185, 204-05, 208, 215, 221, 224-26, 230, 239-40, 246-46, 248, 250, 252, 258-59, 262-64, 267-69, 273, 276, 285
Sussex 8, 13, 15, 19, 33, 38, 51-52, 55-56, 94, 103-04, 107, 111, 114-15, 128, 130, 133, 135, 141, 144, 147, 156, 165-66, 169-70, 187, 198, 200, 204-05, 207, 218-19, 223-24, 230-31, 239, 241-42, 246, 250-51, 256, 258, 265, 267, 271, 273, 275-76, 280-81, 285
Sutcliffe H 20-21, 94, 104, 131, 162, 165, 181, 197, 202, 208, 220, 227, 234, 253, 261, 263
Suttle K G 141
Sutton L D 95
Swallow R 156, 158
Swanwick CC 105
Swarbrook F W 156
Swindon Town 230

Taber B 139
Tait A 56
Tallon D 139
Tarrant F 66
Tarrant G 66
Tasmania 134, 167, 196
Tate C F 136
Tate M W 135-36, 164, 219
Tate F W 135
Tatlow 87
Tattersall R 215
Taylor F 86
Taylor H W 197
Taylor J M 123-24
Taylor R W 139-43, 156-58, 160, 188, 238, 278, 280, 286-87
Taylor T 120

Taylor W T 10, 29, 52, 86-87, 102, 140, 145, **173**, 277
Tendulkar S R 155
Tennyson, Lord 19, 71, 133, 168, 209-10, 249
The Friars 134
The Wednesday 11, 60, 149-50, 153-54, 156, 187
Thomas F (Junior) 51
Thomas F (Senior) 51
Thomson A A 56, 71
Thorn P 57
Thornewell G 149
Thornton C I 90, 124
Timms B 156
Timms J E 223, 242-43, 252, 269
Titmus F J 19, 138-39, 216
Topham E 194
Townsend A F 165, 190, 253, 281
Townsend L F 82, 133, 140-41, 144-45, 156, 162-65, 171, **176**, 183, 186, 191, 198-99, 213, 218-23, 226-27, 229-30, 234, 236, 238-43, 245-46, 248-55, 259-61, 263, 266, 268-70, 272, 281
Trennery W L 123
Trent College 135, 209
Trott A E 108, 215
Trott H 89
Trueman F S 21, 66, 278
Trumble H 72, 97
Trumper V T 102, 107
Tuckett L R 282
Tunnicliffe J 85, 112-14, 116
Turner C 244, 253
Turner C T B 64-65, 72
Tweats T A 187, 274
Tye J 40, 60
Tyldesley E 117, 228
Tyldesley J T 116-17
Tyson F H 278

Ullathorne C 42
Ulyett G 58, 73, 78, 86
Universities Past & Present 113
Usborne T 222

Valentine B H 43, 223, 245, 257
Vandrau M J 46
Vaulkhard P 92, 142, **173**, 184-85, 187, 221, 283
Verity H 70, 143, 189-90, 202, 207, 220, 227, 234, 237, 244, 253, 261-62, 266, 268, 272
Vernon G F 45
Victoria 115, 134
Viljoen K G 235
Voce W 36, 162, 170, 201, 209, 211, 221, 229, 239, 262-63, 266

Waddington A 129
Wade H F 236
Wainwright E 112, 114
Walker G G 11, 47, 54, 59, 64, 73-74, 76, 84-85, 116, **179**
Walker N A McD 190, 250
Walker N G E 126
Walker W 146, 241, 262

INDEX

Walkley E 102
Walsall Town 153
Walsh C A 216
Walters C F 236-37
Wanderers 118
Ward A 71-72, 279
Ward J P 83
Warner A 111
Warner, Sir P F 57, 67, 77, 80, 111, 140, 196-97, 208, 272
Warr, Earl de la 51
Warren A 12, 100-03, 108, 121, 154, **174**, 185
Warwickshire 16, 21, 27, 33-34, 36, 44, 46-48, 60, 78, 83-84, 90-91, 94, 99, 101-02, 105-08, 111-13, 118, 120-21, 126-27, 134, 136, 138-39, 143-44, 151, 158, 162, 164, 167, 181, 189, 197, 203-04, 207, 220, 223, 225, 227-28, 230, 237, 242, 246, 248, 254, 258, 262, 265, 267-68, 273, 275-76, 284, 288
Washbrook C 203, 213
Wasim Akram 289-90
Wass T 119
Watford 106, 151
Watson A 24, 26-27, 41, 60, 65
Watson F 218-19, 238
Watson G S 171
Watson-Smith H **173**
Watt A E 260
Watts E A 240, 264
Webb A 100
Webber R 13, 15, 33
Webster W ('Tagge') 229
Welch G 95, 216
Wellard A W 224, 253, 260, 270
Wellington 163, 183
West A 87
West Bromwich Albion 10
West Bromwich Dartmouth 206
Western Province 146, 270, 287
West Ham United 150
West Indies 46, 49-50, 72, 86, 110, 139-40, 141, 154, 162-64, 182, 200, 202, 206, 225, 229, 232, 276, 285
West of Scotland 47
White, Sir Archibald 137
White, the Hon L R 213
Whitfield E W 239
Whysall W W 132
Wilcox D R 267
Wild H **179**
Wilkins C P 46, 158, 185
Willatt G L 43, 188, 271, 281, 283-85
Willis C B 123
Willsher E 41
Wilmot Rev A A 22, 43
Wilson A 18, 81
Wilson C 54
Wilson G 50

Wilson J V 78
Windhill CC 209
Winlaw R 235
Wisden 7, 9, 14-17, 20, 22, 26, 28, 33-34, 36-37, 40, 42, 47-49, 52, 57, 60-61, 64-67, 71-73, 84, 87, 89, 92, 97, 99-100, 109, 114, 116-17, 130, 137, 146, 155, 162-65, 171, 181, 183-84, 188-90, 201, 205, 212, 220, 225, 228, 232, 236, 271, 276-77, 282
Wodehouse P G 35
Wood A 143, 202-03, 227, 234, 244
Wood B 130, 286
Wood S H (also see B S H Hill-Wood) 83, 118
Woodcock A 111
Woodcock J 65-66
Woodfull W M 195
Woodhead F G 262
Wood-Sims W 55
Woof W 10
Woolley F E 131, 153, 166-67, 181, 208, 221, 241, 260, 270
Wootton J 76-77
Worcester City 157
Worcestershire 33, 44, 46, 48, 56, 84, 92, 103-05, 129, 139, 143, 151, 167, 169-71, 189, 191, 198-99, 205, 224-26, 236-37, 243, 245-46, 254-56, 258, 265, 267-68, 273, 287
Wolverhampton Wanderers 154, 157
Worthington T S 133, 145-46, 156, 162, 165-71, **173, 176,** 186, 191, 196, 201, 209-10, 218, 220-21, 223-24, 226-27, 229-30, 234, 236, 238-46, 248-54, 256, 258-62, 265-70, 272, 278, 281
Wright D V P 202, 204, 210, 212, 250, 263
Wright E 136
Wright J 55
Wright, James **179**
Wright J G 134, 185, 200, 204, 280, 286
Wright L G 56, 61-62, 64, 76, 83, 89, 92-93, 96, 99-101, 108, 114-15, 117-19, 144, 153, 155, 164, 170, **174, 179**, 185, 187, 271-72
Wyatt G 142
Wyatt R E S 167, 181, 196-98, 220, 227, 237, 254, 258, 267
Wynne-Thomas P 57

Yardley N W D 168, 187, 203, 261
Yorkshire 8-9, 13, 15, 27-29, 31-32, 36, 42, 45, 49, 52-53, 57, 60-61, 63, 69-70, 72-73, 76-79, 81, 83, 85, 91, 94-96, 102, 111-17, 119-20, 126-27, 129, 137, 139-43, 146, 151-52, 160, 164, 168, 182, 184-85, 187, 189, 203, 208, 215, 220, 227, 230, 233-34, 238, 241, 244-47, 250, 253-54, 256, 259-69, 271, 273-74, 280-81, 286, 288
Young J 125
Young M 104
Young R 103

Zoehrer T 139